The Forgotten Man: Understanding the Male Psyche

REUBEN FINE

The Forgotten Man: Understanding the Male Psyche

Reuben Fine

The Haworth Press
New York • London

BF
692.5
F56
1987

The Forgotten Man: Understanding the Male Psyche has also been published as *Current Issues in Psychoanalytic Practice,* Volume 3, Numbers 2/3/4, Summer/Fall/Winter 1986.

© 1987 by The Haworth Press, Inc. All rights reserved. No part of this work may be reproduced or utilized in any form or by any means, electronic or mechanical, including photocopying, microfilm and recording, or by any information storage and retrieval system without permission in writing from the publisher. Printed in the United States of America.

The Haworth Press, Inc., 12 West 32 Street, New York, NY 10001
EUROSPAN/Haworth, 3 Henrietta Street, London WC2E 8LU England

Library of Congress Cataloging-in-Publication Data

Fine, Reuben, 1914–
    The forgotten man: Understanding the male psyche.

    "Has also been published as Current issues in psychoanalytic practice, volume 3, numbers 2/3/4, summer/fall/winter 1986"—T.p. verso.
    Includes bibliographical references.
    1. Men—Psychology. 2. Psychoanalysis. I. Title.
BF692.5.F56   1987   155.6'32   87-61
ISBN 0-86656-383-0

The Forgotten Man: Understanding the Male Psyche

Current Issues in Psychoanalytic Practice
Volume 3, Numbers 2/3/4

CONTENTS

EDITOR

HERBERT S. STREAN, DSW

HONORARY EDITOR

REUBEN FINE, PhD

ASSOCIATE EDITOR

LUCY FREEMAN

ADMINISTRATIVE ASSOCIATE TO THE EDITOR

JOSEPH KRASNANSKY, MSW

EDITORIAL BOARD

LAURIE ADAMS,PhD
ROBERT BARRY, PhD
ALBERT N. BERENBERG, PhD
POLLY CONDIT, MSW
LLOYD deMAUSE, MA
JUDITH R. FELTON, PhD
JANET SCHUMACHER FINELL, PhD
JOSEPH FLANAGAN, MSW
LAURA ARENS FUERSTEIN, CSW
JOYCE HAROUTUNIAN, MA
RICHARD HARRISON, PhD
HARVEY KAPLAN, EdD
ROBERT LANE, PhD
SANDA BRAGMAN LEWIS, MSW
MALCOLM J. MARKS, EdD
MITCHELL MAY, MSW
ROBERT N. MOLLINGER, PhD

JAY R. OFFEN, CSW
ELLEN REICH, MSW
PETER D. RICHMAN, PhD
DOROTHY LANDER ROSEN, MA
JEROME ROSEN
NORMAN SHELLY
ANGELO SMALDINO, MSW, JD
TERRY SMOLAR, DSW
SIMONE STERNBERG, EdD
ROBERT STORCH, MSW
RONALD S. SUNSHINE, MSW
RICHARD SYMONS, PhD
MARGOT TALLMER, PhD
GISELA TAUBER, MSW, JD
ELIZABETH REBECCA TAYLOR,
    EdD
DONALD WHIPPLE, PhD

Introduction

Current Issues in Psychoanalytic Practice is pleased to publish Reuben Fine's *The Forgotten Man*. It is a much needed work and in addition, it is a highly readable and insightful treatise.

Although psychoanalysts have often been labelled as "chauvinistic," "patrocentric" and "phallocentric," Dr. Fine has clearly demonstrated that many dimensions of the male's psychic structure and psychodynamics have either been neglected and/or misunderstood by many psychoanalytically oriented clinicians. As a result, professionals of all persuasions and non-professionals as well have "forgotten" about many of the male's dilemmas, presses and stresses.

As our readers reflect on Fine's comments concerning the man's loves and hates, his sexual desires, practices, and conflicts, his problems with aggression, his anxieties, trials and tribulations with women, and his difficulties in maturing, they will become more empathetic and more understanding not only with their patients, but also with their female counterparts who live and work with them.

The thoroughness of Reuben Fine's scholarship and his detailed research places his work on a par with Helene Deutsch's *Psychology of Women*. It is interesting to note that while Deutsch's book was written over forty years ago, it took psychoanalysts many more years to come up with a book on the psychology of men. Psychoanalysts and non-psychoanalysts will be eternally indebted to Reuben Fine for exposing our oversight and doing something substantial about it.

In addition to his brilliant theoretical formulations, Fine provides us with penetrating analyses of men from all walks of life—politicians, business men, psychologists, athletes, and many more. We see healthy men, ill men, loving men, hateful men, those who are too uptight and those who are too loose, winners and losers—the whole range of mankind and the whole gamut of unkind men.

© 1987 by The Haworth Press, Inc. All rights reserved.

While *Current Issues* is devoting three of its numbers to *The Forgotten Man* together with comments on it from several psychoanalysts, Haworth Press, our publisher is making it a hard-back book so that *The Forgotten Man* will never be forgotten and Reuben Fine will always be remembered.

Herbert S. Strean, D.S.W.
Editor

Preface

In the extensive literature on human and sexual liberation, there is one startling omission: the psychology of the man. It has been all too generally assumed that men are strong, domineering, ruthless, powerful and perfectly able to take care of themselves. Little could be further from the truth. Men are all too often weak, submissive, passive, helpless, dependent and depressed. It is this gap in the literature of the two sexes that I have tried to fill in the present work. My thesis is that the problems of the man have been largely overlooked; hence the title: *The Forgotten Man.*

In a brief introduction the central role of the penis is emphasized. Throughout history the main difference between men and women is that man has had a penis, while woman has not. This difference has been handled in many different ways. Not that anatomy is destiny, but anatomy plays a major role in the arrangements the society makes for the destiny of each of its members.

The main discussion of the book is divided into three parts: sexuality, aggression and social role. In each of these the man struggles with a variety of problems. Again the title of the book indicates the direction of the argument: most of the time the conflicts engendered by these three aspects of his life have been forgotten.

In the first part, on sexuality, the development of the boy is traced from that of mama's darling to father's rival. Since much of his earlier life is spent as mama's darling, it takes him a long time to reach a stage of sexual maturity. As every psychotherapist knows, men have just as many sexual problems as women.

By and large, these problems can be divided into too much and too little. Neither one is a really adequate solution. The mythical Don Juan remains a myth; the man who actually does go from woman to woman is full of conflicts. On the surface he is full of vigor and optimism; underneath there is almost always the fear that women will reject him. By going

© 1987 by The Haworth Press, Inc. All rights reserved.   *xiii* from one to another he manages to avoid the rejection. On the other hand, the man who is sexually inadequate is likewise tied to mother's apron strings too tightly. For him the woman is on a pedestal, a Goddess-like unapproachable mother-figure who has little use for him.

Here it becomes clear that the cultural ideal of the macho he-man (John Wayne is perhaps the prototype) is in sharp contrast to the analytic ideal of the loving man. Many men try valiantly to live up to the macho image which is part of the cultural ideal, and many fail in the attempt; some even kill themselves because the standard set up for them is simply unreachable. The highest suicide rate is found among single men over 45; while in people over 80 the suicide rate is reported to be 16 times as high in men as in women.

Hence marriage becomes the desired solution for the great majority of men. Yet here too there are innumerable difficulties. If the marriage turns out to be an unhappy one, as is all too often the case, his alternatives are limited. Many men discover too late that marriage is an economic commitment as well as a commitment to a human relationship, and find this economic commitment a severe burden, sometimes for the rest of their lives.

While the topic of women's liberation is beyond the scope of this book, how men react to it is pertinent. There is no real reason why the interests of men and women should be so diametrically opposed in this area. It is heartening to see that in her latest book *The Second Stage,* Betty Friedan has come back to the position that the ideal solution for both sexes is a happy loving marriage. There certainly should be complete agreement with this attitude.

Part II deals with the topic of aggression. Boys are trained to fight from early age, but fighting is a dangerous sport. We are not too far from the period when duels were fought to the death; today men still fight relentlessly, even when the consequences are disastrous for them. It is well known that ours is an achieving society, and that the achievement motive is a powerful one. Yet paradoxically, the net psychological outcome is frequently to instill a feeling of failure in the man because he has not achieved enough.

A number of types of achievement are considered on the basis of biographies of famous men. Men have looked upon the achievement with awe and wonderment, yet overlooked the human cost to the man who has carried it off.

If the man is looked upon as a human being who is trying to find happiness in his own life, his achievement may well turn out to be counter-productive. Stalin and Hitler both murdered millions in their ruthless drive for power, which they attained, yet as human beings they were wrecks. Lord Acton's famous aphorism that power corrupts, and absolute power corrupts absolutely, should be modified to state that those with absolute power end up with a horrible fate more often than not.

Nor is success any guarantee of happiness. Newton changed man's picture of the universe, but as a man he was unhappy in the extreme: never able to relate to a woman, wasting most of his time on obscure biblical texts to divine God's purpose. Eddie Fisher made millions, yet spent twenty years as a drug addict, victimized by an untrained doctor. Rockefeller, born to the purple, suffered all his life because he could not become president. And so it goes.

Nor is the average person any better off. Thoreau's remark that most men lead lives of quiet desperation is a very apt one.

Part III deals with the social role that the man assumes or is thrust into, since he has less control over where he will end up in the social scramble than over anything else in his life. Various social roles are considered, though with no implication that they offer a comprehensive picture of our society. Politicians turn out to be power-seekers more commonly than statesmen. The witticism is that the politician looks to the next election, while the statesman looks to the next generation. Businessmen spend their lives accumulating money, sometimes sizable sums, then wonder what their goal really was. Creative men are particularly conspicuous for the amount of suffering that they display. The lives of a few therapists are included, to show that the therapist is one who manages to overcome his own suffering, and then teaches this knowledge to others.

Finally, one chapter deals with love, which *is* the answer to the human problem. However, the subject can only be treated briefly here; a full discussion of love is the topic of my next book.

The factual material in this book is taken from published sources. Every attempt has been made to verify all the statements made. If any error has crept in we apologize for it. There is no intentional disparagement of any person, living or dead.

Reuben Fine

Introduction:
The Durable Figleaf

Centerpiece of the great collection of the Sikh Maharajah of Patiala was a pearl necklace insured by Lloyd's of London for one million dollars. Its most intriguing item, however, was a diamond breastplate, its luminous surface composed of 1001 brilliantly matched blue-white diamonds. Until the turn of the century (the 17th) it had been the custom of the Maharaja of Patiala to appear once a year before his subjects naked except for his diamond breastplate, his organ in full and glorious erection. His performance was adjudged a kind of temporal manifestation of the Shivaling, the phallic representation of Lord Shiva's organ. As the Maharaja walked about, his subjects gleefully applauded, their cheers acknowledging both the dimensions of the princely organ and the fact that it was supposed to be radiating magic powers to drive evil powers from the land.[1]

In spite of the many and diverse theories that exist, there are three major differences between men and women that come out of any study of human society. Man is concerned with his penis, he tends to be more aggressive, and he usually dominates in the social sphere. In all of these the man experiences considerable conflict, but his life is necessarily centered about them.

Note the phrase about the penis. It is not that man is more sexual, he approaches sexuality in a different way. For after all the biological given is that woman produces children. The child is for nine months part of her body, and for several years thereafter intimate bodily contact between mother and child remains the rule. This is not going to change for a long time, if ever.

© 1987 by The Haworth Press, Inc. All rights reserved.

1

As you go down the evolutionary scale, the difference between man and woman becomes ever more unclear. Go far enough down, and sexual differentiation is not absolute.[2] Among very simple organisms such as algae, which have threadlike rows of cells one behind the other, one can observe that during copulation the cells of one thread act as males with regard to the cells of a second thread, but as females with regard to the cells of a third thread.

Even among mammals male and female behavior is often not as precisely demarcated as is usually thought. Thus the Big Horn sheep, who live in the Rocky Mountains, present no clear distinction of sex. The female is in heat only two days a year. As a result the males behave aggressively toward subordinate animals, but behave like a female in heat toward their superiors.

Yet once the sexual differences are clearly formed, among almost all animal species the male must take the sexual initiative. As a result, aggressive behavior, sexual behavior and ranking behavior are all closely interrelated, and one can easily turn into the other. The organ and the symbol of such behavior is the penis.

The study of animals, while fascinating, is only suggestive, and I do not want to carry it too far. Whatever his biological heritage, the human being is more influenced by his culture than by anything else; culture determines how the genetic biological basis of life will be molded. Yet culture is necessarily limited by the physiological apparatus, in this case the penis.

Once man became aware of his penis, it became an object of supreme importance to him.[3] In all societies ever investigated, phallic symbols, or more precisely artificial phalli, are found in abundance. Thus among the Greeks the first thing one met at the front door was a phallus. (Today similar displays are found in places as far apart as Timor, Celebes and Borneo and Nias.) In Dionysian processions, devoted to pleasure and release, huge phalli in great numbers were carried forth, and the participants had big artificial phalli strapped on to them.

Even today the otherwise completely naked Papuan warrior in New Guinea wears a cod-piece when armed for warfare. These cod-pieces are made of straw, conspicuously painted in red or yellow, and present the penis in highly exaggerated fashion. A man wearing one is aggressively exhibitionistic.

Civilization has muted such aggressive displays. Within our own culture the cod-piece is the last expression of phallic symbolism openly displayed and publicly recognized and accepted. (A cod-piece is a conspicuous representation of a penis, big and arching upwards.) The closest we come to it today is in the tight-fitting bathing trunks which girls often ogle at the beach. (A patient related that when she went to a nudist colony, she spent the first forty-five minutes looking at the penises.)

Whatever the clothing worn, or not worn, the penis is intimately tied up with man's feelings of worth and self-esteem. The most common feeling that the man experiences about his penis is that it is too small. This derives from the childhood comparison with father's penis. It is so deeply engrained that few men are able to get over it without some help. Analysts see it as part of the castration complex.

The penis is likewise the symbol of man's aggressiveness; e.g., we still say "he's a prick" or "he's a good cocksman." As soon as he knows he is a man the male experiences conflicts about his sexuality and his aggressiveness. To "show the yellow feather" is the worst thing a boy can do in the traditional culture. In order to prove that they are not cowards men have fought and died by the millions.

Vangard comments on the meaning of the word "argr" in old Norse. Applied to man it indicated not only that he was effeminate, but also that he submitted himself to being used sexually as a woman. Evidently the emphasis on machismo has been in existence for a long time.

It is known now that the male hormone testosterone can thus make animals, both male and female, more aggressive. Thus another link between sexuality and aggression is forged. Here too, however, there is a source of conflict. Civilization does not permit man to release this aggression whenever he wishes. Rather the opposite; his entire upbringing impresses on him the need to control himself. Thus he oscillates between displays of aggression, many of which get him in trouble, and the demand that he restrain his aggression, which makes him uncomfortable.

With a few exceptions, in all known societies the leaders

are men. It can be assumed that there is some biological basis for this differentiation, though again culture can force various changes in it. Some societies, like ours, are extremely pushy, driving men on to ever greater feats. Like Don Quixote, a perennial caricature of the nobleman, they pursue an impossible dream. If they do not attain it, as is so often the case, they become depressed, or commit suicide, or resort to some other neurotic outlet.

These are the three poles around which the psychology of any man can be understood—sexuality (the penis), aggression and success. Every culture makes its own provisions for how men should face these three tasks of life. Since we are dealing with our own society, we shall focus on the pressures and conflicts that men in our times actually experience in the course of their lives.

Although no attempt can be made here to summarize everything that has been said about our culture, some preliminary comments pertinent to our subject can be made. The individual is brought up in a certain kind of family, and the nature of this family is the strongest of all the influences that affect his life. By and large families provide most of the care and affection that are so essential to healthy living, but they are also the scene of much of the hatred and destructiveness that is so obvious. In general, it can be said that ours is a hate culture, in which the predominant mode of relationship of people is based more on hateful than on loving feelings.

In this hate culture, the mother tends to loom larger than the father. Perhaps this is one reason why the psychology of men in general, and fathers in particular, has been so sadly neglected, even in the professional literature. The image of the man projected to the average person is that of a forceful, aggressive success-seeking individual, with few warm feelings or any great degree of tenderness. In a recent paper in a psychoanalytic journal the author wrote "In Search of a Loving Father,"[4] stating frankly that his interest in the father began only after his psychoanalytic training had been completed; i.e., even the psychoanalysts have paid almost no attention to the father. This omission calls for correction, and we shall have much to say about fathers in the further course of this work.[5]

PART I: SEXUALITY

Chapter 1:
From Mama's Little Boy
to Father's Rival

There is a widespread belief in many cultures that men are somehow more favored by fortune than women. The Bible makes it obvious that man is the basic model—woman being a kind of afterthought created from one of his ribs. The witch persecutors of the fifteenth and sixteenth centuries also thundered that hell knows no fury like a woman (they did not even add "scorned," as Shakespeare did later). In most churches woman is forced into a subordinate role. Arabs commiserate when a daughter is born, while the orthodox Jew thanks God every day in his prayers that he was born a man and not a woman.

Yet in almost every respect the male comes out to be the weaker sex. About 106 boys are born to every 100 girls, yet throughout life there is a slightly greater mortality of males, until, beyond the age of fifty, there is an excess of females. Within the womb embryonic males suffer a higher rate of mortality than females.

Apart from these biological facts, boys are more susceptible to stress at every age. They suffer more from the effects of complications of pregnancy and childbirth; they more often get and more often die from infections in childhood; they are more likely to suffer impairment of growth after radiation. In most illnesses where there is a sex differ-

© 1987 by The Haworth Press, Inc. All rights reserved.

ence, the male gets the disease earlier in life and more often dies from it.[6]

In a sense, this odd discrepancy between the cultural blow-up and the biological reality plagues the man throughout his entire life. In almost all languages, "masculine" stands for striving, power, achievement, while "feminine" connotes passivity, inferiority, and failure. So here we can already see the roots of one of the man's central conflicts: pushed to ever greater heights by his surroundings, he can never really reach them, either in actuality or psychologically. The outcome is a constant sense of frustration and failure which dogs his every footstep.

Most paradoxical is the man who in spite of outstanding accomplishments can never find any inward peace. Freud once devoted a paper to this topic: those who are wrecked by success. An outstanding example in public life is the late Nelson Rockefeller whose real tensions only became apparent after his death. Born to family whose name is synonymous in the American mind with enormous wealth and power he entered politics, and did become governor of New York State, and vice-president. But it was the presidency he wanted. When this eluded him, he sought consolation in women. The pattern occurs every day, though the stage setting is usually less dramatic.

An instance from clinical practice occurred with Frank, a 60-year-old real estate tycoon who had built his business to the point where his income was $2 million per year. Yet even this did not satisfy him. He travelled around the country to make real estate deals, usually carrying at least $5 to $10 thousand in $100 bills, a roll which he would frequently flash. But he was indifferent to the legalities of his business deals, and gradually slipped across the line. Eventually he was caught, found guilty, and sentenced to a year in jail (sentence was low because of his age.) Tortured by shame and disgrace, he died in prison.

The roots of this and other conflicts can be traced back to the boy's relationship with his parents, particularly the mother in earliest infancy. While this has been known for a long time, in the past ten years much evidence has accrued to show how important the *specific interactions* between mother and child can be. Thus instead of the older idea of the mother responding actively to the needs of a passive child, what is emphasized now is interaction, in which both partners take an active role.

Here are some of the newer findings on interaction. As early as the first day of life the infant can move in precise synchrony with the articulated structure of adult speech.[7] Infants aged twelve to twenty-one days can consistently copy facial and manual gestures made by adults, e.g., a newborn can imitate an adult sticking out his tongue, opening his mouth or widening his eyes. At three days the infant can be trained to turn his head to one side for a reward such as a brightly colored object when a buzzer sounds and to the other side when a bell sounds. Within a month the infant will engage in more intense non-nutritive sucking of a nipple in order to see a picture that is more clear or to hear music.

More evidence is accumulating in many laboratories that interaction between mother and infant is intense from birth on, merely becoming more complex as time goes on. And of course the early interactions will frequently play a role, sometimes decisive, in the later interactions.

The new mother is usually in a state of considerable excitement about her baby. Pleasure, frustration, joy, fear, concern, ignorance, rushing for help to doctors or grandparents, her emotions run the gamut. So the interaction of the infant is not with a cool collected model of mental health, but with a flesh-and-blood woman, who still retains many of the anxieties that she experienced in growing up.

A common reaction, which has been noted for a long time, is that in the main mothers feel somewhat closer to their daughters than to their sons. Whether this is universally true is not too important; it certainly is true of many sex-frightened mothers. Even in monkeys more affectionate physical contact between mother and female infant has been noted than between mother and male, even though it is not entirely clear how the mother recognizes the sex of the infant.[8]

What does count here is that when the mother finds it easier to relate to the girl, the boy feels rejected. On top of that it is almost always true that the boy receives more physical punishment. This adds up to another traumatic experience for the boy in his attainment of independence from mother, the universal human striving.

Careful observational studies of young infants by the New York analysts, Galenson and Roiphe (1972 on) have established that a sexual change occurs in both sexes somewhere between fifteen and twenty-one months of age, earlier than had previously been thought. Masturbation in boys starts as soon as the boy can reach his penis, somewhere between seven and ten months of age.

The reaction of the toddlers to the coming of the sex drive differed in the two sexes. The boys were initially quite elated with their newfound powers, which resulted in more masturbation and more physical activity. On the other hand, the girls seemed bothered by their new awareness of the differences between boys and girls. The girls showed a much greater tendency to fall back on earlier pleasures, such as sucking and anal play.

No doubt the reactions of the toddlers vary with the degree of sophistication of the parents. After a while, however, since we are concentrating on the boys, the pleasure in the penis can no longer be expressed so openly. At best, enlightened parents will say to a masturbating boy, "Do it in your own room."

The boy's growing sexuality must be counterpoised against his immaturity on the one hand and the parental reactions on the other. Since he is so immature the parents tend not to take his sexuality seriously, and he feels frustrated. Then again, the parents often feel threatened because the child's wishes are out in the open; thus he may want to watch mama go to the bathroom, or observe the various parts of her body, or compare his penis with daddy's, or crawl into bed with them, or engage them physically in any one of a hundred ways which excites and frightens them. Thus the first direct sexual confrontation arises, between the boy and mother, and between the boy and father.

The reader may object at this point that too much emphasis is being placed on sex, and that there are many other aspects to growth. That is of course true, but with all the later discoveries after Freud, sexuality still plays a major role in everybody's life. It has been forgotten that every man, no matter what kind of front he puts up, has to struggle with sexual conflicts all his life. My purpose in this chapter is to show how the sexual conflicts arise within the family setting.

The boy's sexual wish for the mother has to be seen in relation to other wishes, such as his physical growth and wish to display it, the fear and love of father, and above all the affectionate feelings for mother. To approach her sexually is forbidden after a certain point, yet he wants to, and also wants to hold on to her love. In this way, the first conflict arises between sexuality and affection, as early as the second year of life.

From the second year to the sixth, roughly, the boy has to live through a series of stormy conflicts with mother. For the child these are extremely intense even though they may seem trivial to an outsider. How they are resolved has a decisive influence on the whole future course of his life.

While at first the boy can take pride in his penis, and the fact that he has one, while girls do not, after a while this pride must be subdued. Thus begins the dilemma that haunts the lives of most men, if not almost all: The boy longs for a woman who is not available.

Added to that is the fact that almost all boys masturbate, as Kinsey showed a generation ago, and that for several centuries masturbation has been severely condemned by Western culture. As late as 1940 the U.S. Navy Department had a rule that a candidate for Annapolis was to be rejected for evidence of masturbation.[9]

The incest wish is the strongest of all human taboos. Mother-son incest in particular is almost unknown; when incest does occur it is usually brother-sister, or father-daughter. There is even some evidence that the taboo holds for the higher primates as well. Jane van Lawick-Goodall, who spent fifteen years observing chimpanzees in their natural habitat in Tanzania, could not detect a single instance of mother-son intercourse. The psychologist Maurice Temerlin adopted a female chimpanzee named Lucy, whom he treated as a daughter. When Lucy reached puberty (the rutting season in the monkey), she presented herself "shamelessly" to every male that came along, but she avoided Temerlin, her adopted "father." So, for whatever reason, the incest taboo is deeply rooted in man's biological background.

The incest taboo is involved with the Oedipus complex, the major determinant of personality structure from roughly three to five. In the Greek story Oedipus kills his father, marries his mother, and blinds himself: In modern terminology we see this as patricide, incest and castration. Every boy goes through a stage in which these wishes are very strong, and the fears connected with them (summed up in the term "castration"). There can be no doubt by now that the Oedipus conflict is a deep universal drama, which arises from the biological fact that the boy is first with mother because of his inherent dependency, and then moves on to an encounter with father.

Since the mother is unattainable for the boy, the Oedipus complex ushers in a dilemma which is found in almost all men: the longing for the unavailable woman. Together with this longing goes the hostility, or even contempt, for the woman who is available.

The Oedipus complex is really another name for the family triangle. Sometimes the conflicts involved are intense, at other times rather mild. My own hunch is that the intensity of the Oedipal problem is a reflection of the degree of animosity that exists between mother and father rather than of the biological strength of any of the drives. When mother and father hate one another fiercely, as is unfortunately all too often the case, the child identifies with one or the other, and develops fierce hatreds as well. When mother and father really love one another, the Oedipal wishes surface, but are rather easily handled.

The incest taboo and the Oedipus complex hit at the heart of human psychology. They can neither be gratified nor rejected entirely. Instead they must be defended against, which means woven into the fabric of the personality. Every human being can best be understood in the light of his or her family background, and in this background the feelings surrounding incest and the love/hate relationship of the parents are at the core.

Family situations are so diverse that they have to date defied any kind of standard typology. I prefer the formulation that the boy grows from mother to father to the outside world, and the life of any man can be approached via this outline. All the other facets of personality, such as aggression, fear, siblings, even grandparents, move around this basic developmental profile.

The boy, frustrated in his sexual approach to mother, necessarily reacts in various ways. In sexual terms he is burdened with the feeling that he is not enough of a man to satisfy his mother, which later generalizes to the feeling that he is not enough of a man to satisfy the dream girl of his life. Accordingly a great many men oscillate between a woman they can have but do not want, and a woman they want but cannot have.

This dilemma also influences a man's image of himself, which henceforth plays an increasingly important role in his life. On the one hand he is mama's little darling, infantilized because of the reality and because of mother's fear of her own sexual wishes for the boy. Thus as a little boy he can expect a lot of love, but as a grown man, with sexual desires, he cannot. But as he moves from there to father, he becomes father's rival, often enough in a bitter never-ending competitive struggle which goes on all his life. Obviously the love/hate patterns of the parents play an important role in his self-image as well. If the mother is destructive and hateful, as mothers are all too frequently, the boy will feel weak and helpless. If mother is warm and cuddly, the boy will feel strong and loved. Then too, the father's character enters the picture: He too can exert an influence on his son's self-image in terms of weakness or strength. Above all, it must be realized that this is a powerful psychological drama which every human being has to go through. For the present discussion we have emphasized that the boy generally comes out with the image of a distant desirable woman he cannot have—his own private Mona Lisa. (The great artist Leonardo da Vinci was taken away from his mother at an early age, and a dominant motif throughout his life was to find a woman who was like his mother.)

At the time of the Oedipus complex an important internal change takes place: The boy acquires a superego, or internalized parent-image, which from then on becomes his conscience, and guides his life as effectively as the real parents guided his life throughout the first years of childhood. The continuity of the personality, the creation of hopes, ambitions and ideals, the neurotic conflicts that the individual goes through, can now all be related to the superego. (While I prefer to avoid excessively technical terms, the concept of superego has no good equivalent in ordinary language.) Ideally, if the family is a happy one, the boy will identify with father, form a superego modeled on his father's goals and desires in life, and eventually grow up to be like him. But this does not happen too frequently, especially in a society like ours which historically assimilated large numbers of foreign groups that were in rebellion against established authority and fathers.

Besides the superego, the boy at age five or six goes through another change: He becomes interested in a little girl his age. I call this the first love affair in childhood. Just as his sexual development in general has to move from mother to another woman, in this first love affair the first step is taken. Sometimes this love affair takes on a direct sexual coloring, as in children who play house, or the boy saying to the girl, "Show me yours and I'll show you mine." At other times the love affair remains a fantasy or a pure wish. Either way it is of great significance in the growth of the boy. One who never has such an affair is much more apt to become a schizophrenic, i.e., a man who remains eternally attached to mother.

The next stage in the boy's sexual odyssey comes at around age eight, and involves his sister or other girls of that age, if there is no sister in the family. Anthropologists[9] have shown that at this age all societies have to make provision against the contact between brother and sister. They have to be taught to avoid one another because of the incest taboo. Two methods are available: brother-sister avoidance and brother-sister extrusion. In our own society the approach adopted is clearly brother-sister avoidance: From this age to puberty boys will not be caught dead with a girl, while girls stay away from boys like the plague. It is true that under the impact of psychoanalysis these patterns are changing; nevertheless they are still the norm in most parts of the world, including most of our own country. In brother-sister extrusion, usually the boy is taken away from the family and sent to boarding school or to some other family. Most familiar to us is the English boarding school system; no doubt it arose as one reaction to the incestuous temptations of this age.

However, let us stop for a moment here. With his mother

the boy learns to get stuck on an unattainable woman. In the first love affair, the parents usually force a quick end to the romance. In the conflict with sister, the boy has to stay away from girls. Thus from earliest childhood on, the man is saddled with a series of experiences in which he learns that he can never have the woman he wants. Small wonder then that so many men have problems in love and sex.

The question may be raised here: What of the boy who grows up without a mother? In the first place such a situation is factually rare; all societies have recognized the deep need of a child for its mother, or some substitute female. Furthermore, and more important, the human being grows by means of models and persons with whom to relate and identify. When these do not exist, a cramped, twisted, lifeless personality results. This leads to the need-fear dilemma: The child needs mother, but also fears her, and this combination of need and fear dominates his psyche throughout his life. Later on, as a result of his childhood experiences, he also needs the woman and fears her at the same time.

After the resolution of the conflict with the sister, at about age eight, the boy enters upon a period of chumming only with boys, referred to as preadolescent homosexuality. In the beginning actual homosexual experiences are rare, but later on they become more frequent. In spite of a century of Freud and Freudianism men still fight a losing battle against their powerful drives. The human being has a terrific need for contact with other people and if this need is not gratified in one way, it will be gratified in another.

In preadolescent and early adolescent homosexuality, there is too much of a tendency to regard it as "normal," without linking it with the severe sexual repression to which the boy is subjected. Anyone who has been through such common social groups as the Boy Scouts has probably had some first-hand knowledge of these early homosexual practices, sometimes by indulgence, at other times by observation. Many times the Scoutmasters themselves use the boys, who are by no means unwilling partners. Yet here too the deeper feelings may emerge only after many years. Here is a revealing clinical vignette.

John had had sex with the Scoutmaster a number of times. Usually the older man would be the aggressor in anal intercourse. When he grew up, John entered Naval Intelligence during World War II. In this capacity part of his job was to deal with homosexual transgressions. These reminded him very much of his own early homosexual experiences which gave him a new slant on what had happened to him some fifteen years earlier. When he was discharged from the Navy, John went back to the mayor of the town where he had been a Boy Scout and filed a complaint of homosexual abuse against his former Scoutmaster.

This vignette highlights another point worth emphasis. Heterosexual behavior cannot be understood in isolation from the rest of the boy's life, especially his homosexual longings or behavior. If in this book I seem to deal so exclusively with the heterosexual that is only to make the situation clear; to include everything would swamp the reader in a mass of excessive detail.

After this long preliminary, we finally come to adolescence, the period of sexuality proper. Adolescence is an artifact of our culture; in most societies before the present era, the boy stepped directly into man's estate as soon as he reached sexual maturity, which also involved physical maturity. This period of life is notoriously difficult, and most adolescents have a tough time, especially in the sexual area.

However, a number of other problems come to the fore as well. The boy must also adjust himself to a new self-image, and having reached physical maturity he begins to ask: Who am I and where am I going? He is confronted with vocational choices, and realizes that within a few years he must make some all-important choices. And through all this he has to liberate himself from the childhood ties to his family, particularly the mother, and move on to become a man like father. He is now in every sense of the word father's rival, and how he handles this rivalry determines the future course of his life. Again, if we focus on the sexual aspect, it is only to draw a meaningful and consistent picture of what the boy goes through; we are well aware that sex cannot be isolated from the rest of the boy's life.

The sexual challenge is so basic because it starts with direct visible physical changes, both in himself and in girls, which he cannot shun. A great deal of the bizarreness, rebelliousness and eccentricity seen in the adolescent stems from an attempt to avoid the sexual conflict, even though the connection can only be teased out through careful inquiry.

On the contemporary scene many young people have left their families and drifted off into strange esoteric cults, such as Hare Krishna and others, a great many of which have come from India and other eastern countries. Recently laws have been introduced to allow parents to "recapture" their errant children. While there are many motives for joining these cults, one of the major ones is the inability to come to grips with the newly felt sexuality. The cult represents another family, to replace the family which the young person can no longer tolerate because the conflicts in it are too great.

> In one case Stuart, a businessman with six children, abandoned his wife after thirty-five years of marriage to go off with a younger woman. The other woman resembled his wife to such an extent that she could have been taken to be a younger version.
>
> The youngest son, Roger, was then sixteen years old. At first he took to smoking marijuana; his father caught him and thrashed him. His school work began to slip, and he could not relate to girls at all. Finally he ran off to Chicago to join one of the eastern cults. He changed his name, his style of dress and his entire life pattern. His sex life was nil; he had become a child in a new family.

Cult behavior highlights the two extremes of the lifelong sexual frustration: either too much or too little. Most cults frown upon sexual expression, or forbid it entirely; some cults on the other hand encourage everybody to have sex freely. In psychoanalytic terminology this indiscriminate reaction is called acting out, and experience shows over and over that it does not solve the individual's or the group's problems. The most gruesome example in recent times is the suicide of some 900 members of the Jones cult in Guyana; all their free sexual activity did not prevent them from destroying themselves at the behest of a seriously disturbed leader.[10]

That complete sexual freedom can lead, as in the Jones cult, to suicide or, as with the Nazis and centuries earlier, the Romans, to horrifying mass murders, has been used as an argument by many that sexuality after all is less important. This misses the point. In the first place sexuality, as pointed out earlier, may have a loving quality to it (to "make love") or a hateful quality (the words "fuck" and "screw" have almost entirely hostile connotations in English as well as in other languages). It is only when sex is used in a loving way that it is fully gratifying.

But in the second place, and equally important, the sexual wishes cannot readily be gratified without destroying the social order. Incest is the prime example: you're damned if you do and damned if you don't. The incestuous wish must therefore somehow be woven into the personality structure, and some compromise solution found. In adolescence that solution lies in finding a girl who is like mother, but is of the same age as the boy; at the same time the sexual longing for mother remains with the boy all his life.

In the same way the only solution to the sexual problem for the adolescent is to find some compromise formation which will give him a sufficient realistic amount of gratification, while reducing the suffering to a minimum. Ideally this could be found in a happy marriage, but there are many obstacles to be overcome before that is reached.

The compromise formations in adolescence are numerous. Norman Kiell, in his book *The Universal Experience of Adolescence*, shows that similar reactions are found in adolescents among widely varying cultural groups. Among the most important patterns seen in our own society may be mentioned promiscuity, drugs, withdrawal, intellectualization, fighting, asceticism and adherence to an idealistic cause. These are all radical alternatives which sooner or later end up in disillusionment, despair or destruction.

Since the introduction of the birth control pill, the discovery of penicillin and other drugs to cure and control VD, and the legalization of abortion, all dating from the 1950's, roughly, there has in fact been much greater sexual freedom—the severe sexual restrictions still practiced in so many parts of the world have diminished considerably, and it seems unlikely that they will ever again be reintroduced in this country. Still, the increased sexual expressiveness has led to other conflicts, which have to be understood psychologically.

Consider what happens to a liberated adolescent boy or girl. They meet, have sex. If their parents are willing, they can use their own homes; if not, they find some other place. But after the sex, then what? Are they to continue this way indefinitely, in a promiscuous life? Many try and end up feeling lonely and isolated. And what of the jealousies and other emotions aroused when the old ideals are given up? They turn out to be just as intense as ever.

> A young couple, in rebellion against their previous sexual fidelity, took to swinging. They could watch one another have sex with other men or women without a twinge of jealousy. Then one day the man decided he would undertake an analysis. The wife was furiously jealous because he would then share thoughts and feelings with another person which he would not share with her.

In practice it turns out that sexual liberation is not as easy as it is supposed to be. The older experiences are still with the boy: the mother he could not have; the first love he could not maintain; the sister he could not talk to; the boys who were homosexually attractive; or with whom he had had sex; the self-image of an inadequate male who has not yet caught up with father's achievements; and perhaps never will. It is with such a psychology that he approaches a girl. At every step dilemmas and conflicts arise.

The conquest of VD has proved to be more formidable than seemed at one time, right after the introduction of penicillin. Resistant strains of bacteria have appeared. Not infrequently gonorrhea can cause sterility in a girl by infecting her Fallopian tubes, before she knows what has happened to her; many girls only discover it when they are ready to have children. People are often careless, especially adolescents who feel they have little at stake. If the disease is not too uncomfortable, which is often the case, they do not bother to have it treated. Homosexuals sometimes have syphilis which has been transmitted through anal intercourse and are unaware of it, because this mode of acquiring VD is not taught in college hygiene courses, or the more popular literature. Herpes has turned out to be hard to treat, and easily concealed from the partner. While some people feel free enough to tell their partners they "have something," many others do not.

Perhaps the most unexpected consequence of the sexual revolution is the enormous increase in the use of drugs. As I am writing this, the radio announces that in the Wall Street area in New York drugs are openly bought and sold. More than one authority has stated that we are in the midst of a serious drug epidemic. Again the same extremes dominate the picture: too much or too little.

For all human beings groups are important, for the adolescent, especially so. The values, habits, customs, even dress of the peer group have a compelling quality which may very well replace the family standards that persisted until adolescence. What the group does about sex then becomes the dominant factor, not even whether the sex is gratifying or not. And again the same old story is heard: too much or too little.

Adolescents, especially in modern times, are particularly enamored of action, and tend to see some action as a way out of their dilemmas, rather than psychological reflection. Bombarded with all kinds of suggestions from the most sensible to the most bizarre, they will choose one or the other, and pursue it with religious fanaticism.

Ideally, the solution to the sex problem in adolescence (as all through life) lies in the growth of love feelings toward other people rather than hateful ones. The conflicts surrounding the acceptance of sexuality can be handled provided there is a strong love feeling. When the conflicts cannot be handled it is because too much hatred has broken through.

As we have seen, throughout his life up to adolescence the boy has been confronted by women who refuse him sexually; now for the first time he can encounter women who accept him sexually. This is the positive side of the sexual revolution, which can help society to overcome the mass of neuroses and psychoses that make up human history. However, the negative side, with its display of hostility, brutality and exploitation is still very much in the foreground. The struggle we are going through now is to see whether the positive or the negative side will prevail.

But whatever happens in the larger society, for many individuals, the growth and nurturance of love feelings can assure the victory of the positive aspects of sexuality. In such a framework sex does indeed become one of the greatest pleasures in life. It is just as well to state though that even at best both men and women have to put up with some sexual frustration. Ideally, in a well-organized life this frustration will not be of any major consequence. In a less ordered life the sexual frustration can become disruptive and destructive.

Once the man goes on to marriage, a new set of sexual difficulties arises, in spite of all the happiness that marriage can offer. For most men the demand that they settle down to have sex with one woman for the rest of their lives is one against which they rebel. Many times the wife lets herself go, becomes sloppy, dresses poorly, loses interest in sex, especially after the birth of a child. For the man in this situation his love life becomes a source of constant distress. If he remains faithful, he is condemned to boredom and indifference; if he tries another woman, he feels guilty.

A more detailed examination of some typical marital conflicts will be taken up in a later chapter. Here I merely wish to sketch the general outline, and direct attention to the manner in which sexual conflicts appear at every stage. It is an illusion to think that sexual problems are solved by marriage, or any other social arrangement; at best the problems are focused on a given situation. The way out is always through the growth of the person's capacity to love, though that too is difficult of realization.

Even more important, the unconscious infantile conflicts are revived in marriage, no matter how sophisticated the partners claim to be. One of the many illusions people have to contend with is that these conflicts can be overcome by a move of the wrist or a shrug of the shoulders. Childhood leaves extraordinarily deep impressions, whose repercussions are felt throughout the person's entire life.

As far as the man is concerned, these childhood conflicts center around remaining mama's little boy and growing up to be father's rival. The road to full manhood and fatherhood is a rocky one, nor need it cause any great surprise that many fail along the way. Just as in childhood the boy felt sexually rejected by an unattainable woman, now too he finds his wife or some other woman the unattainable one and loses himself in fantasies about her. And again there are two poles: too much or too little. Some men, frustrated by the family, turn to other women; other men, equally frustrated by the family, turn away from sex altogether, or move away to homosexuality (far more common than is ordinarily believed).

Once the children come, the man has a hard time adjusting himself to the many new situations that arise. In fact, while the woman has a fairly easy transition from being a little girl, identified with mother, to being a mother herself, and her role is fairly well defined, the man's problems are much greater.

Before the baby comes, the man has to be strong and sexual to conquer the woman. After a period of vigorous sexuality, he must then give some of this up for the sake of the unborn child and become more supportive. Once the baby is born, he again has to play primarily a supportive role, with little outlet for his sexuality for a while. As the child grows up, the man's role tends to change every few years. He can be warm and cuddly with either an infant boy or girl, then he has to give up this physical play. Next he finds himself the authority, who has to lay down the law on how the children (and the wife, too, much of the time) should behave. When children reach school age, he may take an interest in the child's progress, but how much of an interest he can intelligently take is limited by his own education. In the preadolescent years, when the boy likes to relate only to males, the father becomes a hero who can show the budding boy how to become a man in his own right. Once adolescence is reached, the father's role has to be given up in favor of the boy's growing sense of independence and insistence on finding his own way. Yet the father still remains a model whom the son would like to imitate. Once the son gets married, the father must again play a ticklishly difficult part, helping his son out, yet fostering independence at the same time. Finally, in the grandparent phase, he recapitulates with his grandson what happened with his own son in the growing-up period.

It is no wonder that with this constant shift in role, many men fall by the wayside. If the wife has a difficult pregnancy, or is preoccupied with the baby after it is born, the husband finds his sex life damaged. Many men at this time begin to search for other women. Ours is in fact the only society known where so much is demanded of the one marital relationship; in many cultures, one set of women become mothers and another set become sexual partners. By going off to another woman when the children are small (the time when divorce is highest) the man in effect creates this social situation for himself.

Or again, when he has to be the authority, he may err in extreme directions, either by being so authoritarian that he beats the child unmercifully ("Spare the rod and spoil the child" is still the motto in many families), or he may retreat into a passive withdrawal, allowing the wife to rule the household any way she wants. When he does that, the child feels him as a distant unrelated individual, even more so than when he is too authoritarian.

Similarly, every other role thrust upon the man as the child is growing up creates difficulties and conflicts. Small wonder then that the literature on how a parent should behave has proliferated to such an extent; unfortunately those who need this literature least are the ones who patronize it most.

Through it all, there is much compensation for the man in his family life. As Ben Franklin said in his time, marriage has many problems, but celibacy has few pleasures. The much-prized singles life, in which almost one-third of the country is now reported to be engaged, looks good only at a distance. The plain and obvious fact is that almost all singles' activities are geared to finding the right mate.

RECAPITULATION

We have tried to trace the course of the sexual conflicts through the span of a man's life. In childhood, he is confronted by a woman he adores, but who makes him feel small and inadequate. Yet this incestuous tie, which cannot be resolved, and cannot be forgotten, enters into the entire lifestyle. The boy must come to grips with it, whether he wants to or not. Generally speaking, there are two extremes in the management of the ensuing sexual conflict: too much or too little. Most men oscillate between these two extremes all their lives.

Many have tried to handle the sexual conflicts by overt action; this is the origin of the sexual revolution. But such sexual revolutions have occurred before in human history, with similar consequences. When there is too much, the effects often include drugs, destructiveness, illness and misery. When there is too little, some other compromise, or a similar one, is sought by the man.

Paraphrasing Santayana's famous remark that those who ignore history are doomed to repeat it, we may say that those who ignore their basic impulses are doomed to be made unhappy by them. Even though there is no solution to the sex problem in terms of simple action, there is a solution in terms of the psychic orientation and love. In childhood the incestuous wish for mother may be abandoned to establish a love relationship with her which is satisfactory in many different ways. This is in fact the normal solution prescribed by most societies, ours included. And in adulthood the sexual conflicts may be handled by a reasonable degree of gratification, and the pursuit of a life style which makes sense, and is satisfactory in most ways. This life style must include loving relationships with people, including the feeling that sex is an act of love, not a form of conquest, or an act of hostility.

Yet it is easier to set up an ideal than to carry it out, especially in a society which has from time immemorial been troubled by so many other problems. Action is easier than thought, and so the man, troubled by his sexual desires, acts out in one way or another. The usual alternatives, mentioned over and over, are: too much or too little. It is to these alternatives as they appear in real life that we now turn.

Chapter 2:
Don Juan's Exploits:
The Man Behind the Mask

As a reaction to the sexual problem there is an almost universal fantasy among men of having a great many women—in today's parlance, of being a "swinger." This fantasy, found among virtually all peoples in all times and places, usually arises at adolescence, as a result of the sexual awakening. Thus 2300 years ago Aristotle could write:[1]

> The young are in character prone to desire and ready to carry any desire they may have formed into action. Of bodily desires it is the sexual to which they are most disposed to give way, and in regard to sexual desire they exercise no self-restraint. They are changeful too, and fickle in their desires, which are as transitory as they are vehement, for their wishes are keen without being permanent, like a sick man's fits of hunger and thirst. They are passionate, irascible, and apt to be carried away by their impulses. They are the slaves, too, of their passion as their ambition prevents their ever brooking a slight and renders them indignant at the mere idea of enduring an injury. And while they are fond of honor, they are fonder still of victory for superiority is the object of youthful desire, and victory is a species of superiority.

Within our own history, the Romans were especially notable for their orgies, sexual profligacy and unbelievable cruelty. Julius Caesar was an indefatigable lecher, and bisexual; he was known as the man who was a man to all women, and a woman to all men. The avenger of his murder, Mark Antony, was an equally disreputable character: In reality he was an

© 1987 by The Haworth Press, Inc. All rights reserved.

unregenerate rake, whose long and gaudy sexual history included a period of adolescent homosexuality as the favorite of
a Roman nobleman, youthful debauches with matrons and
courtesans, the keeping of a harem of concubines (both male
and female) in his house in Rome, and two marriages made
for gain and dissolved when no longer profitable.

As Roman lecheries multiplied and enveloped the entire
upper classes, sex came to be seen more and more as mere
sensation, to be enjoyed until boredom set in, and then to be
enjoyed again with the help of novelty and change. One little-
noted aspect of this, true in our own day as well, is that the
adults had no interest in children. The women participated
willingly in orgies and debauches, so that for them too the
image of motherhood played no great role in their lives.

When sex becomes the paramount preoccupation, children
move into the background, or are neglected altogether. It has
been surmised that in Rome the overwhelming concern with
sex and pleasure eventually led to the disintegration of the
Roman family which, in turn, was one of the major causes of
the decline and fall of the Roman empire. The same pattern
has been seen in other cultures, and in our own day. Thus a
woman who is promiscuous, moving from one lover to
another, has little time or concern for her children.

Many other cultures have been described in which sex is
pursued freely and without the apparent guilt or shame feelings which attach to promiscuity in our own world. Yet there
is almost always some evidence of intense destructiveness
which can be picked up by a careful observer. Thus in the
harems of the Turks (harem means forbidden) the women
were in effect slaves, and not infrequently were sacrificed to
the ferocity of the Sultan. Offenses were punished with dreadful severity; one sultan is reported to have drowned his whole
harem of 300 women just for the fun of picking a new one.
The everyday lives of the women were so restricted that they
frequently became homosexuals, largely because there was
nothing else to do.[2]

There was a period when our own repressive society was
unfavorably compared with other societies which offered
much more freedom, as in Mead's description of the Samoan
adolescent girl who, she claimed, did not go through the terrible ordeals about sex that our girls do.[3] But now that our own

society has become one of the most permissive in the world, this freedom has come to be reevaluated. Every society sets up sexual rules through which it shapes, structures and constrains the development and expression of sexuality in all of its members. Thus the fantasy of free untrammeled sexuality for the man remains just that—a fantasy. Sex cannot be divorced from the family, from children, and from the homosexual conflicts, as well as everything else in the culture.

In the 1930's, when anthropologists first visited the islands of free love in the Pacific, they came back with vivid stories of the happy and free peoples who lived there, unfettered by Puritanical restraints. As time has gone on, however, and as sexual restrictions in our own society have been lifted, both gradually and suddenly, while more information has accumulated about these love isles, the evaluation of their freedom has shifted. In the first place the greatest freedom attached only to adolescents, as in our own society; married people faced restrictions, though not as severe as ours. But second, there was a carefree attitude to destructiveness and violence which did not fit well with the image of a free and happy people. Infanticide was far more common than had been thought.[4] Cannibalism had not been wiped out completely (Captain Cook, who discovered Hawaii, was captured and eaten by the natives on one of his later voyages).

Some have tried to show that with all these special restrictions the freedom in sex and love the people enjoyed was spurious. This goes too far. When all is said and done, the example of other cultures, which makes anthropology the study of nature's experiments, is instructive. There can be no doubt that the freer sexual cultures, in spite of all their handicaps, contributed as an example to the increasing sexual freedom of this century.

Yet whatever has happened in other societies, we must still come back to our own society and its discontents. The fantasy of total sexual freedom remains a powerful one among men, and more recently, among women as well. As a rule this fantasy first appears in the masturbation reveries of adolescent boys. Here are two typical examples:

> Sidney's only pre-puberty instruction in sex came when he was about 10. Another boy on the block told

him that there were houses in which women lay around on couches, with little or nothing on, and sailors would visit them, to get on top of the women.

When he hit puberty, and experienced the delights of masturbation and wet dreams, he would masturbate with the image of a house with secret panels in which flimsily clad women were kept for his pleasure in the basement rooms. Only he knew how to press the buttons to get down there. The women there did whatever he wanted.

What was most important was that Sidney held onto this image of sexuality. When he had his first sexual experience, at 18, with a prostitute he thought that he was supposed to ejaculate as soon as he entered her. When this did not happen, he asked her whether there was something wrong. She took his penis and masturbated him till he was about ejaculate. Thereafter he began to suffer from premature ejaculation, which might not have occurred if his first sexual experience had been more pleasant and more normal.

Ralph's adolescent masturbation fantasy was that he had a pirate boat which roamed the seas, with innumerable women, all at his disposal sexually. At 15 he entered upon a sexual affair with a young girl his age, and they had sex two or three times a day. In spite of this pleasure, the fantasy of freedom remained with him, and he could not settle down to one kind of work or one woman. The wish for freedom would make him angry at the woman, whom he would eventually discard.

In American society in the past two decades much interest has been aroused by the "swingers," or, in more formal language, group sex. Obviously numbers are difficult to ascertain, but some think there may be as many as five million swingers in the country. The anthropologist Gilbert Bartels (1971) gathered data in the late 1960's and summarized them in his book *Group Sex*. In a less formal vein the writer Gay Talese (1980) presented similar data in *Thy Neighbor's Wife*.

Bartels claims that swinging is a distinctly American institution; this is incorrect, since swinging has been on the rise in most of the democratic countries, though still severely curtailed in the communistic countries. What is new in the current swinging movement is not so much the sexual freedom (some of that always existed but was left out of the history books) but its open acceptance among the leading members of society.

What emerges from the studies of Bartels, O'Neill, Smith, Brecher and other researchers is that swinging has been adopted by a group of middle-class persons who view it as a means of getting away from the humdrum routines of everyday life. It operates according to certain well-defined standards; female homosexuality is encouraged, while male homosexuality is severely frowned upon. For many swingers an experience with another couple is a one-time encounter, much like the one-night stands of single individuals.

The question above all is whether swinging makes these people happier. The claims made by the O'Neills in particular, among others,[5] is that swinging allows all the sexual fantasies to be shared by the partners, which makes the whole relationship more open. This would be true if it were not for the unconscious fantasies that cannot even be verbalized.

Above all, there is the question of the unconscious meaning of sex to the person. Here a number of observations arise out of analytic experience (every analyst nowadays sees a number of swingers and others who seek to make up in quantity what they cannot find in quality). In group sex the usual feelings of jealousy have to be suppressed, but they are still there. What is striking in all the reports is the wish for novelty; even a regular group that has sex every week, where all the people are known to one another, becomes boring with such an attitude. The promotion of female homosexuality and the repression of male homosexuality are both important; clearly the wish for group sex is related to a wish to master the homosexual conflict. Drugs, alcohol, violence frequently enter the picture, even though they are played down in the conventional reports. Most of the time people engage in group sex for a while, have their thrills, and then move on to a more secure and lasting relationship. The wish for constant excitement is one that cannot really be gratified in the human being.

On top of that, group sex enthusiasts loudly proclaim: Couples who swing together stay together. Thus they build up a theory that multiple sex somehow manages to preserve the marriage. This is paradoxical, and untrue. Monogamy does involve a certain amount of sacrifice, which usually means abandoning certain thrills, and joining in a common effort to achieve a worthwhile goal. Freely having sex with others after a while has little more meaning than freely engaging in other activities with many. But the swing is a group activity to which certain dangers are attached: All mention VD, but do not take it seriously enough. Many reports say that the women, stimulated by the multiplicity of partners, and the homosexual acts that are carried out, develop a desire to become prostitutes, and in a number of cases do. There is an air of secrecy imposed; the children must never find out what the parents are doing, yet how is one to stop them? Usually children find out, in one way or another, about everything parents do.

In the last analysis, the problem with group sex is the same as the problem with any kind of acting out: It represents an action designed to gratify an unconscious wish which can never be gratified. Such action leaves the person constantly frustrated, even if this frustration is blatantly denied. The life history of the man, whom we are most concerned with here, is one of severe rejection by mother, girl friends and sister figures; to overcome these rejections the man requires therapy, not forced action.

On the current scene, some therapists have turned to various forms of sexual gratification, maintaining that the talking kind of therapy "does not work." This is wide of the mark. While talking therapy has many problems, action therapy has more. In a properly arranged therapy, the person's entire design for living is carefully examined, not merely one or another area where he feels deprived.

Most people who turn to group sex do so with the conscious complaint that their marital lives have become dull and boring. But group sex merely complicates the picture. If the marriage is dull and boring, the reasons for that must be examined, and steps taken to alleviate it or change it. The ideal, which most people can achieve if they try, is that of a happy marriage, but it is an ideal which requires a considerable amount of work and on many occasions, sacrifice.

Most men, even today, are not advocates of group sex. As a rule they feel that their own jealousies would be so aroused that the situation would become intolerable. The more common psychology of the man who wants too much is the two-woman fantasy, or the fantasy of having a long string of women.

Fantasies of this kind capture the imagination and envy of the woman. From her point of view, the man is out having a good time, while she has to stay home and take care of the children. She is rarely aware of the inner suffering that prods a man to go off chasing one or two or many women. Popular heroes are described and glamorized because they can womanize so much. In our own times Errol Flynn is a good example. A handsome matinee idol, his autobiography discloses numerous affairs with women. Yet, he says, behind every girdle lies a lawyer.[6] Flynn also drank to excess, ran off when he was not yet fifty with a young girl who was alleged to be a prostitute, and died in a fit of alcoholism. More recently there have been claims that Flynn was a Nazi agent. Looked at in the cold light of day, his life seems very unglamorous indeed. It can be summed up in this way: His vanity was enormous, his feats prodigious and his personal life disastrous.

Most men struggle with the idea of another woman for a long time, not infrequently all their lives. Movies and plays respond to this fantasy by focussing on themes of adultery and infidelity. Usually the play or movie is presented with a certain moral to it: the man is punished for his wrongdoing. But there is little recognition of the inner suffering that the man goes through before, during and after the affair.

There are many variations of the two-woman fantasy. The movie *The Captain's Paradise* rests on the image of the sailor with a girl in every port. Many men daydream of being in bed with two women, a variation that is acted out with great frequency. In other cases, a man has a mistress, concealed from the wife; he spends time with her which is ecstatically happy, while he finds the wife a bore and a nag. Sometimes there is great hatred of the wife, as contrasted with great feeling for the other woman. Sartre, in his play *No Exit,* has focussed on a dynamic constellation in many men: the hero is there with two women, one a nymphomaniac, the other a Lesbian. Generally a moral tone is taken toward such activities, rather than an attempt to understand what the man is going through.

Let us begin with some clinical vignettes, and try to clarify the dynamic patterns.

John, a fifty-five-year-old business man, had a wife and two children, whom he lived with, and a mistress whom he saw regularly every Saturday. This had been going on for years; what was unusual here was that his wife knew what he was doing, and put up with it, for whatever reasons she had. Trouble arose for John only when the older daughter no longer wanted anything to do with him. It was because of this threat that he came to therapy, since he felt very attached to his daughter, and the loss of her love was a severe blow.

Larry, a forty-two-year-old electrician, was in a severe dilemma with his wife. She was completely indifferent to sex, but submitted to him out of a sense of obligation. During the sex act she would frequently read the newspaper. But there were five children, and Larry felt devoted to them. He tried to get around his problem by taking a mistress. But the conflict was so great that he died of a heart attack shortly after he had entered therapy.

Steven, a thirty-year-old salesman, was married to a passive woman with whom he had one child, a girl. His wife liked sex, was always willing to have it, and was orgiastic. Still, Steven became a womanizer, entering upon one affair after another. In these affairs he would generally play an aggressive, sometimes sadistic role. One of his woman friends was a married woman who demanded to be humiliated. She wanted to be cursed, beaten and made to feel completely inadequate. Her own marriage was very unsatisfactory to her.

Steven's extramarital flings were best understood as expressions of his aggression, and disappointments at his achievements in life. Originally he had wanted to be a boxer, but could not make it. His childhood was very unhappy and he identified with his father, who also felt unhappy in his marriage.

In all three cases, the man experiences difficulties in his marriage and does not know what to do about it. He chooses a conventional solution, an extramarital affair, only to be disillusioned sooner or later. Sometimes the man is sadistic toward his wife, sometimes he is masochistic (seeks suffering). Larry was a typical masochist, Steve the typical sadist.

As analysts we try to draw such men into treatment, where their childhood problems can be worked out; only after they have done that can they manage a happy marriage. In Steve's case the therapy was very successful; in the others it was broken off too soon.[7]

This brings us to the main point emphasized here: In the man who seeks too much sex there is a constant feeling of frustration with his life, whether sexually or otherwise. The wife is blamed for this frustration, and he pushes the illusion that with another woman he could be different. Most of the time that does not work out; the man's conflicts have to be tackled and resolved more directly.

What kind of frustrations in childhood predispose the man to be unfaithful in marriage? Many different kinds, but they all have one dynamic element in common: overattachment to the mother and inability to beat out father. They are literally mama's boys, whose deepest longing is to return to the warmth and security of boyhood. Reluctant to work as a rule, they fall back on daydreams of wealth and ease; the gambling industry thrives on these daydreams.

Every human being faces the problem of liberating himself from mother, but the liberation takes different forms in men and women. Boys, as has been seen, build up an idealized version of mother, all goodness, sweetness and light, and no sexuality. They are not aware of the sense of rejection they experience at her hands, rejection which may in fact often come from her. One of the comfortable myths of our society is that mothers have an unconditional love feeling toward their sons; many mothers do, many others do not. It is particularly difficult for mothers to show the boy that they are also sexual creatures; hence the common conflict of the Madonna-prostitute arises.

One of the most striking examples of this Madonna-prostitute complex came out in the analysis of Leopold. He was married to a woman who was completely frigid, spent little time with him, refused to have children, and had some close girl friends who seemed to be Lesbian; in fact, it seemed likely that the wife was having a Lesbian affair with one particular girl friend, who was her constant companion.

Frustrated by the lack of sex and warmth, Leo finally dissolved the marriage. He then met a woman, Sylvia, who was everything his wife was not: she was warm, devoted, interested and completely free sexually. He had constant sex with her, and had never felt happier. Leo also met several other women who were sexually mature and responded to him very favorably.

But the scars of his childhood, a rigid Catholic environment in which sexual pleasure was taboo, were too much for him to handle. After about a year of enjoying life as a bachelor, Leo returned to his wife, more out of a sense of duty than anything else.

As a rule the mother not only does not encourage sexual freedom, but actively discourages it, and tries to keep the boy at her side. At times this is done directly, at times indirectly. In the movie *Marty*, the mother on the surface is happy to see her son go out, but every girl he brings home has some fault or other in the mother's eyes. As a result Marty, who needs his mother's approval, never manages to marry. It is no wonder that in half the societies in the world a strict taboo is laid down which forbids the mother-in-law to associate with her daughter-in-law in any way.

Part of the attachment to mother, which Philip Wylie properly called "momism," is the boy's unconscious incestuous wish. Because he cannot gratify this wish, the boy puts mother up on a pedestal, and unconsciously sets her up in his mind as an ideal which other women must equal. Naturally, no other woman ever turns out to be as good as mother, if for no other reason than that he must be a man to the woman, not a boy. Thus the man goes through life eternally dissatisfied, always seeking yet never finding the perfect woman.

The mama's boy is in a rage because mother will not gratify his wishes for her. At first this rage is subdued; later it becomes increasingly obvious. Since one of his deepest longings is to remain a little boy with mother, his disappointment necessarily grows as he gets further and further away from childhood. The fairy tale of Jack the Giant Killer brings out the psychodynamics of such a man very clearly. Jack does not want to work. When his mother sends him to town for an errand, he squanders his money for a few beans. These he plants, only to discover to his pleasant surprise that they form a ladder to the sky (erection). He climbs up and finds the Giant there with his golden eggs (testicles). The giant is killed, Jack takes the gold, returns to earth and lives happily every after with mother. Clearly the giant stands for father, whose large genitals Jack envies, and whom he would like to displace. No wonder the story is universally fascinating for boys.[8]

A comment is in order about the women to whom such a man relates. Since he mistreats them, they are basically masochistic and undervalue their own femininity and worth. Every relationship becomes one in which the man conquers the woman, and the woman submits. She is at heart a masochist.

The 18th century model for such a personality is Casanova, who recounted the story of his amours in six thick volumes (1725–1798). Casanova was born in Venice; at the age of one year he was abandoned by his parents, who turned him over to a disinterested grandmother. At fifteen he was expelled from the University of Padua for excessive gambling debts, and at sixteen from a Venetian seminary for immoral and scandalous conduct. For the rest of his life he rang the changes on these two themes.

Casanova described 116 mistresses by name in his *Memoirs*, and claimed that he had been with hundreds of women. His first completed sex act consisted of coitus with two young sisters in one bed, all three of them enjoying the performance both as participant and spectator (the two-woman fantasy discussed above). This stratagem he used over and over, finding that one girl alone was hard to seduce, but in the presence of another would quickly surrender.

Much of Casanova's memoirs recounts his scrapes and fights, in a number of which his life was endangered. As though in anticipation of Freud, the wish to marry only came upon him once when, as an older man, he met a beautiful young girl at the Opera. He was so smitten with her that he proposed at once. Before the matter could go further, he met her mother, recognized her as an old mistress and realized that the girl to whom he had proposed was his daughter. He then made love to the mother with the daughter watching (again two women and this time also a violation of the incest taboo). Several years later he met his daughter, who was then married to an impotent Marquis. Casanova obliged, had sex with his daughter and got her pregnant.

As the years wore on he became increasingly miserable. In his forties he started collecting pornographic pictures, was inflamed by caressing a nine-year-old girl and as part of a swindle had sex with a seventy-year-old woman as participant in a magical ritual.

A clue to his behavior came out when in later years he visited an inn where he had once been with a certain Henriette. She had scratched on the window: You will forget Henriette too. Stunned by this note, he wrote: "What frightened me was to have to acknowledge that I no longer possessed the same vigor." So his many love affairs were designed to convince himself over and over that he was not impotent.

Many men with a Casanova-like psychology are to be seen today. For them sex is a mere sensation, the feelings of the woman unimportant. One man, twenty-eight years old, boasted in a series of tapes on group sex, that he had had intercourse with over 8,000 women. Obviously the woman is of no consequence to such a man; she is merely an object who must be conquered; once conquered she is discarded and forgotten.

Sooner or later these men begin to lose their sexual capacities because they are scoring a victory, not making love in the true sense. Wilhelm Reich coined the term "phallic-narcissistic" for such men: they are interested primarily in the narcissistic pleasure derived from the activities of their penises (the "big prick" in ordinary slang). Since the real goal is never achieved, after a while they tire of the conquests and cannot function properly. Reich also correctly predicted that in the analysis of such men, at some point they would become very anxious and lose their sexual abilities temporarily; this is indeed a frequent occurrence.

Mention must again be made here that sexual behavior, like any piece of behavior, cannot be properly understood without reference to its unconscious meaning. Sex can be either an act of love, or an act of hatred and conquest. For the Casanova type there is no feeling of affection for the woman; many of these men say they have never loved anybody. Or, like Casanova, they "fall in love" immediately, and are out of love the next day. Unfortunately, it is a tragic commentary on our civilization that in the psychic warfare between men and women hatred is much more common than love, and sex can be used to mask and express the hatred.

This discussion of the unconscious meaning of sex brings us back to the connection between sex and aggression. The need to conquer one woman after another, à la Casanova, springs more from hatred than from love. The Romans, who had no feelings or affection for the "inferior" races, practiced murder on a large scale, and delighted in it, as in the gladiatorial battles, where hundreds of people would sometimes be slain in cold blood. It has been said that every Roman city was a miniature Auschwitz. Similarly in modern times the Nazis used the women of Europe sexually, and then murdered them.

Today such a close connection between actual murder and sex would be seen as a symptom of a psychosis. The notorious Son of Sam, who went around murdering young couples because of his own inability to find any love, is a good example. Hinckley, the man who tried to assassinate President Reagan, is another variation. Reagan's murder was supposed to convince the young actress at Yale, Jodie Foster, that Hinckley was a young man worth loving. This is a bizarre variation on the Oedipus complex: Reagan, the father, Jodi Foster, the mother: by murdering father, the boy convinces mother how great and desirable he is.

There are however innumerable situations where the aggression is less obvious, even hidden from the other person. Understandably, in such cases people react to the frightening hostility, not aware of the inner pain. This is inevitable since, with a dangerous man like the Son of Sam (in the nineteenth century they would have used the more graphic term "furious lunatic"), the prime need is to stop him from murdering. But there are any number of milder incidents where there is no real danger.

Typical is the frightened man who calls up unknown women and hurls obscenities at them over the phone, or the exhibitionists who show their penises to little girls. Neither of these is in any way dangerous; quite the opposite. A man who has to utter obscenities to strange women over the telephone does so because he is too frightened to do so in person. A sadist like Casanova would never hesitate. Similarly the exhibitionist generally confines his displays to young immature

girls because grown women could fight back, report him, or
have him arrested. Women, overly concerned, and rightly so,
with the possibility of an actual attack, do not sense the deep
fear that grips these men.

Selwyn was a typical exhibitionist, who was arrested at
16 for displaying himself to a young girl. His background
was horrifying. His mother had attempted suicide when
he was seven years old by jumping off a bridge with his
younger brother, who was one year old. Thereafter
mother was in psychiatric treatment for sixteen years,
until she finally did commit suicide. The brother also
ended up a suicide. Selwyn, after doing well through
college, also went into a long suicidal period, but because of constant therapy he was able to overcome the
worst of the depression.

In the more average man, who goes through one woman
after another, the aggression acted out in sex is less apparent
than the exhibitionist, though present. There is always some
alibi, some fault that is found with the woman, and since no
woman is perfect, it is always possible to put one's finger on
some weakness. The woman becomes too demanding; she
wants more attention, or more sex, or may even insist on
marriage. At this juncture the man flees. His sadism has been
gratified by hurting the woman; his narcissism is gratified by
retreating into himself, and repeating the scene with the next
woman. Some men spend their entire lives repeating this
scene of seduction-rejection, always dissatisfied, never able to
find the "right" woman, and always fearful they will be impotent, or lose their potency altogether (castration). And as
mentioned above, with men who have sex with many women,
sooner or later there comes a time they are unable to perform; they become little boys whose need for affection is
greater than their need for sex, and their greatest longing is to
turn the woman into a mother-figure.

Finally, mention should be made of the close connection
between excessive sexual action and repressed homosexual
wishes. The human being is basically bisexual, but the heterosexual element predominates. Gender identity (whether the

person is a man or a woman) is well established early in infancy, by 18 months at the latest, and is based on how the parents see the child. Yet whichever sexual identity is chosen, the desire to be like the other sex remains strong in the unconscious.

In childhood the boy has sexual desires for both mother and father. When the incestuous wishes for mother are very strong, there is a playing down of the corresponding wishes for father. Parents will often play into this conflict: The mother tries to keep the boy at her side as a little boy, whereas when the boy turns to father for masculine support and guidance he finds himself rejected.

When such a boy grows up, he may become fiercely heterosexual, determined to "fuck" every woman he meets. And in fact he does go through a number of women, always angry, never pleased with them, never understanding why he feels so frustrated. Even without going into the deeper dynamics of homosexuality, it is obvious on the surface that such a man fights shy of men friends. Or, as in Casanova's case, he is always getting into fights with other men, some of them quite dangerous. Here is a typical clinical example.

> Lou, a 30-year-old bartender, was the youngest of four children, all boys. He came from a small town in Ohio, and emigrated to New York to find fame and fortune. His strongest fantasy in the beginning was to make every girl he could find. He did in fact have a number of sexual contacts, though not as many as he had hoped for. Through it all however he was obsessed with the idea that other men thought of him as a "queer." When he tended bar, men would make jokes about him, which hurt him deeply, though he never said anything about it. He married twice; neither marriage was successful.

Worthy of discussion is the role of the woman in the perpetuation of the conflicts of the man who obsessively pursues sexual conquests. It is not too difficult to find women who will submit to him, especially in these days of sexual liberation. But the psychology of the woman tends to reinforce his struggles. As in Sartre's plays, the man finds himself con-

fronted by the alternative between a lesbian and a nymphomaniac. If he goes with the lesbian he finds himself rejected
by a cold woman who prefers the company of her girl friend
(even if the relationship is not sexual, two close women
friends often pair off against the man). If he turns to the
nymphomaniac, he finds himself unable to satisfy the woman,
which then drives her into the arms of other men.

If the woman is more normal, and seeks a satisfactory sex-
love relationship, she does not respond to a man with this
psychology. Part of the pursuit of pleasure is the capacity to
have a rest period after gratification has been achieved. The
man who is obsessed with sex never allows himself a rest
period; the healthier woman does. Hence friction arises, and
sooner or later the relationship breaks up.

With the hypersexual man we again find adult sexuality
used to overcome childhood conflicts. And that cannot be
done; childhood conflicts have to be overcome directly, with
the recognition by the man he is no longer a child and he
cannot keep on repeating an endless search which yields him
no lasting satisfaction.

Of the various childhood conflicts involved, one of the
most important is the notion that sex is a sadistic act. While
the number is increasing, the percentage of married couples
who really enjoy sex is still so small relatively that many, if
not most, men are brought up with the idea that mother
submits to father only because she is afraid of him. Boys pick
up sexual knowledge from the street: One man recalled that
when he was about eight a friend told him how father pees
into mother's behind, which horrified him and made him angry at father. If sex is seen as an act of cruelty, then the man
in a close relationship must always be hurting the woman.
Some men shrink from this recognition and stay away from a
woman; others go after the woman and find themselves disillusioned. They may, and also do, pick a woman who feels
easily hurt and blames the man for whatever happens.

The culture also blows up the hostile side of the sexual
connection. Wife-abuse has become a cause for so much concern that clinics have been set up to help women subjected to
it. The man is depicted as a brutal monster, defeated and
baffled in all of his life's endeavors, who takes out his humil-
iations on his wife. Or, in the alternative, he is seen as a

successful tycoon who wishes to exploit women and gets into positions where he can exploit them sexually.

What is not displayed in all this outcry against abuse is that the man is equally abusive to others as well. It is not that he hates his wife or secretary so much; he hates everybody and is out to conquer and humiliate them. He feels like a failure inside, and the hostile display is designed to cover up his feelings of failure.

The idealization of the woman (the idealized mother-figure) also leads to a misinterpretation of these destructive actions by the man. In human affairs there is more often than not a certain reciprocity, and the man who abuses his wife may very well be taunted into it by a masochistic woman, while in sexual harassment the woman may quite consciously be goading the man on, only to turn against him when he reveals his true colors.

> Sally, a 13-year-old girl in a home for juvenile delinquents, had had sex with fifteen men. In each case she was warm and loving to the man, flattered him by telling him how wonderful he was, and took his name and address so that she could call him, since he was not to call her at her home. When fifteen names were collected, she turned them all over to the police, who prosecuted all the men for statutory rape.

In general, it is well established that ours is a rather violent society, and whoever is stronger takes it out on the weaker. Within the family[9] the father is stronger, and beats the wife more often than the reverse, though many wives fight back and beat the husband as well. In child abuse, since the mothers are stronger than the children and are with the children more, they tend to hit the child more often than the fathers do. Thus the problem of violence, crucial and frightening as it is, cannot be divorced from the structure of society. The main point is that when sexual frustration is widespread, violence is apt to increase.

Chapter 3:
The Sexually Inadequate Man:
Impotence, Premature Ejaculation
and Homosexuality

It was one of Freud's major contributions to the progress of civilization to show that most men in the modern world are so crushed by their repressive childhoods that they become sexual cripples in adult life. The traditional moral code which prescribes sex with one and only one woman is too hard. As early as 1908 Freud argued that experience shows that the majority of people in our society are constitutionally unfit for sexual abstinence. Add to this the fact that conventional marriage frequently involves withdrawal from sex for longer or shorter periods, and it need come as no surprise that a large number of persons are driven into neurosis and psychosis by their sexual conflicts.

Freud's evaluation has been considerably modified by the high incidence of premarital sexuality, especially in adolescence. Yet the plain fact is that our culture continues to produce large numbers of sexually inadequate men who go on to make poor marriages, producing another generation of men who are equally incompetent sexually.

Although Freud's assertions were pooh-poohed for a long time, the first large-scale study of human sexuality, by Kinsey and his associates in the 1940's and 1950's, virtually confirmed Freud in every detail. Erect impotence, Kinsey stated, was "not uncommon."[1] Premature ejaculation was more the rule than the exception. For perhaps three-quarters of all men, orgasm is reached within two minutes and for a not inconsiderable number of men the climax may be reached within less than a minute or even ten or twenty seconds after coital entrance.[2] Characteristically, Kinsey pooh-poohs his own finding, arguing that premature ejaculation is actually a sign of "superiority"![3]

© 1987 by The Haworth Press, Inc. All rights reserved.

Among the other findings of Kinsey and his associates that attracted widespread attention were the frequency of extramarital sex, the absence of orgasm in most women (Kinsey even called vaginal orgasm a "biological impossibility"!), and above all the fact that the conventional prescriptions for sex are so widely defied that the laws, if properly enforced, would put perhaps 95% of the population in jail. In other words, what Kinsey proved statistically was what Freud and the analysts had been urging on the basis of their clinical experience for some forty years, that sexual frustration is widespread in our civilization and relatively few people manage to develop a satisfactory sex life in marriage.

In the thirty to forty years since Kinsey's work, another development of major impact on the society was the study by Masters and Johnson, which eventuated in the publication of their two books, *Human Sexual Response* (1966) and *Human Sexual Inadequacy* (1970). In the wake of the Masters-Johnson inquiry, sex counselors and marriage clinics were set up all over the country, taking as their theoretical basis the techniques used by Masters and Johnson, but going far beyond them as well. The ease of transportation after World War II also encouraged familiarity with a wide variety of other cultures, and not merely on the part of professional anthropologists.[4] Consequently, since the early 1970's everyone has been speaking of a "sexual revolution."

The impact of this sexual revolution is hard to evaluate. While objective evidence can easily measure such items as frequency and number of partners, it cannot offer any answers to questions of satisfaction and, above all, love. On top of that, the free release of sexuality, pursued by so many from time immemorial (cf. Chapter 2), has brought in its wake a host of other serious problems such as increased incidence of VD, release of violence, use of drugs and increased homosexuality, which are even more difficult to handle than the preceding sexual repression. The pendulum has swung so far that someone has seriously written a book advocating chastity as the answer.

To grasp the situation more clearly, it is necessary to clarify the original Freudian theory. In the description of normal sexual development, Freud delineated three main stages: infantile sexuality, latency (the school period) and adolescence (or puberty). Sexual difficulties arise from a failure to complete development. Further, there is a parallel between sexual problems and fixation, or incomplete development; thus, the voyeur who confines his sexual activity to watching women dress and undress is behaving like the little boy who was excited by watching his mother around the house, while the exhibitionist who shows his penis to little girls is like the little boy who displays his penis to his mother.

However, the end point of development was, for Freud, the union of tender and sexual feelings toward a person of the opposite sex. Such a union is also the essence of love; it has also been called genital primacy, indicating that the highest pleasure is derived from actual intercourse.

In the sexual revolution this emphasis on love is almost always forgotten. Primarily, as in the Masters-Johnson techniques, the improvement in sexual performance is stressed without regard to the feelings that prevail between the two people. Hence its therapeutic claims are open to serious question, since it leaves out of account the most significant aspect of the whole conflict.

It is not surprising then that, in spite of all the emphasis on open sexuality, men still suffer from many of the same difficulties obvious in Freud's day. Thus in George Vaillant's study of a group of superior men (the Grant Study), whom he calls "the best and the brightest," of the ninety-five men followed up over a period of thirty years, almost all had to cope with sexual problems at various times in their lives.[5]

Typical is the case of Edward Keats (the name used by Vaillant in the book). He was like the storybook rich boy. Everybody loved him, everybody described him as the most satisfactory sort of child. It was not until college that his sexual conflicts emerged; up to then he had been able to hide them behind the facade of making himself well liked. He approved dirty jokes if not accompanied by sexual feelings. He did not believe in kissing girls because such behavior was "immature and disrespectful." The male genitals he thought "ugly."

When he was thirty-one he discovered he was full of hostilities; this self-revelation he could never master. He became increasingly estranged from his wife, his job and the Germans, working in Germany after the war. He moved to Boston and devoted himself to encounter groups—giving others the freedom to enjoy the emotional expression he denied himself. While he practiced philanthropy, there remained little pleasure for him. By midlife he had lost his energy and effectiveness.

Another man described by Vaillant, Dylan Bright, became a professor of literature. From earliest childhood his mother had taught him to beware of instinctual pleasure, which of course meant sexuality. Before he was one year old he was cured of thumbsucking, bedwetting and soiling himself. At two his mother made him wear mittens to bed because of his "perfectly revolting habit of masturbating."

In childhood Dylan was constantly trying to prove that he had no fear. Later, in the sexual period in adolescence, typical conflicts emerged. Suddenly he found the first girl with whom he had slept "revolting." With his next girl friend he gave up intercourse "just to see if I could."

A critical period occurred in his life when at thirty-five his wife began to break up their very close marriage. At the same time he realized he was not going to get very far as a scholar. As a way out, he lost himself in alcohol, careless affairs and stock car racing. The drinking went so far as to threaten him with alcoholism and he went on the wagon twice. Eventually he was able to overcome his bad period and make a second marriage which provided him with much happiness.

There is some reason to believe that with all the talk and education about sex there will eventually be fewer sexually crippled men. However, at present clinically we still find many men who need a lot of help to enable them to function adequately sexually.

The typical pattern of the generation Freud encountered was that of a man overly spoiled by mother, toilet trained too early, forced to give up his aggression, made to feel guilty about masturbation, separated from girls at an early age, and then when the conflicts of puberty broke loose, could not come to grips with his sexual maturity and fell back on a variety of neurotic and psychotic defensive postures. In spite of all the changes that have occurred since, and the "new rules"[6] which so many people are trying to adopt, this is a pattern of development that for many men has not yet changed in any significant way. The inroads psychoanalysis has made on the general culture are still not too extensive, the handicaps of an anti-sexual childhood still too great. Usually the sex problem does not become manifest until the boy reaches adolescence or his early twenties. But more and more people are beginning to notice the signs early in life. In the army induction centers of World War II, the psychiatrists would ask one crucial question: Do you go out with girls? If the draftee had never dated, this was regarded as an ominous sign and many such men were rejected.

It is generally realized now that marriage is a stage in development, like school, or camp, or entry into the work life. Gail Sheehy's best seller *Passages* gives a good description of the numerous stages in life, and the pitfalls that await at each one.

The boy who grows up with the image of an unattainable woman, the outcome of a repressive childhood, has great difficulty in making a happy marriage in which he can find a suitable resolution of his sexual conflicts. Instead, when the sexual pressure becomes intense in adolescence, the boy resorts to a variety of defensive maneuvers. As time goes on, these defensive reactions become more and more disturbing to the young man. In the New York atmosphere it is commonly assumed that a man who is not married by thirty should have some therapy, while a man who is not married by forty may well have some concealed homosexual leanings.

The young man's feeling that he is sexually inadequate, whether in terms of performance or in terms of finding a real love match, represents a serious problem. Sometimes it comes on after a disappointing try in early adolescence; sometimes there is not even a try.

The withdrawal from sexual adventure begins to color the young man's entire life. He withdraws from much social life as well, since that usually leads to sexual challenges he does not wish to face. He may become a "jock", building up his body to the point where girls will accept him more readily, for he has the mistaken idea that the average girl will reject him because of his sexual fantasies. The concern with his body will make him more self-centered (narcissistic), which leads to a further withdrawal. There is always something that can be found wrong with the body, and if the young man is constantly preoccupied with these imperfections he will not be able to feel comfortable with a woman.

Another common defensive manuever is to throw himself into some fantasy world, such as books, or the theater, or music, or just lying around and daydreaming. The more isolation there is, the worse the ultimate outcome, for this is the soil in which a severe neurosis or even psychosis may grow. Neurotic and psychotic problems come from an inner feeling in the man that he cannot have a gratifying relationship with another person. The stronger this conviction (regardless of its objective truth) the more likely he is to develop symptoms. A man who cannot love a woman is bound to fall ill at some point in his life; while the precise point cannot be predicted, the direction in which he is heading may be noticed early.

The description of the adolescent boy described above, full of guilt and feelings of sexual inadequacy, fits Freud himself to a "t." In his last published dream in 1900 Freud saw himself seated at a table with a woman who is making a pass at him. He turns her away, to reflect on the picture of a woman. The shy adolescent today does the same: he turns away the real girl and loses himself in the fantasy of what a woman is like.

> One of my patients used to engage in the following frustrating bit of behavior. He would stand outside a dance hall, hoping to pick up one of the women who frequented the place. But his greatest sexual urge was to perform cunnilingus on a woman (to "eat her out"). Yet he "knew" that no decent self-respecting woman would submit to such an act (he obviously knew little about women). Accordingly he would stand there, find a woman attractive, daydream of talking with her, yet unable to do so. After three or four hours of desire and self-punishment he would give up and go home.

By now this dynamic is well known, described in innumerable self-help books. What is less well known is that the sexually inadequate adolescent boy is caught in a painful dilemma from which there is no good escape. Consider the various possibilities, all of which are tried on the current scene.

In spite of the permissiveness of the day, many boys come into puberty with a strong feeling of sexual inadequacy. At sixteen the boy cannot yet legally have intercourse with a girl, even though many do. The more usual solution is masturbation, which is forbidden by the traditional code, and which is not really satisfactory anyhow, as compared with the full pleasure of a sexual relationship.

One of the greatest preoccupations of the adolescent boy is the "first time." The age at which sexual experience begins is certainly getting earlier, as the atmosphere of sexual permissiveness increases. However, exact figures are always hard to come by. Kinsey found that among men with eighth grade education 6.5% had sex by the time they were twelve, 14.5% by age thirteen, 28.0% by age fourteen, 42.2% by age fifteen. However, there was a marked difference at the upper levels of education. For those with education of thirteen years or more (study after college) only 3.1% had intercourse by age thirteen, 6.0% by age fourteen, 9.5% by fifteen, 15.5% by age sixteen, and 23.1% by age seventeen. In a report of a generation later, though without the careful statistical controls that Kinsey had, the social psychologist Sorenson found that 59% of all adolescent boys had intercourse, and 45% of adolescent girls.[8]

Our culture is changing so rapidly that statistics for any period may be outdated by the time the next large-scale report is issued. Clearly, adolescents are beginning to have sex earlier, but its meaning to them is much less clear. Religion still has a strong hold on many people, and to the religious person all sex outside marriage is bad. St. Augustine in his *Confessions* has given us one of the most vivid statements of the extraordinary guilt aroused in the young boy by transgressing the code. He wrote:

> . . . foulness and carnal corruptions . . . out of the dark concupiscence of the flesh and the effervescence of youth exhalations came forth which obscured and overcast my heart, so that I was unable to discern pure affection from unholy desire. Both boiled confusedly within me, and dragged away my unstable youth into the rough places of unchaste desires and plunged me into the gulf of infamy.
>
> I must now carry my thoughts back to the abominable things I did in those days, the sins of the flesh which defiled my soul. I do this, my God, not because I love those sins, but so that I may love you. . . .

> I cared for nothing but to love—and be loved. But my
> love went beyond the affection of one mind for another,
> beyond the arc of the bright beam of friendship. Bodily
> desire, like a morass, and adolescent sex welling up
> within me exuded mists which clouded over and ob-
> scured my heart, so that I could not distinguish the clear
> light of love from the murk of lust. Love and lust to-
> gether seethed within me. In my tender youth they swept
> me away over the precipice of my body's appetites and
> plunged me in the whirlpool of sin. . . . I was tossed and
> spilled, floundering in the broiling sea of my fornication,
> and you said no word. . . . I was in a ferment of wicked-
> ness. I deserted you and allowed myself to be carried
> away by the sweep of the tide. . . . Nothing deserves to
> be despised more than vice; yet I gave in more and more
> to vice simply in order not to be despised. . . .

Clinical experience teaches us over and over that mere sexual experience does not erase the inner feelings of "unchaste
desires" and the "gulf of infamy" of which Augustine speaks.
If society really wishes to rid itself of sexual guilt, it must
begin much earlier and embrace the whole design for living of
the child and later the adolescent. Some countries have ex-
perimented with fairly early and intensive sex education (e.g.,
Sweden) but while they seem to have erased some of the
guilt, much of it still remains.

Wherever one looks in western history one finds evidence
that men of the day were dominated by fears of impotence
and other sexual conflicts. The French historian Ladurie[10] has
described a kind of castration-by-magic fear which became
virtually epidemic in the period from 1550–1600. The castration was supposed to be performed with a small instrument
known as the aiguillette, a cord with metal tips at both ends,
like a shoelace. The castration by the magical device of the
aiguillette was carried out by women on newly-wed husbands.
Fear of this punishment was so great that, according to Ladurie, most couples were married secretly, rather than in the
open in the church, to avoid the magic spell. These magical
beliefs, as we know, correspond to inner fears, and the prevalence of the epidemic testifies to the enormous anxieties the
men of that time had about performing their marital duties.

Since this point is so crucial to the development of the man, it is worth our while to discuss it in a more systematic way. Because of the early disappointments with women, and the guilt instilled in him about sex ("unchaste desires" and "a gulf of infamy") the boy reaches adolescence with a deep-seated sense of sexual inadequacy. At the same time he is plagued by desires and physical reactions, such as erections, or wet dreams, over which he has no control. As a result he is in a state of constant conflict.

Confronted by such a severe conflict, the boy has the choice of a number of defensive postures: (1) repression, (2) masturbation, (3) acting out, (4) early marriage, (5) submission to societal rules and postponement. On top of this conflict, the boy is also going through other changes of enormous consequence, especially freeing himself from his parental ties, and finding his place in the social-vocational order.

Repression is the most common solution adopted: The boy blots out as much of the sexual desire as he can. The trouble is that the drive is so strong at this age that complete repression is virtually impossible. Kinsey has shown that almost all boys masturbate, while the few (less than 1%) who do not are in bad shape psychologically. This pattern of sexual repression, and enormous masturbatory guilt, creates a climate from which the most disastrous consequences may follow. It is one of the frequent pathways through which a schizophrenic illness gradually develops. Many men become schizoid, or excessively narcissistic, or develop some neurotic problem of varying degrees of severity. This was the area Freud first uncovered almost a hundred years ago and which led him to write about it in 1898. It will take mankind a hundred years to get over its sexual repressions.

Acting out when the occasion permits, without worrying too much about the girl, is the solution adopted by many strong-willed adolescent boys. One of the subjects in Vaillant's study, a man who became a top corporation executive, described it as follows: "Sex is a continuous nuisance. I take it when I can get it, and for the rest I am content. Though not a supporter of free love, I will accommodate almost any enthusiastic amateur." After an adolescence of this kind, the man married in his mid-twenties, and lived out a stable, fairly happy marriage.

But many others who act out are much less fortunate. Some comments have already been made about this pattern in the previous chapter. Today especially the pattern so often is accompanied by the use of drugs that it offers no real way out. Most boys, unless they have a steady girl, learn to suffer through this stage.

Going steady, or what the sociologists have come to call serial monogamy, is another reasonable solution adopted by many young people. It involves a sharing of intimacy and affection which is much more gratifying than the isolated catch-as-catch-can acting out of casual relationships. Here the parents, if they are permissive, can play a positive role in the growth of the boy. In effect, he gains the emotional gratification of a good marriage without the concomitant responsibilities. Many times these early relationships go on to marriage; many times they break up. Even when they break up, at least there has been a degree of intimacy which contributes to the emotional growth toward manhood.

Finally, there is the alternative of a real marriage. Paradoxically, marriage in the teens was by no means rare in the nineteenth century. The twentieth in its stead has created a period of adolescence which creates more problems than it resolves. Still, marriage in the teens is possible only with the active support of the parents, since few teenagers have the material resources to take care of themselves.

Numerous studies have shown that prediction of what will happen in people's lives is a hazardous procedure. There are too many imponderables, too many accidents of fortune and fate, quite apart from the fact that man at every stage is able to stand still, assess what he is doing, and make an effort to change, efforts which are often successful even without therapy. But then again there are others who are seemingly driven by inexorable forces to a tragic fate. We can only work with probabilities. Here are two contrasting examples:

Jim (this case history has been presented in more detail in my book, *The Intimate Hour,* 1979, under the title "Jim the Drifter") was a 38-year-old bookkeeper-accountant who had stumbled his way through life. When he entered therapy he did not know what he wanted to do or where he was going. Dissatisfied with his work, with no friends, few outside interests, his life seemed bleak indeed. Nor was there any reason to be optimistic about the future, in the light of what he had been through.

He was the second of three children. The parents were lower middle-class of Jewish descent who ran a store in Brooklyn, a store around which their whole life was centered. The other two children were girls. The older had managed to marry and make some kind of life for herself; the younger seemed mentally retarded and was still living at home.

Childhood was a period of extreme domination by mother. She ran the family with such an iron hand that she even measured out the food beforehand, giving each person his or her allotted portion, no more, no less. Jim's father was completely submissive to her; one of his few rebellions came when at one point in a fit of rage he simply threw his entire meal into the garbage pail. Otherwise his only act of defiance was to join a synagogue where the men sat separately from the women; at least there he could be by himself.

From an early age Jim ran into arguments with his mother. She tried to punish him by merciless beatings, to which he responded by gritting his teeth and refusing to cry, as though daring her to hit him harder. From an early age he resolved to get as far away from her as he could.

With such a background it is not surprising that there was no sex life in puberty except masturbation. Adolescence was a miserable time for him; his main consolation was the daydream that a rich man would come along and adopt him.

Entry into the army in World War II offered him a chance to get away from home. Because of a physical disability, he did not see active service. In spite of that, at one point he had a breakdown and was hospitalized. He stayed in the hospital for several months, crying continually. When he was discharged he rejected the suggestion of therapy.

Shortly after discharge he met up with a strong, domineering man, a successful writer whom he came to worship. With this man, Greg, he established a homosexual relationship which lasted for ten years. Mostly the sex involved mutual masturbation. What was more important was the aura of greatness with which he endowed Greg.

Finally the affair broke up, and it was at this juncture that Jim undertook psychotherapy. Surprisingly from the very beginning he formed a very positive relationship with the therapist. He would listen to him intently, and seemingly memorize every word that was said to him. He never missed an appointment and never came late.

After about one and a half years of therapy Jim met an old acquaintance, Sally, who had felt attracted to him for a long time. In the past he had always spurned her, as he had spurned all women. Now, with his newfound sense of confidence he accepted her interest. Soon they moved into a sexual liaison. Although he had rarely had sex with a woman he reported no difficulties.

Sally had a son by a former marriage who was nine years old. Jim took to the boy very quickly, thinking that he would never have a son of his own (Sally was in her forties). The love relationship flourished and six months after they had met the two were married. So far as could be ascertained, he lived a fairly happy life thereafter, with a new family, a wife he loved, and work he enjoyed. The change was dramatic.

Still, it took Jim a quarter of a century after his miserable adolescence to find himself. A much more tragic outcome was seen in the life of Oliver Kane, a subject in the Grant Study of George Vaillant, mentioned before.

Kane lost both parents before he was sixteen, his father when he was one, and his mother when he was fifteen. He never really had a home. He and his wife lived in residential hotels and never had any children.

In work he succeeded in a briliant career. He was a management consultant, his job was to make friends with promising executives, put square pegs in square holes, round pegs in round holes and then move onto the next problem. His business success however made him no lasting friends. In spite of his $70,000 a year income (in the 1960's) there was little fun in his life. He showed little interest in athletics, never took vacations, and his only hobby was the elegant manner in which he dressed.

Vaillant judged him to be perhaps the most intelligent man in the study, yet his high intelligence did not permit him to order his life more sensibly. When asked if he found it hard to ask for help, he said, "Yes, I have trouble. That is true of me."

Outwardly brilliant, inwardly miserable, Kane's life ended in disaster. During a period of financial crisis, he flew his light

plane into a mountain. It may have been accidental but Kane
had always been a meticulously careful pilot, and he had
spent the previous week revising his will and putting all his
affairs in order. A year before his death he wrote his last
words to the Study: "Ironically, as I have acquired more external 'success', I have more and more doubts that I have
chosen a way of life that really means anything." The implication that his plane crash was really a suicide seems amply
justified.

With both of these men the sexual conflicts of adolescence,
which in turn went back to miserable relationships with the
parents in earlier childhood, persisted for many years. Had
Jim not entered therapy, he might never have gotten over
them. Oliver Kane, with his stiff upper lip, apparently never
did.

Like Augustine, the modern boy when he reaches adolescence and its overwhelming sexual desires, is often overcome
by feelings of "foul and carnal corruptions" and the "gulf of
infamy" into which he has sunk. The degree of this guilt
depends more on the family background than on anything
else. Even the most permissive kind of adolescence does not
eradicate the guilt feelings entirely, and they may easily come
out at a place and time they are least expected to appear.

Apart from his parents, the influence of the women whom
the boy meets in his search for sexual fulfillment is considerable. What kind of a woman will the sexually inadequate man
choose? The answer is obvious: either exploitative women, or
women who are sexually inadequate themselves. Thus a cycle
is created, in which the sexually frustrated man pairs off with
a sexually frustrated woman, and the two create more sexual
frustration. Marriage, however, is an institution behind which
the blinds are drawn. Without a careful search no one can tell
how a couple gets along. Objective studies point over and
over to the widespread incidence of sexual conflicts in marriage. Now that women are freer to bring out the feelings of
unhappiness in their sex lives, more men are confronted with
sexual demands from their wives. There can be no doubt that
this is a major factor in the high and constantly rising rate of
divorce. But there is no reason to believe that there was more
sexual fulfillment in a previous generation. It is simply that
more people are insisting on finding more pleasure and more

meaning in their lives; ours is the age when self-fulfillment has become one of the most insistent claims on life on the part of a large majority of the population.

One alternative that the sexually inadequate adolescent male can choose is homosexuality. In early puberty, the boy, frightened of his sexual desires, frequently resorts to sexual contacts with other boys. Kinsey in his day found that 37% of the boys in his sample had used such outlets. As time went on, the vast majority of these boys gave up the homosexuality and turned to women. Thus the homosexuality was a passing experience which in most cases gave way to the infinitely more gratifying heterosexual experience. The standard psychological theory was quite simply that homosexuality results from the fear of sex.

One clarification is in order here. When psychoanalysts speak of homosexuality they refer to compulsive-exclusive homosexuality, not the casual encounters described in the previous paragraph. Such exclusivity, in which normal sexual relations are completely absent, is in the common sense of most people a sign of pathology.

Since the 1960's a peculiar shift in the attitudes of homosexuals has occurred. Where before they had generally agreed that homosexuality was a sign of immaturity, even if it could never be eradicated by psychotherapeutic means (which incidentally is untrue), now certain groups began to promote homosexuality actively, as a kind of political cause. "Gay" rights came out into the open, out of the closet, as the saying went.

The gay person was suddenly seen as a victim of social oppression, and he was called upon to fight the evil system. In this fight two questions became completely confused. One was the stupidity of laws which punished homosexual activity in private; all agreed that such laws served no useful purpose. The other, more important question, was that of the genesis and pathology of the homosexual life style. Here the homosexual movement suddenly became very militant. They attacked professionals who tried to understand them, created riots, threatened violence and in every way acted like oppressed victims of society. In their writings homosexuals were compared to blacks, minorities and other social groups society did not leave in peace. Some of them stridently proclaimed that man is basically bisexual (Freud had allegedly said so—a common misquotation and misunderstanding) so that it is just a matter of social pressure which way the man blows.

"Scientific" literature was suddenly called in to bolster their position. No matter that this literature was totally devoid of merit; "authorities" could now be quoted. Surprisingly, the major professional organizations began to behave in peculiar ways. Psychiatrists, psychologists and social workers, in their national organizations, and with little regard for the real facts, agreed with the homosexual groups that there was no pathology in exclusive homosexuality. Most of them did not go as far as agreeing that it is just a matter of chance which way the individual goes. But the American Psychiatric Association did come up with the extraordinary designation of a "sexual orientation disturbance," a term never used before. For the most part the general public remained unimpressed by the surrender of the professionals. Perhaps they intuitively recognized that the actions of the professional societies were more a reflection of their susceptibility to political pressure than a considered scientific opinion.

Numerous studies have shown that in adolescence a considerable percentage of both sexes experiment with homosexual behavior. However, comparatively few continue this experimentation into adult life. Boys remain boys; girls remain girls. Exclusive homosexuality, in which the other sex is completely shunned, is rarely found if the person has had real warmth and love from the parents, and has been given a chance to enjoy himself or herself heterosexually. Any immaturity should not be confused with a real resolution to life's problems.

All this hullabaloo should not blind anyone to the simple fact that continued homosexuality into adult life is merely an adolescent hangover. Boys remain boys; girls remain girls. No one becomes exclusively homosexual if they have had warmth and love from their parents and are given a chance to enjoy themselves heterosexually. Gay immaturity should not be confused with a real resolution to life's problems.

RECAPITULATION

While the previous chapter discussed the hypersexed man (the Don Juan and his mask), the present chapter takes up the sexually inadequate man. It is seen that as a result of his childhood, the adolescent boy is filled with thoughts of his sexual inadequacy; his fears range from the feeling that he cannot perform well sexually to actual castration anxiety. As an aside, it was shown that castration anxiety was virtually endemic in France in the half century from 1550 to 1600, showing once more that the man's sexual guilt runs through all of western history.

The adolescent boy has various ways of handling the "gulf of infamy" which Augustine found in himself centuries ago. He can withdraw to a life of fantasy, narcissism and withdrawal; he can move on to severe neurosis and psychosis (schizophrenia is the typical outcome in many cases); he can try to repress the whole conflict with the traditional denial and "cold showers in the Y," except that such total repression is humanly impossible; he can act out occasionally, taking sex when and where he can get it, without worrying too much about the girl; he can enter upon an early serial monogamy, or even an early marriage, though the rising incidence of divorce indicates that this solution is not a lasting one; or he can give up women altogether and become an overt homosexual—many men adopt this alternative after one or more disappointing experiences with women in the adolescent years.

What has been stressed above all is that no matter what alternative he chooses, the man is saddled with deep feelings of sexual inadequacy and frustration which may take a quarter of a century or a lifetime to overcome, or may never be overcome. Unlike the stereotype of the sadistic rapist, the average man suffers from sexual fears of greater or lesser intensity which color his entire life.

Although the sexual revolution has lessened these fears somewhat, clinical experience indicates that sexual guilt is still the norm rather than the exception. Permissiveness in adolescence, which is tried by many parents, helps somewhat, but runs up against the disturbing psychological fact that these guilts are internalized so early in life that they remain as a permanent feature of the personality. There are of course many other problems that the adolescent boy faces. If we really wish to change his life in a positive direction, a large-scale reform of the total educational process, which would give him a much better feeling·about his body and his sexuality, is required. In some circles such a large-scale reform is being undertaken; in others, there is a surface reordering which does not go deep. As we ponder the life of the forgotten man, it is well to remember that for most men this feeling of evil and wrongdoing about his sex life remains an essential part of his makeup.

Chapter 4:
The Masculine Ideal
and the Analytic Ideal

Of recent years two new Spanish words have entered the English vocabulary—macho and machismo. Literally macho means a he-animal, figuratively it means a man who is very masculine. This is the image pursued by a large number of American men—to be strong, masculine, successful, powerful, rich. And since most men cannot live up to this ideal, the net result is that most men in greater or lesser degree feel like failures.

Look at any newspaper or magazine, and you will see how a man's worth is measured: how old is he, how much does he earn, what are his achievements, how far has he advanced (or did he advance) in life, and the like. William James (the greatest American philosopher) automatically comes to mind: He called it the worship of "the bitch-goddess success." From the day he is born until the day he dies, the man is preoccupied with success; even in death the first question is: how much did he leave, i.e., how successful was he?

Since men are by and large more successful than women in the matter of accumulating earthly goods and honors, they have come to be envied by women for their exploits. Rarely do people ask, "At what price was this feat achieved?" How much did the man have to sacrifice of himself, of his tender feelings, of many of the things that make life count, before he got to the top?

Here lies the core dilemma of the man in our society. Pressed on the one hand to accomplish more and more, he is rarely satisfied with what he has done. No matter how successful he is or has been, a certain sense of inadequacy is apt to overcome him. In his private self-evaluation the man usu-

© 1987 by The Haworth Press, Inc. All rights reserved.

ally finds himself deficient. The historian James Robertson has published a book, *American Myth—American Reality*. Every man at some point says to himself: personal myth, personal reality. The myth of the he-man pursues him at every step in his career.

Other aspects of his cultural ideal of masculinity can be described. Success, power, glory are all part of the picture. If the man cannot achieve them himself, he will project them on his organization, his city, his country. The macho he-man must show no signs of weakness. John Wayne is the prototype in this respect: even when his body was being rapidly consumed by cancer, he insisted he would overcome it.

Toward women there is a dual and contradictory feeling. On the one hand women are weak and subservient, they must be conquered. On the other hand women are idealized and adorable, they must be wooed.

Cultural values, such as music and art, still are relatively low on the scale of what makes a man worthwhile. Any man who chooses to become a musician, or an artist or a sculptor, or some other pursuit the major goal of which is not making money or conquering other men, is still looked upon as somewhat suspect.

Yet even with money there are conflicting demands. Make a lot of money, yes, but if you do and hold onto it you are like one of the robber barons after the Civil War who made huge fortunes by fair means or foul. So, once you had made a lot of money you had to give it away—the country is full of worthwhile cultural institutions endowed by robber barons like John D. Rockefeller, Andrew Carnegie, Andrew Mellon.

On the whole the intellectual is still rather suspect, even in these days when the fate of the world hinges much more on scientific genius than on ordinary bravery. The Japanese, who had the same image of the macho, or he-man, showed extraordinary bravery in World War II, even to the point of having 20,000 men ready to commit suicide for the emperor and country (the "kamikazes"), but all this bravery was useless against the atomic bomb.

So, as the boy grows up, moving from mama's little boy to father's rival, he has to shed his youthful illusions. More easily said than done. Just as his early sexual fantasies have to be tempered to allow him a gratifying love life, the early image that any boy can become president also has to be gradually abandoned. And for this abandonment the man often has to pay dearly.

The masculine ideal is absorbed through all the influences that can be brought to bear on the little boy. The TV teaches him to be a superman (the term superboy has also been used). Space flights portray incredible feats. In the movies there are powerful gangsters arrayed against powerful policemen, and for the rest of his life the man will be obsessed by the battle of cops vs. robbers; which one he chooses to be often depends on the vagaries of fate. In his own family he is put in competition with father, brother, other boys as far back as he can remember. If he flinches he is "showing the yellow feather"; if he accepts the challenge he is set on a life of constant challenges. Sam Bronfman, one of the richest men in the world, founder of Canada's elite society and politics, in spite of all his money never felt a success. Throughout his life he felt defeated.

In contrast with the masculine ideal of our culture, there is the analytic ideal, an image of how men can best hope for happiness in this life. This analytic ideal involves the recognition that the major ingredients of happiness are: the capacity to love, sexual gratification, pleasure, a rich feeling about life yet one guided by reason, a role in the family, a social role, a strong sense of identity, the capacity to work, the ability to communicate, creative outlets, and freedom from psychiatric symptoms. While the cultural masculine ideal stresses success and achievement above all, the analytic ideal places the greatest emphasis on love and inner contentment. Clearly these two attitudes are in diametric opposition to one another. What we are going through now in terms of societal transformation involves a drastic shift in both the masculine and the feminine ideals. Though our focus in this book is mainly on the masculine, the change in the feminine must be given a good deal of weight as well, since how a man behaves in life depends to a considerable extent on how women are going to react to him. Thus an interaction process is set up: the typical man's urge to amass a great deal of wealth is matched by the typical woman's admiration of the powerful wealthy man.

While most people view ours as an upward mobile society, in which everybody has a chance to get ahead in accordance with his abilities, more careful studies do not bear that out. The Harvard sociologist, Christopher Jencks, and his colleagues have published two extensive surveys of the degree of inequality that exists in our society, and how it can be remedied.[1] They found, as have so many others, that those who do well economically typically owe almost half of their occupational advantage and 55% to 85% of their earnings advantage to family background.[2] Thus the economic lines are not drawn as rigidly as say, in a caste society such as India, but there is not as much chance to get ahead as Americans would like to believe. On top of that, the drastic changes in the economy that go on all the time further limit the chances of many who start low down on the economic totem pole.

What this adds up to psychologically is that most men do not achieve the success that they feel they were promised when they were little boys. Add to this the fact that success is not simply an external measure, but depends even more heavily on what the man thinks his lot in life ought to have been. This expectation is based more on the boy's comparison with father than on any other single factor; the boy tries to surpass his father and success is evaluated on the basis of how well that is accomplished. Add to this that these expectations and comparisons are established early in life so that if the boy, for emotional reasons, is made to feel very inferior to father, that feeling may very well stay with him for the rest of his life.

The net result is that the great majority of men, at some point deep inside, and in some important respects, feel like failures. The Swedish writer, August Strindberg, whose collected works run to 55 volumes, and who is widely regarded as one of the giants of 19th century literature, toward the end of his life cried out: "Bless me, whose deepest suffering, deepest of human suffering was this—I could not be the one I longed to be."[3] Strindberg was voicing a feeling which haunts a great many modern men.

Thus what William James called the "bitch-goddess, success," or what is more drily called "achievement motivation" in modern psychology, does breed a good deal of achievement, which is plainly visible, but it also breeds even more failures who are not so readily visible. Just as the early sexual deprivations leave so many men with a feeling of sexual inadequacy, the early stress on conquest and victory leaves many with a feeling of not having conquered enough, and not having been victorious enough. General Douglas MacArthur, a leading military figure of World War II, whose father was a brigadier general with a distinguished military career, was not noted for his humility. His biographer in fact calls him the "American Caesar." Yet whenever the question of his father came up, Douglas MacArthur refused even to consider the idea that he had done more than his father.

MacArthur was heavily dominated by the rivalry with his father, who had become a hero in the Civil War. The elder MacArthur's main military exploits were in the Philippines, where he aroused strong opposition from Presidents Taft and Theodore Roosevelt. At the end of his career he was promoted to lieutenant general, but, as Manchester, MacArthur's biographer says, "No one knows what to do with him, so he goes home to Milwaukee." The son did more than the father but never realized it. He did, however, as Manchester shows, identify with his father's arrogance, lack of humility and inability to get along with political figures.

There are so many changes taking place in our society, and so rapidly, that this description of the man burdened by feelings of defeat may be less accurate or less widespread than was the case a generation ago.[4] Still, it remains today more the rule than the exception.

A recent movie centers around a group of men who have been abandoned by their wives. One of them cries quite openly, wondering how he can live without her; the other men console him. Such a scene would have been unthinkable even a short time ago. For part of the masculine ideal traditionally has been that the man must make no public display of weakness. He must always put up a front of ease and assurance. Hence the sense of lack of achievement has to be kept to himself, which makes it all the more painful to bear.

It is worthwhile to see how the success ethic interacts with the analytic ideal. In every case the constant drive to achieve interferes with other aspects of the man's life, even when there is considerable worldly success. Yankelovitch[5] argues that the urge for self-fulfillment, an aspect of the analytic ideal, is not just a passing fad, but is pursued with utmost seriousness by perhaps 80% of the population. Since we are in the process of remaking a culture, the more the crucial issues are brought out into the open, the more effective will the changes be.

One preliminary comment is in order. When the man feels that he is a failure, he reacts in one of two ways: by becoming more aggressive, or by withdrawing into passivity. Why one alternative is chosen rather than another is a question that has to be answered differently in each individual case. But in reviewing the broad range of reactions it is essential to bear these two possibilities in mind.

In the traditional paternalistic *love relationship* where the man is the breadwinner and authority in the household, the consequence more often than not is that the man conceals his financial dealings from his wife, as well as his fears that he may not be able to maintain the standard of living that has been set. It still happens, occasionally, that men, particularly in the lower classes, are sent to jail for refusal to work and support their families. Thus, even though it is not generally realized, the married man becomes legally responsible for his wife's economic security. Many of the bitter arguments about money stem from this simple fact.

Apart from money, in the sexual area there is, after the early days, no legal requirement on the part of either party that they should engage in sex. Quite the contrary: the bizarre situation is that legally the man can be punished for having sex with another woman, or for demanding too much sex from his wife, or "deviant" sex (which still is defined as any variation from the usual missionary position in sexual intercourse). No wonder then that the man will try to dominate the woman, and bend her to his will.

What happens in a marriage after the honeymoon period depends very heavily on what the woman does. If, as so often occurs, she has married out of a sense of desperation that she will never get anybody, she tries to please her husband in the beginning, and then withdraws, especially after the children come. If the wife does withdraw the husband is forced into a real quandary. If he asks for affection he is rebuffed; if he does not ask for it he is left out in the cold. If, in addition, his work is not the most interesting in the world, and his financial situation is precarious, he may very well pull back behind his own wall of silence. This is more likely to occur in the lower classes, where neither children nor work offer much gratification. In desperation the man may turn to drink, or gambling, or women, or, even worse, to psychiatric illness. A sense of despair about life may overcome him at an early age, which leads him to retreat into a state of passivity, or neurotic illness. If he is overactive he dominates the woman; if he is overly passive, he lets the woman dominate him.

In the traditional moral code there is really no way out. Most couples who face this conflict simply conceal it from the outside world, or shift the battle to a symptom that comes out of it, such as drinking or gambling, both almost universal problems. Unless the family is explored in depth, there is no way of finding out what really happens.

In almost all studies of happiness[5] the overwhelming majority of people stress love as the most essential ingredient. Yet they find it hard to clarify what they mean by it. Psychoanalysts, from Freud on, have scrutinized love more profoundly than other scientists. The solution to the marital dispute, which seems to be getting worse, since more than half of all marriages end in divorce today, lies in clarifying the nature of the love experience, not in blaming either the male or the female.

Sexuality for the man dominated by the success ethic becomes a fight, a matter of victory or defeat. The Don Juan complex in the man has already been considered in the previous chapter. When sex is a series of conquests, it is never very satisfactory; no matter how many women the man has bedded down, he will always want more.

On the surface, *pleasure* is man's normal drive. Man seems to be a tireless pleasure seeker. There can be no doubt that the pursuit of pleasure and the avoidance of pain are among the most powerful of all motives.

Yet if the man must conquer, a subtle change gradually takes place in his pursuit of pleasure. He slowly but surely begins to pursue pleasure in a more and more compulsive manner; it becomes an addiction rather than a real source of gratification.

A theoretical point about the nature of pleasure must be inserted here. In any pleasurable activity there are four stages: desire, gratification, rest and then renewed desire. Eating may be taken as a model. There is hunger, eating, rest and then hunger again. Each stage is essential.

With the compulsive pleasure-seeker, who turns it into a compulsive addiction, there is no rest period. The chain smoker, the alcoholic, the drug addict, the womanizer goes from one experience to another without taking the time or having the ability to lean back and enjoy it for a while.

Underneath this frantic search for pleasure there is an ocean of anxiety which the man cannot handle. He does not stop, he dare not stop, because to do so would unloose this ocean of anxiety on him. The picture of the alcoholic who is panicky because he does not have a drink is a familiar one. If an alcoholic is cured, as a rule he cannot take a single drink; if he takes one, he cannot stop, unlike the normal person.

The other side of the coin is the man who stays away from any kind of pleasure at all. There have been many movements in the history of the United States to foster such a degree of asceticism. The term "puritan" has become part of the language. The harshly restrictive laws regarding sexual behavior are another example. Many Americans still recall with bitterness the "noble experiment" of prohibition which let loose a wave of gangsterism and lawlessness that terrorized the country in the 1920's—and didn't work anyhow.

In times of crisis there are always voices denouncing the country as a new Sodom and Gomorrah, and demanding the imposition of a variety of prohibitions. Today there is a strong call for a "right to life" amendment which would prohibit abortions. Forgotten is the long history of shattered and lost lives resulting from illegal abortions, since abortion can no more be outlawed than sex itself. When restrictions are too harsh, they become ineffectual.

An essential part of the masculine ideal is never to display feelings indicating any weakness—no crying, no depression, no shame. A man who does wear his feelings on his sleeve is said to be effeminate, or sissyish. Feeling is feminine, action is masculine.

Again the trouble with repressing all signs of feeling is that it is only partly successful. There is a price to be paid—depression, or withdrawal or somatic illnesses.

Perhaps the most shattering discovery is that men who repress their feelings are much more apt to develop certain illnesses, such as peptic ulcers, asthma and hypertension (high blood pressure). With the enlarged knowledge of how emotions affect the body available now, this need cause no great surprise, although many pieces remain to be fitted into the puzzle. For an emotion has three components: the conscious expression, the conscious thoughts and the unconscious bodily reactions. Whether or not the emotion comes out on the surface, underneath the bodily reactions will continue. Thus the alternative for the man has really been: let your feelings out, or get sick. Since cultural restrictions have prevented him from letting his feelings out, he has become sick. Granted that the masculine ideal is changing in this respect under the impact of psychological observations, it still has a strong hold over many men.

Man, said the sages, is a rational animal, and ever since this observation the capacity to be reasonable has been the hallmark of the man, as opposed to the release of feeling, whether reasonable or not, which has been the hallmark of the woman. Men complain bitterly that their wives or mothers or other female acquaintances are "hysterical" (a term used commonly to describe any kind of emotional outlet) and inaccessible to logic.

Although men are still frightened to make any public display of emotion, a number of changes in this image of rationality have occurred. Foremost among them is the deeper understanding of the truly irrational which has come from psychoanalysis. For it turns out that no one is really irrational; rather the logic is pursued at an unconscious level. Thus, a paranoid man who believes that someone is about to attack him may shoot first in order to protect himself. His logic is unassailable; what is at fault is the delusional notion that he is about to be attacked.

Since World War II the United States has been engaged in a confrontation with irrationality never seen before. Some 200,000 psychotherapists, and thousands more being trained each year, are at hand to explain any kind of irrational behavior to people, and to help them overcome it by the "talking cure."

In the light of all our experience, there is no particular reason to suppose that men are more logical or rational than women. Thus the effort to keep up with the masculine ideal creates a misperception of both the man and the woman.

This brings up another dilemma for the man in his traditional role. Since he is not really more logical than the woman, but must insist that he is, his human relationships are adversely affected. A constant conflict between his ideal and reality easily arises.

Recently a lesbian woman sued a physician for malpractice on the grounds that he refused to provide her with artificial insemination, so that she could have a child, not only out of wedlock, but without further participation by the man. Although she did not win the case, the suit highlights the deep contempt in which so many women hold men.

Ideally the family is the place where mother, father and children love one another and learn to live together happily. Yet even in the traditional culture the role of the man in the family is difficult. Consider the changes the boy has to go through in the route from being mother's little boy to father's rival. When he reaches puberty he has to restrain himself from being too forceful with women until he marries. Before marriage he has to be an ardent suitor, loving the helpless and often rejecting woman. Once married, it becomes his obligation to start a family. When his wife becomes pregnant, another role change occurs: he has to be provider and protector, and take on more of the burden of running the household. How he reacts during her pregnancy depends on the wife to a considerable extent; sexually he is also subject to the advice of the physician and there are still many physicians, trained without understanding the emotional life of the patient, who forbid sex early on in the pregnancy.

When the baby is born, the father is not allowed much of a role in its nurturance; thus he may and often does feel doubly rejected, first because his wife is preoccupied with the child, and second because he has so little contact with the baby. As usual it may be argued that steps are now being taken to give the father more of a chance to interact with the children, but a drastic change is still a long way off. It is striking that the highest divorce rate occurs in the first few years of marriage, when the little child displaces the father.

As the child grows up, the father must now take over the role of authority and discipline. "Spare the rod and spoil the child" is still the philosophy of many men, especially in the lower classes, who as a result turn the family into a hotbed of violence.

Herman, a 40-year-old accountant, was the father of four children, none of whom had any deep feeling for him. When he had proposed to his wife she was pregnant by another man. He agreed to marry her if she would consent to give the child away when it came. She agreed, but remained bitterly resentful. Herman kept on reminding her of what he had done for her by marrying her in such a condition. For many years she felt guilty in her turn, and the battles between husband wife became legendary. Five times he started choking her, apparently with the intention of killing her, and several times he had to be restrained by the children.

After some ten years of this, the worm turned. His wife asked him to leave and began an affair with another man. Her husband knew about it, but this time he felt so guilty about his rages at her that he put up with it. He worked day and night to keep the family economically secure, but in order to do that he gave up virtually his entire social life. Finally the couple divorced, though Herman remained miserable.

When the child reaches adolescence, the father has to play the role of a model for the boy, and a desirable male image for the girl. This introduces another conflict, especially in a society where the younger generation is given so many opportunities to surpass the older. Most people in fact feel that they have to do better than their parents. In this way the man remains eternally dissatisfied with his role in the family. Small wonder that he is bombarded with so much literature about how to have a happy family.

The social role which the man assumes is likewise full of pitfalls. In the traditional pattern it is the wife who takes care of socialization, but men are frequently irked by their wives' partying, even though they may hesitate to say so. Many men, not having really outgrown the adolescent stage, still prefer a crowd of males; they join clubs, or go to bars, or play games such as chess or racquet ball which keep them more with men than with women or mixed company. The anthropologist Lionel Tiger who wrote *Men in Groups* has argued that these same-sex activities are inherent in human nature, but he disregards the price the man is required to pay for this isolation from women.

In any case male-dominated groups are more suitable for the younger men than for the older. Thus as the man gets older he finds himself increasingly isolated. Nowadays, when many women feel bored or fed up with their husbands this isolation of the man is apt to get worse. It is no accident that the highest suicide rate is found among single or divorced men over forty-five; they have lost their roots and cannot find them again.

What is the image that men have of themselves? Naturally this will vary with age, but one outstanding finding from all studies is that men tend to think of themselves as not having succeeded enough. Like Willie Loman in *Death of a Salesman*, they feel that it is not enough to be liked; you have to be *well liked*. Since hatred is more common in our society than liking, the net result is that they feel their efforts go unrewarded, their true merits are unappreciated, and they do not know what to do about it. During World War II we used to speak of the Navy syndrome: overworked, underpaid and underfucked. To a considerable extent many men apply this designation to their own lives, when they are free to release their complaints.

However, the human being is rarely so simple. In reaction to the various stresses to which they are exposed, men (women too) find some compromise solution to life's struggles. They fall into a certain design for living which gives them certain disadvantages, and then pursue this style for the rest of their lives. To understand any man his design for living, which is the result of earlier compromises, must be grasped.

Typologies are of little value here, though many have been offered. To grasp the dilemma of the man, his self-image must be compared with his notion of what he would like to have become. In the traditional society with its overemphasis on success, he rarely feels that he has fulfilled himself. As Yankelovitch shows, currently perhaps three quarters of the country is trying to make more out of life. They are discontent with the traditional rewards, but do not know how to get more. Or, they fall into various traps, many of which have been pointed out, such as amassing money which never turns out to be enough, or taking up with another woman, or falling prey to one of the numerous escape routes our society offers, such as gambling or drinking.

It is often argued that psychoanalysts have a distorted image of society, since they judge it by the patients whom they treat rather than the "normal" person. Nothing could be further from the truth. Most people realize now that the patient population of the psychoanalyst embraces potentially the entire country, which is why no matter how many patients are treated there are always more who come along. Thus the analyst is in a unique position to penetrate the false front which people put up, and to see what the deeper problems are. Foremost among these is an abiding sense of failure. And again this sense of failure can be handled in one of two ways: by covering it up with exaggerated claims of achievement, or by a gradual withdrawal from the activities that make life most worthwhile.

In the area of work many men find their greatest source of strength and gratification. Traditionally the man's life centers around his family and his work; if the wife is nurturing, and the work satisfying, this is a compromise design for living which is about the best that can be done under the circumstances. It is the style of the organization man, about whom so much has been written.

> John was a civil service worker who became ill at an early age with stomach ulcers which severely restricted his diet and other activities. The one area which he enjoyed most was his work, and in thirty-five years he rarely missed a day. With his wife and two children he had little contact, especially when he started to work at night. His only concern about his daughter was when she decided to move in with her boyfriend without getting married first. This aroused his indignation and he insisted that she marry, which she did. When his son left home at eighteen to seek his fortune in another part of the country, John said nothing. In this way he lived out his life.

Still, what is a blessing for one man becomes a curse for another. On the surface at least many men resent their work bitterly, and dream only of the day when they can put it all behind them, and put themselves out to retirement. Since psychologists appeared on the scene, there has however been a noticeable change in the attitude to retirement. Many men need the stimulation and camaraderie of a job to make life more meaningful; when they retire they may die very quickly.

Part of the individualistic tradition in the United States is that a man should be the head of his own business. Some men prefer an organization, many others yearn for a chance to do it on their own.

> Victor was an executive in one of the largest companies in the world. He did well, both financially and in terms of prestige. But he yearned for his own business. Since he had to do it in his spare time, he tried franchising of one kind or another: lawn mowing, automobile transmission, flowers. With each one he sooner or later became dissatisfied because it took up so much of his spare time. Eventually he gave it up, and settled down to enjoy the success he had achieved in the organization.

Apart from the cultural pressures, what lies behind conflicts such as Victor's is still the rivalry with the father. Victor's father was a man who worked for a large company until he was about forty-five, and then retired; Victor was never quite clear what he did after then. The relationship between Victor and his father was never a cordial one. With such a poor identification, Victor fell back on trying to beat father out. It was only when he realized that he was fighting a senseless battle that he was able to give it up.

In the area of *communication* the traditional man has some of his greatest problems. A man is supposed to make money, succeed, be a pillar of strength; what does he have to communicate? In one study of lower-class families[7] the investigators found that a number of the husbands refused to talk to them at all, and in addition complained that their wives talked too much. They preferred to sit around and watch TV.

From an early age the human being has an urgent need to communicate with his fellow-man. The infant babbles, coos, gurgles, makes all kinds of noises just to be in contact with mother or other adults. Recent studies of early infancy have particularly emphasized the crucial role of interaction as so essential to healthy growth.

Children are normally communicative. But then they run

across forbidden material of various kinds, sex, toilet talk, fantasies, above all dreams and as a rule their communication is interfered with by the surrounding adults. Even though we know how all-important dreams are in human existence, most people outside therapy simply disregard them.

Once communication is halted, or blocked, the child feels restrictive and secretive. He accepts the idea that his private thoughts in certain areas must not be told to adults, yet he is unable to keep these thoughts out of his mind. The result is a severe sense of shame, and a limitation of many kinds of communication to some of his peers. Part of the effectiveness of psychotherapy stems from giving the individual a chance to say whatever comes to mind, no matter how irrelevant or absurd it may seem; this chance then corrects the harsh repressions in childhood.

It has become commonplace for women to come to psychotherapy with the dual complaint: no sex, no communication. These complaints are quite justified, since this is an attitude many men lapse into after a lifetime of disappointments. Men however have the same complaints, even though they are not voiced as often. Traditionally husband and wife lived out their lives side by side, at a considerable emotional distance from one another. Today that has become a solution against which a large number of people have rebelled.

It is well known that women come to psychotherapy more frequently than men; the usual ratio given is two to one.[8] This is mistakenly interpreted by many as being part of the cultural oppression of women; the truth is rather the other way around. Psychotherapy is essentially a liberating experience, and if more women turn to it that is evidence that they feel freer to seek help for their troubles. By contrast, the man will frequently refuse psychotherapy or, for that matter, any form of communication, because of the macho image or the masculine ideal. This is but another of the many instances where the image of the masculine ideal is on a sharp collision course with the realities of experience, thus leading to considerable disillusionment and suffering.

The opening up of avenues of communication between people is but one of the many contributions of psychoanalysis to human welfare. Before Freud wrote his fundamental work on dreams in 1900, no one, least of all the professionals, had ever dreamed that dreams could be so relevant and important. After dreams came fantasies and the uncovering of a whole inner world. Psychotherapy is a procedure which allows the individual to share this inner world with another person, now trained to understand the ideas and images produced. Literature and art are also means of sharing fantasies, which is why the artist appreciated the value of psychoanalysis before the professionals. What is surprising, yet vital to understanding, is that the opening up of this new world should have such a liberating effect on the person.

Creativity functions like communication in many ways. For the traditional man, there is no place in his life for creative outlets. And the man who insists on becoming an artist or a writer or chooses some other creative outlet usually runs up against intense opposition from the conventional family. Go out and make a living is what the father says; even when the son has gathered in some of the huge benefits that fall to the lot of the modern artist, the father remains dubious. It just does not fit in with his image of what a man should be like.

Accordingly it is not surprising that many artistic personalities see themselves as oddballs, or freaks of some kind. Yet the paradox remains that almost all the great names in music, art, literature, architecture or other creative fields are men. Some have urged that man's urge to create comes about because unlike the woman he is unable to bear children. Whatever the deeper reasons the fact remains that every creative man must go through a considerable amount of turmoil before he feels secure and comfortable in his chosen field.

One important consequence is that many men feel very stifled in their creative expressions. To let them out is unmanly, so it is better to hold everything in and become seriously disgruntled or disturbed.

Finally men are extremely reluctant to admit to any kind of *psychiatric difficulty*. When General George Patton, in a celebrated incident in World War II, hit one of his men who had a nervous collapse in battle, he was merely expressing the opinion of the usual man. A soldier, which includes every man, should have no fears and no compunctions about killing. To paraphrase Tennyson: His is not to question why, his is but to do and die.

Since these fears cannot really be done away with by any

verbal magic, the average man goes through life with strong neurotic trends, or outright neurotic problems, which he is compelled to cover up; he is compelled, that is, by his need to conform to the masculine ideal. When the chips are down, these problems break through; thus the largest single source of problems in the second World War was the neuropsychiatric: large numbers of draftees were rejected for mental reasons, and others taken in the service in large numbers received Section 8 (neuropsychiatric) discharges.

It has been made abundantly clear that there is a wide gap between the masculine ideal held up to most boys as they grow up and the analytic ideal which has evolved from the careful study of neurosis and psychosis over the past hundred years. Thus the forgotten man is more often than not on the horns of a dilemma: If he behaves the way real he-men are supposed to, he suppresses his feelings, blocks off his affection, releases his rage and aggression, strives for success by fair means or foul—and takes the consequences. One important consequence is lifelong depression and misery, accompanied by innumerable other illnesses. Charles Revson, a typical pursuer of the masculine image, who built up a $100 million fortune out of nothing, once said: "What's there to say about my life? It's just miserable." Typically, in an era when psychoanalysts were in abundance, he would not consult one; there was nobody he would reveal his innermost secrets to.

On the other hand, if the man admits to his fears and failings, he suffers the other way, since such a stigma is attached to not being a true he-man. Throughout his life the man is confronted by a series of choices which will have a major effect on him, yet in all these choices he is guided more by some mythical image of what a man should be like than by the realities of the situation.

The period when men would fight duels to the death rather than accept any affront to their honor passed away more than a century ago. Today the man is concerned about a "put-down" and he will go to great lengths, though not usually death, to avenge a put-down. To us today duelling is a senseless undertaking; to future generations the great concern of men with their reputation, which leads them to fight any kind of put-down, will seem equally senseless.

Our culture is undergoing rapid changes. A whole new

class of intellectuals (the "New Class") has sprung up to clarify how it is changing and the directions the changes should take. To have a frank discussion of the masculine ideal and how it should change can only be to the good.

While this chapter necessarily stresses the neurotic aspects of the masculine ideal, there is no attempt to deny that this image has had positive and benevolent effects as well. Man needs some model to guide him, and in the absence of psychoanalytic understanding, this model served a useful purpose. It is quite obvious that when such a model is predominant, the energies of the society will move toward expansion, conquest and achievement, which is what has happened. McClelland, in his work on achievement motivation, has provided statistical evidence that this is indeed the case, even within the communist world. He reported that Poland shows a tremendous need for achievement, and we have been witnessing the Polish defiance of the Soviets.[9]

Chapter 5:
Far From Ideal:
Typical Marital Conflicts

A happy marriage, while still the ideal of most Americans, is becoming increasingly scarce. One out of two marriages roughly now ends in divorce. Furthermore, all kinds of experiments with different life styles are found. In the 1950s[1] a typical American family consisting of a working father, a housewife mother and growing children made up 70% of all households. In the 1970s just one generation later, the number of households conforming to this "typical" pattern had dropped to 15%.

The reliance on children and a happy marriage as the mainstay of happiness has steadily diminished. Every year throughout the 1970s a million or so Americans had themselves sterilized. Planned large-scale childlessness is a new experience for our society.

Changes in the ideals and patterns of both men and women are taking place at a rapid rate. While men are trying to get away from work, women are trying to get in. By 1980, more than two out of five mothers of children younger than six worked for pay. Between 1947 and 1977 the number of men in the prime working years (from ages 16 to 65) who dropped out of the work force nearly doubled, from 13% to 22%.

Yet with all this considerable continuity is found as well. A repetition of the famous Middletown study of the 1920s showed considerable change, particularly in the sex customs, but also a good deal of continuity in the ideals held up as desirable, such as obedience to the parents, and belief in the Bible as a sufficient guide to everyday life.[2]

The rush away from marriage is certainly connected with the sexual conflicts that are inherent in it. No society before

© 1987 by The Haworth Press, Inc. All rights reserved.

ours has ever tried to impose such a self-sacrificing ideal on
both men and women. Theoretically both must have sex with
one another and only one another all their lives. Tolerance
was usually greater for the man who practiced a "double standard," but there was none for the woman. True, she was no
longer stoned to death as in ancient times, nor branded with a
scarlet "A" like Hester Prynne in Hawthorne's novel, but she
was still looked upon with suspicion and felt herself filled with
deep shame and remorse if she "cheated."

All of these changes in the society are efforts, for better or
for worse, to remedy the defects in the traditional marriage.
A major source of these defects was the traditional sexual
code. As a rule, Freud found, the men and women who stuck
to this code developed neurotic problems of varying degrees
of severity. Initially, it seemed, psychoanalysts seemed to be
recommending free love, and many did, in fact, urge greater
sexual freedom as a response to marital and non-marital frustrations. Gradually, however, it became apparent that sex per
se was not the answer. So while still urging greater sexual
freedom, psychoanalysts came to focus increasingly on stability and love.

Before discussing these goals for a happy life, it is necessary to see how the conventional sexual code had the man
coming and going. For part of the masculine ideal was the
idealization of woman, forcing her to be either a virgin or a
prostitute. Thus before marriage he was limited to sexual experience with inferior women, while after marriage he was
obliged to have sex with a block of ice. Caught in such a
dilemma, the man pursued one of three paths, the two mentioned in earlier chapters (too much or too little sex) and the
third, the conventional acceptance of the usual code.

The inaccessibility of the good woman before marriage and
her coldness following marriage (often postponed until after
the birth of the children) were both parts of the feminine
ideal. John Dollard, a sociologist who investigated a Southern
town in detail, describes the following ritual pursued by university students:

> One of the rituals of the university dances is that of a
> fraternity of young blades entitled the Key-Ice. During
> the intermission the lights are turned out and these men

march in carrying flaming brands. At the end of the procession four acolytes attend a long cake of ice. Wheeled in on a cart it glimmers in the torches' flare. Then the leader, mounted on a table in the center of the big gymnasium, lifts a glass cup of water and begins a toast that runs: "To Woman, lovely woman of the Southland, as pure and as chaste as this sparkling water, as cold as this gleaming ice, we lift this cup, and we pledge our hearts and our lives to the protection of her virtue and chastity."[3]

In any discussion of sexuality in marriage, the first question that invariably comes up is that of fidelity. And the attitude is generally that reflected in the doggerel: "Higgimus hoggamus, woman's monogamous; hoggamus, higgimus the man is polygamous." This view is buttressed by much historical and anthropological evidence. In about half of known human cultures, extramarital sex is completely prohibited for the woman, with severe consequences if she disobeys. In not a few societies it is the husband's obligation to kill the offending wife, and if he does not do so he finds himself completely disgraced.[4]

These attitudes, though of course not the right to kill (although lesser penalties can be expected for any violence that results from the discovery), have carried over into our culture. Kinsey reflects them as "normal." He found in his studies of women that about 26% of women have had extramarital sex, while about 50% of men had indulged. The percentages were higher for the generations born later, pointing even then (the 1940's) to a change in the society.

Although her sample was much less representative of the total population, Shere Hite in her survey published in 1981, documented the rising incidence of extramarital sex.[5] According to her figures 72% of men married two years or more had had sex outside of marriage; the overwhelming majority did not tell their wives. She found that the major reason given by most men was because their wives were inadequate sexual partners, either unresponsive, or altogether unwilling to have sex. In a way Hite is closer to the average man than Kinsey, inasmuch as the class and religious distinctions that were so important for Kinsey are disregarded by her.

Accompanying this increase in extramarital sex is the decline in the number of births. In 1975 the average number of births was 118.3 for 1000 women. In 1975 it had dropped to 66.7. In the 1955–59 period a woman in her childbearing years could expect to have 3.7 births; in the 1965–69 period, 2.6 births and in 1977 1.8.[6] While few people concern themselves with the vital statistics of the country as a whole, these figures help to dramatize the change in values that has occurred and that is continuing.

We are less concerned with the statistics than with the motives that drive people to act as they do. There is a consistent picture here: women are becoming more demanding of sex, yet by and large (as Hite shows) they are still caught in the trap of the good woman-bad woman, which leads them to repress their sexual desires. The one thing that men uniformly complain about in their wives is their lack of sexual responsiveness, which leads to a dull kind of slam-bam-thank-you-ma'am kind of sexual experience.

In general, and in accordance with the standard images of both men and women, it is the man who is more responsible for extramarital sex than the woman. The man is supposed to be aggressive, macho, take what he wants, let the devil be damned. Woman submits. Many men in the Hite study said of their sexual escapades that marriage is an unnatural state of affairs, and they felt perfectly justified in violating the taboos.

A contrary view is expressed by Mary Sherfey, a psychoanalyst who wrote extensively on the subject at the time of the Masters-Johnson reports. Her contention is that woman is essentially insatiable, and that civilization has set up all kinds of barriers to prevent women from gratifying their lusts.[7]

The truth must be sought in the inner-psychological experiences of people. Sex cannot be isolated from other feelings; the notion that it can represents one aspect of the hate culture that has dominated us for so many centuries. For that matter, no contact between two human beings can be viewed in isolation from the total feelings involved, whether it be something as vital as surgery, or as trivial as boarding a bus. Any interaction between two people which is reduced to an impersonal exchange is bound to arouse frustration and resentment.

The important question about infidelity then is not how often it occurs, relevant though that may be, but what feelings are the people going through? It is here that we have to fall back on our analytic experience, since the usual standard surveys tell us nothing about inner motives.

Here the answer is unequivocal: while there have been vast changes in the outward patterns of sexual behavior, these changes do not yield the desired happiness, and are generally found unsatisfactory sooner or later. The stereotyped notion that men enjoy their extramarital affairs, while women sit home and suffer, or go out and enjoy some of their own, is not borne out by the clinical evidence. However much they may talk of complete sexual freedom, the ideal conjured up by most persons is still that of a love match between two people who can gratify one another sexually as well as in other ways.

The profound significance of love puts the question of infidelity on an entirely different basis. Traditionally the man is supposed to "run around" much more, and to be much less concerned about his activities. In reality, men feel just as guilty and unsatisfied about their sex lives as women. There are enough analysts, counselors, sex therapists and the like who can help any reasonable person overcome the sexual handicaps left behind by a frustrating childhood. Once the sexual inequality is remedied, what remains is more important—the total relationship between the two people. And this is much harder to change by direct action.

Consequently *both infidelity and fidelity* have to be examined more carefully. It is always infidelity that is pushed into the foreground, yet pathological fidelity is just as common, if not more so, and just as harmful. What has to be understood is the total sexual relationship in marriage.

Men engage in extramarital activities for many different reasons. What is common to all of them is a deep dissatisfaction with their marriage, and if any radical change is to be effected, this deep dissatisfaction must be tackled. The man's worst dilemma, and it is one that is far from infrequent, is that he finds himself caught between lifelong sexual frustration and divorce.

It is all very well to say that if the woman has sexual difficulties she should try to straighten them out. In practice the situation is far more complicated.

First of all, like the man, the woman suffers from a lifelong history of sexual inhibition. From time immemorial she has dinned into her the ethics of the good girl-bad girl dichotomy, that if she is "bad," somehow or other she will be punished, and internally she is punished. If she tries sex before marriage, as more girls are in fact doing, more often than not it is sex to please the boy, or to show that she is one of the crowd, or the like. It is not a wholesome acceptance of sexuality as part of the good life. If she has no sex before marriage, as in the traditional code, she almost invariably manifests varying degrees of frigidity. It is a rare woman who escapes the good girl-bad girl problem.

With such a history, sex in marriage is bound to be unsatisfactory. Taboos of all kinds may still affect her, she may be revolted by oral-genital contacts, or it may take her years to let herself go in the marriage-bed, or, as is all too often the case, her husband is sexually inadequate and she does not know the difference.

At a deeper level, the sexual inhibitions leave the girl with a profound feeling of inadequacy about her body. This is what psychoanalysts mean by "penis envy"—it is not so much the wish to have a penis, as the extreme revulsion she feels about certain parts of her body. She may be afraid that her vagina smells, or may think that her breasts are too big, or too small, or may be afraid to use the toilet in front of her husband, thereby making worse the sense that her toilet functions are inherently dirty. The list could be continued indefinitely.

Although there is much loose talk of the "sexually liberated" woman, the psychoanalyst, who actually sees a more representative cross-section of the population than anyone else, still finds sexual conflicts universal. Again in this respect Shere Hite may be a better barometer than the more "scientific" studies, which focus so heavily on the well-educated and the well-informed. One of her findings is that women will in the vast majority of cases find it repulsive to suck the penis, a perfectly normal and healthy aspect of sex play. (In fact, if the husband insists on it, he may find himself legally accused of "cruel and inhuman treatment," since the courts look upon almost any deviation from traditional sexuality as abhorrent to the woman.) Because of the refusal of this pleasure, many men turn to prostitutes or pick-ups, who may not only not be squeamish about sucking the penis, but actually enjoy it. Cultures change slowly, and sexual liberation still has a long way to go.

A woman's sexual coldness is also quite often expressed as a contempt for the man, or a kind of implacable hostility. There is a psychic warfare going on between men and women; the hatred of the man reinforces the hatred of the woman, and a vicious circle is set up which never ends. The sociologist Cuber once called this the conflict-habituated marriage; the term is self-explanatory. What is less obvious is that this constant fighting, physical as well as psychological, is much more characteristic of many marriages than love and affection. Faced by rejection and hostility, neither side is in much of a mood to undertake sexual overtures, thus further widening the sexual gap between husband and wife.

Once the children come, the sexual warfare is intensified even more. For the woman is encouraged to give love and care to the children, even though it may involve pushing the husband out of the way. Further, many women become depressed after the birth of a baby; the term "after-birth-blues" is part of the language. Unable to recognize this depression as an outcome of their childhood, they instead blame the husband. He in turn does not know how to handle children, and does not know how to handle his wife's anger, which he does not understand; on top of that he has his own worries in the world of work.

Thus a typical situation often arises after the first few years of marriage. It has been described more accurately by novelists than by psychologists, as in Jean-Paul Sartre's novelette *Nauséa*. Love has flown out of the window, replaced by constant criticism and dissatisfaction. Sex becomes less frequent, and less gratifying. The wife devotes herself to the children far more than to the husband. Both sides find life more and more depressive. In such an atmosphere infidelity and other reactions arise.

Let us reemphasize that ideally the solution is to educate both parties in happy living, including the healthy enjoyment of sexuality. This is the picture portrayed in the popular press, or by widely read columnists. It is not the reality as it comes to our attention clinically. The reality is that both sides reject therapy, push away any reasonable solution, and enter upon a bitter, virtually endless series of battles in which despair and suffering are the only victors. It is, however, the reality of the forgotten man that we are talking about, not the movie image of what life ought to be.

The solution that many men seek in this situation is another woman—infidelity. This solution is part of the lifelong dream of finding some sexually free woman with whom they can enjoy themselves, the dream that is never fulfilled, and yet never vanishes. Even though it rarely leads to any permanent gratification, it is pursued with the utmost tenacity. Here are some typical clinical examples:

> John, a forty-year-old physician, with two teenage daughters, was married to a woman who demanded anal play and intercourse in preference to vaginal. Although she was a college professor in an allied field, the two actually had little in common. Because he did not want to break up the marriage, John went along with his wife's demands.
>
> In his youth John had been a tutor to two young children. Their mother, a vivacious woman, old enough to be John's mother, seduced him; it was actually his first sexual experience. Then the family had moved to California, and John pined for her. Two weeks during the year he would take a vacation, fly to California and spend the time with her. The vacation made him deliriously happy, but then he had to return to his wife and miserable home situation. Unfortunately, the girlfriend developed a cancer and died at an early age; John was desolate, even blaming himself for having caused the cancer.
>
> After experimenting aimlessly with a long series of chance encounters, John eventually found the only rational way out, divorced his wife (the children were grown up by now) and found himself more happiness with another woman. It took him many years to adopt this course, years full of misery and suffering.
>
> James Boswell, the biographer of Johnson, was a typical product of the traditional morality.[8] The son of a Scotch judge, he was given a small allowance in his early twenties and sent to London. Here his thoughts, as his journal reveals, centered very strongly on sex. Wary of

the diseases he might pick up from prostitutes, he avoided them until he could meet a girl he loved.

Finally he did come up against such a girl, Louisa, a bit actress at one of the local theaters. He fell madly in love with Louisa and pursued her for quite a while before she would agree to have sex with him. They made a date to spend the night together, and he left feeling blissful.

Two things happened then. Having taken his fill of Louisa, he lost interest in her and began to look around for fairer game. Before he could make it with another woman, he discovered to his horror that he had contracted gonorrhea from Louisa. Treatment was long and difficult at that time (middle of the eighteenth century), and he was sidelined for several months. Once cured, paradoxically, he began to pursue prostitutes more and more vigorously, using precautions (the condom had already been invented) and never again contracting VD. But after each sexual encounter he would feel intense disgust and self-loathing.

Eventually Boswell returned to Scotland and married. At first his intended did not want to marry him because he was so unfaithful; she even wrote out a statement that if she were to marry him she should be banished from England. But they did marry anyhow.

The marriage did not turn out well. Boswell could never be satisfied with her (though he does not tell us exactly why) and engaged in innumerable affairs on the side. None of these satisfied him for any length of time. Throughout his journal he stresses his insatiable sexual appetite and his depression—a combination equally typical of twentieth-century men.

General Douglas MacArthur, at one point in his career, somewhere in his mid-forties, was stationed in the Philippines, his favorite spot. While there he took a Eurasian mistress (not further described in the biography). Although already a famous general, and a man in midlife, he was terrified that his mother should discover what he was doing, and as long as he had the mistress his main concern was to keep the knowledge from mother— the typical adolescent guilt. Analytically of course we could also comment on his choice of a Eurasian woman rather than a white one; the white girl would be too much like mother, and would inhibit his sexuality.[9]

Thus, if the course of the extramarital affair is examined in perspective, it is almost always found to be ungratifying. Actually, the affair corresponds more to a fantasy than to a realistic way of life. In the play *Brief Encounter,* two people meet at a railroad station in England, have a sexual episode for an afternoon, and then go their separate ways. The fantasy involved is of no commitment to the other person; sexual pleasure as such really plays a minor or even negligible role. The affair is a protest against the difficulties of living, not a realistic way out.

Yet the whole culture, including the legal system, places an inordinate emphasis on the affair, according it a significance far out of proportion to what it actually has. The main reason for this misplaced emphasis lies in the sexual frustration endemic in the society, which is being handled by the mechanism called *projection.* In this defense, the person denies his or her own wishes and attributes them (projects them) to some other person. So many people have such a strong desire for sexual experimentation that they are only too ready to find the desire in some other person.

Many men, made desperate by a frigid, unresponsive wife, and unable to get her to change by either psychotherapy or any other form of persuasion, naturally think of divorce as the way out. When they do, they all too often come to a rude awakening, discovering that the ex-wife has all the cards, financial, custodial and emotional.

Few people bother with the law unless forced to do so. When they grapple with the laws of marriage and divorce, they soon realize that everything is dead set against them. In spite of all the changes and liberalization that have occurred, especially in the last ten years,[10] custody is automatically given to the wife in 85% to 95% of the cases, a sizable portion of his income is sliced off by exorbitant alimony payments which still reflect the state of affairs in the nineteenth century, the children are not allowed normal visitation rights or the development of a normal relationship with the father, and soon turn against him (the law even recognizes the concept that the child's mind is "poisoned" by a vituperative mother). On top of that he does not enjoy the divorced state and makes plans for remarriage.

When children are involved, it is rare to see a divorce action proceed peacefully. All the concealed hatred of both parties is brought to the fore and used with callous indifference to anyone else's welfare. Immediate need seems to have little to do with it, though that is usually given as the cause of the rage. One woman, a wealthy lawyer in her own right, married to a psychiatrist, had his office broken into and stole all his records. Another took all the money out of a joint account, leaving her husband without the resources to pay the immediate bills. Still another refused to let her husband see the child, and when he brought a writ of habeas corpus to force visitation, she blandly told the judge that her husband was out of his mind and that nothing of the kind ever happened. (The judge, who heard this kind of fabrication all day long, was unimpressed.) The list could be continued indefinitely.

Paradoxically, for the man who has no money the situation is easiest. The courts award a minimal amount of support and he is free from the harassment which greets the man with more resources. He still has to come to grips with custody and relationship questions, but these he would have to handle anyhow.

For the average man, as soon as a divorce is agreed upon, his situation is unhappy and becomes increasingly worse, depending primarily on the vindictiveness of the ex-wife. The first step is to find himself expelled from his home, compelled to start all over again.

Next he is confronted with the need for a lawyer, and is soon told that he must pay both for his own lawyer and his wife's. Nor is it so easy in these circumstances to find a competent lawyer who will not swindle him. Essentially, the demands for property settlement and alimony are a legalized form of blackmail, and lawyers understandably do not like to operate under those circumstances.

If a settlement is reached without court action, that at least minimizes the pain. But because of the attitude of the courts, an angry, vindictive woman is granted the legal power to do whatever she can to destroy her husband's life and livelihood.

Very often when the papers are served in such actions, the

husband is completely baffled by the judicial farce. Slovenko (1973) in his authoritative book on *Psychiatry and the Law,* describes a typical petition by the wife alleging cruelty as grounds for divorce (still the most common):

> Your petitioner avers that the defendant has beaten her severely on numerous occasions, and during these periods of intemperate conduct he has, in addition to causing physical injury to the petitioner, made her highly nervous and apprehensive for the safety not only of herself but of the children as well.
>
> Your petitioner notwithstanding has at all times during the existence of said marriage to defendant been a dutiful and faithful spouse and mother to their minor children, providing the defendant with the respect and devotion of a loving wife.

It will be argued that the allegations of beating and mental cruelty driving the woman to nervous collapse are true. Certainly there is a lot of domestic violence, and the man is generally stronger than the woman. Slovenko reports that of 510 murders in Chicago during a recent year, 396 were classified under the heading of general domestic altercations.

But while there are a number of cases of violence, the frequency tends to be greatly exaggerated, and the slick, repetitious manner in which they are presented to court indicates that in most cases the whole story was fabricated beforehand, or written by the lawyer.

Once the case comes to a court, the husband finds that no evidence is needed to substantiate his wife's charges. Her word alone is usually sufficient, even though legally it is not supposed to be. The judge scarcely listens. The verdict comes out almost automatically in favor of the wife, granting her custody and substantial alimony benefits. Although many changes have occurred, especially in the last decade, and many are taking place now, this still remains the general picture.

Psychologically, what is noteworthy is the image of the woman presented in such divorce actions. She is seen as sexless, helpless, exposed to physical threats and beatings, a "devoted, loving" mother. Yet to the outsider, on closer examination it becomes crystal clear that she is filled to the brim with rage against her husband, and frequently against all men, that she is sexually frigid, anything but helpless, largely fabricating the physical threats, depressed, and a highly inadequate mother.

In terms of the main theme of this chapter, the sexual conflict, it is important to see that the courts actually reward the frigid woman. Divorce actions usually take years to resolve, and in this period she remains completely asexual, sometimes homosexual, although that is never brought up in court. It is automatically assumed that the man is chasing around madly and gaily with other women, neglecting his children, refusing to provide support, while the woman stays home, suffering deeply and caring for the children. The sophisticated person can immediately recognize the projection of the two images of man and woman which are dominant in our society: the brutal sexual man, and the refined maternal woman. By codifying these stereotypes, the courts merely serve to perpetuate the cultural sexual neurosis. In addition, they do everything they can to allow the woman to satisfy her deep-seated hatred of the man.

In addition, the man feels keenly the loss of the woman he once loved. Many times of course he finds another, but the process is a long and painful one. The frigid woman who loses her husband, feels, as one writer has put it, relieved rather than bereaved.

Aware that the courts have merely served to perpetuate a cultural neurosis, many progressive jurists have made a number of suggestions to remedy the situation. Psychiatrists, psychologists and other counselors have been called in; it is often recognized that the hair-raising stories women fabricate about their husband are exactly that, hair-raising fabrications; custody is awarded to the father more often than before, or joint custody is arranged, and many other measures are adopted, especially to protect the children.

Still, the break-up of a marriage remains a deep-seated trauma. Ideally, it would be best if everyone involved were to undergo some sort of psychotherapy or counseling. The more loving wives will accept such a solution more readily than the more hateful ones. Even here, however, the man's need for help is rarely recognized and he often remains forgotten.

Other choices than lifelong frustration or divorce are open to men and often chosen. One that has recently come "out of the closet" is homosexuality. In Kinsey's day (the 1940's), while there was a fair amount of homosexuality in adolescence, this soon gave way to a heterosexual way of life; the incidence of homosexuality among married men was rather rare, though it existed. While no comparable statistics are available for today, there is a strong impression that it is much more common.

Much furor has been generated by homosexual or gay groups who maintain in all sincerity that homosexuality is just an alternative life style. In many cases violence has accompanied their protests at being called sick. The peculiar reclassification of homosexuality by the American Psychiatric Association in 1974 added to the confusion; however, a survey carried out a few years later showed that most physicians stuck to the common-sense view that homosexuality is a form of pathology.[12]

The psychological position that homosexuality is pathological refers to exclusive compulsive homosexuality, in which there is a total exclusion of the opposite sex. There can be no doubt that men who are exclusively homosexual become so by virtue of a long history of sexual frustration, going back to earliest childhood. This does not negate the fact that as a variation in adolescence, or at some other time in life, some men may find a homosexual experience interesting, but the basic gratification will always come from the heterosexual relationship unless the man has deep-seated problems.[13]

It is of these men with deep-seated problems whom we are talking of in this section. They are married, in a state of severe sexual frustration. Divorce seems out of the question for a variety of reasons, as does infidelity. It is common enough for men to go out with the boys when their wives are cold, complaining and rejecting. This is precisely the way a great many men experience their wives. As Shere Hite notes, the most frequent replies from men about women's sexuality is that women are too cold, too uninterested in sex, too turned off to the marital bed. And they do not know what to do about it.

It is in such a juncture that some men turn to homosexual affairs, or leave the marriage and become exclusively homosexual. Not that the homosexuality makes them much happier; on the contrary, after a while, it too degenerates into terrible quarrels, fighting, jealousy and desertion. But it is a temporary respite, and that is more than they can find anywhere else at that moment. Here is a typical clinical instance.

Malcolm was an only child, of hard-working, prosperous middle-class (later wealthy) parents. He was particularly unable to compete with his father, who, besides running a good business, was an all-around sportsman. The father naturally gave him no encouragement to compete with him on any kind of equal terms.

Mother was a cold housewife, who let herself decline after marriage. Malcolm particularly remembered how run-down and shabby her clothes were; her stockings never seemed to be free of runs. He could hardly remember any physical affection from his mother, even in earliest childhood.

In adolescence, Malcolm could not handle the sexual conflicts well. He dated a little, even had sex with one girl, who performed fellatio on him, and enjoyed it, but then he dropped her—she was in his mind a "bad" girl. In fact, he could not understand how any girl in her right mind could knowingly suck a man's penis.

Malcolm married at an early age, and entered his father's business. Both business and love were sources of terrible disappointment. His wife was completely frigid, indifferent to sex, and they had intercourse perhaps three or four times a year.

When he was about thirty Malcolm met another man his age, a gay, vivacious bar companion who brought him out of his depression. The other man was homosexual, and soon the two were having sex; quite important was the fact that the friend would suck his penis.

Somehow Malcolm's wife found out about the homosexual affair. She threatened to expose him which terrified him, since he lived in a small town. As an alternative she was willing to accept all his money, and a substantial allowance from his family. In desperation, he agreed.

Thereupon Malcolm became a complete homosexual.

He could never again relate to a woman in any meaningful sexual way.

It is often argued that the analyst sees only "sick" homosexuals in his practice; he does not pay attention to all the
"healthy" ones who do not come to his office. This argument
is completely incorrect. First of all, the homosexual in analysis tells of dozens, often hundreds of other homosexuals with
whom he makes contact. One man in Hite's study[14] said that
he had had sex with over 2,000 men. And second, the notion
that therapists deal with only "sick" people has gone out of
the window along with many other myths. Psychotherapy today affects more than half the population, those seemingly
sick as well as those seemingly healthy.

Psychologically, homosexuality is an inability to develop
beyond a certain point. Boys relate only to boys in the school
years and in the early years of adolescence. Then life forces
them to move on to relate to women. Men who are unable to
do that, or who start to relate (as in the case of Malcolm) and
then give up, suffer from profound and disturbing conflicts,
even though they may function well in a number of other
ways.

The question of whether homosexuality is an illness or not
is often confused with the question of how society should
handle it. No therapist in his right mind is in favor of the
numerous and onerous legal restrictions that often dog the
lives of homosexuals. But while these legal restrictions should
certainly be done away with, or modified, that does not alter
the fact that homosexual behavior is a symptom of emotional
disturbance.

To return to the main theme of this chapter: What is a
man to do when he discovers that his wife is sexually unresponsive and will never change in that respect? We have
discussed infidelity, divorce, homosexuality. There are many
other outlets.

Least obvious, but in a sense most important, are the variety of neurotic and even psychotic reactions that may result.
If a rat is placed in a cage, the floor of which gives him
constant electric shocks, he does nothing but try to escape.
Similarly, if a man is faced by lifelong sexual frustration he
resorts to a variety of escapes; it is of such people that Tho-

reau said more than a hundred years ago: they lead "lives of quiet desperation."

Perhaps the most common male reaction is simply withdrawal: after trying over and over to interest his wife in sex and enjoyment, he just gives up. Usually the man withdraws to the TV set, to the basketball and football games where he can see his dreams realized by others. Wives of such men often complain that their husbands do nothing but watch TV, never even bothering to talk to them or the children. On the surface that is true; underneath lies the undisclosed fact that the sexual relationship has gradually faded away, sometimes into nothing.

After a certain point the sexual refusals become part of a vicious cycle. The wife refuses the husband, then the husband loses interest, when the wife asks for sex he is too tired, or not in the mood, she in turn feels rebuffed, next time rebuffs him and so on. Both sides have retreated to their fantasies, or, equally frequently, to a sense of despair and hopelessness about life.

Another common reaction on the part of the man is to bury himself in his work. This is especially true of more successful men, who constantly get ahead and derive a great deal of satisfaction from their accomplishments. Yet it is equally true of the less successful, who at least find in the job the security, the regularity and the acceptance they could never find at home. Some men choose jobs, such as their own businesses, where they never have a free moment; others work full time at one job, then take on part-time jobs to escape the pressures of their sexual frustrations.

More obvious pathology is seen in the man who turns to drink, or, as is increasingly seen today, to drugs. With little to attract him at home, he begins by stopping for a drink with the boys after work, then gets more and more involved. At times this may include picking up strange women, but men who drink are rarely strongly sexually motivated. Women who put up with alcoholic husbands as a rule see the man as a baby they can mother, thereby forgetting about their own problems and difficulties in living. Here too, as in so many of these problems, after a certain point a vicious circle is set up, the pathology of one reinforcing the other, so that by the time a professional comes along it is hard to disentangle who started what. Invariably, however, serious sexual frustration is found in all drinking and drug problems.

Less obvious but equally important is the resort to illness. Here the wife becomes the mother-substitute the man always longed for, and to whom he returns when his sexual needs cannot be met. In other words, if his wife will not be a woman to him, at least she can be a mother. And so he becomes sick, and gets attention and care, much as he did when he was a little boy from his own mother. If the background of such men is traced, it is found that they were good little boys with mother, but when adolescence came along and they had to relate to other women, they could not make it. These mama's boys manage to leave mother, but then when the new woman lets them down fall back on the old longings of childhood.

The illness the man suffers may be real or imaginary; here it is essential to find competent medical advice that includes an understanding of psychological conflicts and can differentiate them sufficiently from real medical problems. There have been many periods in medical history when doctors went to extremes in the effort to find some hidden physical cause, such as the period of the 1920's, when it was customary to extract all of a man's teeth if he complained of vague, poorly defined complaints. Today there is too much of a tendency on the part of the medical profession to resort to drugs, which has created a virtual epidemic in the country. Illness can, of course, be very real, but it can also be a way out of an unhappy marital situation. Freud in fact once commented that the two most common ways out of a neurotic impasse are physical illness and an unhappy marriage.

It must be recognized that when both a man and a woman because of their sexual conflicts wait a long time before getting married, the neurotic (and psychotic) reactions that may result may be quite severe. For the infantile wishes that caused them to be single so long but were kept in check as long as they were unmarried may suddenly break out into the open. Here is a typical instance.

Clara, a forty-two-year-old woman, had been unable to marry for a long time. She finally met a forty-five-year-old man who was interested in her, and after a long courtship, proposed. The man in turn had been unable to break away from his family before then.

At first the wedding seemed to bring them both great bliss. But then he fell into a deep depression, unable to work, unable to have sex, unable to go out. The depression responded to shock treatment, but the husband remained seriously incapacitated. In effect, Clara had become his mother. Actually, because of her neurotic conflicts, Clara was not too unhappy in this situation; at least she had a man who could not get away from her, as the others all had.

SUMMARY

The focus in this chapter has been on the sexual conflicts that are characteristic of the far from ideal marriage. These conflicts are much more widespread than is commonly thought, since they go back to the sexual frustrations that the man has experienced all his life.

When a man is mired in a marriage where he is doomed to lifelong sexual frustration, either because of his own or his wife's incapacity, or both, he has only a variety of undesirable alternatives. The most obvious is infidelity—to seek out another woman. This is more easily said than done. When the affair is followed up over a period of time, it soon becomes clear that it offers no permanent solution. The man's sexual conflicts are repeated in the new situation sooner or later, and similar problems arise. Divorce confronts him with the realities of an anti-sexual culture, in which all the cards are stacked in favor of a vindictive anti-sexual wife. Some men resort to homosexuality, still others to a total withdrawal from the situation. Physical illness is likewise commonly resorted to, the psychology being that of a little boy who is crying for mother's love and attention.

Ultimately, the only real solution is to help both husband and wife outgrow their sexual conflicts by means of psychotherapy. Short of that, many men and women resort to any one of a large number of compromises, none of which is really satisfying in the long run.

Chapter 6:
The Man's Response
to Women's Liberation

Except for the civil rights movement, no social protest in modern times has had the force of the women's liberation movement. Women's consciousness-raising groups have formed, the term "male chauvinism" has become part of the popular vocabulary, an Equal Rights Amendment has been introduced (though not passed) and in general the demand of many women for greater rights has permeated every fabric of our civilization. One book introduces the topic with four quotes:

> Every woman ought to be filled with shame at the thought of being a woman.
> *Clement of Alexandria c. 150–215*

> The five worst infirmities that afflict the female are indocility, discontent, slander, jealousy, and silliness. . . . Such is the stupidity of women's character, that it is incumbent upon her in every particular, to distrust herself and to obey her husband.
> *Confucian Marriage Manual*

> Nature intended women to be our slaves. They are our property, we are not theirs. They belong to us, just as a tree that bears fruit belongs to a gardener. What a mad idea to demand equality for women. . . . Women are nothing but machines for producing children.
> *Napoleon Bonaparte*

> The fact of the matter is that the prime responsibility of a woman probably is to be on earth long enough to

© 1987 by The Haworth Press, Inc. All rights reserved.

find the best possible mate for herself, and conceive children who will improve the species.

Norman Mailer

These quotes, ranging from one of the fathers of the
Christian church to a prominent modern author, are illustrative of what women have been protesting against: that they
are second-rate citizens, that they have no other function
than to produce children, that they are slaves to men, subor-
dinating their every wish to his commands.

While movements to give women more equality are virtually
as old as recorded history, it is only since World War II that it
has become a worldwide movement with branches in every
country of the world. Simone de Beauvoir perhaps sounded
the clarion call with her book *The Second Sex* (1949). In the
United States, Betty Friedan's work *The Feminine Mystique*
(1963) voiced an eloquent plea against the traditional image of
domestic bliss held out to the woman. Kate Millet (1970) in her
book *Sexual Politics* offered a widely-publicized, though not
too accurate, historical account of female subjugation.

There is no doubt that many women are looking for a new
kind of identity. No longer satisfied with being housewives
and mothers, they want more out of life. What they should
be, how they should realize their true potential is the subject
of considerable debate. The rules are new, the game is new,
the answers yet to be found.

If woman is to change the identity that men are brought up
to look for, the man's reactions are bound to be profound.
And indeed they are. Shere Hite found that when asked what
they thought of women's liberation, many men brought out a
huge amount of anger at women. Much of it was directed
against men's position in society as well. Men felt that now,
with the women's movement and the emphasis on helping
women achieve more independence and equality, they were
being falsely maligned and misunderstood. Here are some
typical replies from her book:

> All I ever hear about these days is how brutal men
> are, how women are always getting fucked over by men,
> and how the sisterhood is gonna go it alone. Well, men
> get the same kind of shit, and I do not like being put in a

category. I'm no better or no worse than anyone else, regardless of gender. Just like a woman, I want to be loved and give love in return.

There seems to be a growing stereotype of what bastards men are. Although I suppose some do live up to this stereotype. I know many men who don't (including, I believe, myself). I don't like this trend and find it similar to the black backlash against all whites once they achieved greater control over their lives . . . alienating even those whites who had fought alongside them for equal opportunities, etc. Some men are stronger feminists than many women. Why condemn all of us?

I'm in favor of it when it comes to getting rid of discrimination, but it's overblown. Women have always been able to get what they want.

I am grateful for their telling me how I've unthinkingly been insensitive to women's needs. They've made me aware of my own inflated male ego, which has caused me to make an ass of myself more than once. But I happen to be fairly handsome and have been used as a sex object on a number of occasions, so I get sick of hearing that women are "treated as sex objects." That whole game is a two-way street. I'm also turned off by all the unthinking propaganda. I also don't like it when women close their own eyes to their own nagging, bitchiness, hypocrisy, cheating, castration complexes, superficiality, etc.

Responsible women's lib is good. But I don't agree with the idea that women have been down so long that they now need to be "on top," so to speak. (Sounds like sexual positions, doesn't it?)

I'm all for real equality, but I think women want to eliminate their disadvantages and keep their special privileges and morally superior attitude.

These quotes all point in one uniform direction: whatever women may mean by the liberation movement in theory, in practice its major claims are that women are being mistreated by men. Men take their money, men run their lives, men beat them up, men force them to stay home and take care of the children while they go out and have a good time, men won't let them develop themselves and so on—the list becomes endless. Perhaps the most obvious example of the deep envy involved is the common cry: What a woman needs is a wife. A man has a wife to take care of all his needs, why shouldn't a woman have one, too?

Thus, in general, the women's movement has assumed a belligerency which seems out of keeping with its original character. And, in fact, the original movement has splintered into a number of different ones, some of which make no disguise of their intense hatred of men. One group devotes itself to finding men whom they can literally beat up. Another is committed to the defense of lesbianism, an entirely extraneous issue. Still another is attempting to recast everything in history and sociology from the standpoint of the woman, as though men did not exist at all. As usual, with any such powerful social movement, a reasonable discussion of the issues becomes very difficult or utterly impossible.

Many have observed the paradox of the sudden surge of women's liberation in the 1960's, when many of the gains for which women had fought for a hundred years were an accomplished fact: they could go through universities, enter professions, work, have property of their own, were regarded as independent human beings. Yet they complained bitterly about their lot.

The 19th century actually saw the beginning of a real attempt to raise women from the level that they had been in for centuries. The effort was obstructed not only by outmoded legal enactments, but also by incredible medical misinformation and mismanagement. It was acceptable, even stylish, to retire to bed with "sick headaches,"[2] "nerves" and various unmentionable "female troubles," and that indefinable nervous disorder named "neurasthenia" (literally: nerve weakness) was considered, in some circles, to be a mark of intellect and sensitivity.

Thus it became an acceptable lifestyle for a woman of the middle or upper classes to become a lifelong invalid. There is a marked contrast in the histories of the three James children. William James, depressed, neurotic, became a famous philosopher and psychologist. His brother, Henry, a hypochondriac who retired from life because of back injury, nevertheless wrote one novel after another. But Alice, the sister, is famous only for the fact that she was a lifelong invalid.

At one point she wrote:

> And then these doctors tell you that you will die or
> recover! But you don't recover. I have been at these
> alterations since I was nineteen and I am neither dead
> nor recovered. As I am now forty-two, there has surely
> been time for either process.[3]

Medicine contributed to the woman's psychological depression by maintaining that the woman's normal state was to be
sick. Menstruation was a real illness; one popular health manual in 1871 warned that "we cannot too emphatically urge the
importance of regarding these monthly returns as periods of
ill health, as days when the ordinary occupations are to be
suspended or modified . . ."[4]

Even worse was the commonly accepted medical theory
that woman was by nature inferior to man. And the source of
her inferiority was the uterus, around which the whole woman
was built. This uterus, it was widely believed, was inherently
diseased, or lent itself very readily to disease. Any symptoms,
headaches, indigestion, or the like, were referred to the sexual organs. The local treatments adopted at that time must
have done more harm than good. Historian Ann Wood describes those used in the mid-19th century as follows:[5]

> This (local) treatment had four stages, although not
> every case went through all four: a manual investigation,
> "leeching," "injections" and "cauterization." Dewees
> (an American medical professor) and Bennet (a famous
> English gynecologist) . . . both advocated placing the
> leeches right on the vulva or the neck of the uterus,
> although Bennet cautioned the doctor to count them as
> they dropped off when satiated, lest he "lose" some. . . .
> The uterus bcame a kind of catch-all, or what one exas-
> perated doctor referred to as a Chinese toy-shop. Water,
> milk and water, linseed tea, and decoction of marshmal-
> low, tepid or cold, found their way inside nervous
> women patients. The final step, performed at this
> time . . . with no anesthetic . . . was cauterization . . .
> even the actual cautery, a "white-hot iron instrument."[5]

It requires no great stretch of the imagination to realize that these incursions into the uterus represented a form of sexual pleasure for both the doctor and the patient, the patient's pleasure being masked by the pain that accompanied it.

If the woman was not bled white in her crotch, she was infantilized by the Weir Mitchell rest cure. Weir Mitchell, known as the greatest "neurologist" of the 19th century, is remembered today chiefly for his notion of the rest cure; it took medicine fifty years to get past the damage inflicted by that.

Charlotte Perkins Gilman, one of the leading feminists of the nineteenth century, once consulted Mitchell about her depression and lassitude. He would not even bother to listen to her complaints. Instead, he directed her to show "obedience." His prescription was:

> Live as domestic a life as possible. Have your child with you all the time. Lie down an hour after each meal. Have but two hours intellectual life a day. And never touch pen, brush or pencil as long as you live.[6]

This last bit of advice was due to the commonly accepted notion that intellectual activity weakened a woman badly. Charlotte Gilman came close to having a breakdown by following Mitchell's advice; she escaped only by leaving her husband and the doctor and going off to California to an active life as a writer and an activist.

While American medicine has, of course, outgrown, at least in large part, these barbaric practices, that is not true of other parts of the world. In 1979 Fran Hosken, a journalist, published what has since become known as the Hosken Report,[7] an impassioned account of the genital and sexual mutilation of girl children in a wide geographical belt of the African continent running parallel to, and north, of the equator. She documents three forms of genital mutilation: sunna circumcision, excision, and infibulation. Sunna circumcision means removal of the clitoris prepuce and the tip of the clitoris, while excision means removal of the entire clitoris (clitoridectomy) sometimes with parts of the labia minora and labia majora.

Most brutal is infibulation. This is an extensive operation in which the clitoris, labia minora and parts of the labia majora are cut out, the soft tissue of the vulva scraped raw, and the sides of the vulva sewed or clamped together. Infibulation is done most frequently on young girls before puberty; after the procedure, the legs of the girl are tied together and she is immobilized for several weeks until the sides of the vulva have grown together. A small opening is left for passage of urine and menstrual blood by insertion of a sliver of wood or bamboo into the wound. The virginity of the child is thereby guaranteed and she is ready to be sold in marriage.

In these cultures female sexuality is seen as a threat to male control and a danger to marital stability. In infibulation the sealed wound must be cut open on the marriage night and the scar tissue must be cut again during labor and childbirth. Such extraordinary brutality must obviously be tied to the fear of the woman's retaliatory wishes. But once again, these practices occur in Africa and not in the United States.

What Hosken does not mention is that in the countries in which these barbarous practices are carried out the man's lot is equally miserable. Slavery, summary executions, constant civil wars (in the Sudan it is stated that the civil wars from 1955 to 1972 cost half a million to a million lives), malnutrition, disease are the rule rather than the exception. In other words, the cruelty of the man toward the woman is matched by the cruelty of man toward men.

It seems highly paradoxical that the greatest protest of women should have come in the last twenty years. In the first place many women enjoy the life of domestic bliss, in which they love their husbands and bring up happy children. Nor can it be denied that a happy family life is one of the best guarantees for a happy life for both men and women.

Furthermore, a closer look at patriarchal societies shows that women, even when confined to domestic duties, often managed to acquire a good deal of power. Ann Pescatello (1976) in her study of women in Iberian society, finds that in both matriarchal and patriarchal societies and families, the female has been the most important person, in the figure of the mother-matriarch, in the family household. She writes:

> So while, in theory, the female often has been an out-caste, a pawn, in practice throughout history, she often has been the wellspring of power.[8]

In an article in *Harper's* of October 1981, Barbara Harrison reexamined the women's liberation movement as it stands today, and came out puzzled. The cover of the magazine shows a girl baby with the caption" "Will she be a Feminist? Having everything may not be enough." The article itself is entitled: "What Do Women Really Want?" It is based on a visit to Smith College, one of the outstanding women's colleges in the country. Ms. Harrison argues that the word "liberation" has lost much of its meaning, and that many women do not know what they want to be liberated from.[9]

Almost all the women at Smith were determined to have careers, but then again the entry of women into the work force has been increasing steadily since 1900. The middle-class family is now generally supported by two working parents; this is more a consequence of the economic situation than of anyone's wishes as such. A powerful contingent of lesbians seemed to be present, though the president stated that there were no more homosexuals at the college than in the population at large. (It has long been known that whether male or female, unisex schools promote homosexuality, and literally hundreds of unisex schools have been replaced by coed schools in the last twenty years.)

Everywhere she went Ms. Harrison asked: "What do women want?" The usual answer was: "Don't ask me what women want, ask me what I want." Most of the women wanted a good family life, and a career, certainly not a radical suggestion in this day and age. Some said bluntly: "Why can't I have everything?"

The impression one gets from her article is that the women at Smith (and in general in the women's liberation movement) are searching for a happier life, and blaming men for their lack of it. In much the same way many men today are searching for a better life and blaming women because they cannot find it. The old values are disappearing; in the face of tremendous economic and social problems (which are distributed equally among the sexes) people are looking for the "new rules." Thus looked at from a broader perspective the women's liberation movement is part of a broader human liberation movement, and not really confined to women at all.

It is most unfortunate that one prominent aspect of the women's liberation movement has been its vehement attacks against psychoanalysis, and particularly against Freud. Because these attacks are based largely on ignorance or distortion of what psychoanalysts and Freud have said, it is appropriate here to set the record straight and clarify what the psychoanalytic view of women is, if there can be said to be one psychoanalytic view (which is not the case).

Historically, Freud's first great contribution was to show in the 1890's and 1900's that the severe sexual repression to which women were subject in the Victorian age led to illness, primarily hysteria. At first he thought that girls were made hysterical by the attacks of older men, later he abandoned this as a fantasy of the girls and attributed the illness to the frustration of the infantile sexual wishes, which arose inevitably in the course of every girl's life. *That he made exactly the same point about men has also been overlooked.* Sexual repression leads to illness in both sexes, and he made this point so tellingly that the twentieth century in a very real sense may be examined in the light of this striking discovery.

The full history of psychoanalytic discussion of women's psychology, including the various changes in Freud's views, would take us too far afield. Through them all, however, there has always remained the basic and indisputable finding that excessive sexual repression leads to illness, often of a serious kind, sometimes, either directly or indirectly, fatal in its consequences.

It is primarily against this background that the psychoanalytic position must be traced further. As we view it today, the biological (or anatomical) differences between boys and girls, while important, are secondary to what the parents and the culture inculcate in them. Mountains of research, outside and inside psychoanalysis, have not demonstrated any fundamental differences between boys and girls other than the obvious physiological ones. But what they do with their bodies is of vital importance.

The boy, in exploring his body, soon comes on his penis and testicles. The penis gives him great pleasure, the testicles are extremely sensitive and easily hurt. He thus learns to masturbate and avoid any great shock to his genitals. Masturbation is frowned upon by the parents, which produces castration anxiety in him.

The analogous process in the girl is different because her

anatomy is different. When she learns to masturbate, the center of her pleasurable sensations lies in her clitoris, and there is no sensitive area comparable to that of the little boy. The vagina, however, is an opening in the body, and she discovers it at about the same time that she has to control her bowel movements; hence the vagina tends to be seen as something disgusting and dirty; the girl must eventually learn the difference between the anus and the vagina.

When the sexes grow up to be old enough to have sexual intercourse, again different reactions occur. The boy, who has previously known his penis only as an organ of urination, now must also learn that it is an organ of pleasure, to be used to penetrate the woman's body and in masturbation to produce sperm and extremely pleasurable sensations. The girl, on the other hand, continues to derive pleasure from her clitoral sensations, and now must cope with the flow of blood from her vagina. Without going into all the details, she too learns that penetration by the penis is an extremely pleasurable experience, especially since it involves the close union with another body.

When the culture forbids early intercourse, as ours has, and still does, in large measure, the boy reacts with castration anxiety and heavy masturbation. The girl, however, reacts by not allowing herself the enjoyment of penetration by the penis, and even after it becomes "legal" it frequently takes years for her to reach a stage where it is fully pleasurable. Thus she has to shift from clitoral to vaginal pleasure to get maximal satisfaction from sex and life, while the boy has to shift to see his penis as an organ which can penetrate the woman and bring both pleasure.

When the culture interferes with such activities, each sex reacts in a characteristic way. The girl takes a long time to make the shift from clitoris to vagina, the boy takes a long time to become fully potent.

But the physical aspect of sexual competence presents only half of the total picture. The other half is love. And this other half has always been more important in psychoanalytic thought, though so often neglected by lay and professional critics alike.

Freud described the growth toward love in terms of passing through a number of developmental stages—oral, anal, phallic (penis-centered) and so on. Eventually both sexes reach a stage, ideally in puberty, where the tender and sexual feelings are united toward a person of the opposite sex. The truly liberated person is not the one who can have sex with anybody, but the one who can have a gratifying love experience with another human being.

In this respect Freud's view is echoed by every sociological survey on the subject ever done. What people long for more than anything else is love. Jonathan Freedman begins his book with a quotation from Marlowe: "Come live with me and be my love/And we will all the pleasures prove."[10] In his surveys he found that love is mentioned more than anything else as the one element missing from people's lives that, if supplied, would bring happiness. Many people who seem to have everything else are unhappy or even miserable because they do not have love. People look to love as the key to happiness.

Angus Campbell[11] approaches it in terms of the need for relating, and finds that of all the various mechanisms societies provide to meet this need, marriage and the family appear to be the most universal and the most fulfilling. Andrews and Withey[12] even though they eliminated questions about love found that being married did make a difference in a number of measures of global well-being, and not being married made a big difference in unhappiness.

It should be borne in mind that however popular writers and some professionals may distort it, this is and always has been the orthodox traditional theory, from Freud on. Other questions such as masochism, or submissiveness, or narcissism, are secondary, and essentially neurotic malformations which the psychoanalyst makes every effort to help the woman get over.

It is therefore all the more remarkable that so many leaders of the women's liberation movement have put Freud and psychoanalysis in the position of oppressors of women. One writer (Phyllis Chesler) views psychotherapy and marriage as the two devices men have used to hold women down. In the Hite report on women, when Hite discovered that most of her women respondents derived more orgastic pleasure from masturbation than from intercourse, she came to the extraordinary conclusion that intercourse is a male device used to subjugate women.

Even in a journal as serious as the *American Journal of Psychiatry,* in a recent issue devoted to women, two female physicians blithely state that "marriage increases stress for women," totally ignoring the enormous stresses that marriage produces for men.[13]

It can scarcely escape anyone's attention that in the literature of women's liberation a great deal of hostility toward men is released. An extreme is seen in the manifesto of SCUM (Society for Cutting Up Men), which states categorically that life being at best an utter bore, one of the few remaining goals left is to destroy the male sex completely.[12] Even if this is admittedly a lunatic fringe group, others iterate and reiterate that women are oppressed by men, that they have always been oppressed by men, and that men are the root cause of all their troubles.

Women's studies have developed, and properly so, in many colleges and universities. Much has been uncovered about the indignities foisted on women by society at many points in history. What has been overlooked is that parallel indignities, including torture, murder and enslavement have been foisted on men. And there is as yet not a single college in the country that has a department of men's studies. Thus even here the information is being collected in a one-sided manner.

HATE CULTURES VS. LOVE CULTURES

In order to place the women's liberation movement in proper perspective, it is essential to elaborate on the distinction between love cultures and hate cultures. In love cultures the predominant mode of relating between people in a positive affectionate one, in hate cultures the predominant mode is a negative hostile one. In the most essential respects, our culture qualifies more as a hate culture than a love culture, and has been that for thousands of years.

Theoreticians have been so impressed with the ubiquity of hatred that they have often postulated it as an instinctual force which must always be found and reckoned with in every society. Among the biologists who have taken this position the foremost is Konrad Lorenz, whose book on *Aggression* specifically emphasizes how deeply rooted aggression is in man's evolutionary past. Freud actually had two theories of instinctual aggression, one in his earlier years and one in the later period. But while analysts today generally agree that hostility is a powerful instinctual drive, they also argue that it can be tamed and put to constructive use, rather than let loose in the demonic world—shattering forms that have dominated in the past and that still dominate today.[14]

Love cultures are in fact so rare that many have doubted that they exist. But they do. Ashley Montagu, the noted anthropologist, has assembled data on a number of them, offering a spirited refutation of Lorenz's contention. Montagu insists that aggression is due to human nurture, not human nature.[15]

Particularly important for the present discussion is the differing notions of love that are prevalent in the two kinds of cultures. In a love culture love is a (a) more diffuse; (b) less intense; (c) more gratifying; (d) less ringed with violence (in cases of unfaithfulness or desertion); and (e) less confined to marriage. In the hate culture the opposite of all of these would be true. Clearly our own culture qualifies as a hate culture in every important respect.

Instances of love cultures may be quoted. Ruth Benedict describes cultures in which the concept of warfare is so foreign to their thinking that they cannot even understand it when it is described to them. Among the Zunis, in the Pueblos of New Mexico, all things are pursued in moderation. Sex is an incident in the happy life. Plesant relations between the sexes are merely one aspect of pleasant relations between human beings. Their phrase of commendation is: "Everybody likes him; he is always having affairs with women." Or: "Nobody likes him; he never has trouble over women."

Spiro has investigated the people of Ifaluk, a small atoll in the South Pacific. The outstanding sentiment in their ethos is the feeling of kindliness. Obedience is exacted by love rather than by reward or punishment. The only form of aggression he found was that they believe in and exorcise malevolent ghosts. Their main art is in gesture and song; love songs are composed principally by women. They are frankly sexual, followed by some feelings of parting and abandonment (apparently not marked).

Margaret Mead, in her comparison of thirteen cultures,

found that there is a high correspondence between a major emphasis upon cooperation, a social structure which does not depend upon individual initiative or the exercise of power over persons, a faith in an ordered universe, weak emphasis upon rising in status and a high degree of security for the individual. Even in animal groups the great significance of love and cooperation has only recently been appreciated. Almost all animal groups manage to work out amicable relationships among their members so that destructive encounters are avoided. In fact, as has been pointed out, there are few animals as destructive as man.

All of this is highly relevant for the proper evaluation of women's liberation. Much of what women have been saying, about oppression, deprivation of rights, is true but equally true about men and many other groups in society. In a hate culture such as ours everybody lives in a state of considerable insecurity, never knowing where the next blow may strike.

It is in the light of the prevalence of hate cultures that women's situation has to be evaluated, and men's, as well. Actually, the notion that women are more oppressed than men is a dubious one anyhow. Equal pay for equal work is certainly a commendable idea, but that women receive less pay for comparable work than men has to be balanced against the greater financial obligations of men. In order to assay the relative rewards of the two sexes the obligations must be considered as well, and the man in general is saddled with obligations of a financial nature which are far greater than that of the woman.

Besides, the demand for the "right to work" is a paradoxical one. Most men regard work as an unavoidable curse and spend their time dreaming of inheriting a million dollars, or engaging in get-rich-quick schemes such as the lottery or gambling which will free them of work. Some recent data do in fact indicate that while more women are being drawn into the work force, more men are withdrawing from it.

The attack on analysis is also the result of misunderstanding, and entirely misplaced. What Freud and other analysts said about women was descriptive, not prescriptive. If girls have penis envy (a simple clinical observation) that is not the desirable attitude. Psychoanalysis seeks to rid them of it, while education, along psychoanalytic lines, seeks to prevent it. However, neither psychooanalysis as a therapy nor psycho-analysis as an educational philosophy rule the culture. The great prevalence of sexual malfunctioning is borne out by one survey after another. In the individual this sexual malfunc-tioning stems from the inhibitions about the use of the body—penis envy in women, castration anxiety in men. Both may be reduced to the feeling that their body is inadequate. In a culture where sex education is still largely taboo, where a vocal group pretending to "high moral standards" wishes to do away with legal abortion, returning women to the criminal conditions that existed before, where millions of people live under the most appalling economic conditions breeding crime, disease and social disorder of all kinds it should scarcely be surprising that sexual inadequacy is more the rule than the exception. And this sexual inadequacy is found among men just as often as among women.

To some extent the initial furor set off in the 1960s has died down, and a more sober view of the realities is beginning to take its place. In her review of Betty Friedan's most recent book, *The Second Stage* (1981), Erica Jong[16] rightly comments that what the right-wing nostalgia mongers and the feminist extremists have in common is that they are both fulminating about something that no longer exists.

In fact, Friedan in her latest book reverses her position entirely. She now puts it:

> The second stage cannot be seen in terms of women alone, our separate personhood or equality with men.
> The second stage involves coming to new terms with the family—new terms with love and with work.
> The second stage may not even be a women's move-ment. Men may be at the cutting edge of the second stage.
> The second stage has to transcend the battle for equal power in institutions. The second stage will restructure institutions and transform the nature of power itself.
> The second stage may even now be evolving, out of or even aside from what we have thought of as our battle.[17]

But if family is the new frontier, as she now maintains, and if women are to liberate themselves by having a happy family, then it merges into the traditional democratic ideals of our society, and its acerbity and virulence are largely outmoded.

This second stage, as she calls it, however, is exactly what the psychoanalysts have been talking about for the past hundred years. The problem, however, is that marital happiness and family harmony are not as easy as they seem. What tears the family apart, and interferes with a gratifying love, is the internal conflicts that stem from childhood. Once people realize this, a third stage will be reached, where the early problems will be tackled and eventually resolved by a combination of psychoanalysis and education. It is this inner revolution which represents the real heart of the psychoanalytic vision.[18]

INNER CHANGE VS. OUTER CHANGE

Once more it is necessary to clarify the psychoanalytic position. While the recent feminism agrees with analysis that a healthy family life is the desired solution, the two differ widely on the means needed to realize this change. For psychoanalysis stresses the indispensability of an inner change, while all the other approaches, including all the social sciences, only think of outward change.

The family has been the core of all social structures from time immemorial. If family life were the only requirement, it could be accomplished overnight. But this is exactly where psychoanalysis from the very beginning found that there was something rotten in Denmark. Looked at close up, the family turned out to be a hotbed of incestuous desires, suppressed (or expressed) violence, rivalries, jealousies, schizophrenia, neuroses of all kinds and all the other evils that the world has suffered throughout the ages. It was these discoveries which led the early analysts to feel that marriage as such was not the answer to humanity's problems. As Ernest Jones put it:

> Every form of marriage relationship so far attempted . . . has been accompanied by serious disadvantages. Polygamy, monogamy, easy divorce; none provides a satisfactory solution.[19]

Subsequently various research studies (Rennie, 1962) have confirmed what analysts had surmized from their early limited experience: The vast majority of people in the world suffer from neurotic problems of varying degrees of severity. Merely living in a family does not overcome these problems.[20]

I have elsewhere argued the case for a universal psychotherapy, and would refer the interested reader to my earlier book for a fuller discussion of the topic.[21] The urgent need for psychotherapy means that we will have to move into a third stage, in which there is not only a family, but one based on love and harmony, rather than on hatred and discord. In other words, there has to be a transformation of the hate culture into a love culture before any real resolution of man's problems can be effected. The form of the family in which this occurs is really of secondary importance.

The emphasis on inner change means that outer changes, no matter how desirable, must be carefully evaluated. The most extraordinary changes in society have come about in this century (as well as in previous centuries) without noticeably adding to the happiness of the average man. The notion that women are oppressed runs up against the observation that many groups are oppressed in a hate culture. The prime need is to overcome oppression, wherever that may occur.

The real problem is that of searching for a new way of living in a society in a constant state of flux. The women's liberation movement has emphasized certain problems for women, but has tended to forget the man and the family structure, to which it is now returning. Man's problems are in fact in many respects far more burdensome and far more difficult to overcome than women's, yet there is not a single college in the country that has a course devoted to men's studies. If the role of women in history has been neglected or misrepresented, which is certainly true, that is part of the large-scale misrepresentation that conventional historians have offered about what has really happened in the course of the centuries.

From the point of view of inner change, the goal should be the pursuit of the analytic ideal without ignoring the outer changes needed to alter the hatred and oppression that make the lives of so many millions of people miserable. There is no real reason why the pursuit of such an ideal could not be one constructive outgrowth of the women's liberation movement.

PART II: AGGRESSION

Chapter 7:
Trained to Fight

From earliest childhood the boy is trained to be a fighter. This has been covered over by arguments about whether hostility or aggression is instinctual or not. While it is true that there is a biological basis for the aggression, it can be manifested in so many different ways that the decisive factor becomes the society, rather than the physiological drive. In terms of the traditional masculine ideal, our culture has emphasized more than anything else the fighting qualities of the man.

Consider how the average American boy is brought up. As soon as he is born, often before, the parents speculate on how big, strong and successful he will become. When he is developed enough to get around, he begins to fight with his parents and with other children. He is taught that it is not manly to hit girls, but is praised and encouraged in many subtle ways for his aggression toward boys. If there is a younger brother, the two are often engaged in battles. In these early years much of his aggression is directed toward his father. Only excesses are curbed; ordinary aggression is stimulated and favored.

Once he is old enough to go to school, fighting becomes one of the main centers of his existence. Girls are shunned; boys will play only with boys. And their play revolves around fighting in all its variations—literal fights, using weapons (sticks, stones), contests, games. Many times when boys have

© 1987 by The Haworth Press, Inc. All rights reserved.

nothing else to do, they start a friendly fight, to see who is the stronger: "Put up your mitts." This reflects the constant pre-occupation with strength and power which makes up such a large part of the growing up of the American boy.

Even fairly early in childhood some of the aggression may spill over into violence. Rock fights, which occur everywhere among schoolboys, are dangerous. One of Nixon's brothers was killed in a rock fight at an early age.[1]

When the boy is old enough to react to the larger world outside, fighting and violence are the order of the day. Movies depict fights; cops and robbers, whites against Indi-ans, battle scenes of all kinds. The immature boy learns to glorify war because he does not as yet have an adequate concept of death. Even adults hold on to the notion of the heroism of war. McArthur's father made a daring assault on the Confederates when he was an eighteen-year-old lieuten-ant in the Civil War. The assault succeeded and became almost an obsession with his better-known son Douglas MacArthur. During World War II MacArthur kept repeating that the greatest thing a man can do is die in battle.

Other stories likewise glorify violent heroes. Davy Crockett is often a craze with American boys, even though he was only a boastful frontiersman with little to recommend him except personal courage. The hero of the Alamo died with all his men, when it made more sense to retreat; the battle was lost from the beginning, with less than 200 Americans against 4,000 Mexicans.[2]

Mythological heroes also fill the mind of the boy. Super-man flies through the air, is impervious to guns and other weapons, and can only be brought to heel by the use of kryp-ton. Tarzan is like a primitive superman, defeating all of his enemies with ease.

Beatings of children are common, and are still supported by the old adage: Spare the rod and spoil the child. It is only in the present century that serious objection has been raised against child beatings by children and social scientists; previ-ous to that it was considered normal and even necessary, to drive out the beast in the child.[3]

In a national survey of 1968, a considerable percentage of children were found to be seriously abused by their parents. The greatest abuse came in the age period three to six years,

when about 20% of the children were hurt. The injuries inflicted were by no means light, and included scalding burns,
bone fractures, and even on rare occasions poisoning and
brain damage. Beating with the hands was found in 39% of
the cases, with instruments in 44% of the cases.[4]

It is known that parents who beat their children are generally poorly educated and themselves very unhappy. Almost all
were beaten by their parents when they were children. Thus
one generation of disturbed people passes on their disturbance to the next generation.

In the average family, a strong antagonism between father
and son may arise very early. Fathering is something for
which the average American man has neither training nor
understanding. The situation is beginning to change, with the
"new rules" urged by the mental health profession, but
changes take many years, and in the meantime the old patterns persist. Such newfangled notions as paternity leave are
unheard of in most places, with the result that the mother
takes care of the children all day, and when the father comes
home from work in the evening he stays away from them, or
battles with them.

After a great deal of frustration in the family, the boy goes
out into the world of peer groups, from about the age of eight
on. Here once more the gang prods him to fight and repress
his fear. "Don't show the yellow feather" is the motto. To be
branded a coward is literally for many boys worse than death.
There is little modifying effect from women, since at this
time, boys will not go near girls.

Naturally many attempts are made by the parents and
school authorities to get the boy to restrain his aggression.
But this only leads to confusion. All around him he sees the
fighting spirit idealized, yet he has to hold his back. Naturally
most boys do, but at the cost of enormous inner resentment,
which soon becomes chronic.

A further psychological conflict arises. Fighting after all
makes anybody fearful; you can get hurt, and the boy often is
hurt. Yet he is not allowed to say that he is afraid. And so he
learns to go through life willing to fight if anybody tries to
"put him down," yet inwardly terrified of what he is doing.

A comparison can be made with earlier centuries when
dueling was the accepted means of avenging one's honor. A

leading American statesman of the revolutionary period, Alexander Hamilton, was killed in a duel, as were countless others. Yet this honor, which today is called the put-down, is after all only a social pretense. Throughout the dueling centuries men must have been as panicky about being killed as they are now, yet they were caught up in the grip of a conflict they could not escape. This conflict takes a different form today, now that duels no longer occur, but it is still a source of tremendous tension in the man. Just as he is sexually frustrated from an early age on, he is filled with foreboding about fights he does not know how to avoid. Again the forgotten man does not know where to turn.

Increasingly with the school period, aggression is shifted to sports and games. Not infrequently these take on a violent character; "kill the umpire" is a common reaction. Adult sports heroes, like John McEnroe in tennis, or Reggie Jackson in baseball, also fight openly about trivialities, setting a bad example for the spectators.

Once the boy enters adolescence he finds himself saddled with these two unnerving conflicts—about sex and about aggression. Now there come the added problems of reaching the end of the growth period, which had always seemed a way out before, and the need to face adult responsibilities. Added is the fact that for a large majority of the teens in our society, senseless restrictions are imposed, particularly with compulsory schooling and lack of preparation for adult work.

The result is the enormous amount of sickness, mental and physical, and violence that erupts. Everybody today is properly concerned with the terrible toll that violence takes on our society. Even though remedial measures are started when the boy is an adolescent, it becomes too little and too late. The boy has been trained to fight, and he will fight on for the rest of his life. The consequence is the hate culture that we see all around us (all over the world, not just in this country).

WILLIAM DOUGLAS[5]

Of course there are positive sides to fighting. In adult life this expresses itself as the capacity for hard work, the ability to achieve, the quality of initiative and the satisfactions attached to success. With the Protestant ethic, which gave work a religious sanction, Americans and Europeans have performed unheard-of feats—men on the moon, conquest of space, elimination of many diseases, prolongation of life and health—the list is truly endless. Yet if we look at the man behind the mask, there is always a price paid for success. William Douglas, who rose from poverty-stricken beginnings to become a justice of the Supreme Court and one of the eminent legal luminaries of our century, is a good example. His father was an itinerant preacher who died of ulcers (usually associated with conflicts about success) at the age of forty-seven, leaving his widow with three small children to bring up.[6] From earliest childhood he was dominated by the wish for success. His biographer James Simon titles the first part of his biography: "The Achiever." Chapter 2 is titled "Born for Success."

Determination, grit and inborn talent all combined to lead Douglas far early. He was born in Maine in 1898 and moved around a great deal as a child because of his father's profession. The family went to the northwest (Washington) when he was still a small child; at that time the country was still pacifying some of the Indians in the area. All his life Douglas retained some of the characteristics of an Indian fighter.

His father died when he was only five, which left an indelible feeling of loss in his life. On top of that he was always a sickly child, and developed infantile paralysis at a very early age, which affected his legs. The doctor called to attend him predicted he would lose the use of his legs and die before forty.

In spite of this gloomy prognosis, his mother tended to him indefatigably. His legs were massaged constantly; at one point she did not sleep for six weeks. Fortunately, the illness left no lasting after-effects. But Douglas continued all his life to strengthen his legs and his body by long hikes and other physical exercises.

In his teens he once went on a long hike with his younger brother, Arthur. Without telling Arthur, William decided on a twenty-five mile hike with thirty pound packs on their backs. They made it, but both boys became ill. William that night slept fitfully, aroused by nightmares and a splitting headache. The next morning he was too ill to move. But, though sick, he was satisfied. He later wrote:

Inwardly I felt a glow because of my achievement. I had walked twenty-five miles with a thirty-pound pack in one day. My legs had stood up. I had conquered my doubts. So far as my legs were concerned, I knew that I was free to roam these mountains at will, to go on foot where any man could go, to enter any forest without hesitation.[8]

The same single-mindedness that led him to overcome his childhood physical weakness is plain in his brilliant legal career. Regarded as the country's outstanding law professor when he was still only thirty[9] Douglas became chairman of the Securities Exchange Commission in 1937 when he was only thirty-eight, and a Supreme Court justice two years later. He remained a justice for thirty-six years, the longest period anyone had ever remained on the Court. There he was always the outstanding liberal, dedicated to the needs of the oppressed, and forever alert to the removal of liberties from helpless or disadvantaged individuals. He survived four attempts at impeachment, and continued to try to maintain himself on the Court even after a stroke had left him physically incapable of doing his job.

But in spite of the honors and accolades Douglas remained inwardly a most unhappy man. He had always suffered from a certain amount of nervous tension. His second wife, Mercedes, correctly said of him: "He is a great man, but an unhappy one."[10]

Apart from his inner insecurities which were known to relatively few, his problems came out most clearly in his relations with women. Brought up in a strict Puritanical code, he evidently stayed away from sex altogether until his early marriage to a girl from his hometown, five years his senior. The marriage was a conventional one, serving as emotional support while he climbed the ladder of success and power. One friend said of the family: "I could feel the unhappiness. He never touched her or showed affection or appreciated her. He bossed her around and he bossed the kids around, too, and they resented it."[11] His children rebelled, and an emotional closeness with them never really ripened.

As with so many other prominent men, after his achievements had reached a sufficient pinnacle, he turned away from the coldness of family to seek comfort in other women. Staying within the limits of his judicial stature, and performing his duties brilliantly, he nevertheless began to have a number of affairs. Publicly all that is known is that he made three further marriages after divorcing his wife in 1953, when he was in his mid-fifties. All three were notable in that the new wives were very much younger, in their early twenties.

His later marriages were apparently no happier than his first. One friend said of him: "Bill was always happy just before a marriage and a week afterward."[12] His second wife, Mercedes, showed keen insight into his character. "When a Supreme Court judge lays a babe, it isn't an ordinary man doing so—it's the 'robes' and very little sex is needed."[13] At another time she wrote: "My theory is that he never ran around as a young man and hence his problem. Also he needs adulation to the nth degree—she (his third wife, Joanie, who was twenty when he met her) wrote her senior thesis on him—the answer is in that. Also he has a tremendous self-destructive instinct—whether that enters this I do not know."[14]

With all his amours Douglas achieved little lasting happiness. At one point he consulted a doctor (a self-trained psychiatrist, Dr. George Draper) for his inner insecurities. But primarily he wanted to get over some fears, particularly the fear of water. This he did overcome but deeper insight into his life pattern was not forthcoming. Clearly his great need was to win, to achieve success, to dominate people, whether men in the law or women in sex. This is the Don Juan pattern with women which emerges later in life and the man behind the mask remains miserable and unhappy, even if he is a great Supreme Court judge.

Douglas' behavior aroused so much gossip and criticism that a move was actually made to impeach him in 1970. Although he pooh-poohed it at first, later he had to hire a lawyer and take it seriously. A committee investigated his activities, which included earnings from associations outside the bench but eventually the impeachment move was discontinued.[15]

HENRY VIII[16]

Many similarities may be noted between the rulers of various epochs. Henry VIII, England's most famous and notorious monarch, was a man favored by birth and early environment. But he too became more and more paranoid as he grew older. He wanted to be the omnipotent ruler of Britain, as well as head of the church. Gradually he became the troubled anxious ruler of the mid-1520s (he was born in 1491) harried in mind by fear of divine vengeance, then the fearsome murderous king of the 1530's whose wrath was fatal to those about him. The Catholic Church puts at fifty the number of martyrs whose deaths he brought about by execution or starvation. Two wives, at least a dozen blood relatives and a similar number of onetime counselors and friends lengthened the list of his victims. By the 1540's, as he entered his fifties, he had become a monstrous figure to his people—an inhuman tyrant of mythic proportions, whose valor and integrity had dissolved under the corroding influence of adultery, sacrilege and blood lust. One of his biographers referred to "the inwardness of that majestic childishness, that absurd mixture of naivete and cunnning, boldness and poltroonery, vindictive cruelty and wayward almost irresistible charm."[17] Much of this might have been said of Nixon. But the times were different. Henry had the right to exert all power, which he maintained by almost indiscriminate murder, of both friends and foes. Nixon liked to destroy men, but he was prevented from doing more harm by the limitations placed on his power by the system into which he was born.

OSWALD T. AVERY[18]

Though spurred on by the same drive for achievement, the life course of many scientists takes an entirely different turn. Oswald T. Avery (1877–1955) whose name is unknown to the general public, is responsible for one of the greatest biological discoveries of modern times—the role of DNA in the transmission of hereditary characteristics. Through this discovery, and the later one of the chemical formula for DNA, the way was opened for a biological transformation of man, a transformation with incalculable consequences.

Avery's life was totally uneventful; all his energies were poured into the single-minded pursuit of his work. Born the son of a minister who later emigrated from the most vice-ridden area of New York,[19] Avery at first studied the liberal arts. Once he had graduated from college he entered medical school. For some years he practiced medicine, but it did not interest him. Then he got an appointment as a researcher for the Hoagland Laboratories. In 1913 he moved on to the Rockefeller Institute, where he stayed the rest of his life.

Like many other scientists he was extremely reticent about his personal life. His student René Dubos, who himself became a scientist of great renown, described him as follows:

> Avery ate very little, was extremely fastidious about the nature of his food, shunned public gatherings, and resented being entertained. Although a very effective lecturer, who loved to advise those who came to him, he virtually gave up public speaking after joining the research staff of the Institute. He kept shy of social responsibilities, and instead devoted all his energy and talent to laboratory work in collaboration with a small number of colleagues . . .
>
> He elected to withdraw almost completely from public life. He has left no written document to account for this choice, nor does he seem to explicitly have stated his reasons for it to either family or friend. His conversation was always sparkling and often penetrating, but he was very selective in what he revealed of his complex personality. To the end he kept his own counsel.[20]

A small man (100 pounds) of slight build, Avery never married and was never known to have taken any interest in women. Nor did he have very close men friends after the early years; his entire life was wrapped up in his work. His closest associate was his brother, Roy, also a bacteriologist. From 1909 to 1950 he produced an enormous number of scientific papers, culminating in the discovery of the role of DNA in heredity.

A life such as Avery's, with its stupendous achievement toward the end, stands in marked contrast to the previous lives discussed. Superficially, no sex, no aggression, no fear; a

Christ-like figure, perhaps in imitation of his minister-father's ideals. Underneath, however, he too was trained to fight. The one extra-scientific interest he had was in the cornet, which he mastered so well that he was once invited to play in a symphony orchestra; thus another notable achievement.

In men such as Avery, the aggression is channeled entirely into their work. Withdrawal as severe as his is not common; most scientists at least get married, fight for their places, and many have a number of other interests besides their main work. The degree to which Avery blocked off his instinctual life is extraordinary; how he did it we can only guess, since he left no written documents, and no one, even his closest associates in the laboratory, knew anything about his inner thoughts and feelings. Nor could he have predicted in 1907, when he left the practice of medicine to enter research, that in 1944 he would unlock one of the great secrets to life. There is in fact no indication that he consciously hoped he would unearth some scientific facts or theories that would make him deserving of the Nobel prize. It should have been awarded to him, but his extreme shyness led to a down-playing of his contributions. They were appreciated by the Rockefeller Institute but he was indifferent to outside awards. He did receive recognition from a number of scientific societies, here and abroad, but he rarely went to collect any of them, because he abhorred traveling. Various excuses were offered, his health or the cost of travel, but obviously any public display of praise for his work would have aroused storms of emotion in him which he might not have been able to control, so he withdrew.

In his personal life, the withdrawal must have caused him suffering to some extent, but he could shift it to the kind of work he did. As is well known, a scientist of his type has to perform thousands of experiments before one comes out well. So his favorite expression became: "Disappointment is my daily bread. I thrive on it."[21] Since he was confronted with disappointment in his research all the time, he could block off the disappointments in his personal life.

The fighter sets himself a task which he may not be able to communicate to others. When he sees himself fail, he may and frequently does, turn the violence against himself by committing suicide. The modern country which still has the most peculiar attitude to death and suicide is Japan.

YUKIO MISHIMA[22]

Yukio Mishima, author of forty novels, eighteen plays, twenty volumes of short stories and numerous essays was in the forefront of the Japanese writers of the post-war generation. His dominant theme and obsession was the westernization of Japanese culture.

Mishima's autobiographical novel, *Confessions of a Mask*, was published in 1949. In it he revealed himself to the public—his homosexuality (although on the surface he seemed to be happily married with two children), his erotic fascination with the well-tanned naked bodies of young men, and with blood and death; his adoration of the portrait of the death of St. Sebastian, the Christian martyr. He also exposed his pathological obsession with violence and death:[10]

> There, in my murder theater, young Roman gladiators offered up their lives for my amusement; and all the deaths that took place there not only had to overflow with blood but also had to be performed with due ceremony. I delighted in all forms of capital punishment and all implements of execution.[23]

From 1966 to 1970, Mishima led two lives. One was his normal one as a writer, husband, father and prominent man of letters. The second was the Shield Society, a private army founded by Mishima with a group of students. Nationalistic in spirit, the purpose of the army was to defend the emperor with their lives against any enemy, from the political left or right. When he announced the formation of the Shield Society to the press, the reaction was one of amusement; for the average Japanese such suicidal emperor worship was a thing of the past.

But he persisted. His chief aide was Masakatsu Morita, a young student and orphan, who fervently shared Mishima's extreme right-wing political ideas.

By 1970, the Shield Society had grown into a rigorously trained and uniformed force of eighty young men. In that year he began to work out the scenario of his hara-kiri. They wanted to exalt Japan's army again (the Jieitai), as a protest against what he felt to be the gradual undermining of Japan's history and traditions through westernization. This was patently ridiculous in the light of Japan's defeat in World War II, but reality played little role in his schemes. He wrote:[11]

> Our fundamental values, as Japanese, are threatened. The Emperor is not being given his rightful place in Japan.
> We have waited in vain for the Jieitai to rebel. If no action is taken, the Western powers will control Japan for the next century! . . .
> Let us restore Nippon to its true state and let us die.[24]

True to his philosophy, on the morning of November 25, 1970, the Society executed a bizarre scene at the office of the commandant of the Eastern Army Headquarters. With four companions Mishima went to the commandant's quarters, seized him and gagged him. They demanded that the soldiers convene to listen to his speech, otherwise the general would be killed. The soldiers did convene, but the noise was so great no one could hear his speech.

Mishima then committed suicide in the ritual manner by driving a sword into his belly. This was followed by having his assistant Morita behead him. Then Morita did the same thing. The instructions Mishima left were:[12]

> Dress my body in a Shield Society uniform, give me white gloves and a soldier's sword in my hand, and then do me the favor of taking a photograph . . . I want evidence that I died not as a literary man but as a warrior.[25]

Everyone agreed that the suicide was an act of insanity. Yet it imitated the suicides of more than one million Japanese soldiers who had lost their lives in the attempt to conquer the world during World War II. The obsession with death was part of a whole romantic movement that flourished during the war years. As Mishima put it once: "It was in death that I had discovered my real 'life's aim'."[26]

The facts of Mishima's life can scarcely explain his odd death. It is true, he had an overprotected childhood, in which he had been brought up by his grandmother until he was twelve, then overprotected by his mother and despised by his father. It is also true that he was refused by the army during the war because of his physical disabilities. But primarily he was acting out some peculiar fantasy about death which derived from his reading of Japanese history.

LENNY BRUCE

A more American version of life and suicide is found in the story of Lenny Bruce, once called "the most radically relevant of all contemporary social satirists."[28]

Bruce was born in 1925, the same year as Mishima. His parents were divorced when he was eight. His mother was an amateur dancer and comedienne who passed her life dreams onto her son. In the fall of 1945, he got himself dishonorably discharged from the Navy by claiming homosexual urges. Thereafter he tried to make it in the entertainment world.

In 1950, he met Honey Harlow on a club date in Baltimore, a stripper, twice divorced, once jailed. In a few months he had married her. Together they went out to Los Angeles to try their luck.

In a seedy club, one night after the conclusion of a long strip act, in which he was master of ceremonies, he walked out on stage stark naked. The story was the first Lenny Bruce legend.

Both he and Honey became heroin users in Los Angeles. The marriage broke up in 1956; there was one child, a girl, whose custody was given to the father because the mother had been sentenced to two years in jail for possession of marijuana.

In 1958 he received his first big break at Ann's 440, a risqué nightclub in San Francisco. His reputation grew and he was soon earning $1,000 a night, in addition to records. *Time* proclaimed him the most successful of the new "sickniks."

While the violence he released against society earned handsome dividends, he increasingly lost control of himself. For the next few years there followed public obscenities, hearings, arrests, and trials. After a while he could no longer get bookings. He filed for bankruptcy and was officially declared a pauper. Fueled by amphetamines, he spent the last eighteen months of his life lost in a private labyrinth of legal books, petitions and briefs. When he was found guilty in 1964 he fired his lawyers. In 1966 he died of an overdose, aged forty. It was apparently a suicide.

Like Mishima, Bruce must have had some fantasy of what his suicide would do to society. And again, like the Japanese, he was merely denying his own uncontrollable rage.

SUMMARY: THE FIGHTER'S DILEMMA

Enough examples have been given; more will be cited as we go along. The man is and always has been in a serious dilemma about fighting. Trained to fight, he does not know what to do with his rage. If he becomes too aggressive and beats up the other fellow, he risks the danger of retaliation. If he is not sufficiently aggressive, he tends to turn the anger against himself, becoming excessively shy and withdrawn. At best, life is a fight which always leaves him with some underlying sense of fear; at worst, life becomes a disastrous defeat from which he may not recover.

Like the sexual experiences, the aggressive shape his entire style of life. And again, to begin with, there are two alternatives: too much or too little. Fighting is after all a dangerous business, and many men are literally killed trying to cope with it. Others are seriously hurt or damaged. Boxing, for all its popularity, is a highly risky sport; after some time the boxer may emerge permanently damaged. Even superficially it is noted that fighters are often "punch drunk," a description of damage to the brain which results from the pounding it has received over a period of years.

We are understandably concerned about the men who make violence a part of their lives. Unfortunately historians and other social scientists have generally paid too little attention to the role violence has played in the world. One reason is that violence is generally rationalized; no one admits he kills others for the sheer pleasure of killing. People argue about these rationalizations, overlooking the frenzy and fear underneath.

For underneath the violent man is terrified. This comes out most clearly in political dictatorships. Stalin, according to one recent historian (Ovseyenko) either directly or indirectly caused the deaths of 100 million people. As time went on, his suspicions of others grew and his murderous proclivities increased. Toward the end he even deluded himself into thinking that he could live to be 150 years, a longevity some people in the Caucasus allegedly reached, and everyone who did not contribute to his theory of longevity was suspect. Thus it comes as no surprise to find that, like Oriental despots of old, he accused his doctors of trying to poison him, put several to death and was preparing to execute more when he died (see also Chapter 8).

In the same way that dictatorship breeds paranoia, the ordinary violent man becomes increasingly suspicious of everyone around him. There is a joke about two neighbors which exmplifies the process. Smith wants to borrow a lawn mower from his neighbor, Jones. On the way over he begins to think that the lawn mower will be defective, Jones will accuse him of damaging it, and an annoying lawsuit will follow. When he finally gets to the door and rings Jones' bell, as the door opens he shouts: "Keep your Goddamned lawn mower!"[11]

While people are understandably frightened of the violent man, his ability to hurt others leaves him no inner peace. On the contrary, as time goes on he becomes increasingly frightened of what others might do to him and steps up his own violent tactics, often bringing about his own destruction in this way.

From time immemorial religions have urged men to give up their violent ways and pursue love in its place. For centuries the Christians were persecuted and hounded to death by the sadistic Romans. But when the Christians later assumed power, they did exactly the same thing to those under their control. The wars of religion, which decimated Europe for centuries, were as bloody as any fought by pagans; many times more so, in fact.

Nor did Christians act only in self-defense. The Crusades, spread over several hundred years, were conducted under the direct sponsorship of the popes, known as "the princes of peace." The message to the Crusaders was: "Go and kill the infidels." There were also crusades against many dissenting groups of Christians. Most startling is the so-called Albigensian Crusade. The Albigensians were a group, mostly in southern France, who believed in direct communion with

God. They wished to dispense with priests, monks, bishops, popes and live a simple Christian life. With its authority so seriously questioned, the Church waged an active Crusade and massacred all the Albigensians. Naturally expropriation of all their goods enriched the northern Frenchmen who carried out the actual crusade.

Again, the violence of Christianity can be tied to the underlying fear. In the year 1000 A.D. a large part of Europe was convinced that the world was coming to an end. Ghosts, demons, witches, supernatural visitations of all kinds were everyday matters. Unpredictable illnesses were common occurrences. The worst was the Black Death of 1347, when at least one-third of Europe was wiped out, but the occurrence of large-scale plagues did not disappear until the twentieth century, when they were finally understood and could be brought under control.[30]

In recent years increasing attention has been paid to violence in the family. There are now laws about wife abuse and child abuse, and centers where help can be found when it happens. Usually the man is the aggressor because he is stronger and because of the tradition that "my home is my castle" which gives him carte blanche to do anything he wants. But often women are the aggressors as well, especially against the children.

It goes without saying that such violence is found among men who are desperately insecure and unhappy. Like a dictator, they blame the family for their troubles, and lash out against them. One authority states:

> The element of power in human relationships is more pervasive in family life than is often recognized. Family members always stand in relationships of power towards each other; the power may be that of adults over children, income earners over those who do not earn, the healthy over the sick and aged, some have legal authority over others. These imbalances are unavoidable, and they are usually counterbalanced by the ties of affection and the common need for the maintenance of a tolerable family life. There is, however, always the possibility that the expectations of the more powerful members may in some ways not be satisfied, and one or more may then resort to

force in order to get the desired response. The force may take many forms—verbal assault, ostracism, constraint and physical force. All of these can be subsumed rather loosely under the term "violence", although its impact and after-effects will vary immensely. The damaging possibilities of violence in the family immediately raise the question of how it is to be regulated.[31]

The question the author raises at the end is a very important one. It is extraordinarily difficult to regulate violence in the family; even the police, when they are called, are most apt to say: "It's a family quarrel, I can't interfere." Only the most extreme forms of violence are brought to public attention.

While men with open violence obviously suffer from many psychological problems, to repress the hostility leads to another set of difficulties. Chronic resentment is one root of all the major psychological disorders, such as schizophrenia and depression, and of many of the psychosomatic disorders, such as hypertension (high blood pressure) and heart disorders. The coronary-prone man, driven to achieve more and more, with less and less personal satisfaction, has become well-known, though it is less often realized that unexpressed rage is an essential part of the pattern. Lynch, a cardiologist, in his book *The Broken Heart* maintains that all the emotions usually connected with a broken heart, such as rejection, loneliness and rage lie at the root of the coronary disorders.

Thus again there is a parallel with sexuality: too much or too little. Releasing the hostility has one set of consequences; repressing it has another. The only really effective solution is to get over the hostility and the frustrations which underlie it. The man who is condemned for his aggression but cannot find a way out is again forgotten.

Little has been said in this chapter about the positive side of aggression, leading to initiative, work, success and social leadership; a detailed study of that pattern is reserved for a later section. But once more while success stories impress by their outstanding achievements, when the man is looked at from the inside a different picture emerges. Examples have been given of men whose achievements or roles in life have been truly stupendous—Douglas, Henry VIII, Avery; yet when their inner lives are examined they reveal enormous lacks.

Arthur Lewis in his study of business tycoons comments that the one quality never found in them is compassion for their fellow men. Their determined drive for fame, fortune, their single-minded effort to win, no matter what the cost, all too often leaves out those qualities of mercy, compassion, affection, love and similar feelings which create the real basis for a truly happy life.[32]

Chapter 8:
The Powerful Can Be Ruthless

ERVIL LeBARON

On May 10, 1977, two young women entered the office of Dr. Rulon Allred in Murray, a prosperous suburb south of Salt Lake City and without any warning shot him dead.[2] Thus exploded one of the most bizarre episodes in American history, and an excellent example of the dangers of power, in this case religious power.

Dr. Allred was a naturopath, not an M.D., but one who believed in treatment by herbs and other natural remedies. At the time of his murder, he was 71 years old. He was also the leader of a dissident group of some 2000 Mormons who revered him as a religious Caesar.

The Mormons are a Christian sect which broke with established churches in the 19th century on the issue of polygamy. Seeking a safe haven, they finally reached Utah, where they remained and continued in the practice. But polygamy was declared illegal in the U.S. in 1862 and renounced in 1890. Yet despite the ban by the official church, it is still practiced. One authority estimated that in spite of government raids and prosecutions, there are still some 30,000 polygamists in the west.[3]

After the official Mormon church banned polygamy, a number of heretical sects arose which continued to practice it. One of these was Allred's. After arrest and imprisonment on the charge of polygamy in 1944, Allred was paroled on the promise that he would abandon it. Instead, he continued it secretly; at his death it was estimated he had about eleven wives.[5]

Allred's mortal enemy was another Mormon ex-communicant, Ervil LeBaron. But while Allred was a harmless, kindly old man, LeBaron was a murderous maniac. Power in the

© 1987 by The Haworth Press, Inc. All rights reserved.

hands of Allred led to secret polygamy; in the hands of Ervil LeBaron, to large-scale murder.

Some of the Mormons who wished to continue polygamy emigrated to Mexico, where they were tolerated. Ervil LeBaron's father was one of them. Father LeBaron had only two wives but incesantly preached polygamy. His thirteen children tried to carry out his doctrine.

Of these thirteen, two were particularly outstanding, Joel and Ervil. The first-born, Benjamin, originally hailed as the brightest hope, soon turned out to be insane, preaching he would someday lead the world in the Lord's name. Most of his life was spent in mental institutions.

Joel, dissatisfied with the older Allred's group, soon tried to disassociate himself. In 1955 he announced the formation of the Church of the First Born.[7] His brother Ervil was one of his earliest disciples.[8] By 1961 they claimed to have about 500 members.[9]

There then ensued a battle between Joel and Ervil for the dominance of the Church of the First Born. Joel was a peace-loving man, whose only failing was a fondness for polygamy. He remained the head of the sect until Ervil embarked on his policy of extermination.

Perhaps because he knew how to temper his claims, Ervil's mental illness did not become as apparent as Benjamin's had been. While Benjamin lost himself in notions of grandiosity, Ervil sought power. Soon he set himself in opposition to Joel as head of a rival sect. This, however, was not enough for him. He declared himself the Patriarch who would establish God's rule on earth by exterminating all his enemies. At one point he preached:

> I the Lord God will send forth flies upon the face of the earth, which shall take hold of the inhabitants thereof, and shall eat their flesh, and shall cause maggots to come in upon them; and their tongues shall be stayed that they shall not utter against me, and their flesh shall fall off from their bones, and their eyes from the sockets.[10]

The next step was to get rid of Joel, whom he arranged to have murdered in 1972.[11] Others followed, and Ervil became known as a man who would deal death to the unbelievers.[12]

With his fourteen wives and innumerable children, he still was alone, like so many dictators a victim of his own hatreds.

Since he was only the leader of a small sect, and not the head of a country, Ervil could not maintain his position as head of the church too long. Eventually his murder of Allred led to a fuller investigation and he was convicted in 1980. While waiting for the appeals to run their course, he died in prison of massive heart failure.[13]

THE PATHOLOGY OF POWER

Ervil LeBaron's case is unimportant in itself. What is important is the light it sheds on the pathology of power. Polygamy was for LeBaron merely an excuse for his narcissistic grandiosity. He wanted power, he wanted to be the Lord's vicar on earth, he wanted to conquer the world, he wanted to exterminate his enemies. As he grew more powerful, he became increasingly paranoid, suspicious of anyone who did not agree with his ravings and worship him as the true Patriarch. Eventually his empire crashed down around him and he died in prison, a broken man. He is a good example of Acton's famous remark that power corrupts, and absolute power corrupts absolutely.

Yet there are other ways in which the hunger for power can express itself. With Ervil's older brother Benjamin it came out in bizarre claims, without any concomitant action, that everybody recognized as clearly delusional so Benjamin ended up in a mental hospital. With Ervil's brother Joel, a much less angry man, it came out as a wish to head a new church. Allied to this wish was the wish to rule the world, but Joel was content with his small domain. His aggression turned the other way, against himself rather than against others. When reliable friends reported that Ervil was planning to kill him, he burst into tears. He even anticipated he would be killed and took no precautions to prevent it. Why the three brothers directed their lust for power in three different directions is hard to say. To answer the question, we would have to know a lot more about the details of their childhood. But whatever motivated their various drives, once set in motion they acquired their own momentum.

This latter point is crucial for an understanding of both sexes. A certain mind-set appears early in childhood. It then plays itself out for the remainder of the individual's life. But this mind-set is only the internal structure. Equally important is the external environment. A murderous zealot like LeBaron could move almost inexorably on his path to grandiosity (the Lord on earth) and eventual self-destruction. Yet, had the circumstances of his social milieu been different, he might have ended up in a mental hospital like his brother Benjamin, or as an ordinary criminal, or even gunned down by one of his enemies.

In all societies ever known, the drive for power has been significant. More recent research has even shown that among animals there is a dominance-submission pattern which governs the interrelationships of the group, and allows it to proceed on a peaceful course. Somehow, it might be said, every animal knows its place. How this is managed remains a mystery, yet it is observed over and over. Perhaps best known is the pecking order among chickens, so that when food is offered to a group, a hierarchy is formed which determines who will eat first, second, third.

In all human groups, no matter how primitive, somehow a chief is found who takes charge; again how this is done originally is a mystery, though its perpetuation can be traced easily enough. How this chief uses his power, and how his followers obey him varies widely. Each one, both leader and follower, builds up a certain mind-set which tends to move him in certain ways. This can also be called his prized self-image—what kind of person he would really like to be, and how he would like to mold society to fit in with this image of himself. In all of the following discussions, the nature of the prized self-image will be at the center of our inquiry.

The degree to which power struggles around trivial issues can be continued for centuries is amusingly brought out by the Falkland Islands crisis of 1982. Over 200 years before, in a similar scenario in 1770 they caused a major international crisis and nearly led to war between Britain and Spain.

Then, too, the initial coup was made from Buenos Aires, which was part of the Spanish colonies. The British defenders were surprised by a massive invasion. Then, too, Britain responded by mounting a great naval force. The islands themselves had no indigenous population. Then, too, the crisis was out of all proportion to the immediate occasion. Then, too, British opinion was divided. Samuel Johnson described it as "a bleak and barren spot in the Magellanick Ocean, of which no use could be made unless it was a place of exile for the hypocrites of patriotism."[2] Then, too, the only issue was titular sovereignty. The crisis was resolved when Spain agreed to restore Port of Equion to Britain without renouncing its claim to sovereignty.

HITLER AND STALIN: THE TWO MAD DICTATORS OF THE TWENTIETH CENTURY[15]

There are libraries full of literature on both Hitler and Stalin and it is not my purpose to review the historical events here. What I do wish to do is to show how similar they were in their inner psychological structure, even though they were the bitterest of enemies politically, and later militarily.

Also, the story of the atrocities they committed, though known to many during their lifetimes, was vigorously denied by their official defenders. It is only afterwards that the full enormity of their crimes has come to light. Once the facts became known, and with the expertise added by the progress of psychoanalysis, and psychoanalytic psychiatry, the question became more and more insistent: Were they insane? To this a further question must be asked, in the light of the discussions in this book: Were they happy? The first question has been raised by psycho-historians, virtually ignored by conventional historians; the second, surprisingly, has never been asked. Yet they were, after all, human beings, and we can legitimately inquire, what did they think about their own lives and deeds?

To begin with, they can be approached in terms of their sexuality, their aggression and their social role, for it is here that the deep similarities can be found. Both had abnormal sex lives, though each in a different way. Hitler had a physical abnormality, one testicle, and according to later psychiatric research, a masochistic perversion. He rarely had normal sexual intercourse in his life.[16] Instead he preferred to spend hours looking at lewd and pornographic pictures.[17] It also

seems probable that he liked to have a woman (his niece
Geli) squat over him while he was lying down, so that he
could see her anus and genitals.[18] Geli, daughter of his half-
sister Angela, was the only woman for whom he reportedly
ever had any strong love feelings. She committed suicide in
1931, before he had come to power. He was so shaken by her
suicide that he fell into a deep depression for months, and
even contemplated suicide himself.[19] It seems odd that Hitler,
whose lieutenants certainly omitted no concievable sadistic
act toward women, could not allow himself any.

Stalin's sex life was also abnormal, though in a different
way. Like Hitler, he was a loner and never showed any great
passion for women. In an early marriage about 1902 or 1903
(when he was in his early twenties), he took a plain Georgian
girl to wife. She died of some illness several years later, after
bearing him one son, Yakov. The only other contact with
women is reportedly the rape of a teenage girl, some time in
the years before the Revolution. Then he remarried, when he
was forty, a girl of seventeen, Nadya Alliluyeva, then attached to Lenin's secretariat, where she had access to top
secret documents.[20] (This interesting fact has largely been ignored by his biographers. Stalin was always described as a
cold, emotionless individual with no feelings for any human
being other than his mother and Lenin, with whom he was
obviously identified.)[21]

Stalin led a seemingly normal married life from 1919, when
he remarried, until 1932. His second wife bore him two children, a son and a daughter, Svetlana. The internal events of
this marriage are completely unknown. Nadya died in 1932
under mysterious circumstances. The official story is that she
committed suicide; for this no reason is given. The rumor,
widely believed, is that Stalin, in a fit of rage, choked her to
death. In 1932 Stalin was still only fifty-two years old. Yet
from then on until his death in 1953, he showed no interest in
any woman, in spite of the sexual atrocities his lieutenants
were freely committing.

For his three children Stalin had no real feeling. His first-
born, Yakov, attempted suicide in the late 1920's; the attempt
failed. Stalin's only comment was that his son was a weakling
who bungled everything. During the war, Yakov was taken
prisoner. The Nazis offered to exchange him; in reply Stalin

said that he had no son called Yakov (all the Soviet soldiers taken prisoner by the Nazis were later executed when they were returned to the U.S.S.R. after the war). Yakov died in a Nazi POW camp. Vassily, the second son, was promoted to general in the air force, but he was a complete drunk. After his father's death, he also died, apparently of alcoholism; in any case, he disappeared from the pages of history.

Stalin's daughter Svetlana, for whom he perhaps had some fondness when she was younger, later escaped from the U.S.S.R. against the wishes of the ruling clique, leaving behind her two children. In her book *Twenty Letters,* written when she was outside the Soviet Union, she repeatedly commented on her father's coldness and vindictiveness. If anybody opposed him, she said, he would never forgive: "No matter how long and well he had known the person concerned, he would now put him down as an enemy." At this point—and this is where his cruel implacable nature showed itself—the past ceased to exist for him. Years of friendship and fighting side by side in a common cause might as well never have been: " 'So you've betrayed me,' some inner demon would whisper. 'I don't even know you anymore.' "[22]

In their hatred of people, total indifference to human suffering and the callousness with which they sent millions to their death, Hitler and Stalin were almost identical. Erich Fromm suggested the term "necrophiliac" (lover of the dead) for such men, but the term pales when compared with the realities of the horrors that they perpetrated. They were in fact most similar to murderers, a point which is obscured because they either concealed their murders or gave them a political sugar-coating. Yet they can best be understood as murderers who somehow rose to positions of enormous power.

Lust for power, capacity to murder and the inability to love a woman are again what the two had in common. The lust for power expressed itself in grandiose fantasies about remaking the world. Hitler was building a "thousand-year Reich," and even in the last few days of his life he was sketching designs for enormous new cities. Stalin saw himself as the leader of a world-transforming revolution, compared to which nothing else was of the slightest importance. It seems likely that secretly they even admired one another, though that could not be admitted in public. Hitler is reported to have said of Stalin once that he was a cunning Caucasian, who commanded unconditional respect, and who was "in his own way, just one hell of a fellow."[23] Stalin is not known to have said anything about Hitler.

As is well-known, the Hitler-Stalin pact of 1939 unleashed World War II. The pact was signed on August 23, 1939, and Hitler attacked Poland eight days later. In the celebrations in Moscow when the pact was signed, a German participant reported:

> In the course of the conversation Mr. Stalin spontaneously proposed a toast to the Fuhrer in the following words: "I know how much the German people love their Fuhrer and I therefore should like to drink to his health . . ." In parting, Mr. Stalin addressed the following words to the Reich Foreign Minister: "The Soviet Union takes the new Pact very seriously" and said he could guarantee on his word of honor that the Soviet Union would not betray her partner.[24]

With all due allowance for the complete untrustworthiness of both sides, these toasts of Stalin and his parting words betray the deep respect he really had for Hitler. It can even be recalled that both were pursuing national socialism, though each from different directions; the techniques, however, were largely identical: intimidation, lying, mass executions. After the war, it was even revealed that in a secret supplementary protocol the two parties had agreed on a division of Europe, which would then join up with Japan in a division of the world. Truly Hitler and Stalin were brothers under the skin.

A further point in common is the deep-seated paranoia of both men. At first Hitler directed his primarily against the Jews, though he later extended it toward all "non-Aryan" peoples. Stalin too in later years became paranoid about the Jews when he fabricated his famous "doctors' plot," alleging that the doctors in the Kremlin were trying to poison him. After Stalin the anti-Semitism of his followers also became apparent.

Since the last war the question has frequently been put: Were these men mad? The historian Adam Ulam considered this problem in detail, concluding that while Stalin was insane in his domestic policies, he was sane in his foreign policies.[25] Likewise historians who have studied Hitler have been reluctant to say that Hitler was insane because he reached such an extraordinary pinnacle of success before he was defeated. These arguments stem from a basic blunder of organic psychiatry (with which the historians as a rule work) and from a misreading of the record.

From the time of the Greeks organic psychiatry has viewed the schizophrenic as having a thought disorder and probed the brain unceasingly to find out what it might be. Following the common sense notion, a "crazy" person is one who cannot function in everyday life. Up to the advent of psychoanalysis the discipline did not have the conceptual tools with which to understand men who function well in one area but are completely mad in another. This was the case with both Hitler and Stalin. In their paranoia, lust for power, grandiosity, wish to conquer the world, hatred of women and ruthless indifference to the murder of millions, they were like many schizophrenics. But they still retained the capacity to organize, the ability to capitalize on good fortune and maintain leadership of large countries. Thus the question of whether they were "insane" or not cannot be answered by a yes or a no; rather it leads to a revision of psychiatric theory which recognizes that men may be quite sane in one area of their lives and quite demented in another.

Furthermore, the element of luck cannot be ignored in the case of either man. Had Lenin not died in 1924 and had Trotsky not been such a vain narcissist blind to everyday realities and the enormous hatreds engendered by the revolution, Stalin would never have succeeded. Had the allies not been so frightened of social revolution in the 1930's they would have had the courage to stand up to Hitler and fight earlier. For it now appears that at any time prior to 1938 the French army was overwhelmingly stronger than the German; even when Hitler attacked in 1940 the French were just as strong; they were simply unwilling to fight because of the memories of World War I.[21]

Furthermore both men, instead of being military geniuses, interfered so much in military affairs that they seriously damaged the war effort. Stalin had decimated his entire military command before the war broke out, and was virtually defeated in the first six months; his men would not fight, and did not have the necessary leadership. Had Hitler possessed the good sense to make allies of the Russians instead of massacring them, he could easily have formed a Soviet Army under Vlassov or some other Soviet general, and the Russians, exhausted by Stalin's senseless purges, would have been overrun.

THOMAS PITT [27]

The lives of Stalin and Hitler could be compared with someone like Thomas Pitt, the 2nd Baron of Camelford in England, who lived from 1775 to 1804. His biographer calls him the "half-mad Lord." Pitt was related to some of the most prominent families in England at a time that country was the center of a mighty empire. One cousin was Prime Minister, another was First Lord of the Admiralty; Pitt's brother-in-law was Foreign Secretary.

Instead of pursuing the easy political career into which he had been born, Pitt spent his brief life in senseless violence. His biographer says of him: "He was responsible for the death of more than one man, and he himself died in violence. He was handsome, athletic, arrogant, immensely sensitive on the subject of his honor, and, with pistols or swords, ever ready to meet an opponent on a lonely spot at dawn. He was constantly in physical and legal conflict with others. Some doubted his sanity, but none his courage."[28]

Pitt, like Hitler and Stalin, knew only unhappiness as a child. Born into a prominent family and great fortune, his parents showed him neither affection nor attention. Their days were spent abroad or at Petersham and London. The two children were brought up on the family estate at Boconnoc, where Pitt's education was conducted by a private tutor. There seem to have been no other children around, other than his sister, who, for some reason, was away much of the time. Thus he was essentially alone.

When he was eleven his parents decided to send him to school in Switzerland. After a few years there, which young Tom found the happiest of his life, his father decided to send him to a regular English public school. But the boy, in his lonely childhood, had acquired an overpowering love of the sea. He refused to go to school. Reluctantly his father allowed him to take a post as midshipman on a boat going to New South Wales.[29]

His next voyage was on a warship under a Captain Vancouver. This ship had the mission of surveying unknown areas in the Pacific. One early port of call was Tahiti, where the women were famously beautiful and willing. To the fifteen-year-old Tom it must have looked like paradise. But the stern captain forbade any traffic with the natives. Tom violated orders by flirting with one girl. The captain saw him, sentenced him to a flogging of two dozen lashes. This incident determined Tom's future course: For the rest of his life he was determined to get even with Vancouver and anybody like him. As with Hitler and Stalin, the dominant themes of his life became revenge and promotion (in the Navy, for Pitt).[30]

In 1795 he sent a challenge to Vancouver to fight a duel, which was refused. Shortly thereafter, Pitt saw Vancouver and his brother on the street and beat him up. Vancouver took legal action and Pitt was required to put up a bond of 10,000 pounds (a huge sum in those days) to insure that he would keep the peace.

After this incident Pitt (known as Lord Camelford) was determined to fight a duel with anyone who offended his honor, which was easy to offend. Dueling at the high level he held in society (he had taken his seat in the House of Lords in 1797) was strictly forbidden. Still, Camelford could not avoid getting into fights, the common belief was that he was mad. An early historian of dueling described him as a "murderous ruffian" who sought quarrels on every occasion. It was said he dressed eccentrically and cruelly ill-used his horses to provoke bystanders into providing pretexts for duels.

Unable to fight enough duels, Camelford then turned to boxing. Soon he was renowned as an excellent boxer and the foremost patron of prizefights. In 1801 he concocted a daring scheme to assassinate Napoleon. Reported by spies, he was apprehended by the French police and sent back to England, since there was really no evidence against him.

Camelford's love life was largely confined to prostitutes. The only woman he ever loved was his cousin, Hester Stanhope. But she, possibly alarmed by his reputation, turned down his offer of marriage.

To us today Pitt's life seems strange indeed. He was out to fight, and scarcely cared whom he fought. His only redeeming virtue was kept secret. At that time the poor in London lived in such unsanitary conditions that there was a very high death rate from typhus and other diseases. Camelford secretly arranged to give thousands of pounds to the poor to help keep them alive.

But most of his time he spent looking for a fight. The end came with one. His mistress of the moment, a certain Fanny Simmons, a lady of easy virtue (the polite name for a prostitute at the time) apparently egged him on to fight a duel with a man named Best, then rated the best marksman in England. At the duel Best aimed his pistol away from Camelford but the latter motioned him to make it a real duel. The result was a fatal shot. Camelford died in 1804, not yet thirty.

Pitt, Hitler, Stalin, Ervil LeBaron all had certain psychological features in common, yet all came to different ends. Clearly the social circumstances facing each accounted for much of the difference. In particular, the attitude toward aggression held by the authorities of their day, and enforced, was the primary factor.

This brings us to the oft-repeated question: How is it that two murderous madmen, like Hitler and Stalin, acquired such an enormous following? The answer is not reassuring. Psychological studies of leadership have invariably shown that the successful leader has followers who are much like him. If the difference is too great, they will not follow him. This principle has been applied to political events as well. In the Eisenhower-Stevenson contests for the American Presidency, Stevenson was clearly the better informed and superior candidate. Yet he was an "egghead" with whom the average voter could not identify so easily; Eisenhower was a soldier, a war leader, and an easy object of identification.

The combination of sexual disturbance, aggression, lust for power and paranoia has occurred many times in many countries. A comparison of different societies shows that the consequences depend on social conditions as much as on the personalities of the rulers. In the Watergate conspiracy, after

President Nixon had been impeached, it was reported that the Joint Chiefs of Staff had given orders that any orders he gave had to be approved by them before being carried out. At other times, with other conditions, a military coup might have resulted instead.

In the Ottoman Empire, under the all-powerful Sultans, there was no peaceful way to assure the succession. Since the Sultan had so many wives, there were often dozens, or hundreds of young men, sons of the Sultan, ready to take over the Sultanate. For several centuries the new Sultans, to forestall any such rebellion, as soon as they took over power would have all their possible rivals put to death. One Sultan modified this system by putting all his possible rivals in a "cage" for life. This produced a spineless and impotent regime, which eventually fell apart in World War I.

Unfortunately, as Harold Lasswell showed in a brilliant work as far back as 1930, the paranoid personality, especially of the kind described here, is strongly drawn to politics. Thus a functioning society must be constantly on guard against such men, who can easily develop an insatiable lust for power.

The question can still be raised, especially of the four men discussed in most detail, LeBaron, Hitler, Stalin and Pitt: Were they happy? What were they like after all as human beings? To ask this about Hitler and Stalin is something like asking it about God. God rules the world in traditional theology, but is He happy about it?

Of both Hitler and Stalin it can justifiably be said that they were lonely miserable men who found in their enormous hunger for power an antidote to their personal conflicts. Both were pampered by an indulgent mother who had lost several other children (each of them three, by coincidence), while they were brutally knocked around by a drunken father who died when they were still young (Hitler was thirteen, Stalin was eleven). Their family lives were severely disrupted, the normal gratifications of home and hearth were denied them. Their paranoia made them continuously suspicious of everybody, and steadily grew as they became older and more powerful. Khruschev reports that toward the end Stalin said to him: "I trust no one, not even myself."[32] They were both terribly fearful of death; their boasting about 1000-year reigns or creation of a new world covered up their terrors, which everyone shares. By preserving Lenin as a mummy, and giving orders that he be preserved in a similar way, Stalin might well have been giving expression to a magical belief that somehow this would keep him alive forever. Thus while one recoils from these two men as the embodiment of evil in our time, they too were forgotten men, with thwarted sex lives, aggressive impulses that could never be satisfied, and a lust for power that was insatiable.

Since this book is about men, what happens to women when they acquire excessive power has not been discussed. Usually the result is no different. Catherine the Great of Russia, who reigned in the latter part of the 18th century, is a good example. She married the existent czar, then engineered a coup d'état deposing him and making herself Empress. Shortly thereafter he was murdered, evidently with her knowledge.

Catherine followed a policy similar to that of her predecessors. Serfdom (read: slavery) was increased. Her armies fought one war after another, taxes were high, working conditions abominable; her rule was military. In 1773 one of the worst rebellions in Russian history broke out, the Pugachev revolt. Bloody revenge on the part of the oppressed peasants was put down ferociously by force of arms. Eventually Pugachev and his accomplices were put to death in the barbarous fashion common at that time. The empire was saved, but it had come close to collapse.

To later generations Catherine has become best known for her extraordinary licentiousness; just as male emperors took female mistresses, she took male lovers. There were favorites from time to time, but the most original feature of the system was the way in which she picked men for straight sex. If a man pleased her, he was first examined by her personal physician to see that he was not diseased. Then a female assistant, known as an *eprouveuse* ("tryer-out") would have sex with him to assure competence on that score. Finally he was admitted to the Empress's chamber, where he received 100,000 rubles in gold, with a promise of more to come. When she tired of him, she would pick another man. How many lovers she chose in this way no one can say, but the number seems to have been considerable.[33]

POSITIVE USES OF POWER

While as a rule excessive power tends to make men increasingly ruthless and destructive, especially as they get older, there are many exceptions. Perhaps the most striking in our century is Franklin Delano Roosevelt.

Roosevelt was born in 1882 to a wealthy New York family of Dutch extraction; he was distantly related to Theodore Roosevelt. His mother was only 20 when he was born, his father 57. Naturally he was adored by both parents. There were no other children.

From his earliest years Franklin was bitten with the presidential "bug." He did passing well in law school, from which he never bothered to graduate, then entered the political arena as soon as he could. As early as 1910 he was elected state senator. There followed other political activities, culminating in Wilson's wartime cabinet. In the meantime he had married Eleanor, a niece of Teddy Roosevelt, and sired five children. Although feelings for Eleanor later cooled, the family was a happy one for many years.

Then in 1921, when he was only 39, a terrible tragedy occurred: he contracted poliomyelitis. It left him with a severe weakness of the legs which prevented him from standing or walking with ease. With grim determination he fought the illness, and made every effort to regain the use of his legs. A spring at Warm Springs, Georgia turned out to have strong beneficial effects, and he spent much of his time there. It is possible that had he persisted he might have regained a normal use of his legs, but politics lured him.

In spite of his physical disability he entered the race for governor of New York in 1928. That year Al Smith challenged American prejudices by being the first Catholic to run for President. He lost, but on the same ticket Roosevelt won the Governorship of New York. Two years later he was re-elected by an overwhelming plurality.

After two terms as governor of New York, Roosevelt was ready for the Presidency. In 1932 the country was in the throes of the deepest depression it had ever known. Roosevelt introduced a spirit of optimism and proposals for reform which had never before been equalled in American history. His victory over Hoover was again an overwhelming one.

Once he was President, Roosevelt unfurled his "New Deal" for the American people, which brought an entirely new climate to the country. Although the Depression actually persisted, though in milder form, until the country entered World War II, the people's spirit under Roosevelt was entirely different from what it had been under Hoover. In effect, a social revolution was brought about—unemployment insurance, social security for old age, insurance for bank deposits, the government's willingness to create jobs, regulation of the securities markets and many other reforms came from the brain trust he created. When war broke out, Roosevelt elected to stay on, supported by the mass of the people in his feeling that he should be allowed a third, then a fourth term, unheard of before him. He died in office in 1945, just a few weeks before the Nazis surrendered.

During his tenure in the Presidency, Roosevelt had more power than any other American President. His early dream was realized. Yet, what did he do with his power? He brought about a transformation of the country which favored the common people as they had never been favored before. It was the rare example of a patrician who snubbed the class into which he was born, and strengthened the democratic process and the lot of the common man wherever he could.

If Roosevelt is compared with Hitler or Stalin, several salient facts emerge. Although all three were in effect only children, and doted on by their mothers, Roosevelt was the only one who had a father who took an interest in him. While the other two suffered brutal beatings all through their childhood, there is no record that Roosevelt was ever beaten. Sexually he did suffer the repressions of the Victorian Era, but he loved his wife and five children and created a happy family atmosphere. His wife Eleanor, in spite of her shyness and possible homosexual liaison, was one of the best-loved women of her time. Had there been such a post, she could have been elected first lady of the world.

As far as his aggression goes, Roosevelt was a vigorous fighter for the causes in which he believed. But in spite of the cries of some of his enemies, he fought fairly, in the democratic way. One of his biographers has called him "the lion and the fox"—a rare combination of strength and cunning.

Nothing like it was possible with either of the dictators, who knew only force and violence.

SUMMARY

Power is one of mankind's greatest passions. Men fight for it, kill for it and die for it. The powerless envy the powerful, dreaming only that if they had so much power they would be blissful.

Yet studies of the exercise of power do not bear out the notion that the powerful are so happy. On the contrary. Power immediately sets up a conflict, in that the powerless wish to deprive the powerful of what they have, whether it is hereditary or won, legitimately or illegitimately. Hence power cannot be separated from aggression, hatred, violence and murder.

The wish to maintain power, once acquired, is so great that it attracts the energies of millions. Powerful men have no difficulty attracting others to their standards, others who in their turn yearn for the power of the leader, or the "boss." In Germany Hitler's power was sustained by millions of little Hitlers; in Russia, Stalin's by millions of little Stalins.

Hitler and Stalin are two examples, both of world-shaking importance, of the profound pathology associated with power. There is a lust for power, a fear of losing this power, which leads to an ever-increasing paranoia and fabrication of "enemies." These enemies must be hunted down and killed; hence the paranoid fantasies of a dictator lead to endless murders. The longer this power lasts the more the dictator yearns for immortality; in olden days he sought deification, in modern times he sought to impose a thousand-year reign. The dictator who hungers for power usually has little use for women; many are often sexual perverts. None can enjoy the normal love of a woman. An almost invariable feature of the childhood of those who yearn for power is a tortured and brutal family life.

Less often, but still frequent, are those who can wield power constructively. In our own country Franklin Roosevelt is perhaps the clearest example. And Roosevelt's childhood, unlike those of his dictator rivals, was a fairly happy one.

Acton's aphorism that power corrupts and absolute power corrupts absolutely, certainly holds for most human societies. The moral of the story is that society will not be able to gratify the aggressions and hatreds of those who seek power.

And finally, are powerful dictators happy? Envied, feared, despised, hated, but happy—never.

Chapter 9:
Successful Men Suffer

Most American men prize success highly. They wish to get ahead, beat out the next fellow, acquire more money, conquer more women, make their mark in the world and exhibit the achievement-success motive in a thousand other ways. Within our culture there is a good deal of opportunity for getting ahead, and many are successful. There are also a large number of failures. And even the successful, by the standards of other people, often judge themselves a failure.

To begin with, the meaning of success depends on the family and cultural background. Most basic is the competition with the father; if the man cannot surpass his father's exploits he never feels that he will amount to anything. This is why the sons of famous men so often fade into oblivion, even though under other circumstances their accomplishments would seem considerable. Nelson Rockefeller (whom we shall consider in more detail later) was governor of New York State for sixteen years, longer than any other man, and instituted a number of significant reforms and improvements. Yet compared to his famous grandfather, the founder of the dynasty, who made a billion dollars, it seemed insignificant to him. He had to be president—or he was a failure. President Franklin Roosevelt's sons have virtually escaped notice, even though James was a Congressman for a number of years. John Foster Dulles would not rest until he had risen to be Secretary of State, like his uncle Robert Lansing, who was Secretary of State under Wilson, as was his grandfather John W. Foster under Benjamin Harrison. And so the story goes. Every man has a rival in mind in his life struggle, and the most important rival is usually his father.

Then the environment within which the man is brought up leads him in certain directions, and bars him from others. A boy is most impressed by the men in his family, who serve as models. Blacks see so few men in their families who have

© 1987 by The Haworth Press, Inc. All rights reserved.

gone far in intellectual pursuits that they give up in school before they really start. Jews have never seen a Jew become President of the United States so they never even try to enter the race. Before Kennedy was elected President in 1960, it was considered a hopeless cause for a Catholic to try: Al Smith had been defeated on this issue in 1928. After Kennedy it became perfectly acceptable. To rise to the top of the military ladder without being a West Pointer is so unusual that again few even make the effort, except in the emergency situation of war. Even then as the experience of the Civil War shows, after the early years almost all the generals on both sides were West Pointers. The list could be continued. The point is that whatever a man aspires to is limited by what he sees other men of his social station have achieved.

There is often a notable difference in the character of the man before he is successful and afterwards. Nobody could have predicted the vast changes in the social system brought about by Roosevelt in looking at his background before he was elected. Einstein, by temperament a most reclusive man, took pleasure in travelling around the world and lecturing on relativity to lay audiences once he had been recognized as one of the makers of modern physics. Since success is rarely attained before mid-life, the change of personality is nowadays often referred to as the mid-life crisis. As we shall see, one very common pattern is that of the man who devotes himself completely to his work until he reaches fame or fortune, or both, with a fanaticism which seems completely puritanical. Once he gets there, he then lets himself go with women.

The kind of suffering attached to success differs in the period when the man is getting there from the period when he has made it. On his way up he is often a "workaholic," so dedicated to his goal that nothing else counts, not even wife, or children. The suffering at this time is one of deprivation.

Once he has made it, the suffering may take many different forms. The most difficult for the layman to understand is that the success is never enough for the man. While to the outsider he seems to have everything, inside he does not have enough. Aristotle Onassis had mae a million dollars by the time he was twenty-three yet the only thing he could think of doing with the rest of his life was making more millions. Einstein, having changed man's way of looking at the world, then tried to go on to an even higher synthesis, the value of which is dubious.[1] Bertrand Russell, after bringing about revolutionary changes in mathematics, gave up the field and became a popularizer and a commentator on the human scene. Since no one can be a master of all trades, the only work that lives on is his reformulation of mathematical theory. Thomas Edison, it has now been revealed, made his most famous inventions, the electric light bulb and the phonograph in his earlier years. After that, though he was referred to in the popular press as the "wizard of Menlo Park," he does not seem to have done anything of note, though he kept on trying.[2] All these men had one psychological feature in common: They could not sit back and enjoy their laurels.

In order to see in more detail how successful men have handled their exploits, we shall give a number of thumbnail sketches of prominent people, to understand how the "sweet smell of success" was incorporated into their lives.

EDDIE FISHER: FROM RAGS TO RICHES[3]

Eddie Fisher was the fourth of a family of seven children. His father, an immigrant from Russia, made a poor living as a repairer of trunks and suitcases. The parents were always quarreling. Father is described as a tyrant who treated his wife like a slave. Though he never beat her physically, if she talked back to him he went berserk. It seemed like an unlikely environment to produce the golden voice that thrilled millions for so many years.

The realization that Eddie had a marvelous voice came early, and as far back as he could remember (he has written a very frank autobiography) all he wanted to do was sing. Still, it is one thing to have talent, even genius; it is something else to climb to the top with it.

Eddie's childhood was miserable. He never got along with his father. As a poor Jewish boy without outstanding intelligence, school never meant much. He had lice in his hair, and was always afraid the kids who sat behind him in school would notice them. Following a practice that was common in the Great Depression (he was born in 1928) the family moved repeatedly in order to avoid paying rent.

One incident he recalls highlights the way in which seemingly trivial childhood events can have a lasting influence. In grade school he won the marbles championship of South Philadelphia. For the city-wide championship he changed his shooter from a small marble to a big one. A girl beat him out. His father never let him forget it. The seeds for his fear of success were already sown.

His introduction to sex was likewise humiliating. He found a dirty picture and sold it to a friend in school for two cents. The teacher found out about it and demanded that his mother come in. She slapped his face in school; then when he got home his father gave him a vicious beating, "the worst of his life," he says. His first sexual experience was at fourteen, with a girl named Tootsie Stern, who had a reputation for fooling around. It was such a let-down he vowed, "I am not going to have any more sex. Sex is out for me."[4]

Although he began singing professionally when he was only twelve, it took many years before he was a recognized star. On the way up he suffered from the disappointments, lack of money and dashed hopes that are the lot of an aspiring young singer. His voice was great but so were many others. Finally two breaks came. He acquired a well-known manager named Milton Blackstone, and Eddie Cantor discovered him. At twenty-one, he went on tour with Cantor; shortly thereafter Blackstone booked him into a New York night club at $5,000 per week. He had a contract to make records for RCA Victor, which eventually netted him millions. At twenty-two he was rich and famous.

When he was drafted he was already so well known that he was sent out to entertain the troops, rather than to fight. After an unhappy romance with a girl named Joan, he began an active sex life. It was, however, as he put it, pure physical release. He realized the truth of the remark that "when you are in the theater, you are married to it." Love had not yet reached him.

When he was released from the army in 1953 he resumed his career. But unexpectedly he lost his voice. Instead of seeing a reputable physician or psychoanalyst, he was rushed by friends to Dr. Max Jacobson, who gave him an injection which restored his voice. What he did not know was that Jacobson had given him a drug to which he eventually became addicted. Fearful he would lose his voice, or not sing at his best, he began to rely on Jacobson's drugs.

The addiction lasted twenty years. Eventually Jacobson's unprofessional conduct was brought to public attention, and he was deprived of his medical license.[5] Fisher could have discovered that in 1953, had he gone to some responsible person, but the "quick fix" was always so tempting he could not escape.

His career was typical of many stars. He was romantically involved with countless women, among them Marlene Dietrich, and Judy Garland (who died of an overdose of drugs). He married and divorced Debbie Reynolds, Elizabeth Taylor and Connie Stevens.[6] He made and spent millions. By the early 1970's, his career in ruins, he was fighting for survival against his addiction to drugs.

As he tells the story, it was the need to be in the spotlight all the time that was his undoing. He says:

> I always seemed to be on stage. The dramas in any man's life—love affairs, marriages, even divorces—I played out in glaring spotlights. But I myself sometimes permitted my need to be loved to dominate my life. And a love that feeds only on the self destroys.[7]

Between the lines, it becomes clear that his early miseries stayed with him to prevent him from enjoying the success he deserved. It was as though his father was still reproaching him for being beaten out by a girl, while mother was still bawling him out for sexual misdeeds. What saved him later is hard to say from his autobiography. I would be inclined to attach major importance to the effect of his children, now grown up. When he speaks of his daughter Carrie, in particular, it sounds like a new love affair.

CHARLES REVSON:
NAIL POLISH, MILLIONS AND MISERY[8]

Charles Revson, founder of the Revlon empire, is a prototype of the American millionaire whose main goals in life are to make money and to impress others with how much he has.

Starting from nothing, he built up one of the 300 biggest industrial enterprises in the country, and one of the 200 most profitable. Married three times, he could not even remember the name of his first wife. Women he went through wholesale, one source claims three a day. He was on good relations with nobody; everything was bought, from friends to women. Money and power were his passions; the business was his life. Born in 1906, he drove himself so hard that he had a heart attack at forty-nine. He built himself a yacht so expensive to run that Henry Ford could not afford to buy it.[10] Glitter, polish, ostentation were the mainstays of his life. He made a fortune out of fingernail polish for women, yet he had nothing but contempt for them, and for almost everyone else. His own brother sued him for fraud.[11] He was in every respect a showy miserable millionaire.[12]

Too little is known about his childhood to guess at the roots of his personality. He was the middle of three brothers; both parents were Russian-born Jews. Father was a cigar-maker; mother worked as a saleswoman. There is nothing in the early history that foreshadows his later life.

At an early age (twenty-four) he ran off with a showgirl to Chicago. He did badly there, came back to New York where the family had in the meantime emigrated. Then in 1932 he started the Revlon firm; for the rest of his life nothing else mattered. It was, as his biographer notes, the obsession of his life. Revson himself once said of it:

> In terms of marketing, you've got to have the will to win. You've got to see the blood running down the street. You've got to be able to take it. You've got to be able to shove it. If you're not, you're nobody. You never will be. You think you are? Fine. Love it. Go on—have happiness, have love, have this, have everything. But as far as marketing is concerned (which is what really counts)—niente. Nothing.[13]

His aggression and need to win were obvious to anyone who had the slightest contact with him. Revson's fear was the dominant emotion. The tension started at the top. Charles brought his two brothers into the firm, and all three spent a lot of time quarreling. The firm became notorious for the high salaries it paid newcomers and the speed with which they went into and out of the firm. Longevity, says his biographers, was inversely proportional to proximity to Charles.

The turnover among the personnel was unbelievable.[14] Although he paid them handsomely he treated them like dirt, and in short order they were either fired or quit. A purchasing post was filled six times in a single year. One Wall Street analyst started a report on the twelve top executives at Revlon; by the time he finished it only two were left. Perhaps one factor in this enormous turnover was that Revson was paranoid about what people might be saying or doing, and he bugged his whole office to have a record of everything that went on.

Frequently his aggression centered on competitors, and he would not rest until he had defeated them. The only exception was Helena Rubenstein. Yet in spite of all his tricks he never did manage to become the biggest firm in the cosmetics business, and this always remained a sore point with him.

In his private life he was equally pugnacious. When he set out to play golf he took along a golf pro to make sure that the ball was set up properly whenever he teed off. Nor did he play with people who could beat him; he had his own circle for the golf course and kept everybody else away.

His pugnacity contained a bit of the swindler as well. It was he who started the $64,000 quiz shows, which brought him tremendous publicity at a low cost, and helped his business enormously. Then it turned out that the show was a fake, in that the answers were given to some of the people beforehand, or they were prompted to act in certain ways. Since the show at one time had 82% of the TV audience in the country, this blew up into a huge scandal that led to a Congressional hearing.[17] Eisenhower publicly stated that the whole mess was like that of the Chicago Black Sox in 1919,[18] and no one would rest until it was cleared up. With the help of a prominent lawyer-politician, Clark Clifford, Revson escaped prosecution, but the show had to be discontinued.[19] By that time (three years after it started) the boom to his business was so great that it no longer mattered.

His sex life was indeed most extraordinary. The biographer relates the facts, as known, but does not have the psychological acumen to see where they point. As part of his ostentation and machismo Revson needed a long string of women desperately. One of his aides stated that he had sex with three women a day for years, and paid every one of them, as though this were some virtue.[20] Obviously women were contemptible to him, and all, in his mind, were prostitutes. In one case a madam in Chicago brought in a girl who had never (or rarely) had orgasms.[21] Revson undertook to give her one. His staying power was allegedly enormous, and after about an hour she did have an orgasm. Evidently the biographer did not understand that prostitutes are largely frigid and homosexual (Greenwald, 1970) and that unusual staying power in a man (several hours before he ejaculates) is a neurotic symptom, characteristic of paranoid homosexual trends.

Revson's need for false conquests over women was demonstrated in other ways as well. He would have open sex sessions with some of his executives or salesmen, in which he would have sex in front of the other man, or force the other man to have sex with one of the prostitutes in front of him. This peculiar behavior is also one step short of open homosexuality.

Another aspect of his homosexuality came out in the fact that he never went to bed without putting lipstick on his lips and nail polish on his nails. He would leave a call with the desk to wake him at two and at four and at six to see how it was wearing.[22] Thus every night he would pretend that he was a woman.

It is not surprising that his biographer describes him as nasty, crude, lonely, virile, brilliant, inarticulate, insecure, generous, honest, ruthless and complicated. Once he said of himself, "If it wasn't terrible, it wouldn't be my life."[23]

ISAAC MERRITT SINGER: THE DRAMATIC POLYGAMIST[24]

To most people the Singer sewing machine is a household word, and indeed it has revolutionized the life of the average housewife. Although Singer held several patents on the machine he was never the sole, or even the main inventor; his skill lay rather in commercializing the machine, and in the introduction of such innovations as mass production, loss leaders and installment purchase. But the drama of his life is even more extraordinary.

Again Singer's is a Horatio Alger story, from rags to riches. He was born in 1811 to an immigrant from Germany, about whom little is known. The most salient features of Singer's father's life are that he married twice and lived to be 102 years old.[25] With nothing to keep him at home, Isaac, at the age of twelve, left for Rochester, New York, then a boom town, without money, without friends, without education, possessed of nothing but a strong constitution and a prolific brain. After knocking around for a number of years, at nineteen he entered a machinist's shop and became a skilled mechanic, an ability which stood him in good stead later in life.

Isaac's real dream, however, was to be an actor. At that time, acting was not even considered a respectable profession, condemned by the clergy and all morally-minded citizens. One historian of Rochester commented that "In 1838 neither theater nor circus are now to be found in Rochester."[26] In spite of the bad reputation acting held, Singer was determined to act and joined a strolling troupe. At the same time, at nineteen, he married a girl named Catherine; she was then fifteen. Two children were soon born to the couple. Singer was described at this time as a jack of all trades, master of none. Most of his time he devoted to theatrical performances. He was rarely home, out traveling about the country, taking whatever jobs he could find in the theater.

In 1835 or 1836 the family moved to New York City. Singer then joined an acting company which took him to Baltimore on its tour. There he met an eighteen-year-old named Mary Ann, whom he soon promised to marry. He deserted Catharine, and although unable to marry Mary Ann he went to live with her in Baltimore, where they announced themselves as man and wife.[27] Shortly thereafter their first child was born. Although he made some money by the invention of a rock drill for moving earth, for many years Singer lived the hazardous life of an itinerant actor. The theatre remained his great passion all his life. But after fourteen years as a traveling actor he developed a machine which would carve wooden type, and made that his business. He finally patented his machine as a "machine for carving wood and metal."[28] By 1849 he was sufficiently successful to move back to New York City with his family. By this time he was thirty-eight years old, with two wives and eight children;[29] each wife knew all about the other, but seemingly did not object, especially since he was punctilious about supporting all his children.

The type carver was no money-maker. Singer moved his business to Boston, but made little progress until he discovered the sewing machine. Here the story becomes complex and intriguing.

It appears that the sewing machine had been invented many times over. The first patentee was an Englishman named Thomas Saint, in 1790.[30] The first American was Elias Howe, in 1846.[31] But Singer found the machine in 1849, made some improvements, and then capitalized on it as no one had before.

In the course of his commercialization he swindled his first wife, Catharine, and his first partner, the man who lent him the capital for his business. He also engaged in a long-lasting patent infringement legal battle with Howe and others. Some battles were lost but in the long run Singer emerged with the most practical and most marketable of the various sewing machines. The transition finally came in 1858 and 1859. The other manufacturers were eventually squeezed out and by 1869[32] the Singer Manufacturing Co. emerged as the largest and most prosperous. prosperous. Singer himself had become a millionaire; at his death his estate was valued at $13 to $15 million.

In the 1850's the fantastic story of his personal life began to unravel. On the surface he seemed a happily married man, with Mary Ann as his wife, and presumably Catharine as his former wife, with ten children by Mary Ann and two by Catharine. He entertained lavishly and was highly esteemed.

In 1860, when he was forty-nine, he decided to divorce Catharine, who in the meantime had gone to live with another man. In the puritanical world of that day such conduct for a woman was enough to stigmatize her, regardless of what the man had done. Still, knowing what his business was worth, and realizing that Catharine did not, he bribed her to admit to adultery and be divorced.[33]

Mary Ann, who by this time had lived with him for twenty-three years, now expected marriage. She was bitterly disappointed. No marriage, said Isaac, that would "put him in her power."[34]

In 1860 Mary Ann, driving along in her carriage, saw Isaac driving in the opposite direction with a woman named Mary McGonigal. When she reached home, Mary Ann and her daughter, Voulette, raised a scene, whereupon Singer beat the two so badly that they both lost consciousness. Mary Ann thereupon filed a complaint with the police, who arrested Singer and required him to post a bond to assure that he would keep the peace.[35] Extensive legal battles then occupied him for the next three years.

In the course of these battles, it was revealed that virtually since his arrival in New York in 1850, Isaac had been running three families actively, and maintaining some contact with a fourth, which was the legal one. By 1860 Isaac had fathered and recognized *eighteen* children by four women, of whom sixteen were alive, and supporting them all in reasonable style. It was also claimed, and not denied, that he regularly seduced most of his operatives.

Around this time (early 1860's) he found still another woman, Isabella, half French, half English. Mary Ann, in a curious decision in a suit for divorce, denied the marriage and conceded the adultery. A settlement was reached for $8,000 a year alimony, the largest such award ever given at that time. Mary Ann shortly thereafter married a man named Foster. This faux pas was immediately pounced on by Singer and his lawyers. Singer accused her of bigamy, and had the settlement substantially reduced. He also took custody of the two youngest children.

Therupon in 1863 Isaac married Isabella, settled down with her and had five more children. But as an actor he yearned for recognition. He retired from active participation in the business, with a large and secure income. He had a house built in Yonkers for himself and his new family, and set out to entertain on a lavish scale. But the scandals had rocked New York, and few visitors came. Disappointed, the couple went to Europe, where they finally settled in Torquay, in England.

In Torquay he again built an elaborate house, named the "Wigwam." (In his father's time, in upper New York State where he was brought up, Indians were still being pacified.) Again, lavish parties were offered. The nobility spurned him, not because of his scandalous life in New York, but because he was an untitled American. So he invited all the tradespeople who were only too happy to partake of his hospitality. His house even had a private theater. For the people of the town his parties were a most spectacular fare, and he was warmly regarded by all, who knew nothing of his past. Thus his final years (he died in 1875) were spent as an actor offering entertainment. Histrionic to the last he even left instructions about how his funeral should be conducted. He was buried in three lavish coffins, the funeral cortege was drawn by his own twelve horses, three abreast, and the funeral procession was nearly three-quarters of a mile long, containing between seventy and eighty carriages.[38]

In all Singer, though legally married only twice, in his will acknowledged the children of five women. He made provision for all, though he skimped on the bequests to his first two children by Catharine. What was astounding for that time was that he publicly acknowledged all of his illegitimate children.

In this extraordinary life, his first forty years were spent knocking around without being able to make a living; the typical suffering of the man who later made millions. The next ten years were spent actively living in three households with sixteen children; how he managed it remains a mystery to this day. His last ten years were spent in a retirement in which his main interest was in displaying his huge wealth to a foreign audience who knew nothing about his past.

Was Singer a happy man? He was never described as markedly morose or depressed or fearful. But his defense was to conquer women, beating them into submission when necessary. With little concern for others, he swindled wherever he could to make himself a fortune. For women he admittedly had nothing but contempt; with all his millions he allowed Mary Ann, who had lived with him the longest and borne him ten children, a paltry $15 per week. Like other men of his day, he was a robber baron. As a born actor, he revelled above all in displays of his prowess. Such men cannot be called happy in any meaningful sense.

MOZART: THE TRAGIC GENIUS[39]

Regarded generally as the greatest natural musical genius of all times, Mozart's life was a tragic combination of spectacular accomplishment and overwhelming misery. He was born in Salzburg, Austria in 1756, where his father Leopold was vice concert master to the Archbishop of Salzburg (whom Mozart was later to hate) and a competent composer in his own right. There were seven children; only Wolfgang and his sister, also an accomplished musician, survived.

He was, as everyone knows, a child prodigy. At three he was picking on the harpsichord. At four he was studying minuets. At five he was composing them. His ear was so accurate that it was bothered by quarter tones, and so delicate that the close-up sound of a trumpet made him faint dead away. At six his genius was so outstanding that he was taken by his father on his first tour. Then followed tour after tour.

Apparently he could do everything in music without being taught. He could play string instruments, and improvise and compose and fluently play any keyboard instrument, and name and repeat any combination of notes on hearing them played.

It is obvious that he could not have a normal boyhood. There were no playmates, except his sister, five years older, no formal schooling, only his father and music, music, music. He grew up hating his domineering father and dreaming of the day when he could escape parental domination. In the meantime father exploited him mercilessly, and earned a comfortable living from the boy's performances.

In 1777 he went on a trip with his mother to Paris where he hoped to find some permanent employment. This did not materialize, but he did meet Aloysia Weber, with whom he fell in love. He also liked the Webers so much that he virtually adopted them as a kind of second family. Aloysia did not reciprocate his love, but her sister Constanze did. He married her in 1782, over his father's strenuous objections.

Once he was grown up, he had trouble making a living. The life of a musician in those days was almost entirely dependent on official patronage. Mozart, as might be expected, was arrogant, rude and at times insulting; he made fun of lesser musicians and was always ready to "die laughing" when they played. Naturally he was extremely jealous of any competence that came close to his own.

An incident typical of the times, which would be virtually unthinkable today, was his "competition" with the great Italian pianist Muzio Clementi. The Italian's history was in some ways similar to Mozart's. A wealthy British musical connoisseur named Peter Beckford discovered him at fourteen, and virtually adopted him. Beckford took Clementi to England, gave him a good education, and prepared him for a musical career. When he gave his first concert at twenty-one he created a furor, and immediately became known as the greatest pianist of the day apart from Mozart.

In 1781 the Emperor Joseph II arranged (or should one say ordered) a competition between Mozart and Clementi. Victory was left undecided. But while Clementi had nothing but praise for Mozart, the boy wonder sneered at his opponent's music. Competitions of this kind were not uncommon in eighteenth century Europe, where the kings and lords held the money bags and called the tune.

The last ten years of Mozart's life were filled with bitterness and disappointment. Because of his arrogant attitude he could get neither lasting patronage nor worthwhile pupils. A musician on his own in those days could barely survive: There were no records, no great sums for concerts, no adequate royalties from publishers. The former prodigy struggled with an unhappy marriage and a terrible burden of debt. Yet in the midst of all this he composed one piece after another of immortal music. He even introduced technical innovations in the manufacture of the piano, just beginning to be the instrument it now is. Clementi had the good sense to start a manufacturing company which made him a rich man; Mozart had no such business acumen. Finally he died in 1791, at the age of thirty-five and was buried in a pauper's grave.

Mozart's fate·is a fitting commentary on the civilization of his time. The greatest natural musician of all time, exploited by his father, given no adequate education, sneered at by sadistic kings and princes, intrigued against by inferior musicians who were jealous of his genius, without real love in his life, he could only live in his music. And even that was neglected—most of his major works were not printed until after his death, and his sublime talents were not fully recognized until the end of the nineteenth century. His early successes brought him no lasting happiness. Truly a forgotten man!

NELSON ROCKEFELLER: THE PRESIDENTIAL BUG[40]

Nelson Rockefeller, born in 1908, was the grandson of John D. Rockefeller, then the richest man on earth, whose vast wealth was estimated at $900 million, in an age when no income taxes were paid, and the dollar was worth far more than today. Considerable controversy surrounded the Rockefeller fortune, which had been accumulated in the manner of a ruthless steamroller. Senator Robert Lafollette called John D. "the greatest criminal of his age." Teddy Roosevelt dubbed the family "malefactors of great wealth." John D. was the most famous of the robber barons who dominated the American business scene after the Civil War. He was widely known as the most hated man in America.

Nelson was the third of six children of Rockefeller's only son, John D., Jr. The size of Nelson's inheritance has never been revealed in detail, but it is known that in 1934 his father gave him and the other children each a trust fund of $40 million. Thus Nelson was born to a fortune greater than the net worth of many countries.

As always with the sons of the very wealthy, Nelson had a highly sheltered childhood. Although not as strictly as some others, he was always under the watchful eye of numerous guardians, understandably, since kidnappings of the children of the rich were by no means uncommon.

His mother, Abby Aldrich Rockefeller, was also wealthy in her own right. She was the daughter of Nelson Aldrich, a Rhode Island farm boy who had risen to become the iron-fisted ruler of the United States Senate and an avowed spokesman for big business in government. She was also much warmer than the rather puritanical father, who had been brought up in great seclusion as an only child, and was exposed all his life to the social bitterness the Rockefeller fortune had created. From his mother, Nelson acquired a love of art which remained one of his enduring passions all his life.

What was a man to do with such extraordinary wealth? Brother David opted to stay in business and became the head of the Chase Manhattan Bank. Brother Winthrop, after a lurid life as a playboy which led to a much-publicized divorce,

entered politics in Arkansas, where he became governor.
From an early age Nelson wanted to enter the political arena;
he had the presidential bug.

In school he was not outstanding. Perhaps the most important detail of his college career is a forty-five page paper he
wrote on Standard Oil, in which he rejected the contention
that the company had crushed its competitors by ruthless
competition; to him it was simply a more efficient monopoly.
He argued:

> If things had developed without the Standard monop-
> oly, prices would probably have been somewhat lower,
> but the profits would have been proportionately much
> lower and the industry most likely would not have devel-
> oped nearly as fast. The Standard took in profits that
> would have otherwise gone to waste.[41]

Throughout childhood he was dominated on the one hand
by the "Olympian" rectitude of his father and the warm and
spontaneous personality of his mother. The father sermonized
and offered to pay each of his children $2,500 if they reached
the age of twenty-one without smoking. At college, where his
allowance was only $30 per week, Nelson was admonished
that if there were too much publicity his allowance would be
cut. Father also held him back by a peculiar method of cor-
recting his left-handedness: Whenever Nelson reached for his
fork with his left hand, his father yanked on a string attached
to a rubber band around Nelson's wrist. Later it was also
revealed that he·suffered from a reading disability all through
childhood, which psychoanalysts usually attribute to an unconscious rebelliousness.

In 1930 he married a girl who won the approval of his
father. Then, despite his unwillingness he entered the family
business. A family of five followed.

At the outbreak of the war, in 1940, he sensed a chance to
enter politics, and offered his services as an expert on Latin
America. But the administration was Democratic and he was
a Republican. So his position was of little consequence.

Although it was only revealed after his death, through the
years he had his share of mistresses. But discretion remained

the rule, and none of this was known to the public. His allowance might be cut should such news get out.

After years of minor government appointments and service in the family business, he finally saw his chance at politics in 1958, when he ran for the governorship of New York. To the surprise of many, he was elected. That made him the brightest star in the Republican firmament. Immediately the notion of the presidency came to the fore. For almost twenty years he was to pursue it with dogged tenacity.

He served four terms as governor of New York, from 1958 to 1974. On the whole his administration was constructive and successful. But his sights were aimed higher.

Before his first term as governor expired, two momentous events occurred. He fell in love with "Happy" Murphy, wife of a microbiologist at the Rockefeller Institute. And his son, Michael, disappeared on an expedition to New Guinea and was presumed dead.

Happy's divorce from her husband was secured at the cost of giving him custody of their four children. When later she was married to Rockefeller and wanted the children back, she lost in a sensational trial. There can be little doubt that this incident damaged his presidential chances badly.

In 1968 he formally announced himself as a candidate for the first time. But it did not help him. The country was tired of the Vietnam War and Nixon was riding high. The image of the Rockefeller fortune in the White House was repugnant to too many people.

His last days, sudden death and the manner of his passing were a let-down. It appeared that he had hired a young woman, Megan Marshak, to "help him" classify his art collection at an extraordinary salary. In 1979 he suddenly died, while he was with her. It was obvious she was more than an art assistant, and that she was only the last of many amours in his life.

The image of the happy-go-lucky millionaire politician was punctured once and for all. It became apparent that Rockefeller was dominated by the same urges that bedevil many men in their older years: conquest and women. He had evidently already broken up with Happy. The frustration of never being able to gain the Presidency cut deeper than appeared on the surface. In spite of all his wealth and conquests, he remained deeply insecure.

SUMMARY

Although success and achievement dominate the lives of many men, they do so at a price. If the men are born poor, they suffer on the way up. The Horatio Alger story is not a total myth; it does occur. But Horatio has a rough time, whether in trying or in winning.

Some men are born to the purple, either because they have a native genius, like Mozart, or because they inherit great wealth, like Rockefeller. Yet the circumstances of their times and the experiences of their childhood still remain the decisive factors in how happy they will be. Mozart was ruined by a greedy father and by a society that did not know how to appreciate great music. Rockefeller was aware of the stigma on his family name, and wanted to correct it by becoming president. His failure to do so was the tragedy of his life.

Is there then no successful man who does not have to suffer? Certainly no such generalization would hold. Many men manage to reach their goals and lead fairly happy lives. But many more win in one area and lose in another. Pomp, ostentation and victory take the place of happiness.

As far as the battle of the sexes is concerned, it is particularly noteworthy that the man when frustrated in his personal ambitions often seeks to take out his frustration on the women in his life. When Louis XIV reached the age of sixty he is said to have told his mistress: "You make me feel that I'm thirty." The same illusion dominates the thought of many successful men. In Rockefeller's case, whether or not he died in the act of sex, as was popularly supposed, his ignominious end brought light to the shaky foundations of his sense of self-esteem.

Chapter 10:
Narcissistic Men Are Lonely

The topic of narcissism has in the last ten years become of central importance in psychoanalytic theory. It must not be supposed, however, that narcissism itself is new. Nero, who fiddled while Rome burned, and committed every crime conceivable, from incest to murder, was a pure narcissist, as was Louis XIV, who grandiloquently proclaimed "L'État, c'est moi," (I am the state).

And of course there is Narcissus himself, the hero of the Greek myth. As formulated by the Roman writer Ovid, it became the favorite myth of writers through the ages.

The myth of Narcissus contains some profound psychological observations. Narcissus was distinguished for his beauty. His mother was told that he would have a long life, provided he never looked upon his own features. In one version, he then consoled himself for the death of a favorite twin sister, his exact counterpart, by looking at his reflection in the pool to recall her features by his own. He looked so long that he drowned in the pool.[1]

Thus the myth first of all embodies the idea that a narcissistic man is one who is told by his mother that he is great; if he ever tries himself out in reality (looks at himself) he will be disappointed. The incestuous material is contained in the part about the twin sister. The divorce from interpersonal contacts is embodied in the idea that he looks at his own reflection in the water. Eventually this self-absorption will kill him.

Narcissism is essentially self-involvement. All human beings are narcissistic to some extent; to give up the self entirely, as many religions and philosophies have urged, is psychologically impossible. But the self-involvement alternates with interpersonal relations. If there is an imbalance between the two, either by being too self-deprecating or too self-aggrandizing, then the man suffers. In the interplay between

© 1987 by The Haworth Press, Inc. All rights reserved.

narcissistic pleasure and interpersonal contacts lies much of
the human conflict.

The structure of the narcissistic individual is by now well
understood, and the term "narcissistic personality disorder"
has been coined to describe those who are too involved with
themselves. Although all people are narcissistic to some degree, when it becomes excessive, the narcissism is a way of
warding off interpersonal suffering. It begins with the relationship to the mother. The boy who remains too tied to the
mother becomes narcissistic, the test is then whether he can in
his growth move on to the father, eventually leave the family
and love another woman. Although there are autistic (self-
involved) children, by and large the narcissism does not become fully apparent until the boy reaches adolescence, when
he has to make a relationship with a girl, moving away from
parental domination, and mother in particular. It is here that
many men flounder; in the extreme they become schizophrenics, seriously, often permanently impaired in their capacity to
communicate or relate to other people.

Since the narcissist wants to hold on to mother, resents
father and other rivals, he always suffers from a great deal of
jealousy and rage. As Richard III says in one of Shakespeare's plays, since he cannot be a lover he will be a villain.[2]
Narcissists are permanently frustrated by their overattachment to mother. In response to the frustration, they either
withdraw into themselves, as in the myth, or they rage against
others. Many of the men we have discussed in previous
chapters, such as Hitler and Stalin, fit the pattern perfectly,
and their unbelievable rage is the compensation for the lost
Garden of Eden of childhood. It has been observed that in
almost all images of paradise in the world's religions and mythology, the setting is most similar to that of early childhood,
when there are no demands made upon the man and sex has
not yet entered the picture. In the Biblical story of the
Garden of Eden, it is only when Adam and Eve partake of
the tree of knowledge (read: discover sexuality) that they
notice their nakedness and fall from grace.

Thus in the three major areas we have been discussing, the
narcissist is always at a loss. Sexually he soon experiences the
forbidden incestuous desire for mother, and can never find
satisfaction with a woman. His aggression is either turned

inward, making him withdrawn and morose, or transformed into a rage against other people. A social role is difficult because he always wants to be preferred to all others. Unfortunately when such men reach a position of power, they may wreak havoc, and equally unfortunately, many of these men are driven to seek power.

DUDLEY: A CLINICAL INSTANCE

We would like to begin with a clinical example in order to highlight the features of the narcissistic personality. One of them is that through his constant preoccupation with himself, he frequently achieves a great deal. Yet no matter how great the achievement, the narcissist is never satisfied with himself.

Dudley was an identical twin who could never marry and remained in psychotherapeutic treatment all his life. He was one of six children born to immigrant Italian parents. When he was about six years old, his mother became ill, and the children were sent to an orphan asylum, where they remained until they were old enough to be on their own; in his case he returned home when he was eighteen. His mother had in the meantime recovered from her illness, but she preferred to leave the children in the asylum. Father died when the children were in the orphanage and mother never remarried.

The orphanage was run in an authoritarian way. Discipline was strongly enforced by a rigid director who demanded strict obedience. The military character of the institution was emphasized by the use of old Civil War uniforms for the boys. Spankings and other punishments were common. In this atmosphere Dudley grew up with a deep hatred for the director, even vowing that if he ever had the chance he would kill him. When the director died a peaceful death long after Dudley left the home, he felt a twinge of disappointment that he had never been able to carry out his threat.

Once discharged from the asylum, Dudley returned home to find himself emotionally isolated from everyone. On top of everything else, his mother was alleged to be a typhoid carrier, so that no friends could be invited to the house. The family remained poor, so that Dudley could not exercise his wish to go to college. Instead he trained as a cook, an occupation in which he continued all his life until retirement.

World War II gave him the first chance to really leave his home environment, and he was pleased to be drafted. He fought through the war in Europe, on the Italian front. There he met a girl Isabella, whom he dated on and off for several years. She was divorced, with one child. He considered the possibility of staying on in Italy after the war and marrying her, but decided against it.

Upon his return home, he moved out on his own, since he had some money saved up and could easily find work in restaurants. Then began his steady withdrawal from his childhood contacts. The tie with his twin brother was strained when the brother had a mild nervous breakdown. In general twins are either very close or very distant; in this case they became more distant.

Dudley became increasingly ashamed of his family, all of whom had menial jobs, although his was not at a much higher level. But he did have intellectual inspirations and read extensively, which they never did. However, he never went back to school, fearful he would not be able to make it.

Gradually the distance from his siblings widened, and after he was thirty-five he saw less and less of them, finally ending up cutting himself off from them altogether. He found friends where he worked, but feared any lasting ties with people. Even in his personal habits he was always on the run; he used paper tissues rather than linen handkerchiefs so as to avoid any commitment to laundry. He liked to read in public libraries rather than at home, even though he knew none of the people there.

In his relations with women, he also kept distant. There were occasional sexual experiences and pick-ups of prostitutes. He did attempt a more serious affair in his late thirties which went on for two years, with a woman named Jean. After a short time Jean began to display symptoms of severe neurosis, screaming, feeling easily hurt, suffering from various bodily complaints. He did not feel that he could marry her, and the relationship broke up.

There followed a very lonely life. On the one hand he was eager to marry and start a family, on the other he was tormented by the idea that the woman would be as "crazy" (his word) as Jean. His fear produced a self-fulfilling prophecy, and every woman he became involved with did show signs of mental disturbance. One broke down so badly that she had to be taken to Bellevue in the middle of the night, from where she was transferred to a state hospital for a while. When she was released, she began to call him, but he did not respond.

As time went on, the intervals between affairs with women became longer and longer. Sometimes he would go for years without touching a woman. Always the same excuse—women could not be trusted. His main recreation became going to piano bars, where he could drink with the habitués, but never get closely involved. When he did on rare occasions try to get closer to some of the women he met there, he was invariably rebuffed.

In his late forties he turned to psychotherapy for help. By that time the fears had become so deeply entrenched that little could be done for him. On top of that, as might be anticipated, it took him a long time to build up any trust for the therapist; he remained suspicious throughout, thinking that all the therapist was after was his money. The therapy did help him to enjoy his solitary activities, but could not get him to move closer to other human beings. He filled up his time with various hobbies. Surprisingly he became a rather competent painter, and found in art an outlet for so much of what he had missed out on in life. Unlike Narcissus, he did not drown in his reflection. Instead he learned to derive some satisfaction from the solitary activities—reading, painting, movies, to which he had become accustomed.

Dudley had no special abilities. Of him it can be said, as in *The Rubaiyat of Omar Khayyam,* that the moving finger wrote and having written, passed on. The other men we shall discuss in this chapter, however, have in one way or another made a lasting impression on other men and women. This derives in part from some special ability (as in Eddie Fisher), and in part from the healthy part of their narcissism, which allows them to devote a large part of their energy, for a short or long time, to a specialized field. Yet when examined more closely, in spite of their great contributions, their narcissistic exploits left them miserable. They achieved fame, but neither love nor happiness.

ISAAC NEWTON: GOD'S SPOKESMAN[3]

We are all familiar with Alexander Pope's famous couplet about Newton:

> Nature and Nature's Laws lay hid in night
> God said, Let Newton be!—
> And all was light.[4]

Newton is so important in the intellectual history of the world that for centuries men spoke of the Newtonian world revolution. He was the first to demonstrate the universal law of gravitation, and how it explained the structure and functioning of the solar system; he (at the same time as Leibniz) invented the calculus, thus fostering great progress in mathematics, and he was the first to clarify the nature of the spectrum of light. Yet his eccentricity immediately becomes apparent when it is noted that all of these discoveries were made in a period of two years when he was twenty-three years old, and that in their essentials they remained unpublished for some twenty years, and then were only published with the assistance of others.[5]

Recent research has disclosed the bizarre character of his life, especially when it is realized how preeminent he was in science. He was born in 1642, three months after his father died. His mother was alone with him for the first three years of his life, then she left him to marry a man of sixty-three (she was then about thirty). She went to live with her new husband, Reverend Barnabas Smith, about a mile and a half away, while Isaac was brought up by his maternal grandmother, a woman then in her fifties. When Isaac was eleven the Reverend Smith died and Hannah (Isaac's mother) returned with the three children of her new brood. It is recorded that father Barnabas was still siring children when he was past seventy.[6] Thus Newton was left without mother, father or siblings from the time he was three until he was eleven. This is enough of a background to make anyone introverted, and he was always described as absent-minded, daydreamy, narcissistic (if the word was then in use).

Thrown back upon himself, Isaac from the beginning took an intense interest in the world outside. From an early age he was known for the "pregnancy of his parts," meaning that he was extraordinarily gifted at mechanical objects and inventions. There were many stories about his mechanical skills, his clocks, sundials, kites and other ingenious devices.

It is not surprising that he remained fixated on his mother, Hannah, and that he supposedly lived and died a virgin. Only one contact with a girl in his life is recorded, and that when still a little boy, with another child in the neighborhood, who became a Mrs. Vincent. For her he retained a certain affection all his life, though it never resulted in any kind of emotional or physical contact.

Although he was reported to be very shy and retiring at school, one story foretells his future psychology. When the school bully tried to pick on him, young Isaac turned on him and beat him soundly.[7] In later life too whenever anybody tried to criticize him he reacted with rage and an attempt at a verbal thrashing.

In general, from an early age he was the subject of what Milton called the "great Forbidder." He was scrupulous, austere, disciplined, industrious, fearful and overwhelmed by a typically repressive morality. As his biographer, Frank Manuel, reports, there is not much laughter in Newton's life and no echo of "merrie old England" in his notebooks. He had an image of himself as sinful, close to death and tending toward consumption, though he was a healthy specimen who lived to the ripe old age of eighty-three.

In spite of his mother's objections—she wanted him to take over and manage her estates—Newton went to Trinity College in Cambridge when he was just past eighteen. At this point it is important to recall that in 1661, when he first went to college, science was still so rudimentary that it was not beyond reason to try to master all knowledge and weave it into one unified system of the world, including the inner world. Nor was college necessarily the best place to study, for many of the best minds were found in non-academic settings, and the restrictions of the university life were numerous and severe.

The plague, which had destroyed almost half of Europe in 1347, still recurred in less virulent form time and again. Its cause was unknown; the only rememdy was to get away from other people. In 1665 it hit Cambridge, so he went home to his mother's place in Woolsthorpe Lincolnshire, where he remained for two years. It was in these two years, 1664–1666, especially the latter, that he made his great discoveries.

In 1667 he returned to Cambridge. In 1669 his predecessor Isaac Barrow resigned and Newton became the Lucasian Professor, one of the most prestigious posts in English universities. Here he remained until 1696, when he was appointed Warden of the Mint, and moved to London. There he continued until his death in 1727.

In the meantime, Newton had presented his first paper on his theory of colors to the Royal Society in 1672. Here he encountered his first major enemy, Robert Hooke, who tried to tear the newcomer to pieces and he and Hooke remained bitter enemies until the latter died in 1703. Hooke continually claimed that Newton was plagiarizing him, a claim that does not stand up to serious scrutiny. But Newton was so outraged that he withdrew into silence, then into a period of total isolation after the death of his mother in 1678.

It was only through the astronomer Edmund Halley that the *Principia Mathematica,* one of the greatest books ever written, came to be published at all. Newton had put it to one side, and only brought it out when accused by Hooke of plagiarism. Halley noted the book's extraordinary importance, and prevailed upon the older man to let it be published. It was finally brought out in 1687.[8]

With the publication of the *Principia* Newton became the most eminent scientist on earth, even though it took time for the scientific world to digest all of his ideas.

Another major change in his life occurred when he was appointed Warden of the Mint in 1696,[9] so that he could sustain himself in London, where he lived with his niece Catherine Barton as housekeeper. But amazingly he took the office very seriously. Counterfeiting of the coinage was then a very serious problem, and Newton went after the "clippers and coiners' with great relish. He personally supervised many of the interrogations, and reportedly took pleasure in seeing the offenders go to the gallows. His rage against "falsifiers" knew no limit. He never forgave Hooke, broke off relations with him, and would not accept the presidency of the Royal Society until Hooke died in 1703. Newton was equally angry and vindictive toward John Flamsteed, the royal astronomer, who provided essential astronomical observations to verify or refute Newton's theories, and against Leibniz, who had independently discovered the calculus.

In the latter part of Newton's life he also became the autocrat of the British scientific world. Because of the authority conferred upon him by his great discoveries, he assumed the right (by then he was president of the Royal Society) to determine all appointments to posts in the British universities. Evidently, this position of power was also very dear to his heart.

After the publication of the *Principia* he undertook no meaningful scientific work, even though he lived for more than forty years. Instead, he devoted himself to alchemy and religion. In addition to trying to disprove the Trinitarian hypothesis of the Father, the Son and the Holy Ghost, he tried to elaborate an exact chronology of the history of the world, according to the Scriptures, and to explain the true meaning of prophecy. Evidently he thought that since he had shown that God had created a self-regulating mechanical world, God had also created a self-consistent psychological-historical world. And Newton was there to divine where God's hand lay. This latter part of his work is too fanciful of course to be taken seriously, but to Newton it was part of his essential mission on earth, just as important in its own way as the *Principia* was in its way.[10]

Even to his contemporaries it was rather clear that Newton was a bit mad. He had no intimates; either he isolated himself in his work or he was lord of the manner. Twice in his life, once after the death of his mother, and again in 1693, he apparently had nervous breakdowns which led to complete isolation. In 1696 we find him suddenly breaking off with Samuel Pepys, and accusing the philosopher John Locke of trying to fix him up with women.

His personality is similar to that of other narcissistic men who work on their own and have visions of greatness. What has obscured his psychology is that he did achieve greatness in one field; this has concealed the absurdity of his claim to greatness in another, prophesy and alchemy.

It has also led his standard biographers to overlook the depths of his unhappiness. Always busy with one thing or another, always alone even when in company, always in some rage ·at some real or fancied rival, always lonely, always frightened and insecure, from his earliest days life could not have been much of a pleasure to him. And above all the inability to break away from mother and enjoy the love of a mature woman bore down heavily.

FRANZ KAFKA:
THE CHRONICLER OF INNER TORMENT[12]

In Franz Kafka (1883–1924), the writer whose publications have created such a deep stir among modern intellectuals, especially those familiar with psychoanalysis, we have another kind of narcissist. Unlike Newton, he was not physically isolated from other people. But the emotional distance and despairing loneliness were more than he could bear.

Kafka was born to a Jewish middle class family in Prague in 1883. The two brothers nearest him in age died in infancy; there were three younger sisters.[13] Thus he became the oldest and the only son. Ever in rivalry with his father, the struggle to break the attachment to his family became the dominant theme of his life. His father wanted him to enter the business but he rebelled, insisting that he wanted to be a writer. His goal was the literary recording of his dreamlike inner life. Yet even here he was filled with pessimism and foreboding; more than half of his writings were never published during his lifetime, and his fame only grew after his death.

His rebellion was not total. He studied law, took his degree and got a job in an insurance firm. Here he finished early in the afternoon, giving him time to go home and write.

But writing could not resolve the great problem of his life, the struggle with his father. Kafka's wish was to marry and become a father in his own right, a goal which he could never reach and which left him feeling impotent, helpless and despairing, at times suicidal. It was the classical Oedipal struggle which he could never resolve. "Man cannot live with a permanent faith in something indestructible in himself. At the same time this indestructible part and his faith in it may remain permanently concealed from him," he wrote.[14]

In one of his best-known pieces, a letter to his father, he puts the following words into his father's mouth: "You have in fact made up your mind that you want to live on me altogether. I admit we fight each other, but there are two kinds of fight. There is the chivalrous fight. . . . And there is the fight of the vermin, which not only bite, but at the same time suck the blood on which they live. . . . You cannot stand up to life, but in order to set yourself up in it comfortably, free from care, and without self-reproach, you'll prove that I robbed you of your capacity to stand up to life, and shoved it in my pocket."[15] This image of the vermin appears in one of his best-known short stories, *The Metamorphosis*, where the hero wakes up one day to find he is a giant insect. The family makes strenuous efforts to keep him out of sight, but they cannot succeed.

It is clear that the struggle to express his rage at his father for not valuing his literary and artistic work paralyzed his existence. At one point he wrote: "The tremendous world I have in my head! But how can I release it and release myself without tearing myself apart?"[16] Then again in 1914 he wrote in his diary: "My preoccupation with portraying my dreamlike inner life has relegated everything else to a secondary position, other interests have shrunk in a most dreadful fashion, and never cease to shrink. Nothing else can ever make me happy. But it is impossible to calculate how much strength I have for this portrayal."[17]

The main events of Kafka's short life can be briefly recounted. After he took the job with the insurance firm, he continued to write, and to struggle with his feelings about his family. His yearning for marriage and children could never be gratified, which made him feel useless, he had passed from youth to "ancient," as he put it, without ever becoming a man. He finally became engaged to a girl from Berlin, but he could never make up his mind to marry her. After five years the engagement was broken. There were other brief unhappy affairs. In 1917 he developed tuberculosis, which did not respond well to treatment and he knew he was dying. Only in the last year of his life could he leave his family, go to Berlin, and meet a girl he loved, Dora Dymant. By then it was too late; within a year he was dead.

In one of his best-known novels, *The Castle*, the anxiety and alienation of modern man are beautifully depicted; they were Kafka's own. The hero, whom he calls simply K., passes through life alone. He is a man of good will, strives after a useful career, wants to marry and found a family, but everything goes wrong with him. One notices more and more that the chilly layer of isolation around K. is nothing accidental. He is a stranger and has entered a village in which strangers are looked upon with suspicion. Everywhere he goes he meets with rejection. When one man invites him in, he discovers that his host is weak in the head. When he makes a comment, he is told, "You are new here and yet you already know everything." If only he could get a woman, but this proves impossible. He learns he belongs nowhere. Finally he discovers that he even disturbs the sleep of the children. Everything takes place in an atmosphere of ill-concealed hostility.

The novel, like many of his writings, expresses the existential dilemma felt by so many in a world which has gone through genocide and fears nuclear destruction. There is no security; no safe place. In another famous novel *The Trial* Kafka feels accused of God knows what, he is judged by an unknown interrogator, he is locked up in an unfamiliar place.

But while Kafka could provide a beautiful poetic expression of this dilemma, in his own short life he experienced terrible suffering. His narcissism lay in his unconscious revolt against the business mentality of his father on the surface, but at a deeper level he was afraid to grow up. Even with the father he had, he reached a stage of independence (law degree) where he could do what he wanted. What undid him was his inability to leave his father psychologically and reach a love relationship. Consciously he longed to do so; unconsciously he was too tied down by his infantile conflicts.

LAWRENCE OF ARABIA:
THE MOHAMMED FROM BRITAIN[18]

T. E. Lawrence has gained international fame as the man who sparked the Arab revolt during World War I, which played a role in the collapse of the Ottoman Empire. Apparently Lawrence did view himself in some ways as a possible Mohammed, who could inspire hope and unity in the Arabs, a people with a glorious past who had been reduced to a virtual slave status for centuries by the Turks. Lawrence has described his activities during the Arab revolt in his book

Seven Pillars of Wisdom. But his life was in its own way quite extraordinary.

Lawrence once spoke of his own work:

> If I have restored to the East some self-respect, a goal, ideals: if I have made the standard of rule of white over red more exigent, I have fitted these peoples in a degree for the new commonwealth in which the dominant races will forget their brute achievements, and white and red and yellow and brown and black will stand up together without side-glances in the service of the world.[19]

Lawrence was the illegitimate son of an Irishman, Sir Thomas Chapman, who had escaped both marriage and Ireland by running off with the nursemaid of his daughters.[20] Nevertheless, the two lived together as man and wife in various parts of the continent and England. Even though it was the Victorian era (Lawrence was born in 1888) the shock at the father's behavior did not affect the family noticeably. In all they had five children, all boys.

Lawrence trained in archaeology, especially medieval architecture, and from 1911 to 1914 worked on excavations at Carchemish on the Euphrates. Here he acquired his knowledge of Arabic language and customs that was to underlie his major achievements.

When the war broke out, he was dispatched to Cairo as an intelligence officer. Shortly thereafter he began his epic effort to spur the Arabs to revolt, and form one unified nation, even though he realized that unity at that time was virtually impossible because of the intense rivalries among Arab factions. Still, a dream is a dream.

There is some question about how great a part Lawrence played in the victory, since at the same time Allenby was advancing on Palestine. In any case whether true or false, when the news of his exploits reached the outside world, he was dubbed "Lawrence of Arabia," and has been looked upon as that ever since.

After the war ended, he continued for several years to be the advocate of the Arabs, at the Versailles peace conference, and other diplomatic conferences.

When he found he could do nothing for the Arabs,

Lawrence abruptly deserted the entire fight, and in 1922 enlisted in the Royal Air Force under the assumed name of Ross[21] (his assumption of one fictitious name after another will be discussed below). Here his presence was discovered and because of the incongruity of having such a famous man a mere private in the Air Force, he was discharged. The next year he enlisted in the Royal Tank Force as a private under the name of T. E. Shaw.[22] He endured all the rigors of a raw recruit in the army, which he described as an essential violation of man's humanity. Later he was transferred back to the Air Force, where he remained until his discharge in 1935. When he was discharged he said of himself: "There is something broken in the works . . . my will, I think." A few months later he was killed in a motorcycle accident: he was driving along at high speed, when he saw two young men on bicycles directly ahead of him; in order to avoid running into them, he swerved the motorcycle, hit a rock and was fatally wounded.

The switch from Lawrence of Arabia, a modern Mohammed, to Private Shaw, an absurd raw recruit, is remarkable enough. But as the details of his life emerge, it becomes even more remarkable. The urgent question is: after all his extraordinary successes in the Arab world, why did he not settle in one or another of the Arab countries for good? Why did he retreat to humiliation, mistreatment and self-effacement?

The first point that is striking is his lack of a sense of identity. He assumed in his life at least five different names; the last one, Shaw, became his legal name. It was adopted because George Bernard Shaw and his wife took a great interest in him. Thus if he could not be an Arab he would be reborn as the son of a great writer.

The second point is that Lawrence remained a virgin all his life. During his military activities with the Arabs, at one time he was captured by the Turks and homosexually assaulted. But he is not known to have been an overt homosexual. At another point in his campaigns he is said to have ordered the execution of 200 Turkish prisoners at Tafas, but such an act of cruelty was also uncharacteristic.

Again, the question has to be raised: how can a man go through life without close physical contact with either woman or man? One answer lies in the discovery of a peculiar perversion of his. He would make up a story that he had done something bad, and at the request of an uncle he was to be punished; the implication was clear that the punishment had to be a physical beating on the behind, like a boy spanked, but the beating had to be severely painful, not imitation, or a mere token. Later the beatings were to be done with a metal whip and were to produce an ejaculation.[24]

Thus once he gave up his preeminent role among the Arabs, he went steadily downhill, endured one humiliation after another, culminating in self-imposed severe flagellation. Even his death could be interpreted as a kind of suicide, since he might just as well have run down the boys on the bicycles and taken the consequences; at worst he would have been condemned for unintended manslaugher, at best the boys might merely have been hurt.

Lawrence spoke Arabic fluently, dressed like an Arab (he appeared in Arab clothes at the Peace Conference) and was thoroughly familiar with Arabic customs. If he did not take the final step of settling in an Arab country, the answer must be sought in his sexual perversion. For the Arabs are notoriously dominant and cruel with their women (in a number of Arab countries little girls still have their clitorises cut out in order to deprive them of sexual pleasure later in life). To become an Arab would have meant marrying Arab women, and playing a sadistic rather than a masochistic role. While he could do this under the pressure of war, he could not bring himself to do it in times of peace. Thus his career after his retreat from the Arab world was an unconscious form of suicide, and it is not surprising that he sought pain, humiliation and suffering so often. To some extent he must also have been paying the price for his heroic deeds when he was with the Arabs, since in such a man victory was so dangerous psychologically that it had to be followed by some kind of punishment.

JOSEPH LISTER: A HEALTHY NARCISSIST[25]

Many men make good use of their narcissism by devoting themselves wholeheartedly to their work. This pattern is perhaps most often seen among scientists. Joseph Lister, the dis-

coverer of antisepsis, one of the cornerstones of modern surgery, is a good example.

Lister was born in 1827, the son of two Quakers. His
father, a dealer in wines, was also an amateur physicist and
microscopist who achieved such competence in the field that
he was elected a fellow of the Royal Society.

With such a family background Lister naturally drifted to
medicine. At that time the mortality rate from surgery was
enormous: 50% and higher. Nor was it at all understood.
Lister devoted his life to the problem, and eventually resolved
it by the introduction of antisepsis, chemicals which would
combat the infections set off by surgery. Later asepsis, or the
total avoidance of any possible infection, became the treatment of choice, but Lister's discoveries provided a notable
link in the chain.

The facts of his life are briefly told. After taking a medical
degree in 1852, he received an appointment in 1853 as assistant to James Syme, in Edinburgh, regarded as the greatest
surgical teacher of his day. Later he married the daughter of
Symes. Though the marriage remained childless, it seems to
have been a happy one.

Once Lister became acquainted with Pasteur's discovery
that microorganisms cause fermentation and disease, he saw
the answer to the problems with which he was struggling.
Prior to that, it was not known why surgery so often produced
infection and death. Lister found in carbolic acid an effective
antiseptic which would kill the infection. The results were
dramatic: on the male accident ward the mortality rate fell
from 45% to 15%.

Although there was some early opposition, eventually he
saw the almost universal acceptance of his basic principles
during his working life. Had it existed then he would most
certainly have been awarded the Nobel prize. Yet in spite of
his fame, he remained a gentle, shy, unassuming man, firm in
his purpose because he humbly believed himself to be directed by God. Neither social success nor financial reward
meant anything to him; his great joy lay in his work. He lived
to a ripe old age, and died in 1912 at eighty-five.

There was obviously nothing flamboyant or dramatic about
Lister. He set himself a scientific problem and eventually
solved it. His narcissism came out in his absorption in the
problem. That he could make a happy marriage with the

daughter of his esteemed teacher helped him to create a new family similar to the one into which he was born.

LEWIS CARROLL: THE MAN WHO LOVED LITTLE GIRLS[27]

Lewis Carroll is the pen name of Charles Dodgson, who has become famous as the author of *Alice in Wonderland,* one of the most popular books ever written. It is still a universal best seller after more than one hundred years.

The story of his life, however, reveals an entirely different kind of man from the one who casually told stories to little girls. Born in 1832, he was the eldest son and third child in a family of seven boys and four girls. His father was a clergyman. Charles was a gifted student, passed his examinations easily and became an instructor in mathematics at Oxford, where he remained for the rest of his life.

How *Alice in Wonderland* came into being has often been told. Carroll had friends, the Liddells, who had young daughters. Unable to relate to adult women, Charles spent a great deal of time entertaining young girls. Alice Liddell was the Alice of the book; the book was the record of stories he wove for her and her girlfriends. He was merely playing with words and fancies; when the book had such extraordinary success he was astounded. For many years his favorite pastime was to photograph young girls, age eight or so, in the nude.

As mentioned, Charles was unable to relate to adult women and never married. He suffered from lifelong insomnia, which he tried to correct by writing a book called *Pillow Problems.* He was deaf in one ear and stuttered. Today we would look upon him as a narcissistic individual whose problems came out in his eccentric behavior. Toward the end of his life (he died in 1899) he even renounced the name Lewis Carroll and sent back mail addressed to him, an indication of the severe conflicts aroused by the assumption of a new identity. His mathematical work is said to have been undistinguished.

Like so many narcissistic artists Carroll could use his fantasies to cover up deep wounds. In one verse he wrote:

> He thought he saw an Elephant
> That practiced on a fife.

He looked again and saw it was
A letter from his wife.
At length, I realize, he said
The bitterness of Life.[28]

What comes out here as whimsy is really a reflection of the
real bitterness he experienced at the idea of a wife, and his
inability to obtain one.

SUMMARY

The narcissistic man, as in the myth, turns to himself because of his over-attachment to an incestuous figure, mother
and sister. This over-attachment then makes it impossible for
him to relate to adult women. The narcissism makes him
lonely, a feeling frequently covered up by activities of various
kinds. But no matter how talented or successful he becomes,
the inner sore never heals. Many of these men at best become
eccentrics in adult life. Others develop serious problems of
one kind or another, which may not be recognized by their
contemporaries. The fiction that a man "chooses" to be a
bachelor rather than that he is forced into it by his inner
conflicts has been demolished by psychoanalytic scrutiny.

In some men, the narcissism is healthy in that it leads to an
extraordinary kind of devotion to work; in others it is harmful
in that it lends itself only to fantasies or escape mechanisms.
But even the healthy narcissist finds himself lonely and unhappy if he cannot adjust to women.

Chapter 11:
Criminals Die Young

The life of the criminal holds endless fascination for men. As boys, their favorite games are cops and robbers, or cowboys and Indians, or good guys and bad guys in one form or another. Many men engage in petty criminal acts at one time or another, such as stealing something from a store, or sneaking into a movie without paying for it, or cheatinig at cards or other games. Many others restrain themselves from criminal activity with such force that they become too good to be true; in analysis we call that a reaction formation. Often enough men who have built up such reaction formations, when faced with great stress, cannot maintain their facade and resort to violence of one kind or another.

In this chapter our concern is with those men who actually engage in a life of crime, whether minor, such as pickpocketing, or major, such as armed robbery or murder. The attraction of murder is enormous, even though as a crime it is statistically rare. When two young men brutally murdered a family of four in Kansas in 1959, Truman Capote wrote a book about their trial and subsequent execution; the book sold four million copies, emphasizing the strong unconscious identification with the murderers. Usually murder leads to lurid headlines in the newspaper; unfortunately the glare of publicity sometimes tempts unbalanced men to kill in order to have the limelight for a day or a week. The famous or rather infamous Son of Sam, who murdered young girls out of frustration at his own inability to relate to a girl, is a case in point. For months he was the center of attention for an army of policemen and newspapermen.

Although criminals have come from all social classes, there is a strong likelihood that the lower classes will resort to crime more readily than those better off. The poor have less to lose, and at one extreme of poverty even a prison looks better than life outside. However, this generalization should not be over-

© 1987 by The Haworth Press, Inc. All rights reserved.

done, since criminal behavior has existed at every level of society, including the very rich and the very powerful politically (the president).

While the sociological factors that lead to crime vary, the psychological factors are more consistent. A criminal has little regard for the welfare of others; his wants come first. This narcissism is coupled with a good deal of rage about his predicament in life. To others this rage may seem without motivation, yet as we have seen in previous chapters, men are often dissatisfied with their successes for internal reasons.

As the narcissistic rage grows, a loosening of the ordinary constraints that inhibit crime occur. The criminal almost always feel fully justified in his actions, exhibiting neither contrition nor remorse. What annoys him most is that he is caught. Nor does harm done to others or their possessions mean much to him; he comes first.

The criminal often tries to justify his actions by the claim that we live in an immoral society, that everybody else does the same thing he does, and that the only difference is that he was foolish enough to be caught. All of this serves to obscure the fact that he feels no guilt about what he is doing to other people. This explains why the most hardened criminals will murder without the slightest compunction.

There have been numerous theories offered about what makes people criminal. The notion of a "criminal personality," or innate evilness, has existed from time immemorial, but there is no evidence that it has any validity. Today, too, there are those who maintain that the criminal has a "defective" brain, yet no matter how often this theory is exploded it comes back in one form or another. Almost all students of the topic are agreed that the root causes are psychological and social, though why within any given socioeconomic group some become criminals, while others do not, remains something of a mystery.

There was a time when even slight crimes, such as the theft of a loaf of bread from a bakery, were punished with death. Debtors' prisons also existed in those days (several hundred years ago) to make sure that the established order would not be overthrown. Severe punishment by society is now looked upon as somehow counterproductive; Dr. Karl Menninger has even written a book entitled: *The Crime of Punishment.* Such an argument tries to generalize from the analytic position, but there is a wide gap between the analytic situation and the social. Mankind has not yet reached a stage of inner equilibrium where police are no longer necessary.

Since the criminal has so little regard for others, it is inevitable that there will be something wrong with his love life. A loving marriage and a happy family are not found among criminals; the closest they can come is a domineering patriarchal kind of marriage in which the man is the supreme boss.

Generally speaking, psychotherapy, no matter what variety, has little effect on criminal behavior. This would indicate that the criminal mind-set is learned so early in life that it is extremely resistant to change. While there are many exceptions, it remains true that social and police measures are more effective than psychological ones.

The incidence of crime is higher in this country than anywhere else in the industrial world. Yet there is a peculiar paradox, for the degree of freedom that exists here has prevented the government from engaging in wholesale violence in order to suppress or punish troublesome minorities. Still, while the degree of governmental violence is equally low in most countries of western Europe, the frequency of crime and violence is by and large much lower there than here. It is no secret that American cities have become increasingly unsafe, and poll after poll shows that people regard crime as one of our major public problems.

Even though crime is rampant, and most criminals are not caught, in the long run the criminal does not succeed in his way of life. Many, tired of the chasing, hiding and constant fear, give it up; others persist until sooner or later they are caught, or come to grief in other ways. In the case of prostitution, one study (Greenwald) showed that two-thirds of the girls had attempted suicide at one time or another; many others had died. Hence the title of this chapter: criminals die young. The prospect of an early arrest and/or death always haunts the mind of the criminal, and helps to account for much of the despair, need for immediate gratification, and disregard of others that exists.

THE BLACK EXPERIENCE:
MANCHILD IN THE PROMISED LAND[1]

The black experience in the United States has made crime a significant way out for many blacks. Born into a broken and unhappy family, with the father often absent, the boy grows up with little hope for the future. Sex begins early, at puberty or before, though it is anything but a love experience, since so many of the girls become prostitutes and drug addicts. In school, the odds are heavily against the boy. Without much education he stands little chance of getting ahead in the business world. Religion, involving strong group consciousness and powerful repressions, is one alternative; crime is another; he has little to lose. The legacy of slavery is still with us, and will take a long time to overcome.

Yet no stereotype can be set up showing that the black is a born criminal, or that all blacks are dangerous. Many have escaped from the rat race, and lived happy, productive lives. One who managed to get out, Claude Brown, has told his story in an excellent book: *Manchild in the Promised Land.*

The book begins with an account of a shooting when Claude is thirteen years old.[2] For months before, his gang had been stealing sheets and bedspreads off clotheslines. His mother was frightened; father was brutal.

In one scene he recalls, he is thinking about the tenement in which he lives, where he has written "pussy" and "fuck you" on the walls. The superintendent of this building, Mr. Lawson, had once killed a man for peeing in the hall; he was never punished. Claude's younger brother, Pimp, began writing dirty words on the wall, following Claude's example. Pimp was caught by his father, who vowed he would kill him. He began to beat Pimp with the ironing cord so brutally that Claude thought he would kill him. Mama was crying, insisting Pimp was too young to be beaten so severely. She ran out of the house to get a policeman, returning with one who stopped the father from beating his son so mercilessly. Claude told Pimp not to cry any more, to wait until Claude got older and then he would kill their father and Pimp could help him.[3]

By and large Claude's family background seems to have been better than most. The family of two boys and two girls remained intact. The father worked regularly, though what he

worked at is not related. Emotionally, however, there was
much amiss. Father beat the boys harshly and regularly. The
rest of the family believed the sons were just "bad" and
looked for the "roots." Father drank and had little to do with
the children; mother cried and prayed, but did have affection
for her offspring.

From an early age Claude was on the streets. By the time
he was eight or nine he hung around with a gang that was
always playing hookey and beginning to engage in petty thiev-
ery. Eventually the thefts, hookey and other offenses caught
up with him. All the father could think of doing was to "beat
his ass." Mother was of little help. The boy was sent to hospitals and to various homes for juvenile delinquents, particularly the well-known Wiltwyck School for Boys; he mentions
Ernst Papanek. In these homes at least he had some chance
to air his emotions. At one point he writes:

> As a child, I remember being morbidly afraid. It was a
> fear that was like a fever that never let up. Sometimes it
> became so intense that it would just swallow you. At
> other times, it just kept you shaking. But it was always
> there. I suppose, in Harlem, even now, the fear is still
> there.[4]

Around puberty drugs and prostitution entered the picture.
The slang, he says, was always changing for heroin. They
called it duji or shit or stuff or poison. After 1952 nobody
called it horse. He always referred to it as the shit plague
because that had more meaning to him.

Eventually, his brother Pimp, of whom he was genuinely
fond, was "hooked" on the stuff. A good deal of the book is
devoted to the efforts to prevent Pimp from getting too involved. But Pimp took part in an armed robbery to get money
to buy the stuff and was sentenced to one to five years in jail.

It seems odd that a child should be called "Pimp." The
explanation given is that when his mother was in labor and
going to the hospital, the only one around to help her was a
young prostitute, who spent a valuable seventy cents to take
her to the hospital. The prostitute became the godmother of
the baby who was called Pimp.

The book relates the fate of the boys and girls with whom

Claude grew up. Most of the "cats," he says, had not made it; they were either dead or in jail. He calls the cause of their fate the "plague" that hit his people; a sad commentary on our civilization.

Something, perhaps the understanding and affection he received from counselors in the detention homes, or an unknown factor, helped to save Claude from the fate of his buddies. One commentator called his book "a guided tour of Hell conducted by a man who broke out." He became a law student at one of America's leading universities, able to leave Harlem behind.

THE MURDERER IN CHAINS: IN THE BELLY OF THE BEAST[5]

The history of Jack Abbott is unusual in that it is tied up with recognition by one of America's best-known writers, Norman Mailer. Abbott wrote letters from prison which eventually reached the attention of Mailer, at that time working on a book about a famous condemned murderer, Gilmore, called *The Executioner's Song*. Mailer was considerably impressed by the literary measure of Abbott's writings on prison. He wrote of him:

> There is a point past which any prisoner can get nothing more from prison, not even the preservation of his will, and Abbott, I think, has reached these years. Whereas, if he gets out, we may yet have a new writer of the largest stature among us, for he has forged himself in a cauldron and still has half of the world to discover. . . . I love Jack Abbott for surviving and for having learned to write as well as he does.[6]

Perhaps because of Mailer's intercession and recommendations Abbott was released in 1981. Shortly thereafter he went into a restaurant in Greenwich Village, flew into a rage at a waiter and stabbed him to death. He was returned to prison where he will probably remain the rest of his life.

In his book, *In the Belly of the Beast,* which consists of his letters to Mailer, Abbott gives a grim picture of his life. In a brief autobiographical statement he says:

I was born January 21, 1944, on a military base in Oscoda, Michigan. I was in and out of foster homes almost from the moment of my birth. My formal education: I never completed the sixth grade. At age nine I began serving long stints in juvenile detention quarters. At age twelve I was sent to the Utah State Industrial School for Boys. I was "paroled" once for about sixty days, then returned there. At age eighteen I was released as an adult. Five or six months later I was sent to the Utah State Penitentiary for the crime of "issuing a check against insufficient funds." I went in with an indeterminate sentence of up to five years. About three years later, having never been released, I killed one inmate and wounded another in a fight in the center hall. I was tried for the capital offense under the old convict statute that requires either *Mandatory* death if malice *afore-thought* is found, or a sentence of from three to twenty years. I received the latter sentence. An "indeterminate" sentence is what justifies the concept of *parole*. Your good behavior determines how long you stay in prison. The law merely sets a minimum and a maximum—the underlying assumption being that *no one* serves the maximum. A wrong assumption in my case. At age twenty-six I escaped for about six weeks.

I am at this moment thirty-seven years old. Since age twelve I have been free for the sum of a total of nine and a half months. I have served many terms in solitary. In only three terms I have served over ten years there. I would estimate that I have served a good fourteen or fifteen years in solitary. The only serious crime I have ever committed in free society was bank robbery during the time I was a fugitive.[7]

From this autobiographical sketch one learns little about the inner dynamics of the man. But the book as a whole is revealing. Abbott quite openly admits he is paranoid, sayng, "Paranoia is an illness I contracted in institutions."[8] Themes of murder and rage are found on almost every page. When he is with a crowd of prisoners, he has to restrain himself from attacking them, he feels such hatred.

He distinguishes between the prisoner who spends some

time in jail and then leaves, and the prisoner who spends his entire life there. The latter he refers to as "state-raised." These state-raised prisoners, obviously referring to himself, are mentally unstable.

In order to have a chance for parole, a prisoner has to be on good behavior; everybody knows that. But Abbott is unable to go a month in prison without violating rules. He is so enraged at guards that he still sometimes stutters when he talks to them.

In spite of this constant "persecution" he states that there are not many books "of philosophical importance I have not read."[9] How did he get them, and how did he manage to find time to read them if he was mistreated so miserably? He prides himself that he never went to a prison school, this in spite of his intellectual ambitions.

He relates that he received a number of the tranquilizing drugs while in prison, and had adverse reactions to all of them. The only purpose he can see for the drugs is to ruin him, "ruin me completely."

Abbott makes much of his years in solitary confinement. But what he says is unclear. He speaks of the "hole" as though it were the usual prison cell. On one page he says:[5] "Most prisoners I know who have been in prison off and on all their lives will tell you they have served *five years* in the hole. Everyone is lying . . ."[10] Why then should we not assume that Abbott is lying, or at least in this understandable way looking for a little more sympathy? At one point he discovers the term "sensory deprivation," and compares his prison life to that.

His hatred of the guards is open and overpowering. He always calls them pigs: "The pigs are so weak that it takes five or six to whip an inmate." A prisoner, he says, cannot be subdued, even with a knife at his throat, only murdered.

As he goes on, we begin to suspect we are dealing here with paranoid delusions. A great conflagration is coming that will tear the whole world apart (the typical schizophrenic world-destruction fantasy). He denies his fear: "If I was afraid I was never aware of it. . . . You could say I was paranoid: bloodthirsty to establish my place."[12]

Then he discovers Marxism. The revolution will save the world. There is no other country on earth that has a tyranny as profound as America.[13] Solzhenitsyn is a traitor to his country, Abbott interprets the Russian author's book as showing how *lenient* the Soviet Union is to its prisoners, certainly a most extraordinary distortion.

There is no contrition whatsoever for his acts. In one poem he says: ". . . . your eyes . . . I think that I shall gouge them from your skull, and crush them in my fist."[14] Then he writes a poem *Paranoia,* following which he expresses his perplexity (justified) that he can write something like that.

If one looks at the book dispassionately, it becomes clear that we are dealing with a delusional schizophrenic. All the drugs given him have had no effect. He relates to no one; only his sister is mentioned once. Parents are never discussed. His writing is an anguished cry for help, but typically he blames everything on the "pigs," takes responsibility for nothing, not even for the murder he committed.

What requires explanation is why Norman Mailer viewed him as so gifted, and encouraged his release. The murder of the waiter in the restaurant after his release is a typical paranoid murder: the pretext was trivial, the waiter had delayed in giving him his order. He called the man outside and stabbed him to death. Obviously Abbott, fearful that he would be hurt, lashed out first: this is the paranoid mechanism.

Mailer is a writer fascinated by violence, murder and narcissism. His most famous book, *The Naked and the Dead,* comes out of his World War II experience. In his works Mailer freely admits to experimenting with a number of drugs and to deep depressions, for which he took the drugs. Another book, *Advertisements for Myself,* is certainly a highly narcissistic endeavor. At one point in this book Mailer writes:

. . . I've burned away too much of my creative energy, and picked too slowly on the hard, grim and maybe manly knowledge that if I am to go on saying what my anger tells me it is true to say, I must get better at over-riding the indifference which comes from the snobs, arbiters, managers and conforming maniacs who manipulate most of the world of letters and sense at the core of their unconscious that the ambition of a writer like myself is to become consecutively more disruptive, more dangerous and more powerful.[15]

This passage provides an essential clue to what might best be called the Mailer-Abbott affair. Abbott is as much a creation of Mailer's imagination as some of the characters in his novels. Writing, art, is more important to Mailer than anything else. When he received Abbott's letters the unrestrained violence in them must have intrigued him. The paranoid killer was forgotten. Actually, if one looks at Abbott's book as literature, the question must immediately be raised: how much of it is fantasy and how much fact? De Sade, who also put together some of the most sadistic works in print, spent most of his life in a mental hospital, and his works were written there. What Abbott is writing about is his own almost unrestrainable rage, his hatred of people, and his interest in no one except himself. At the trial for the murder of the waiter Abbott again showed no contrition and Mailer, somewhat chastened by the experience, merely remarked that Abbott's literary gifts should not be forgotten. Mailer, like many artists (as will be discussed below) was still thinking of art and disregarding the human cost.[16]

As for Abbott, his life history is indeed a tragic one. Something might have been done about it when he was a child (as happened with Claude Brown); now it would appear too late to expect any real change in him.

WHEN THE JAILERS ARE THE CRIMINALS: JACOBO TIMMERMAN[17]

Jack Abbott's claim that all of his troubles stem from the sadistic actions of the jailers has been echoed many times by criminals in all cultures and in all countries. In the Russian Gulag system it has generally been reported that few men ever get out alive; a sentence to jail is a sentence of death. Though there are certainly many abuses in the American system, by and large that is certainly not the case here. But there are many countries where it still remains true.

The Argentine system in 1982 is a case in point. For many years the country had been run on a dictatorial basis in which thousands of innocent people were jailed, tortured and murdered. One of the most outrageous aspects of such despotic rule is the practice of "desaparecidos," the Spanish for "disappeared." Men and women simply disappeared and nothing was ever heard from them. Sometimes their bodies were found mutilated and unrecognizable; at other times their bodies were never found. Any inquiry cast extreme suspicion on the person inquiring who, in turn, might be subject to arrest, torture and death. The only exception allowed is for the mothers who demonstrate occasionally in the Plaza de Mayo in Buenos Aires. The whole system is well known, yet no one can do anything about it until the government is overthrown or mends its ways (which appears to be happening now).

Jacobo Timmerman, the former editor of a prestigious Buenos Aires newspaper, is one of the lucky few who got out alive after being held and tortured. His account of his experiences is related in his book: *Prisoner Without a Name, Cell Without a Number.*

Timmerman traces his ancestry back to the Spanish Inquisition in the fifteenth century, and the Spanish occupation of the Netherlands in the sixteenth; in both cases many Jews in his family were murdered. The survivors managed to escape to Bar in the Ukraine, where they lived for several centuries. In 1648–49 the Cossack chief Chmielnetski passed through Bar and, "of course" massacred all the Jews he could capture.[18] The survivors pulled themselves together. The final extermination came in 1942, when the Nazis killed all the remaining Jews.

Timmerman's father emigrated to Argentina in 1928, when the boy was five years old. There the family prospered and Jacobo rose to become an important figure in the newspaper world. In 1977 a new dictatorship imprisoned him, this time not for being a Jew (though there were strong elements of anti-Semitism in their actions) but for somehow being allied with the "terrorists."

He was imprisoned in a narrow cell; when standing at its center he could not extend his arms. Because the floor of the cell was permanently wet, he had to sleep standing or seated. Then followed the systematic torture.

Timmerman describes the first phase of the torture as follows:

> This is the first phase of torture: to take a man by surprise, without allowing him any reflex defense, even psychological. A man's hands are shackled behind him,

his eyes blindfolded. No one says a word. Blows are shattered upon a man. He's placed on the ground, and someone counts to ten, but he's not killed. A man is then led to what may be a canvas bed, or a table, stripped, doused with water, tied to the ends of the bed or table, hands and legs outstretched. And the application of electric shocks begins. The amount of electricity transmitted by the electrodes—or whatever they're called—is regulated so that it merely hurts, or burns, or destroys. It's impossible to shout—you howl. At the onset of this long human howl, someone with soft hands supervises your heart, someone sticks his hand into your mouth and pulls your tongue out of it in order to prevent this man from choking. Someone then places a piece of rubber in the man's mouth to prevent him from biting his tongue or destroying his lips. A brief pause. And then it starts all over again, with insults this time. A brief pause. And then questions. A brief pause. And then words of hope. A brief pause. And then insults. A brief pause. And then questions.[19]

Timmerman was lucky: after the torture he was finally released. Not so the others. As he says: "It's a world for either the resigned or the mad."[20]

One little item in his book is quite revealing. In the area of Buenos Aires where the prison was located, there was a night life. The torturers and their officers were entitled to control over prostitution in certain bars, to exploit some of the women and to enjoy immunity in their protection of secret gambling operators. Three very beautiful girls in their early twenties were incarcerated in the prison. They had been tortured, violated and gradually corrupted until in resignation they submitted to their jailers' sexual demands.

ARCHIE HILL: THE HEALING POWER OF LOVE[22]

Generalizations about human beings are always risky. While it is true that criminals seldom escape from the trap of crime—prison, drugs, further crime, early death—there are many exceptions. One is described by an Englishman named Archie Hill in his book *The Closed World of Love*.

This is the story of an aimless, hard-drinking ex-con named Archie who drifted through life after his release from prison. He was living in a one-room set-up in North London. A bed, a drunken-door wardrobe, a cane-bottomed chair, a small washbasin and an electric-element cooker made up his home. For work he was doing a variety of jobs, all casual and impermanent. He described himself as follows:

> On the outside I was normal. On the inside I was empty. Going through motions. No purpose, no ambition. Just working, drinking, mixing with floaters and drifters.[23]

In this state, on one job as a salesman he met a woman who had an extra room to let. After some hesitation he took it. The woman was divorced, with a crippled son who required a great deal of care; his name was Barry.

After a short time Archie proposed to the woman (whose name is not given). At first she refused, saying he would never accept all the hardships connected with Barry and she could not leave Barry to have another child. When Archie pressed his suit, assuring her he would love both her and Barry, she finally accepted, with the proviso that they would not have another child.

The marriage proved a very happy one. He willingly assisted in the care of Barry. Eventually he told her he wanted a son of his own and she changed her original proviso and agreed to bear his child.

In the meantime he had been writing and educating himself. She sent one of his stories to the BBC which accepted it. He was launched on his career as a writer. With the work and love problems resolved, he was a happy man.

The story comes out of a published book, and no one can vouch for its authenticity. Yet it sounds real and convincing. There are many people whose lives are turned around by some other person. William James called them the twice-born, as contrasted with the more stolid people, the once-born. Often the inspiration comes from a religious source, but often it comes from a warm and affectionate person. Whether the particular story told here is authentic or not, the whole scenario—a life that feels worthless transformed by a loving woman—rings true. It is stirring how even in the most unhappy childhood one kind person may stand out and become a beacon for future growth and change. Two dangers must be guarded against in lives of this kind. It would be too Pollyanish to believe it occurs frequently or regularly. On the other hand, it would be too cynical to deny it ever occurs.

GORDON LIDDY: THE POLITICAL CRIMINAL[24]

Of all the scandals that have rocked American history, that of Watergate was by far the most disturbing. Earlier, Vice-President Agnew, caught red-handed taking bribes, resigned. As a result of Watergate, President Nixon, under impeachment proceedings, also resigned. the Attorney General and a series of high-placed officials in the government admitted to complicity in varying degrees in a number of crimes, and almost all spent some time in jail. The one who has described his life background most candidly is G. Gordon Liddy, "Will." Liddy was also the one who stubbornly refused to talk, as a result of which he served almost four and a half years in jail.[25]

Liddy's autobiography reveals the psychology of a typical criminal, even though for most of his life he was a lawyer, police officer (assistant district attorney) and member of the government. He shows no remorse or guilt about what he did; he repeatedly attacks Judge Sirica, who sentenced him, for dishonesty and incompetence. He speaks blandly of conspiring to kill Jack Anderson, a move that was only stopped at the last minute apparently because it went too far. Throughout, he admits he was a great admirer of the Nazis from childhood on; he even ends his autobiography with a variation on a slogan the Nazis sang before the attack on England: "Today Europe, tomorrow the world." Liddy ends with: "Tomorrow belongs to them."[26]

Liddy came of a good family. His father was a successful lawyer who gave his children a fine education; there was even, as Liddy describes it, some feeling of affection and camaraderie between father and son, and in the home. But his inner life was dark and foreboding from an early age.

The book begins with a description of his various childhood fears. Before he was two, he says, "I began to speak immediately, to articulate my first memory absolute, overwhelming fear."[27] A surprise fire drill several years later in Washington again produced "absolute, overwhelming fear." Other horrifying memories from childhood abound. Lying on the floor as grandmother lashes him with a leather harness shouting, "Bad! Bad!" Unable to understand why he is being forced to use his right hand, when he is by nature left-handed. Terrified that a vacuum bag on the street will suck him in. He writes, "Soon my every waking moment was ruled by that overriding emotion: fear."[28]

Then came the most frightening menace of all: God. Brought up in Catholic schools he was threatened and severely punished. An imprecise sign of the cross was an insult to God, punishable by a sudden crack on the head from monitoring nuns. Only the year before a boy who had not made the sign of the cross properly woke up to find his right arm withered, twisted and paralyzed for life.

Once in school came the next fear: that of the older boys who wanted to beat him up. He became ashamed of his fear, and this led to deep self-loathing.

The average family, as was his, has no understanding of the depth or persistence of childhood fears. His mother told him stories of great feats by his ancestors and others, including Glenn Cunningham, whose legs were burned so badly he was told he would never walk again, and grew up to become national champion in the mile run.

Since Liddy got no help from his family, he decided he would conquer his fears by sheer willpower and would make himself strong and powerful, so that nothing would ever threaten him. His mother's brother Ray was an FBI agent and Liddy's earliest ambition was to emulate him, become an agent too, face his fears and conquer them one by one.[29] What he did not realize was that he overcame his fears by assuming the personality of the cop who instills fear into others. Hence Liddy's constant rage and lifelong destructiveness.

Since Liddy was born in 1930, the evils of the Nazi regime were unknown to him as a child. But he had a German maid named Teresa, who became an ardent Nazi as soon as Hitler came to power, and she successfully indoctrinated him. Although he hesitates to say so openly, the social role into which he would fit most comfortably is that of a Nazi storm trooper, ready to kill at the slightest bid from his superior. As he puts it at one point: "I would make myself into a machine."[30] Omitted from this self-description is that it is a machine for killing.

After school he drifted quite naturally into his father's profession, law. Though he had a secure job waiting for him in his father's firm, he chose at this point to join the FBI. Few policemen relate with such obvious glee how they polish their weapons, stalk their prey and swoop down on the enemy.

But the FBI did not pay enough money. He and his wife had decided to have six children, so he resigned and went into law practice. After three years of this, chiefly with his father, he tired of it, understandably, since there was no killing involved (his father was an expert in trademarks) and he went back to a governmental position, in a district attorney's office. Politics led to some disappointments, but it did bring him to the attention of Richard Nixon. In 1968 he threw himself into the Nixon presidential campaign, and shortly thereafter he received an appointment in Washington, this time again as a law enforcement officer. In this and other capacities he first came to attention when he broke into the office of Dr. Fielding in Los Angeles, the psychiatrist who was treating Daniel Ellsberg, then accused of radical sympathies because he was opposed to the Vietnam war. It is obvious to anyone that "break-in and entry" as the police call it, is totally illegal, but this never seemed to bother Liddy.[21]

Eventually came his master stroke—the Watergate affair. Of all the Watergate conspirators, Liddy was the only one who refused to cooperate with the government at the trial, and for that reason received the heaviest sentence (twenty years). No good reason is given why he should have been different from the others, but silence was his way of proving to the judge that he was not afraid. In his memoirs the only thing he does reveal, not spelled out before, is that the break-in at Watergate was for the purpose of finding out what the Democrats had on the Republicans, not for the purpose of uncovering the Democratic plans as such.[32] His silence gives one the impression he was playing out some imaginary role in the cops and robbers battle that had always been the design of his life.

One of the most gruesome sections of his book is where he cold-bloodedly discusses his offer to the Republican high command to kill columnist Jack Anderson. After discussing various alternatives, the chief method he recommended was to kill Anderson in a simulated robbery so it would appear he was just another victim of the high crime rate. At this Mitchell and the other conspirators drew the line; outright murder was too much for them. But Liddy showed no compunction, and had they agreed, he would have proceeded to kill Anderson.[33]

An interesting sidelight on his psychology is the comment that the Ten Commandments do not forbid killing, they only forbid murder (he does not explain the difference). Then he goes on to describe the many situations in which killing is perfectly justified.[34]

In the whole Watergate affair Liddy does not display any great admiration for Nixon or the Republican party, nor does he attempt to justify what he did. Here the cop simply becomes the robber. The only thing Liddy sees as wrong is that he was caught. And in such a case you shut up; his silence was part of his criminal code. For the others, all of whom except Nixon confessed their guilt, he had nothing but scorn. That holds as well for Judge Sirica who found him in contempt of court; he says he considered Sirica contemptible.[35]

Liddy's behavior after release from jail is an amusing counterweight to his previous existence. In order to make money he arranged a series of debates with his former arch-enemy, Timothy Leary, whom he once arrested for the use of drugs.[36] He and Leary spent the evening arguing about various matters, each on opposite sides of the fence. Evidently Liddy no longer cares about his stern principles of law and order; anything that makes money for him is acceptable. This, too, is characteristic of the criminal mind, which places narcissistic advancement above everything else. (Incidentally, the same comment applies to Leary.)

ORGANIZED CRIME: THE MAFIA[37]

Organized crime has long been a feature of life in America. Perhaps its best-known form has been the Mafia, or Cosa Nostra (our thing). At present, the Mafia is reported to be diminishing in importance. A number of books about it have appeared, its methods and techniques are no longer so secret. Other forms of organized crime may be taking its place. Yet the common impression is that the Mafia is still a powerful entity.

The Mafioso is sworn to silence and loyalty on pain of death. Yet some have escaped its clutches and informed. The highest-placed informer has been Jimmy the Weasel (real name, Jimmy Fratianno). His experiences are described in a book by Ovid Demaris (1981). Fratianno had been the Mafia's top enforcer on the West Coast. Through a series of double-crosses, he discovered that a "contract" had been let out to kill him. He then went to the Witness Protection Program of the FBI and told them everything he knew. While in this program he was allowed to tell the story of his life to Demaris.[38]

Fratianno was born in Naples in 1913, was brought to this country four months later. His father was already here, in Cleveland. While his father was an honest but stern man, the neighborhood in which he was brought up was criminal in the extreme. At six he saw three men murdered in front of a speakeasy. In school he was rowdy and got into fights, which finally led to his being sent to a reform school.[39]

Money was always central in his mind. At eleven he was working with his father. At twelve he was a waiter in a speakeasy. He dropped out of school in the ninth grade. At fourteen he became acquainted with a gambler who initiated him into the racket. At seventeen he had become the gambler's partner.[40]

At nineteen he was out with a girl and five Polish boys attacked him, beat him badly. True to his upbringing, he swore revenge. Systematically he sought out four of the boys and beat them so badly they almost died; the fifth boy had moved away. Vendetta was the name of the game.[41]

There followed more petty crime. He became a bookie, labor racketeer and crooked gambler. When he was twenty-two he married, though when asked later whether he had loved his wife he characteristically replied:

Love her! Are you fucking crazy? I've never loved a
broad in my life. What the fuck's love? Do you know?[42]

Soon he discovered it was a lot quicker and far more profitable to rob gambling joints than to run his own crooked
game. So he went in for armed robbery. A year later he was
caught and sent to jail.[43]

After release from jail Fratianno went to Los Angeles, re-
marrying the wife who had earlier divorced him. Again,
bookmaking became his specialty and made money for him.
But soon he discovered the Mafia. Through connections he
was finally allowed in.

Fratianno was initiated into the Mafia when he was thirty-
three. He recalled the initation ceremony. On the table when
he came in were a revolver and a dagger crossing one
another. The Master of Ceremonies said:

> We are gathered here this evening to make five new
> members. . . . Now Jimmy, you are entering into the
> honored society of Cosa Nostra, which welcomes only
> men of great courage and loyalty.
>
> You come in alive and you go out dead. The gun and
> the knife are the instruments by which you live and die.
>
> Cosa Nostra comes first above everything else in your
> life. Before family, before country, before God. When
> you are summoned you must come, even if your mother,
> or wife, or your children are on their death bed.
>
> There are three laws you must obey without question.
> You must never betray any of the secrets of this Cosa
> Nostra. You must never violate the wife or children of
> any other member. You must never become involved
> with narcotics. The violation of any of these laws means
> death without trial or warning.[44]

Someone asked him to raise the index finger of his right
hand. A pin pricked his finger and a bubble of blood burst
forth. He was told, "This drop of blood symbolizes your birth
into our family. We're one until death."

In the ensuing years Fratianno faithfully functioned as a
member of Cosa Nostra. When ordered to kill he killed.
When ordered to rob he robbed. He at one time accumulated

a considerable fortune, which he put in his first wife's name, apparently to avoid any inquiry by the IRS.

He was married twice. The first wife was a young Italian girl of eighteen, to whom he was never faithful. Since prostitution was one of the rackets, there were always easy women available to him. His second wife had been a prostitute. Toward the end of the investigation, in his sixties, he had a new sweetheart, much younger, and boasted he could "outlast" a man half his age. This image of the powerful man who can have intercourse for hours is a popular fantasy among men; actually it represents a psychological problem. But it is important to men such as Fratianno to be the strongest, the most powerful, to have no feelings, to be a killing-robbing machine.

Had Fratianno not been willing to turn state's evidence, he would no doubt have been killed by the Mafia. Many times earlier his life hung by a thread. In spite of his connections he served several other jail sentences. There were never any really quiet or secure periods in his life. The happiest time he seems to record is during his first long jail sentence, when he played softball with the boys all day long, playing out the carefree boyhood he had never had.

While organized crime is a serious menace to society, the members of the Cosa Nostra can be looked at another way, as human beings. What kind of lives do they lead? What do they feel about it themselves, consciously and unconsciously? It certainly is a bitter lonely existence. Always on the go, always hiding, always fearful of being betrayed, and occasionally being betrayed. Women are just objects to be possessed; no love or affection is wasted on them. The tough exterior of silence and loyalty hides the terrible inner fears. Most of the men come to grief early in life, but they are *soldati,* and when they are expended more soldiers are available, as in any army. Looked at from the inside, they are truly forgotten men.

SUMMARY

Under a surface veneer of inscrutable toughness, the criminal is a bitter, lonely man. From childhood on he has been harassed, punished, beaten, jailed and mistreated in every conceivable way. Little or no affection is noticeable in his life. Instead he is dominated by overwhelming fears, which he can never share with anybody. Driven by impulses over which he has little control, he usually gets into situations where he either lands in jail or is murdered. Whatever their story, criminals still die young.

Chapter 12:
The Average Man

Up to now we have of necessity focused on men who have led lives conspicuous enough to merit some biography or autobiography. But what about the average man? How does he live? What does he do with his sexuality? How does he handle his aggression? How does he feel about his social role? There are a number of statistical surveys in print which could be quoted or summarized here. But they never get to the inner soul of the men they are describing, and that is what we are looking for. So, while no large-scale answer about the average man can be forthcoming, I will pass in review some of the fathers of men and women who have been analytic patients. While they are not known as well as their children to the analyst, their lives do come through in reasonable fullness. I shall focus on those men who have stayed with their families, sired children, lived, and died in the everyday world of work—not too narcissistic, not too successful, not criminal. Some comments about their effect on their children will also be in order.*

JOHN: THE CIVIL SERVANT

John was a civil servant all his life. After graduation from high school he took a job with his local public utility as a staff member. No great skill was required; only regular attendance.

Since he was Polish Catholic John married early. There seemed, in the son's eyes at least, to be no great love lost between John and his wife. She was a housewife, taken up with the daily chores; he went to work, came home, listened to the ball game. There was little family around on either

---

*All names are fictitious. Identifying data and other particulars have at times been changed to avoid implications about any man, living or dead. The overall picture is important, not trivial or arbitrary details.

© 1987 by The Haworth Press, Inc. All rights reserved.

side, so the couple led a rather isolated life. John's main form of recreation was to play cards with his fellow-workers on the job.

Throughout his life John was never unemployed. He took his first job when he was twenty-two and stayed there until he died forty years later. Except for occasional illness, he never missed a day's work. He had no outside interests or hobbies, other than an occasional game of cards.

At an early age he developed a severe stomach ulcer. Treatment in those days was inadequate, and he was severely restricted in his diet. This further limited any kind of social activity he might have wanted to engage in.

For some reason (which the son did not know) the couple could not have children. Accordingly they adopted two, a boy and a girl. But why John consented to the adoptions is somewhat of a mystery, since he never took any interest in the children. The son could hardly remember any contact with his father; from the age of eight he was out on the streets making money selling newspapers. The daughter hid herself behind a wall of silence where she had nothing to do with anybody. She lived out her life as a lonely recluse.

The son could give no information about his parents' sex life. From the descriptions he gave, it looked as though it had come to an end very early. Statistical studies show that it is not at all unusual for such couples to discontinue sex in their early forties, or even in their thirties. And up to then there is very little sexual contact.

The sociologist John Cuber (Significant Americans, 1965) has offered a five-fold classification of marriage which is very useful: conflict-habituated; devitalized; passive-congenial; vital, and total. Clearly the marriage of John and his wife was a totally devitalized one. Cuber describes this relationship in the following way, which seems to fit John to a 'T':

> On the subjective emotional dimension the relationship has become a void. The original zest is gone. There is typically little overt tension or conflict, but the interplay between the pair has become apathetic, lifeless. No serious threat to the continuity of the marriage is generally acknowledged, however. It is intended, usually by both, that it continue indefinitely despite its numbness.

Continuity and relative freedom from open conflict are fostered in part because of the comforts of the "habit cage." Continuity is further insured by the absence of any engaging alternative, "all things considered." It is also reinforced, sometimes rather decisively by legal and ecclesiastical requirements and expectations. These people quickly explain that there are "other things in life" which are worthy of sustained human effort.

This kind of relationship is extremely common. Persons in this circumstance frequently make comparisons with other pairs they know, many of whom are similar to themselves. This fosters the comforting judgment that "marriage is like this—except for a few oddballs or pretenders who claim otherwise."

The devitalized marriage of John had a strong effect on both children. The father, as mentioned, had little to do with them. At an early age the girl withdrew from the entire family into herself. When she reached maturity she took a low-paying job, and spent the rest of her life at it, never marrying and apparently having little personal life.

However, the son rebelled at the idea of such a life. Perhaps contributing to this rebellion was an incident with his leg. When he was ten, the doctor prescribed that he sleep with his leg on his mother's lap, which both probably enjoyed, though they could not say so. This went on for six months.

The boy, whom we shall call Patrick, soon found his meaningful experiences outside the home. He was a "gang" kid at a tender age, and engaged in much of the petty law-breaking kids of that age favor: breaking into movies without paying, stealing items from department stores, gambling. But since he came of a solid family, crime did not appeal to him. His high intelligence led him into business. Patrick was determined that he would make a fortune.

However, sex was a problem, so he married at twenty-two, before he was really ready, either sexually or emotionally. The marriage was based on convenience, not love: it was the thing to do. He was brought up in a repressive period; without marrige sex would be limited to prostitutes.

His wife was a virgin and as naive sexually as he. After the honeymoon period, which was not too exciting, she withdrew more and more from sex, until it was limited to once a month. In the meantime she too proved unable to have children, so they, like his parents, adopted two, again a boy and a girl. Both children turned out poorly since they were rejected by both parents. The girl drifted into a pseudo-criminal life. The boy became delinquent before he had left high school.

Patrick meanwhile had unexpectedly prospered. He was secure in a good job, with a wife and two children. But he was possessed by some inner pressure to make more and more money. Analytically, we can understand this in terms of his reaction to the miserable life his parents had led, and to the lack of sexual gratification in his own life. Realistically, it led him to give up his job and leave for another part of the country.

When his wife joined him there he again began to prosper; clearly he was a man of superior talents. But because of the sexual frustration, he began to have affairs with other women. When his wife discovered this, she tried to run him down with her car; he narrowly escaped with his life. He left her, dissolved the marriage, gave up his lucrative business and moved to another part of the country.

For the third time he built up a business, as the manager of a small factory. But the company was family owned and he stood little chance of ever getting much further. So he left the company, started one of his own.

By this time Patrick had found another woman who, in spite of various problems, was sexually responsive. This led to marriage. Eventually he was able to settle down in the fourth business, even though it would not make him a millionaire. By this time he was well into his forties and had lived out his rebellion.

This case has to be looked at from the vantage point of both father and children. The father lived out a conventional, empty life, plagued by a bad stomach and other physical ills, but he stuck to a meaningless devitalized marriage. Both children rebelled against this way of life, each in a different way. The girl never really did anything with her life. The boy turned out to have unusual gifts and succeeded in business. But sexual frustrations led him from one business to another. He finally calmed down when he became the boss of his own business, and when a new marriage offered him a satisfactory sex life.

ARNOLD: OUT OF THE GHETTO

Arnold was the youngest of ten children in a desperately poor family living in a slum section of Brooklyn. Father made a fair living in the garment industry but since there were ten children, there were always money problems.

As far back as he could remember Arnold was ordered around by his older brothers and his mother; father was rather retiring and did little at home. Life became a series of shoulds and oughts, with few rights or pleasures for Arnold.

When he was ten his father unexpectedly committed suicide by jumping off the roof of the tenement. No explanation was offered to Arnold. Since the older children were independent by now and earning money, the financial consequences of his father's death were not serious.

Arnold continued school and thanks to the free education provided by the city, attended college. Though only a fair student, he managed to graduate, got a job as a clerk for the city. While in college he had made money by selling newspapers on a stand. Occasionally someone would give him a five dollar bill, he would give change as though it were a one dollar bill, the customer would not notice and Arnold would pocket the difference. This system would as much as double the income from the stand.

Arnold's sex life began when he was seventeen. The wife of one of his older brothers deliberately seduced him, telling him he was much nicer than her husband. Fearful of vengeance, Arnold never repeated the experience and guilt feelings about what he had done persisted.

At twenty-three, he met Sarah, who later became his wife. She was an artist who made a living teaching art. But her main attraction to him was her sexuality and soon they had sexual relations.

Though Arnold only found out later, Sarah had a history of promiscuity. In childhood she had been seduced by a teacher and had sex play with an uncle for several years. When she reached puberty she became very promiscuous, picking up men on the street and having sex anywhere, in a hallway, on a dark street, on a cot. Three times she had been pregnant, required abortions; twice she had contracted VD. She felt little guilt about her sexuality but was always in mortal fear of getting pregnant. In spite of her experience, she knew little about birth control. When she met Arnold she abruptly ended contacts with other men. Somehow she sensed he was a kind, sincere man who would take care of her. They started going steady, in a short while they married. What Arnold did not know was that Sarah had nothing but contempt for him; all she wanted was someone around. She was terrified of going out on the street and resuming her old ways, so she made him stay in the house with her, or if she did go out he would have to go with her.

About a year after the marriage they had a bitter fight: Sarah accused him of being inept sexually, of not being a man but a worm, and left him to go back to her mother's. In a rage he went to a dance hall and picked up one of the hostesses, Sally, with whom he had sex. Unfortunately he acquired syphilis from her, but did not know it right away.

Then he and Sarah were reconciled, resumed their life together. She then contracted syphilis. When it was discovered, both were treated, fortunately with good results. But the experience left them both quite frightened.

Sarah was still terrified of going out alone. She insisted Arnold remain with her in the evening and for twenty years he never left the house without her, apart from his work routine. In the meantime she found a regular job as an art teacher, went to her school and came home immediately after work.

In a few years a son was born and became the apple of Sarah's eye. She lived virtually the rest of her life for him. She became extremely seductive with the boy, would dress and undress freely in his presence. Later she asked him to help her put on her brassiere, a request that became the core of a constant family quarrel, since Arnold was opposed to it. However she was the boss and had her way. When the boy was eight he began to urinate so frequently that the school recommended a medical examination. A doctor did not find his penis was small, he could not give any reason for the frequent urination. He recommended that his mother watch her son's penis carefully, to see that it would grow properly, a request to which she complied with great gusto.

Sexual relations with her husband were poor. Sarah submitted to Arnold compliantly, as she had with so many men, without pleasure. He in the meantime had frequent bouts of impotence. Her main gratification was anal and he often had to play with her anus instead of having intercourse.

It is not surprising that in this atmosphere divorce was constantly brought up. On innumerable occasions they had drawn up papers and seen a lawyer to settle their dispute legally, only to change their minds at the last minute. It was truly a conflict-habituated marriage.

At one point Arnold was so desperate that, like his father, he tried suicide by taking an overdose of pills. The attempt did not succeed and he was advised to seek psychiatric treatment. This lasted only a few months. It did help with his impotence but could not free him from his wife's almost total domination. Though treatment was also recommended for her she refused, on the grounds that the marital difficulties were all his fault. He acquired a lifelong interest and admiration of psychoanalysis from his treatment and would have pursued it further, but his wife was set against it.

The boy, as might be anticipated, developed serious problems. In adolescence he finally reacted to his mother's seductiveness by tearing off her dress in a rage when she again asked him to fasten her brassiere (she always asked him to fasten it in the back, stating that in that way she avoided showing him her breasts). Thereafter she stopped. He made a very bad marriage and also had sexual difficulties; since he was still young, he sought psychiatric treatment and improved. However, the unconscious attraction to his mother remained so strong that he left psychotherapy prematurely and never did fulfill a considerable potential.

Another source of conflict was the mother's habit of refurnishing whenever the couple managed to save some money. She would throw out the old furniture and replace it with new, not much different from the old. As a result they could never succeed in building up any capital.

Thus the marriage went on for many years—anal play instead of sexual intercourse, constant fighting, constant depreciation of Arnold by his wife, intermittent episodes of depression and occasional brief treatment. The treatment he sought was always second-rate—hypnosis, behavior therapy and the like—and never did him much good. He could never shake off the domination of his wife, with his unhappy childhood he could not strike off on his own. He could not live with her and he could not live without her—a situation which typically leads to a conflict-habituated marriage. She, for her part, frequently wanted to leave him but remained fearful of her history of promiscuity.

In his early seventies he experienced a severe depression. By this time lithium had come into vogue and the psychiatrist he consulted recommended lithium treatment. Arnold, though he was knowledgeable about psychotherapy, was frightening and willing to submit to any authority. He received lithium on and off until shortly before he died at the age of seventy-eight.

In any statistical investigation, this couple would probably have been scored as happily married. They stayed together for fifty years, had one child, expressed some satisfaction with one another, were in fact almost inseparable most of the time. Yet when a look is taken behind the facade, the inner misery becomes apparent.

Arnold's case is also typical of many marriages in which the husband is meek and submissive, while the wife is powerful and dominant. There is no infidelity on either side, partly because of their fears and partly because of their history. Analytically we look upon it as a mother-marriage, in which the husband is the little boy submitting to whatever his wife does to him, because of his overpowering fear of her anger and her threats to leave him.

SHERMAN: THE FRIGHTENED SCHOOL TEACHER

Sherman, the youngest of three sons of an immigrant tailor, was a good student and a devoted son. Even in his sixties he visited his parents every Friday for the traditional Sabbath meal.

During his teens he began to go steady with Alice; there were no other dates in his life. She was a vivacious, quick-tempered girl who charmed him completely. Since she was also planning to become a teacher, the match seemed to be made in Heaven.

Everything seemed to go well for the first few years of their marriage. They had a son and a daughter, and Sherman began a career as a high school teacher of mathematics. The only fly in the ointment was that Alice did not get along with his mother. He shrugged it off as common mother-in-law trouble.

As the children grew up, Sherman became more devoted to his daughter and more antagonistic to his son. At this point Alice's past entered the picture. In her family a younger brother had become mentally ill at thirteen and been confined to a mental hospital for the rest of his life. There seemed no hope for him. Alice was afraid (encouraged by articles in the press) that the illness was hereditary and she began to become increasingly concerned about her son. As happens in so many marriages, she also convinced herself that Sherman was not the strong father the boy needed. She urged Sherman to be more forceful, to punish the boy more, to see to it he "behaved." Sherman retaliated by withdrawing from her and spending as much time as he could with his daughter. The daughter, ten years older than her brother, had married early and was out of the house when the boy was still in his early teens. Once she had left, fierce battles erupted between Alice and Sherman. Everything became his fault, he was not a good model, he could not handle his son, the boy was becoming incorrigible. At the same time the sex life of the couple began to deteriorate.

Outsiders are often puzzled as to why a relationship which starts out with such great promise turns sour. The reasons lie in the psychology of the individuals, as well as in their conception of marriage. For Sherman marriage meant regaining his mother, to whom he was still attached. He wanted Alice to be warm, affectionate and motherly. She in turn wanted him to be a strong powerful father-figure, to reassure her about her own fear of mental illness, for she felt her brother's illness would strike her sooner or later. The two drifted further and further apart.

As usual, the real quarrel could never come out into the open because it was carried on at an unconscious level. Instead, the couple fought about the discipline of the son and about money. Even though their income was quite adequate, Alice still insisted on refurnishing the house well beyond their means. Sherman, meek and compliant, agreed to her every

demand. Soon he discovered he was in debt. Since he was a
good credit risk, he borrowed more money to cover his earlier
debt. But his management of money was disastrous. One loan
led to another, he never seemed to be able to get out from
under.

As time went on, Alice became increasingly frustrated. She
blamed everything on Sherman, who accepted the responsibility since he felt Alice could do no wrong. After a while she
became physically abusive of both her son and husband. She
flew into rages, attacking either one or the other, usually the
son. She refused to visit her mother-in-law, forbade Sherman
to go. But that proved too much, he faithfully continued to
see his mother every Friday until she died.

The couple sought counseling. At the first session Alice
told the counselor she thought nothing could be done for
Sherman, as he sat in her presence. Clearly she was project-
ing her feelings about her psychotic brother on her husband
and son.

For a while family therapy was tried. At the sessions Alice
would dominate completely. She became increasingly narcissistic and self-righteous, saying her son was no good and her
husband did not know how to straighten him out. She scarcely
listened to the comments of the famly therapist. The therapy
ended in failure.

Individual therapy was then tried. Sherman was full of guilt
during the sessions, covering himself with self-reproaches.
One day he came in and told the therapist, "See what I did
now." The therapist could see fingernail scratches on his face.
Sherman explained, "I forced Alice to scratch me." He made
this remark in all seriousness.

Alice paid a visit to another therapist who advised her to
continue. Instead, she stopped, then told the family that the
therapist had dismissed her with the comment, "There's absolutely nothing wrong with you, it's all the fault of your husband and son; the boy may have some hereditary illness."
Later, in the worst of the quarrels, she made up a story that
she had been going to therapy regularly.

Little could be done for Sherman in individual therapy
either. Because of his mismanagement of money, he was
forced to discontinue therapy at an early stage. He ran up a
bill and the therapist decided to sue him. Once the suit began,
he paid what he owed and told the therapist, "You were quite

right to sue me." He settled down to his unhappy life, in despair that nothing could be done for him.

The son became increasingly unable to handle his mother's constant yellings. Even when he apologized for what he had done (minor misdeeds) she would say, "You did not apologize in the right tone of voice; I won't accept that." As father and son became more upset, she turned more and more into the castrating woman. Sex had long been out of the picture for the couple. The son, with a woman like his mother as a model, became an overt homosexual.

This case illustrates what happens in many marriages—a slow deterioration of the relationship because of the childhood disappointments of both parties. Sherman could never grow up and leave his mother's apron strings. Alice could never get over the stigma of her brother's hospitalization and the fear that it implicated her as well. And the son—he was ruined by the family battles.

JAMES L.: THE AVERAGE MIDWESTERNER

It has been argued often enough that Freud was deceived by his Victorian background and that analysts by and large have generalized too much from "sick" people. It would be more correct to say that once Freud discovered how neurotic or emotionally disturbed the average man can be, his findings were applied to all known cultures. Every society seems to have ingrained in it certain defects, as measured by the analytic ideal. It accepts these defects as "normal" for them and does not see how the lives of those who live in that society can be frustrated, sometimes quite severely, by the prevailing ideals.

In his book *The Psychological Frontiers of Society*, Abram Kardiner (1945) includes a section on "Plainville USA," a city somewhere in the midwest. This section was written by an ethnographer, James West. He selected four biographies, more or less at random, and notes that three of the four people were quite disturbed. One is James L.

James was born in Plainville in 1897, the oldest of four brothers. From eleven to fifteen he had to do all the farm work because his father was very ill. When he left home for a visit for the first time in his life he reports feeling "scared."

He left his family at fifteen, with the vague notion that what he wanted most was money, not education. He wanted to live better. Later he changed his mind and wanted an education but could not persist. He began to read which aroused in him the wish to be a writer. At eighteen he wrote a movie scenario but it was never accepted.

After a few years knocking around, he returned home, where he fell ill with typhoid fever. When he recovered he went off with his cousin to become a helper on a farm. He did not want to desert his cousin, who had a nervous illness and could not work. They rode freights for a while, then his cousin deserted him and he went on alone.

He then held a number of jobs. He joined the IWW even though he despised them. They tried to get more pay from the farmers, would threaten to set on fire a farmer's house if he "didn't come across." Then in 1916 he joined the army. He thought it would be an adventure to visit the Philippines or Hawaii. He also wanted to get a pension.

In 1917 as a soldier he found himself on the West Coast. He went out with a girl for three weeks, had sexual relations and then married her. She was not a virgin but he did not care. One day he came home to find her in bed with another man and he divorced her. His reasons for marriage were vague: "I thought it would be nice to have someone to come home to; I'd be going to France." He also said: "My marriage was not an enriching experience" and "I made many innocent girls suffer," referring to the number of girls he had victimized.

During the war he never saw service overseas but felt somewhat shell-shocked nevertheless. He had repeated nightmares, some of which would throw him out of bed. He disregarded these.

Once out of the service, he went back to Plainville but soon felt all the people there were hillbillies, poor and ignorant. He left for the nearest big city but did not stay there long. He had sex with a girl from the West and, for the first time in his life, felt satisfied with sex. He tried song-writing and had several songs printed. But he had no success with them and returned to Plainville.

This time he was more content with his home town and its denizens, including his brothers, one of whom drank too much. He decided to find a "good" girl in Plainville, marry her. He met Elinor, saw her as an ideal romantic mate and promised himself they would never quarrel, be ideal companions. This rosy image soon faded but he accepted "that's the way it would be."

Soon his marriage proved a disappointment because Elinor was frigid. He tried to "wake her up" sexually but to no avail: "Elinor was different; she wanted me to talk to her and worship her and kiss her." For a brief period after the birth of her second child, she became sexually responsive but during their nineteen years of marriage she never wanted intercourse, responding to his overtures only two or three times a month.

As a result, he was unfaithful to her twice. Both were anxious bout having too many children. Sex was frustrating and all he would think of was how he had to suppress his desires.

He felt no favoritism toward any of his children. They all preferred their mother and he accepted this as natural. His greatest problem was that the children did not want to help him with the farm work, which he disliked, and his wife encouraged them in their refusal. She would not permit him to leave the farm to seek work in a city, fearing he would become involved with other women.

His feeling about one brother who drank heavily was strong. His daughter married a man who also drank and James wanted both men sterilized. He resented another brother and feared his son-in-law, dreading the prospect of having to take care of his own grandchildren. His attitude toward his wife was one of extreme jealousy and he was extremely envious of all potential rivals.

His chief preoccupation was with the education of his children. Unable to gratify his own ambitions, he shifted to them: "I couldn't be a great writer, but my son will."

James is typical of his community. He is accessible, guardedly confidential and honest within the limits of telling as good a story as possible. Obviously everything in his life became a disappointment to him sooner or later—his wish to be a writer, his marriages, his sex life, his work, his children, and now even his grandchildren. He has not reacted with any classical neurotic symptoms; like so many others, he became resigned to his fate.

SIMON: THE FATHER OF THE SCHIZOPHRENIC

Schizophrenia remains the number one problem of mental health. Although if caught early it can be considerably ameliorated or even drastically altered, usually it is overlooked until too late. The tranquilizing drugs offer a little relief but in the long run do nothing to help the schizophrenic attain a meaningful life. The best treatment is long years of psychotherapy, which few have the patience or the means to accept.

Usually the plight of the schizophrenic is attributed to an overattachment to the mother. This is the most obvious aspect of the illness. The child never outgrows his mother. Frieda Fromm-Reichmann, one of the great pioneers in this field, even coined the term "schizophrenogenic mother," referring to the kind of mother who creates schizophrenia in her children.

Yet the father plays a significant role as well. A boy, in his growth, turns from mother to father and seeks encouragement and a model from him. If the father fails, then the boy falls back on mother, infancy and dementia.

Simon was an immigrant from Russia who came to this country around 1900. He was an orphan who had lost his mother and father at an early age. He was brought here by an uncle who took care of him through the formative years.

With little education, Simon got a job as a salesman of men's haberdashery, traveling for a large company. He married, prospered sufficiently enough to open a store in the early 1920's. As long as times were good, he managed adequately. The only drawback was that he had to be in the store day and night, even Sundays. The blue laws of that day forbid stores opening on Sunday but when the cop came around to give him a ticket he slipped the officer five dollars and was allowed to keep open.

Then the depression hit. The neighborhood changed from a lower middle-class to a lower-class area. In the early thirties Simon was bankrupt. He was then fifty. What was a man of his age, with no special talents, no education, no background to do? Fortunately his wife had some skill as a seamstress and she supported the family. Simon retired from the world, never worked again.

Simon had married after eight years of courtship. Premarital sex was taboo, he was a virgin who married a virgin. Sex for him was not very exciting and after a while it tapered off, eventually disappeared. The couple had one son, Albert.

Albert was a bright boy, but rather withdrawn and overprotected from the very beginning. When he was six he came down with St. Vitus' Dance (a convulsive disorder) which no doctor knew how to treat but in a short while it passed. He was regarded as a shy but talented boy.

Nothing seemed amiss until Albert entered college. In his first semester he complained that one of his teachers was "picking" on him. Instead of looking into this, his parents let him drop out of college. He then busied himself with a variety of activities—radio, photography, gardening, painting (he was a gifted artist). In all of these he would go a certain distance, do well, and then stop. It was clear neither parent wanted him to leave them. His only foray away from home was in the Civilian Conservation Corps which President Roosevelt set up in the early 1930's. His parents strongly opposed Albert's leaving them because he was too "delicate" for rough companionship but he threatened to run away if they did not give the necessary permission.

When Albert returned from the CCC, he went back to his old ways, staying at home, puttering about with one or another of his numerous interests, locked away from any male friends or female companionship. One day, in a fit of rage, he tried to choke his mother. His parents were frightened by this act, sent Albert to live with his aunt, his mother's only sister. Nobody in those days thought of psychotherapy.

Albert stayed with his aunt for a number of years, unreasoningly furious with his mother, though he would speak with his father. He continued his lonely life.

Then, after five years he attacked his father, trying to choke him as he had earlier tried to choke his mother. He ran away, was found unconscious in the park by a policeman. Sent to Bellevue Hospital, he was diagnosed schizophrenic and released. A psychiatrist who was consulted recommended electric shock, which was administered, and psychotherapy, which the psychiatrist discontinued after a few sessions.

Following shock treatment Albert returned to his parents' home. By this time some relatives who believed in psychotherapy realized how much Albert needed help and urged the parents to find treatment. In the meantime he was rejected by the army as unfit for military duty and again diagnosed schizophrenic. But the parents, especially the mother, felt he only "lacked ambition" and would not permit any kind of professional consultation. The father had completely retired, now well into his sixties, and could offer no opposition to his wife. Albert relapsed into a kind of stuporous silence. He would pass his days staring at the ceiling.

Thus the family continued to live out a typical domestic tragedy: father unemployed and useless, Albert silent and infantile, the mother working and providing support. Consciously no one believed anything was really wrong. The trio would spend their time together doing nothing in particular or on rare occasions socializing with a relative or a friend from the old country.

Nothing much seemed to happen in this climate of emotional exhaustion. Eventually Simon died of natural causes at seventy-two, his wife, of cancer a few years later. Albert, left to his own devices, could not cope. He was rehospitalized, developed malignant hypertension and died at fifty-two, alone and friendless.

One could only say of this father and son: two empty wasted lives. Literally two forgotten men.

SUMMARY

If the life of the average man is explored in more individualistic detail, a great deal of despair and tragedy is uncovered. These are the men of whom Thoreau said more than a hundred years ago: Most men live lives of "quiet desperation." (Thoreau himself, who died of unknown causes at forty-five, could never win the girl he wanted, could never become really self-supporting, was, in spite of his feelings about Walden Pond, also one of the despairing ones.) Many such men manage to make marriages in which the wife is the dominant figure. Psychologically, in these marriages the man still remains a boy, depends more on his wife's neurotic traits than anything else, seemingly helpless. Invariably the children of these marriages, as Albert did, experience immense suffering, sometimes complete insanity.

PART III: SOCIAL ROLE

Chapter 13:
The Politician:
Leader or Power-Seeker

Man, said Aristotle, is by nature a political animal. And indeed, as this philosopher noted more than two thousand years ago, the political system under which a man lives plays a more important part in the vicissitudes of his existence than anything else. As a rule, the system is something over which he has no control. Either he rebels or seeks reform or adapts himself to the system. Most men just adapt.

The only real rebellion against the American system was the Civil War; the only slavocracy in history that fought to maintain its slaves was the American south. It was put down in a bloody war which has still left its traces of bitterness; in the southern states the term "civil war" is forbidden, in its stead the term "war between the states" must be used.

The United States is a country which repeatedly has called for and brought forth reforms of all kinds. The politicians have either been reformers or conservatives. How successful their reforms is a matter subsequently discussed passionately and at great length by historians.

In other countries rebellion or conquest have been the rule. Europe has known peace only for the period after World War II, and then limited to western Europe. For two thousand years before then, one country after another set itself up by force of arms as the arbiter of Europe's destiny: Romans,

© 1987 by The Haworth Press, Inc. All rights reserved.   *225*

Frenchmen, Spaniards, Swedes, Austrians, and last, but by no means least, Germans.

Whatever the system, politicians have been the subject of intense scrutiny in every country. Biographies of national heroes and of other important figures in public life abound. Subsequent generations debate at great length whether their actions were beneficial or harmful to the country. The image of a nation, or country, has been such a pivotal one for the last two centuries that everything connected with it is of immense interest to its people.

The politician has two functions: he is a leader, and he holds the reins of power. If his leadership is inspiring and advantageous we refer to him as a statesman; yet few men are called statesmen. If his activities merely entrench him in power, and there are all too many such men, we call him a demagogue or a crooked politician. Between these two extremes lie most of those who have held office. Open demagogues or true statesemen are both rare.[1]

In a position of power, the politician must also adopt some attitude toward violence. He controls the organs of the state that are permitted legal violence: the army, the local militia, the police, the prison system. How he handles this control of violence is another factor in our estimation of him.

In our country the politician must also maintain the support of the electorate. Although the recall process is rarely found, except in local situations, every politician on the state or national level is acutely aware of how he is doing. Every president has a "popularity ratio" which is computed almost weekly and published in all the mass media. Whether he wants to or not, he pays careful attention to public opinion and molds his actions accordingly. Thus, President Franklin Roosevelt obviously wanted to support the British and French in their war against Hitler, but refrained from doing so because of a strong anti-war sentiment in the country. In fact, had Hitler not made the mistake of declaring war on the United States four days after Pearl Harbor, he might have avoided having our country as an enemy for several years.

Politicians also have the power of patronage. How they use this is another measure of their worth. In South American countries there is usually a law that a man must declare his wealth on entering and leaving office—the intent is obvious.

No such law exists here, but should a man in office enrich himself too much there are cries of outrage and possible prosecution. Officials at every level from governors to senators to Supreme Court justices have been sent to jail or threatened with jail for corruption in office; twice presidents have been impeached, though not convicted. From time immemorial corruption has been an ever-present facet of American public life. It is no secret that the chance to make a great deal of money is one of the factors that leads men to seek public office; even if they do not make it directly while in office they do so afterwards by writing (a president's memoirs will net him at least one million dollars), or using the influential contacts they have made.

Thus politics involves leadership, power, violence, money, prestige and other factors which act as powerful incentives. It is no wonder that when so much is at stake the politician should equivocate and at times lie. "Fourth of July speech" has become synonymous with worthless promises. There is always some gap between what politicians say they will do and what they actually do. Perhaps such a gap is inevitable, but for some it is much greater than for others.

The political leaders chosen for more detailed consideration here have been picked more or less at random. Since so many men aspire to be, and become politicians, generalizations about them are tenuous in the extreme. Each one has to be evaluated in accordance with the considerations mentioned above.

LYNDON JOHNSON AND THE AMERICAN DREAM[3]

Lyndon Johnson was a politician par excellence. He came to Washington at twenty-three as a legislative assistant, and he stayed there for thirty-seven years, as congressman, senator, vice-president, and finally as a result of President Kennedy's assassination, president. He was in many ways a typical American politician, with all the virtues and faults of the breed.

Toward the end of his life he was seized with the desire to write his memoirs. He found a young woman, Doris Kearns, instructor in government at Harvard University. She was also psychoanalytically sophisticated, and consulted with a number of psychoanalysts as she wrote his biography. Her work therefore is an invaluable source of data and insight on the man.

Johnson was born in Texas in 1908, the son of a small-time farmer and trader in real estate and cattle. The marriage of his parents was not a happy one. Lyndon worshipped his mother, who he felt had married beneath her. Her father had been a lawyer, educator and lay preacher in the Baptist church, and was viewed by his daughter as the paradigm of religious ideals, moral thought and civic duty. In the late 1870's he had served as secretary of state for Texas and afterward a member of the state legislature. With his encouragement Johnson's mother attended Baylor University where she majored in literature and planned to write a novel about the old South during the Civil War. But when her father died she married Sam Johnson, and gave up her ideals. Undoubtedly it was her inspiration that led to her son's championing the Great Society in his period in congress and as President. Lyndon's father also drank, which created further divisions within the family. No doubt the wish to rescue his mother from an unhappy marriage was one of the psychological roots of his concern for the underdog.[4]

Early in childhood, when the family had moved into town, Lyndon had a recurring nightmare: He would see himself sitting absolutely still in a big straight chair. The chair stood in the middle of the Great Plains. A stampede of cattle was rushing toward him. He tried to move but could not. He cried out again and again for his mother, but no one came to rescue him.[5] In another dream later in life, also recurring, he had become Woodrow Wilson, whom he regarded as too intellectual and too idealistic. In the dream his head was still his own but, from the neck down, his body was dead, victim of the paralysis which had held both Wilson and Johnson's grandmother down in their last years. Both dreams highlight his fears of being immobilized and attacked—all through his life he was constantly on the go.[6]

As he grew older, his father became politically active and spent several periods in the state legislature. He was a liberal fighting the Ku Klux Klan and defending civil liberties on all levels. Lyndon loved going with his father to the legislature. He would sit for hours in the gallery watching all the activity on the floor. The only thing he loved more was going on the trails with his father during the campaigns for reelection. But his father could never get beyond local politics.

For nearly a year when Lyndon was sixteen he went off with some friends to California, where he lived a vagabond life. Then he went back to Texas, with his future all mapped out in his mind. As he put it:

> I would become a political figure. Daddy would like that. He would consider it a manly thing to be. But that would be just the beginning. I was going to reach beyond my father. I would finish college; I would build great power and gain high office. Mother would like that. I would succeed where her own father had failed; I would go to the Capitol and talk about big ideas. She would never be disappointed in me again.[7]

No sooner said than done. He returned to college, where he preached the philosophy of success and where he involved himself in political activities on the campus to further worthy causes. "Do and dare"; "be brave and bold"; "strive and succeed" were the recurrent themes in his college editorials. He regarded ambition and self-mastery as the mainsprings of American activity, the driving wheels of cultural, social and economic progress. With a true Horatio Alger philosophy, he was convinced anyone could get ahead and succeed who wanted to and worked hard at it.

While in college and for fifteen months after graduation Johnson became a teacher—and loved it. Then he received an invitation to join the staff of Congressman Richard Kleberg, which he eagerly accepted. For the next thirty-seven years he remained in Washington, moving steadily ahead and enjoying every minute of it. Politics was truly in his blood. Yet underneath, as he told his biographer, he was lonely. On the one hand he was happy to be in the public eye; on the other he could use the public eye to hide his private fears.

Johnson arrived in Washington in the winter of 1931, when the country was in the throes of the Great Depression. Shortly thereafter President Roosevelt arrived on the scene, inspiring new faith and new hope in the country. With the liberal background he had acquired from both his father and father-in-law, it was only natural that Johnson should hitch his wagon to President Roosevelt's star. He did so immediately and enthusiastically; to the end of his days he remained the advocate of the New Deal for the common man.

There is no evidence in Johnson's career of any serious corruption. The one suspect activity is the radio station that he bought in 1943 for $17,500. In the first year the station showed a profit of $18. In ten years the assets of the station rose to nearly ten million dollars, and by 1964, the net earnings, with profits accruing to the Johnson family, exceeded $500,000 annually. No doubt there was some use of influence, since a broadcasting station was highly dependent on favorable decisions from the FCC, but there were never any accusations that Johnson used his power dishonestly or even unethically. Politics was the thing he cared most about in life, not money.

Once he became senator, Johnson siphoned more and more power into his office, until he exhibited an impressive mastery over the Senate unequalled in modern political history. While he was criticized for monopolizing so much power, no one claimed that he had any ulterior purpose. He felt his cause was right and that power was needed to put it into effect. And his cause remained that of the man he had admired above all others—FDR. In all his actions except one (the Vietnam War) Johnson remained the champion of the common man.

Yet with all this he did not have the charisma to reach the presidential pinnacle. His campaign against President John Kennedy in 1960 fizzled out, and he graciously accepted second place on the ticket.

After an early romance that collapsed, Johnson met Claudia Taylor in 1934. With his typical forthrightness he proposed and they were quickly married. Since childhood she had been known as "Lady Bird," and their children (two girls) were each given names beginning with the letters LB, so everyone in the family was LBJ. The marriage proved a happy and secure one.

Johnson became president by the accident of an assassination, but once at the top he pursued his "great society" program with absolute determination. Harriman later observed that if it had not been for Vietnam Johnson would have been the greatest president we ever had.

In retrospect Johnson was certainly faced with extremely difficult decisions when he assumed the presidency in 1963. Vietnam and the communist threat seemed like a bottomless pit. If he abandoned Saigon, the communists would overrun southeast Asia, including Indonesia, perhaps the Philippines. If he did not give up, he knew he was cooperating with a weak, unpopular dictatorial government which he must have privately despised. At first he temporized; an election was around the corner.

Johnson's position in the electoral campaign of 1964 was exactly the opposite of Goldwater's. The Arizona senator breathed fire and brimstone; he would defoliate Vietnam, use every available means of warfare and defeat the enemy totally. His position seemed so extreme to the average voter that Johnson won by the largest plurality in American history, his margin in the electoral college was second only to FDR's in 1936. Johnson could be satisfied that he was well loved by all the people.

Then, like most candidates in high office in American politics, he reversed his course and his electoral promises. The catchword became "escalation." In part Johnson seemed caught up in his own rhetoric, believed that the American threats would bring the North Vietnamese to their knees. In part, however, he did not know what to do, since retreat meant a communist victory and an American loss of face, with incalculable consequences.

Johnson inherited the Vietnam quagmire; he did not create it. Unable to resolve it, he temporized. Strong criticism and even civil disobedience were the consequences. Men fled to Canada and other countries to escape the draft; others simply refused to go. Unable to find a reasonable way out, Johnson finally gave up in 1968 and retired from politics altogether. Between 1964 and 1968 his support rating in the standard polls had dropped thirty-six points. He had lost control of the course of events, and he knew it. With all the discontent created by the war, it was inevitable that a Republican candidate would win the election in 1968; the candidate was Richard Nixon.

Upon his retirement Johson said: "The long hard effort was over now, and I was glad to see it end."[10] No doubt he meant what he said. His health was no longer so good (a heart attack in 1955 had been a premonitory warning) and he felt he had done as good a job as he could. After five years out of office he died in 1973, of a heart attack.

If it had not been for Vietnam Johnson might well have reached the status of statesman. He was basically an idealistic politician, who used the political arena to further the idealistic causes in which he believed. Scandals that had rocked other administrations did not occur in his. But after a certain point the politician displays his real weaknesses: the realistic problems of the world become more than he can handle. Nevertheless, for all his faults Johnson led a vigorous and on the whole a happy life. He realized his ambitions to a far greater degree than most other men.

RICHARD NIXON: THE PARANOID REALITY[11]

The experience of Watergate remains one of the most shocking in American history. There have been other scandals, including in some cases the presidency, but none where the entire administration acted in such a brazen manner with so little provocation, and where so many, including the attorney general, were sent to jail. While Nixon was pardoned, he remains the kingpin of the affair.

All through his life Nixon felt under severe attack. His battle with the media was notorious; when he failed to win election as governor of California in 1962, he said to the media: "Now you won't have Dick Nixon to kick around." In 1973, before his resignation, he said to John Dean: "Nobody is a friend of ours; let's face it."[12]

The mystery of how a man with such a warped psychological outlook could rise to be president is indeed worth pondering. He was born in 1913, the third of five sons of Frank Nixon, who had successively been through a variety of occupations— streetcar motorman, farmer, carpenter, grocer and butcher. Frank had endured a harsh childhood. His mother died of tuberculosis when he was seven and he was sent to live with relatives. At eleven he returned home to a stepmother he hated and who beat him. Frank's brother said of him: "He became aggressive . . . slow to anger but a wild bull if things went too far."[13] He fled from his stepmother at fourteen and became a drifter. Somehow he reached California, and there he married, though his wife's family felt she had married beneath her. Frank Nixon is described as a chronically angry man, ulcer-ridden from the early years of his marriage, crude, brittle, who invited hatred in his own family. Richard tried consciously to be as unlike his father as possible.[14]

Marriage and home life were not happy for Richard. Of the five brothers, one was killed in a rock-fighting affray with other boys,[15] while a second died of tuberculosis. For several years his parents were separated while the mother took care of the tuberculous son.[16] The scars of his childhood remained with Nixon all his life.

Still, he showed great determination to get ahead. Once in college he became president of his freshman class, president of his fraternity, president of the History Club and campaigned against what he called "political dictators" to become president of the student body. Everywhere he was out to win—power had already become a life goal for him. Although he had musical training, he had no talent for innocent abandon. Life was a grim business for him. Nor was he, in spite of all his activities, particularly popular. When his alma mater honored him with a doctorate in 1954 a line formed that refused to shake hands with him.[17]

Once out of college, he went to law school, where he led what his biographer calls a "monastic existence." As a lawyer he did not get too far. Admitted to the bar in 1937, as late as 1940 he was considering a move to Havana. In his first case the judge was so shocked by his behavior that he said:

> Mr. Nixon, I have serious doubts whether you have the ethical qualifications to practice law in the state of California. I am seriously thinking of turning this matter over to the Bar Assocation.[18]

It is of course difficult to evaluate anybody's marriage from the outside. But most observers are agreed Nixon's marriage to Pat was never a happy one. In public he almost never touched her. It was believed, on fairly good authority, that he suffered from experiences of impotence fairly early, that he drank too much, that he slept poorly, and had other neurotic problems. In later life his closest friend was Bebe Rebozo, while Pat had a woman friend with whom she spent a lot of time. As Nixon once said of himself:

> I can have fun playing poker, being with friends. But any letting down my hair, I find that embarrassing, even with Pat.[19]

Again Nixon stands in marked contrast to Johnson, who felt so free about himself that he could suddenly take off all his clothes in the middle of a gathering at the White House, invite all and sundry to do the same and take a dip in the White House pool.

Nixon's record during World War II was not distinguished. He was an operations officer in the Pacific, saw little combat. What he and everybody who knew him then has emphasized is that he was a great poker player and did very well at it during the war years.

Shortly after leaving the service Nixon entered politics. His first campaign, against Jerry Voorhis, was typical of his approach. He attacked Voorhis as a dangerous socialist with ties to the communists, though he knew not a word of it was true. In the post-war hysteria he won.[20]

Vigorous unsparing attacks became his stock in trade. In Congress his main achievement was to spearhead the trial and conviction of Alger Hiss. Without any reluctance he even attached himself to the McCarthy slander campaign which attacked everybody in sight, once even President Eisenhower by insinuation.[21]

In 1952 he had his great chance, when Eisenhower picked him as running mate. But then came a grave crisis: It was revealed he had used campaign funds to bolster his private life to the tune of about $1,000 per month. In the public outcry many urged Eisenhower to drop him, but he refused. Finally Nixon himself had to offer an explanation in his famous Checkers speech (Checkers was the name of his dog). He denied any wrongdoing, was exonerated and the whole incident became papered over.[22]

In the years before 1968 he led an undistinguished life as a conservative politician. In 1960 he lost by the narrowest of margins to Kennedy; in 1962 he could not be elected governor of California. He seemed finished. But a new chance came in 1968, when the country was weary of the Vietnam nightmare.

Nixon was nominated and won easily; no democratic candidate could have won that year.

As president his most dramatic action was taking the initiative to reopen relations with China and Russia; however what long-term effects these contacts produced can be questioned. The same result could have been achieved with fewer histrionics.

Then came Watergate, and the facade collapsed. At first Nixon denied any complicity; gradually his role in the affair came out in the open more and more. Once he was impeached by Congress, he decided to resign. The scandal rocked almost every member of his administration.

The motives that led Nixon and his buddies to authorize a break-in into the Democratic Party headquarters at Watergate, an apartment complex in Washington, are still obscure. Liddy says in his memoirs that the Republicans only wanted to know what the Democrats knew about them.[23] Still, Nixon's entire conduct in the affair was saturated with such arrogance, dishonesty and self-righteousness that he left in complete disgrace, the only president who has ever resigned while in office. Had he not been pardoned by President Gerald Ford, he might very well have gone to jail.

Once he was out of the White House, people started asking how did this happen, and a more rounded picture of the man began to appear. For years he had been consulting a physician in New York by the name of Arnold Hutschneker, an internist with no specialized psychiatric training. A variety of problems came out which led to the consultations. Nixon's associates all wrote revealing memoirs which plumbed the depths of political deviltry. Even murder was cooly contemplated. Nixon, it was seen, had a strong paranoid streak, which always made him feel that people were out to get him.

It is clear that Nixon represents in the political arena the man whose major goal is power. He gave his intimates the feeling he was in power and that they could do anything they wanted. And, like any paranoid individual, to this day he denies the evidence of any wrongdoing.

THE KENNEDYS: A POLITICAL DYNASTY[24]

The Kennedy family has had four members active in politics—a president, an ambassador, an attorney-general and a

presidential aspirant, and a senator and a presidential aspirant. Before the present generation, two others had been in
local politics in the Boston area—Joseph Kennedy's father
and the father of his wife, Rose Kennedy. It was thus a family
born and bred to money and politics.

Joseph Kennedy was the progenitor of the more famous
Kennedys. He acted in his life with admirable determination
and clearness of purpose which became a legend. Born in
1888, he first went into business. Before he was forty he had
amassed a fortune, enough to give every one of his nine children a million-dollar trust. Then he retired from business,
with excellent timing, for he left Wall Street in 1926, three
years before the crash. Money no longer interested him, nor
did he encourage any of his sons to go into business. Politics
became his obsession as long he could function at it, and he
single-mindedly pushed all his sons into the political field. But
tragedy stalked the family.

Joe, the oldest was accounted by all the most charming and
the most promising. Then he was killed in an airplane accident in 1944, during World War II. John, always a sickly
child, the next oldest, became senator, then president in 1960,
only to be assassinated three years later. Next was Bobby,
attorney-general under his brother, presidential favorite in
1968, assassinated by an Arab fanatic, without apparent reason. Of the boys, there remained Teddy (Edward) whose
presidential hopes were temporarily spoiled by a wild party at
Chappaquiddick in which a young woman was mysteriously
drowned while in his car. This incident still clouds his future.
Of the Kennedy girls, one turned out to be retarded. Another
married an Englishman killed in World War II; she died later,
also in an airplane crash.

Three of Joseph's sons followed the path he had laid out
for them. Given enough money to make them independently
wealthy, they entered politics as soon as they could. It was
only natural with their Irish heritage that they should become
democrats and champion the cause of the underdog. James
Joyce has one of his characters say: "History is a nightmare
from which I am trying to awake."[25]

Joseph Kennedy, Sr. was a devoted family man, though he
was also, as was well-known in his day, an avid womanizer.
But his major concern was always the future of his sons.

Arthur Schlesinger describes the family environment in this way: the athletic code was accompanied by equally incessant pressure for intellectual development. At mealtime the father liked to preside over a family seminar. Among the children the two older boys did most of the talking. Their father sometimes took the other side in order to sharpen the discussion. There was no frivolity; but the meals were always exhilarating and fun.[26]

The forbidden topic was business. The father had made enough money not to have to make any more, and he saw no reasons for his son to do what he had done. None of the children showed any interest in business later in life. In any event, Joseph Kennedy thought, the reign of money as such was over: "The boys might as well work for the government, because politics will control the business of the country in the future."[27]

The father's concern followed the children everywhere. He made comments about John's penmanship. His whole effort was to make the children independent of him. They were given tasks of responsibility. He even sent them to teachers or political leaders who held views quite different from his. Courage, accomplishment, victory were the virtues and goals he drilled into them and which they internalized. The children seemed to love the father; the home in turn was a very happy one.

As was to be expected, all three brothers (Joe had died during the war) became lawyers and entered politics early. In their academic work they were not distinguished. Teddy, in fact, was dropped from Harvard because he persuaded another student to take an examination for him. Eventually he was readmitted and graduated.[28] But none of the boys were unusually bright; perhaps they all realized they were headed for politics and did not care about the academic world.

In accordance with the family code, all showed unusual courage. John was wounded in a PT boat encounter with the Japanese during World War II; he helped save a number of his fellow-soldiers behind the lines. But as a result of war injuries he became saddled for life with a bad back. Teddy broke his back later in an airplane crash. Bobby, physically fit, sought out one dangerous sport after another. He climbed a 14,000 foot mountain named after his brother; he skied down precipitous slopes; he shot rapids in western rivers; on a trip down the Colorado he dove into rushing water. One of his skiing companions said of him: "He obviously enjoyed approaching the brink of the impossible."[29]

All three Kennedys were womanizers; it was well-known and kept quiet. John's amours were revealed more fully long after his death; Bobby's were less prominent. Teddy finally divorced his wife after much sorrow and unhappiness. The mishap at Chappaquiddick dogged him many years after the event.

What kind of politicians did the Kennedys make? They certainly were not corrupt; there was no need to make more money. They were not inordinately hungry for power. The greatest political mistake any of them made was John's approval of the Bay of Pigs invasion of Cuba in 1961, and secondly, their apparent approval, or at any rate, lack of strong disapproval, of McCarthy's witch-hunting in the early fifties. But on the whole they were the champions of the underdog, they pushed civil rights. Bobby Kennedy succeeded in breaking the hold of Jimmy Hoffa and other labor racketeers, Teddy Kennedy consistently introduced his programs for making medical care available for the poor and indigent. They enjoyed being in positions of power without abusing it, and they fought for their ideals, giving whatever it took. The deaths of John and Robert were woeful tragedies; had they lived, the course of world history might well have been different.

HUEY LONG: AN AMERICAN DEMAGOGUE[30]

In 1935 a group of men in Louisiana gathered and swore they would overthrow the regime of Governor Huey Long by force. He had oppressed the people, violated their liberties, set up a system of government answerable only to him. His nickname "Kingfish" was fully deserved; when he was still in high school he had announced he could sell anything on earth to anybody. And he had sold himself to Louisiana and now controlled it hook, line and sinker. A few weeks later he was assassinated.[31]

Although a lawyer by profession, Long was fascinated by

politics as far back as he could remember. He entered politics at an early age, became governor of Louisiana in 1928 before he was thirty-five, a senator several years later, and a figure of national importance between 1930 and 1935, when he was killed.

His father was a farmer, comfortable but not rich. A number of members of his family went into politics, even though he himself remained on his farm. Long's younger brother Earl was the only three-time governor of Louisiana.

Long was not particularly close to his family. Once in power, when he controlled a large amount of patronage, he gave some of them jobs, but of minor importance. He once said: "I'd like to get as far away from my damn kinfolks as I could."[32] He married in 1913, when only twenty, but never seemed particularly close to his wife and children. When he became governor in 1928 they did not even live with him, though there was never any official separation. There were rumors of his long-standing affair with a pretty young secretary, but they were only rumors; he never seems to have been strongly attracted to women. Power and politics were his consuming obsessions.

On his way up the political ladder Huey espoused a program of social and economic reform. When he became nationally prominent in the early 1930's he preached a Share-the-Wealth program as a way out of the Great Depression; in this respect he resembled Father Coughlin, another demagogue of the depression, who at one time was said to have commanded a radio audience of eight million.

On his way to the governorship Long had played fast and loose with just about everybody. He had hardly been installed in the governor's office than impeachment charges were introduced against him. One of the claims was that he had ordered the assassination of a long-time enemy. Although the charges were of course denied, and an impeachment trial never came to pass, the hatred Long had engendered was enormous.[33]

Long made no secret of his presidential ambitions. When President Coolidge visited New Orleans in 1930, a picture was taken of the two men which Long described as a "picture of past and future presidents."[34] He wrote a book, *My First Days in the White House,* published in 1935 shortly after his death.[35] He preached economic revolution in the senate and one columnist described him as "strong, bitter, merciless and inflaming." President Roosevelt, for him, was much too conservative; his opinions of most of his senatorial and governmental colleagues were spicily unprintable. Few, however, believed that he was after anything other than power, much as had been the case in his career in Louisiana.

As a politician Long's craze for power is his most obvious trait. After a while no one believed any of his promises, or anything he said; it was clear his main goal was to get rid of his enemies and consolidate his power. During his lifetime he was regarded by many as a dangerous man, an American equivalent of Mussolini or Hitler, then startling the world with their political ambitions. In retrospect he merely looks like a small-time politician, narcissistic, vainglorious, poorly educated, who strutted his hour on the stage raucously and moved on.

JOHN ADAMS AND THE AMERICAN REVOLUTION[36]

In marked contrast to the demagoguery of Huey Long and the underhandedness and trickery of Richard Nixon, stands another famous American dynasty—the Adams. Two of them, John and John Quincy, rose to be presidents; many others were prominent in service to the nation. All represented a thoroughly democratic approach to the political scene.

John Adams, the first vice-president and second president of the country, was born in 1735 on a farm near Boston. He trained as a schoolteacher, then lawyer. Not a flamboyant or exhibitionistic man, he was content to quietly do his duty for the new country. Only recently have the achievements of this modest man received proper appreciation.

In 1802 Adams wrote an autobiography for his children; a diary, innumerable letters and several publications have also come down to us. They display a reflective man, with a happy home life, who was an idealistic leader in the political arena.

Particularly noteworthy was an extraordinarily harmonious marriage. Many of the love letters between him and Abigail, married to him for fifty-four years, who bore him five children, have been preserved. Too little attention has been paid to the relationship between personal happiness and the degree to which leaders resort to violence and dictatorship. Consider this entry from his diary in March 1754, when he was only nineteen years old:

> This morning is beyond description. Beautyfull, the Skie bespangled with Clouds which shed a lustre on us by the refraction of the rays of light, together with the healthy and enlivening air, which was purifyed By the thunder, afford most spirited materials for Contemplation. The gaiety of the weather is equally delightful to the phylosopher, Poet and the man of Pleasure.[37]

With such thoughts, it is understandable that he would be particularly apt to believe there is danger from all men who enjoy power and the greatest danger from those who enjoy the greatest power.

Afer an early period as a lawyer Adams devoted the rest of his life to politics. He was active in all the undertakings of the new republic, as a signer of the Declaration of Independence, a member of the constitutional convention, later a diplomat then vice-president, and finally a president. There is no evidence he benefitted in any way from his political labors.

The constant round of labor on behalf of the colonies was not easy. In 1774 he wrote his wife:

> I was first sworn in 1758; My Life has been a continual Scene of Fatigue, Vexation, Labour and Anxiety. I have Four Children. I had a pretty Estate from my Father. I have been assisted by your Father. I have done the greatest business in the Province. I have had the richest Clients in the Province. Yet I am Poor in Comparison of others.[38]

It has often been argued that the American Revolution was a bourgeois revolution, in contrast to the French or the Russian, and that it is to this fact the absence of large-scale violence can be attributed. Our psychohistorical researches suggest an entirely different answer. The men who made the American revolution—Adams, Washington, Jefferson, Franklin among others—were on the whole mild-mannered individuals who had no insatiable lust for power. Many, like Adams, were happily married and found considerable contentment in their home lives. If they are contrasted with men like Stalin, Hitler, or Rasputin (to be discussed below), marked differences are noted. The Americans were men who fought for their ideals; the others fought for power, and once obtained, used it to exercise a cruel vengeance on their enemies.

RASPUTIN: THE SEXUAL MONK[39]

Grigory Rasputin (1872–1916) was a political figure of some importance in the Czarist empire. He is the kind of man who can flourish only in an autocratic climate, since as a politician his influence was limited to the advice he could give to the Czar and the Czarina. There is available a biography of him by his daughter which provides some interesting details.

Rasputin was born in Siberia and led a life as a peasant and a mystic until he became known as an unordained man of religion with unusual abilities to cure the sick. In Russian "rasputin" means "debauchee," and evidently part of his healing method was rather indiscriminate sexual intercourse. It is striking that his introduction to sex follows a classical Freudian model. Irina Kubasova, was married to an artillery officer forty years her senior (it can reasonably be surmised that she felt frustrated in her sex life). She began to seduce Rasputin, still a virgin and smitten with her. She invited him to her summer house and acted enticingly, stroking his penis through his trousers. He was placed in a room and directed to undress. The curtains fell and he suddenly found himself surrounded by Irina and three young girls. It was a cruel hoax. The girls then threw him out naked into the street.[40]

Smarting from this sexual teasing he married, sired some children, then began to wander around Siberia as a holy man, a common enough sight in those days. One time he came across three young girls swimming in the nude. He approached them and seduced them one by one. There and then was born his philosophy of spiritual awakening through sexual assuagement.[41]

After wandering around Russia, he reached St. Petersburg in 1905 and was introduced to the royal family a few months later. The heir to the throne, Alexis, was a hemophiliac (bleeding difficult to stop) and went through much suffering.

When Rasputin by some magic demonstrated his ability to ease the boy's suffering, he was welcomed into the family circle of the Czar as a close and trusted friend. The empress came to revere him as a holy man sent by God to save her son, the Romanov dynasty and the Russian autocracy.

With the royal family Rasputin consistently maintained the posture of a humble, circumspect and holy peasant. Outside court, however, was an entirely different matter. His doctrine was that one must sin before salvation. To this end he kept seducing women, acquiring numerous mistresses and constantly trying to seduce others.[42] By 1911 his behavior had become a general scandal. But since he was under the protection of the royal family, no one could touch him. It was even rumored at one point he had sex with the empress.

During World War I, the emperor went to the front, leaving control in the hands of his wife. She managed affairs badly, relying heavily on Rasputin's advice; he was obviously not fit for the task.

Finally a group of extreme conservatives, horrified by the turn events were taking, plotted to murder him. They felt they were saving the Russian autocracy, completely oblivious of the chaotic social conditions which led to the revolution the next year. In December 1916 he was assassinated and his body thrown into the river.[43]

Another Freudian touch is provided by his daughter. She claimed she had a relic of her father's, found under his picture in a polished wooden box. The relic was eighteen inches long and six inches wide, with an inlaid silver crest on the top. This was said to be Rasputin's penis, which had been cut off by the assassins after they killed him.[44]

Rasputin was obviously a fraud who wanted only power and sex, which he got by convincing the royal couple he had magical control over sickness. His story is a commentary on the kind of culture that prevailed in pre-revolutionary Russia.

WINSTON CHURCHILL: LEADER WITHOUT A FOLLOWING[45]

Winston Churchill was a born leader of men, but because of conflicting ideals in his own mind, and the times in which he lived, he could exercise his leadership adequately in only one period, that of World War II.

Churchill came of an illustrious British family. He was born in Blenheim Palace, named after the great victory of his ancestor, John Churchill, first duke of Marlborough, hero of the wars against Louis XIV in the early 18th century. Winston's father, Randolph Churchill, had been a prominent Tory member of Parliament. By background and temperament Winston was most suited for the conservative party, but at the same time he was fully imbued with liberal ideals, so that he was torn all his life between liberalism and conservatism.

His childhood was unusually unhappy. His father had married a beautiful American, Jennie Jerome, but the marriage was not a happy one. It was soon discovered Randolph had syphilis and,[46] since there was no effective remedy against the disease at that time, he gradually sank to a lingering death and toward the end he went completely mad.[47] Unable to have sex with her husband, his wife took a number of lovers and eventually married one twenty years her junior.[48]

The effect of such a disturbed sexual life in his parents was to steer Winston away from sex altogether. He was once accused of homosexuality but when he brought a libel suit, the accusation was dropped. He married at thirty-four, had several children, but he does not strike one as a man who ever had much of a passion for women. His passions were war and politics.

Both parents neglected the boy and criticized him severely. In school he did poorly and behaved badly. His only solace was his nanny, Mrs. Everest. Since he seemed to have no head for learning he was sent to military school. After graduation, he craved action. No British war was going on so he went to Cuba as a war correspondent. Here he began to make his mark as a writer, and many of his books, especially about campaigns in which he had been engaged, became best sellers.

His first venture into politics came in 1899, when he was barely twenty-five. In this election he lost, but a year later he won and became a member of parliament. There he remained on and off until old age forced his retirement in 1956.

Since he admired his father intensely, and was proud of his heritage, he naturally started out as a Conservative. But three years later he switched to the Liberal Party. Thereafter he veered from one view to the other, never quite sure of what direction to follow. Because of his vacillation he never acquired any large political following.

In World War I Churchill was in charge of the admiralty as a member of the cabinet. The general impression was that he favored the campaign in the Dardanelles and Gallipoli, which proved disastrous for the British forces. Apparently this is only partially true; in any case the defeats in Turkey brought about his resignation in 1915.[49]

Thereafter Churchill was not welcomed by any major party, so he remained an ordinary member of parliament. Then World War II came and offered him his greatest opportunity.

There can be little doubt that without Churchill, Great Britain would have had a much harder time in the war. He promised his people, "blood, toil, sweat and tears" but they worshipped him. Although he made military mistakes here as well, he was not the chief commander of the allied forces so his mistakes were not fatal, as were those of the French high command. Further, his capacity for organization made itself felt, and he participated admirably in the build-up of a powerful war machine which eventually defeated the Nazis.

When the war ended Britain, tired of its far-flung empire, voted the Labour Party in and Churchill out. In peacetime again he was unclear about his ideals and had no great following. Although he held office again from 1951 to 1956, his performance in that period did not compare with what he did during the war.

Mention should be made of his extraordinary literary output, for which he received the Nobel Prize for Literature in 1953.

As a politician Churchill was certainly above reproach. His judgment could be faulted at times, but his honesty could not. Yet, except for the period of the war his record is not a distinguished one. As one commentator has put it, had he died before the war broke out, he would have been considered a magnificent failure.

While he obviously loved power, he did not abuse it in any way. Nor did he have any use for violence, in spite of his predilection for warlike situations he was personally a very peaceful man. Except for his fondness for liquor, he managed to overcome many of the handicaps of his childhood and lead a reasonably contented life full of pleasure and achievement. His chief weakness, as we have mentioned, was his lack of clear-cut ideals, so that men did not know where he led. He once said he had not assumed office in order to preside at the dismantling of the British Empire, yet that is precisely the fate history had in store for him.

SUMMARY

Politicians can be looked at in terms of leadership, power, violence and ideals. A review of a number of political figures in the last two centuries reveals that they come in all sizes and shapes. Men who love power are often drawn to politics, as the political scientist Harold Lasswell showed more than fifty years ago (*Psychopathology and Politics,* 1930). Excessive power and corruption (loss of ideals) have always been the dangers involved in political struggles. The capacity for personal happiness plays a strong role in warding off these dangers.

Chapter 14:
Business Is Business

The life of the business man centers around making money. Yet he must also be efficient, calculate profits and losses carefully, estimate future prospects in a variety of ways; in short he becomes a manager of a firm. Since how a man earns money depends so much on social and economic circumstances, personalities of businessmen will vary more with the times than those of other fields. However, one common element is that the businessman wants to earn money and very often how he does it is irrelevant to him.

Max Weber, the German sociologist, coined the term "Protestant ethic" to describe the ideology of the man who devoted himself to business within the capitalistic framework. According to Weber such a man finds religious sanction for his money-making activities, provided he gives up all spontaneous enjoyment of life. Thus arose the image of the Puritan—industrious, hard-working, religious, forbidding even minor pleasures such as dancing or acting on pain of divine punishment.

It is impossible to determine how many men tried to fit themselves into this scheme of things over the centuries. Certainly many did; many others did not. For if the goal is to make money, the temptation to transgress is great, and obviously many have transgressed. Shady business practices are a matter of everyday observation, and outright crime is frequently countenanced. Laws have to be passed to curb such practices, and an army of lawyers grows up to intepret these laws.

Most interest has always attached to those businessmen who made fortunes. How did they do it? Were they lucky, or was it the result of ingenuity and hard work? Balzac once remarked that behind every fortune lies a crime; how much truth is there to that?

When America was bursting at the seams industrially after

© 1987 by The Haworth Press, Inc. All rights reserved.

the Civil War, a number of men became millionaires by tactics that were legal within the law of that day or could be covered over by rewarding legislators and judges. The millionaires were dubbed "robber barons" by the embattled farmers of Kansas, and the tactics which created such immense wealth have been studied at considerable length. Of these millionaires Francis Bacon's remark seems appropriate: "There are never wanting some persons of violent and undertaking natures, who, so they may have power and business, will take it at any cost."[1]

The rise of the great fortunes induced a counter-reaction, as the disparity between poverty and wealth became increasingly apparent. Reform movements were started by the hundreds. The "muckrakers" (raking up muck) were journalists who dug up all the unsavory activities which had led to the establishment of the fortunes. Laws were passed to curb the excesses; corruption in the police, legislatures and courts was attacked.

Under these circumstances the life of the businessman underwent rapid changes. Although millions still went into business hoping to make it big, more than 80% failed. The percentage of self-employed dropped from 80% in 1800 to 8.5% in 1980. Thus the dream of the businessman to go off on his own and make a fortune has become increasingly unrealistic. Yet the dream persists.[2]

Today big business is stronger than ever before. Technological advances create different opportunities, and fortunes are still made by those who know how to exploit new technologies, like Land of Polaroid, or Wang in computers. But even new technologies usually require large amounts of capital to get off the ground, which limits the opportunities.

As a result the corporation man, or the organization man, as he has been called, has become the latest prototype of the businessman. One study reports that the urge to be a technician, a collaborator, shows most markedly in the kinds of jobs college seniors prefer. They want to work for somebody else. Paradoxically, the old dream of independence through a business of one's own is held almost exclusively by factory workers, the one group least able to fulfill it. Consistently college placement officers who deal with the seniors find that of the men who intend to go into business—roughly one half of the class—less than 5% express any desire to be an entrepreneur. About 5% to 10% plan to go into their father's business. Of the rest, most have one simple goal: the big corporation.[3]

Since the life of the businessman varies so widely with the times, we have chosen men from the past two centuries to examine more closely what their lives and motives have been like. Generalizations are tricky here; it may well be that the next generation will again have a radically new philosophy, especially if the trend toward bureaucratization continues.

JOHN D. ROCKEFELLER: "THE MOST HATED MAN IN THE WORLD"[4]

John D. Rockefeller was the first man to earn a billion dollrs, and with it he founded a family dynasty. He made his fortune by monopolizing the oil industry (much as the Arabs are trying to do today). Yet to a later generation just why he was so hated in his day is somewhat of a mystery.

Rockefeller was born in 1839 on a farm in upstate New York. His father, William Avery, was a rather unsavory character, the details of whose life only leaked out when reporters were trying to ferret out John D.'s past.

The elder Rockefeller, though he lived on a farm, wanted to be in business. He was apparently a roving speculator, dealing in horses, timber, salt and patent medicines. But he was also a good-natured fraud, philanderer, quack doctor and a bigamist.[5] In another city he lived under the name of Dr. Levingston. When John D. was ten, in 1849, his father was indicted for rape, but not convicted.[6] He also held himself out as a cancer specialist, who could cure all cases except "those too far gone and they can be greatly benefited."[7] The biographer calls him a mixture of a charlatan and a puritan.[8] He was a light-hearted man, careless of his morals (he would stay away from home for months at a time), who lived to the ripe old age of ninety-five.

Although John D. admired his father, his own life moved in an entirely different direction. He was a quiet, taciturn man, with few obvious needs (he once said: "I never had a craving for anything"),[9] devoted to the church and his family, whose major interest in life was making money. Apart from money, whatever emotion he needed to release came forth in the Erie St. Baptist church. He was baptized by immersion in 1854 at the age of fifteen and thereafter the church remained central to his life.

School held little attraction for him and it was over by the time he was sixteen. Accounting and bookkeeping fascinated him and he methodically looked for a job in all the firms in Cleveland, finally landing one with a commission house as a bookkeeper at $4 a week. At this job he worked as though he owned the firm. Business became his life. He was at his desk at 6:30 A.M. and often returned to the office at night. Once he tried to stop: "I have this day covenanted with myself not to be seen in No. 45 after 10 o'clock within thirty days. . . . Don't make any more such covenants."[11]

Numbers were as important as money. In his diary he listed every cent spent, including gifts to church and charity. The story went that in his old age it was his custom to give the golf caddies bright new shiny dimes. When the depression hit and he lost $100 million, shrinking his assets from $1 billion to $900 million, he replaced the dimes with bright new shiny nickels. He seemed to have no inner life unconnected with numbers.

The only dream he ever reported was a recurrent one in which he was still trying to collect old bills. He would wake up exclaiming: "I can't collect so-and-so's account."[12]

In April 1859, shortly before his twentieth birthday he opened his own commission house with a friend, Maurice Clark. The firm prospered, especially with the outbreak of the Civil War. They handled all kinds of commodities, including kerosene. Early in 1860 he handled some of the crude oil that was reaching Cleveland. Soon John started a refining business, though not yet sensing the unbelievable profits that lay ahead.

He was always described in pretty much the same way: studious, grave, reserved, never noisy or given to boisterous play, an unassuming youth who never showed any of the hilarity usually seen in boys of that age, usually sitting quietly in a chair listening intently to what was said, invariably courteous to everybody.

Underneath this calm exterior lay an all-consuming ambi-

tion to beat out the next fellow. As an old man he once
reported a dream:

> I was sitting on a lawn, and I was told that someone
> looking rather like a ruffian wanted to see me—and they
> all advised me not to see him, that he meant no good.
> "I'll see him," I said, and he appeared. And I said to
> him nicely, sweetly, "sit down;" and he sat down next to
> me, and I talked to him nicely, quietly and he said, "of
> course, if it's shooting you want—all these people here
> are quite ready to shoot." Well, I talked to him and I
> won him over, and he departed. All good."[13]

The dream brings out on the one hand his need to curb his
own aggression, on the other to beat everybody out.

In 1864 he married Laura Spellman, whom he had met in
high school. She was a feminist of that day and believed very
strongly that a "woman can paddle her own canoe." The
marriage was a close and happy one. He never made any
important decision without consulting her.[14]

Rockefeller soon intuited the possibilities in oil and began
to concentrate on the business. He prospered, and by 1870
had formed the Standard Oil Company of Ohio, with a capi-
talization of $1 million. He had 2667 shares. His career was
launched. He saw the oil industry as plagued by cut-throat
competition, and evidently had made up his mind to conquer
it and end the competition. But that was still many years
ahead.

His plan, like that of most of the robber barons of his day,
involved increasing control of the oil business. First he dealt
with the refiners, either bought them out or forced them out.
Then he faced the oil producers and did the same. Eventually
he had control of the entire industry, which allowed him to
manipulate prices in both buying and selling.

His scheme was not really exposed until Ida Tarbell's famous book *History of the Standard Oil Co.* was published in
1904. There was actually little allegation of fraud or excessively sharp practices in Tarbell's book. It essentially exposed
how a monopoly was set up, paving the way for the later
anti-trust legislation. The worst part of the exposé concerned

the rebates railroads had given him to lower the cost of his products, an era when the railroads were thoroughly corrupt and using rebates to feather their own nests.

By 1875 he was officially a millionaire. Yet he maintained a simple way of life. He never went to the theater, rarely attended a symphony or read books; the newspapers satisfied him. He paid little attention to politics unless it affected the interests of Standard Oil. His pleasures were those he had enjoyed as a boy, ice skating, swimming, driving a team of horses at a fast trot. He was a meat and potatoes man who dined out as little as possible. He favored a glass of milk and an apple before he went to sleep. He was in no way pretentious. When he took his business to New York, he rode the elevated to his office. He belonged to no clubs. Business and business alone was his all-consuming passion.

Then in 1878 he was indicted with eight of his associates on criminal charges. Among them were conspiracy to monopolize the oil industry and conspiracy to oppress the Allegheny Valley Railroad. Soon he had bribed enough influential persons to bring the charges to a dead stop. His activities went unchecked until the Supreme Court ordered his holding company, Standard Oil of New Jersey, dissolved.

By 1913 his fortune had climbed to a third of a billion dollars. He was then seventy-four. After that he no longer took a very active interest in his business, leaving it in the hands of his son John D. Jr. and turning to an extraordinary increase in charitable gifts. He lived to be ninety-seven.

In retrospect Rockefeller's life represents a paradox. What motivated this man, who led an unblemished life, who did not flaunt his wealth, who still regularly taught a Sunday school class, to cheat and lie his way to a great fortune? He remained confident that God was on his side, that he had never done any wrong. His refusal to talk to reporters left them with no story to write. Even when Joseph Pulitzer uncovered his father's unsavory past, he would not say a word.

Rockefeller was neither educated nor introspective. In some way he must have been driven by the image of enormous wealth as representing a great good, blessed by the Lord. Perhaps in him the Calvinist doctrine of predestination, making him one of the elect to go to Heaven, was operative, though taken literally he was a Baptist. Or perhaps, in spite of all his disclaimers, this was his road to immortality, to be anything but a forgotten man.

JAMES HAMMOND:
SOUTHERN PLANTER AND FIRE-BRAND

From John D. we go back one generation to James Hammond of South Carolina, who claimed that planting was "the only independent and really honorable occupation" and compared planters in the South to the nobility in Europe, both standing at the head of society and politics.[18]

Hammond was born in South Carolina in 1807 and became a lawyer at twenty-one. Since his family was poor, he sought out and found an heiress, Catherine Fitzsimmons, whom he married in 1830; she was then sixteen. Through his marriage he acquired 7500 acres, 147 slaves and much farm equipment.[19]

From the very beginning Hammond gloried in his social position. He was opposed to the federal tariff and prepared to oppose it by force if necessary. He advocated the death penalty for abolitionists, since he considered slavery the cornerstone of the Republic and abolitionists reckless incendiaries.

He combined his plantation with politics. In 1834 he was elected to Congress. But he had stomach ulcers all his life and, when physicians advised him to travel, he went abroad. Then he returned to his plantation.

His biographer calls him a "tough son of a bitch."[20] Having wed his wife for her wealth, he proceeded to exploit her property to the fullest. He reentered politics, was elected governor of South Carolina in 1842. Throughout his career he was firm on states' rights, anticipating the Civil War by twenty years.

He wanted to run for the Senate but was blocked by his wife's brother-in-law who was annoyed by Hammond's sexual peccadilloes. Hammond had four nieces ranging in age from thirteen to seventeen and was seductive with all of them; his biographer claims he and his four nieces enjoyed every intimacy but "the ultimate one."[21]

In 1849 his wife bore him their eighth and last child. This did not prevent him from initiating a sexual liaison with a slave, Louisa, whom he refused to give up. His wife left him;

even the servants shunned him.[22] All he could say was: "What have I done or omitted to deserve this fate?" He blamed it all on the "bad blood" he had taken into his life through his wife.[23]

During his long separation from his wife, his sense of persecution increased: "Friends I have none."[24] His major outlet became the acquisition of the land of as many neighbors as he and the sheriff could persuade to sell. At his death he had expanded to 14,000 acres, and he had memorialized on his tombstone the legend: "As a planter, the impenetrable swamps of Cowden and Cathwood turned into fruitful fields bear witness to his creative skill."[25]

In 1858, upon the death of the incumbent, Hammond was appointed to the senate. There he first coined the phrase: "Cotton is king."[26] He also defended slavery by observing that all civilizations had a class of servants to do the menial duties. The North had its working class, the South its slaves.

His dream was to establish a rich, educated and well-bred family of his name. Business was good for him, but he complained that his dilettante sons were running his plantation operations into the ground. He was oblivious of his actions as a father. His friend the novelist William Gilmore Simms wrote to him: "You overawe your boys, overwhelm them, and make them halt and hesitate, if not fear, so that they become distrustful of themselves."[27]

He was so identified with the Confederacy that he expected to be obliterated with it. He died in 1864 after writing: "But mind . . . if we are subjugated, run a plow over my grave."[28]

Hammond's motivations are easy enough to understand. He was a narcissistic, unprincipled man who took what he could and justified his actions by doctrines which look ridiculous today, and were of dubious merit even in his own time. Planting was the great business in which he could engage, and he wanted his plantation to be his monument. It was indeed an irony that Redcliffe, the house he built for himself and his family, eventually ended up as property of the state of South Carolina, a monument to the lost cause and the forgotten civilization of another era. Like many grasping men, women were seen by him as simply objects of conquest, whether they were his wife, his slaves or his nieces. Certainly not an admirable man, yet in many ways a typical businessman of his day.

HENRY FORD II: THE HEIR TO THE FORTUNE[29]

The self-made man has one kind of psychology; his heirs have another. Henry Ford achieved fame and fortune by revolutionizing the manufacture of automobiles. But he was also uneducated and paranoid. All his life he lived in fear of enemies, real and imaginary. At various times he imagined that "international Jews", the Catholic Church and particularly the Catholic Du Ponts were out to get him. His homes were honeycombed with tunnels through which he could escape or where he could hide in the event of danger. And he rarely travelled anywhere without packing a revolver.[30] For his Ford plant he had hired Harry Bennett, an ex-Navy boxer who headed a network of informers. It was said that at one time every fourth man on the assembly line was an informer.[31] Henry Ford paid high wages, and was bitterly opposed to unions; he did not allow one in his operations until he was forced to do so by the government during World War II.

Ford had only one child, a son Edsel, who was taken into the family business. The father bore down heavily on him. In 1943, at the age of forty-nine Edsel died, of stomach cancer and undulant fever, the latter apparently contracted from drinking unpasteurized milk from his father's farm.[32]

Edsel in turn had four children, three sons and a daughter. His oldest son, Henry II, head of the Ford Company for thirty-four years, is the subject of this discussion.

When he was in his sixties, in 1980, Henry Ford II expressed himself pretty dismally about his life. He told Barbara Walters in an interview: "I want to make sure that nobody knows anything about me except what is in the public domain."[33] What was he so eager to hide?

Like many children of the wealthy, Henry and his brothers and sister were under constant guard by husky men provided by the Ford Service Department. This was only prudent, since kidnappings of the wealthy and demands for enormous ransoms were not at all uncommon in that era; the parents' fear was natural, especially since the kidnapping and murder of the Lindbergh baby in 1932.

Knowing he would enter the Ford company, Henry showed little interest in school. The constant presence of a bodyguard must have inhibited him further. At Yale he was caught with a

ghost-written senior thesis and he dropped out without gradu-
ating. In another unfortunate incident he hit a twelve-year-old
while driving through the small town of Oxford in Connecticut;
the damage suit was settled out of court. It was not the last
time his lawyers had to bail him out of embarrassing or dangerous actions.[34]

When he was nineteen he met Anne McDonnell, then seventeen, and fell in love. The only problem was that she was
Catholic and grandfather Henry hated Catholics. In spite of
his grandfather's opposition, young Henry converted to Ca-
tholicism and married Anne in 1940; on the morning of his
wedding he was baptized by Monsignor Fulton Sheen.

Henry was in the Navy when his father died in 1943. Since
the Ford Company was an important manufacturer of war
material, the government released him from the Navy and he
assumed the helm. His grandfather at that time was still alive
but no longer functioning on an even keel.

Old Henry Ford had run his company as if it were a small-
town store. He had not even sold stock to the general public;
it was still family-owned. It was young Henry's job to turn the
company around and bring it into the twentieth-century. With
considerable help from various associates Henry managed it;
by 1953 Ford had by-passed Chrysler and was in second place
in the automobile industry.

Though Henry in those years worked hard at his job, he
gradually acquired a reputation as a bon vivant. His capacity to
drink became legendary.[36] And he was also reputed to be
something of a swinger.[37] He did not care what people thought
of him; at one gathering he flung a cake at someone.[38]

His gradual estrangement from his wife was a well-kept
secret. But in 1963, after twenty-three years of marriage, the
couple were divorced.[39]

From that point on Henry became more rambunctious and
unrestrained. He soon married again, this time an Italian
woman named Maria Cristina Vettore Austin whom he met in
Paris. The marriage to Cristina (as she was called) was apparently not a happy one, though it lasted ten years. He was
unfaithful to her from an early stage. Associates were forced
to listen to his stories of sexual conquests. At times it would
become embarrassing, especially when he boasted of having
made it with the wives of some of the company executives.

Once he claimed he had seduced a woman on a diving board. He could not understand how, with all the women available some of his executives could remain faithful to their wives.[40]

On another occasion he was arrested for drunken driving in California, held in jail four hours until he posted $375 bail. In court he pleaded no-contest. The judge placed him on probation for two years and fined him $375, stipulating that if he was convicted of the same offense in California within two years, he would draw an automatic sentence of six months in jail and a $500 fine. The Michigan authorities also announced that his driving license was suspended for thirty days.[41]

Charlotte, his daughter, once seeking to explain her father's erratic conduct, said he found it very hard to handle his emotional life, had a weak side when it came to women and always fell for "strong, tough cookies." (Her own difficulties with men were highlighted when she married and shortly thereafter divorced the Greek shipping magnate Stavros Niarchos, eight years older than her father.)

In business Henry also became increasingly autocratic. He fired Lee Iacocca, the long-time unofficial head of the company. Henry would fire on a whim, at a moment's notice. The company started going downhill. In 1978 Henry had to face a grand jury probe about bribery in Indonesia.[42] He also had to face a stockholders' suit masterminded by the well-known lawyer Roy Cohn.[43] When Henry announced his wish to retire in 1979, the company's prospects did not look good. A federal loan to bail them out, as had been done with Chrysler, was discussed.

Nor did his personal life show much improvement. He finally settled with his second wife Cristina, then married a former model, Kathleen Ross, whom he had been dating for a number of years. He had developed a heart condition and when the constant drinking would end was anybody's guess. Though still one of the richest men in the world (at the divorce trial involving Cristina he testified he was worth about $60 or $70 million) he was far from happy.[44]

Looked at as a human being, Henry Ford II could have been expected to have serious emotional conflicts. Grandson of a legendary figure who had amassed a huge fortune, but was also a paranoid crank, he found a model he could not possibly live up to. There is no indication he had any unusual ability in business; he merely inherited the firm. He did have the sense to hire some excellent people, but as he became increasingly dictatorial he made bad mistakes. In his personal life he was guarded so closely as a child, and given so much, that he could never get over the idea he was a kind of king. Not surprisingly, he made several unhappy marriages, drank too much, womanized too much, was too arrogant and inconsiderate of others. It now becomes understandable why he told Barbara Walters he wanted nobody to find out anything about him. It is amazing that in this day and age he never involved himself in psychoanalysis or psychotherapy of any sort (though his nephew Benson is reported to have had help from a therapist in California). People envied Henry his enormous wealth, but as a man he deserves pity rather than envy.

ARISTOTLE ONASSIS: THE SELF-MADE MAN[45]

While he was alive, Aristotle Onassis was one of the most glamorous men in the world. Fabulously rich, friend to persons as important as Winston Churchill, he involved himself with some of the most famous women alive—Greta Garbo, Maria Callas, Elizabeth Taylor, finally Jacqueline Kennedy. In one sense, as his biographer says, his life is like a tale cut out of ancient Greek mythology.

It is a fitting reflection on his personality that the bathroom on his yacht was said to be an exact replica of the bath of King Minos in ancient Crete.[46] In Greek mythology, with which Onassis must have been familiar, Minos was the grandest of the grand and the cruelest of the cruel. He was supposed to be the son of Zeus, king of the Gods, and Europa, a Phoenician princess whom he carried across the sea to Crete. Once in control of the area he executed a terrible tribute by feeding young men and women to the insatiable Minotaur. Eventually he was said to have been killed by the daughters of one of his enemies, who poured boiling water over him as he was taking a bath.

This image of splendor and cruelty certainly fit Onassis to a "t". When he was already one of the richest men in the world and asked why he wanted more money, he said, "It's not a question of money. After you reach a certain point, money becomes unimportant. What matters is success. The sensible thing would be for me to stop now. But I can't. I have to keep aiming higher and higher—just for the thrill."[47]

Onassis was born in the Greek-Turkish city of Smyrna in 1906. His father was a well-to-do Greek tobacco merchant. In the aftermath of World War I, when a large number of Greeks took refuge in Smyrna, the Turks entered the city and began to massacre the inhabitants. Somehow Aristotle, then only seventeen, found his way into the good graces of the Turks and was left untouched. Along with thousands of others, his father was arrested and slated for execution. The father had accumulated about $100,000 in available cash. Somehow Aristotle gained access to it and bribed the Turks with $25,000 to let his father go. Although he saved his father's life, the father remained suspicious that his son had pocketed some of the money allegedly used for the bribes. Father and son were always distant from one another.[48]

The family went back to Greece. Aristotle's mother had died when he was a little boy, his father remarried and Aristotle was brought up by his grandmother Gethsemane. She died shortly after the family returned home; evidently she was the only one toward whom he had any loving feelings.

Conditions in Greece in 1923 were poor so Onassis decided to go to Argentina. When he disembarked in Buenos Aires he literally had $60 in his pocket. Nevertheless he quickly turned out to be an astute businessman. Turkish tobaccos were almost unknown in Buenos Aires at that time. He began to import them and soon accumulated a fortune. By the time he was twenty-three he was worth a million dollars.[49]

He turned his attention to shipping, one of Greece's major industries. Seeing the potential in shipping and ship-building, he went back to Greece to secure official status. In 1929 he was appointed the Greek Consul General in Buenos Aires and his life career was launched.

One success led to another. He traded with everybody, made money from everybody. He was apparently completely unprincipled. Had he been able to do business with Nazi Germany during the war he would have done so. Instead he focused on the United States and the allies. Over 450 Greek ships participated in the war effort and 360 of them were sunk yet Onassis did not lose a single one.[50] He was suspected of harboring anti-democratic views, but nothing was ever proved. When the Liberty ships were sold after the war, there was a provision they had to be sold to American citizens but Onassis cleverly put together companies in which he had 49% interest, while Americans had the rest, thereby evading the law. At one point he was indicted, actually arrested and fingerprinted, but the indictment led to nothing.[51] When Arabian countries became the leading exporters of oil in the sixties and seventies, he carried their oil in his tankers. He was among the first to register his ships in Panama and Liberia, thereby evading onerous taxes and restrictions. Taxes were one of his main bugaboos and he managed to evade them, or most of them, all his life. While his exact wealth was never revealed, it was customarily reckoned in the hundreds of millions of dollars. He was truly a modern Croesus.

Unlike the American millionaires, Onassis showed no interest in forming a Foundation or engaging in other philanthropic activities. His money belonged to him and his family, even though there was so much no one could manage to spend it in ten lifetimes.

His personal life was however an entirely different matter. His sex life is reported to have started when he was eleven and he remained active all his life.[52] However, women to him were primarily commodities to be acquired and shown off to the world, not even conquests in the manner of the ordinary Don Juan. The first woman in whom he was seriously interested was a Norwegian, Ingebord Dedichen, part of a family that belonged to the aristocracy of Norwegian shipping. Through his connections with her he was able to expand his shipping operations considerably. They became lovers but evidently marriage was out of the question.[53]

He first married at forty, the bride was Tina Livanos, seventeen, daughter of another fabulously wealthy Greek shipowner. They were married in 1946 but after the first year of marriage spent less than ninety days a year together. They had two children: Christina and Alexander, both of whom became the emotional center of his life.[54]

It is rather difficult from the biography to disentangle all the complex strands of his interpersonal affairs and to see the human being behind the dark glasses he affected at an early stage. When he and Tina were divorced after thirteen years of marriage she said: "It is almost thirteen years since Mr. Onassis and I were married in New York City. Since then, he has become one of the world's richest men, but his great wealth has not brought me happiness with him, or as the world knows, has it brought him happiness with me."[55]

Onassis liked to live in the glare of publicity, and all his activities were widely reported. He affected various personal idiosyncrasies, such as never wearing a topcoat, installing a one-way mirror on his yacht, engaging in risky sports such as a variety of water-skiing in which he was almost literally flying.

But most publicized were his numerous affairs and his marriage to Jacqueline Kennedy. His best known affair was his on-again-off-again romance with the opera singer Maria Callas who once said: "He is obsessed with famous women. He was obsesed with me because I was famous. Now she (Jackie Kennedy) and her sister, they have obsessed him and they are even more famous." It was a true evaluation; what he loved more than anything else in life was notoriety. He even had a brief affair with Maria Constantinesco, a known spy for the Nazis, later convicted and imprisoned.[57]

Most startling was his marriage to Jackie Kennedy, widow of the former president, startling and incomprehensible on both sides. They were married in Greece in 1968, in a Greek-Orthodox wedding. Since she was a Roman Catholic, she was not permitted to marry a divorced man; eventually the Vatican announced she was living in mortal sin. Shortly thereafter the whole religious question was forgotten.[55]

The biographer gives some details of the purported 173-clause marriage contract. It looks like a business deal, with so much money going to Jackie if she lasts one year, so much after two years, and so on, and so much to Aristotle if she leaves him after certain periods of time. One clause stipulated she was to receive $3 million immediately in tax-free bonds, another that she was not required to give Onassis a child, and a third that they need spend only Catholic holidays and summer vacations together; the rest of the time they were free to do as they pleased.

Obviously such a marriage could amount to little, and shortly thereafter they were reported to be splitting up. The newspapers announced she was spending too much money and he had refused to increase her allowance.

Although he allegedly doted on his children, he derived little satisfaction from them. Alexander died in an airplane crash in 1973: His father could have kept him alive another day but refused to do so. In 1971 Cristina, then twenty, married a forty-seven-year old Jewish real estate man in Los Angeles; Onassis was in a rage and threatened to cancel her trust. After nine months the couple separated.[59]

Toward the end of his life he developed myasthenia gravis and died at seventy-one in 1975. Only Cristina was at his bedside.

Though not an American, Onassis is a perfect example of the adage that business is business. His only goal seems to have been the accumulation of an enormous amount of wealth. With this wealth he could secure fame, publicity, and women. And yet, looked at from his point of view, what did he get out of all this frenetic activity? A bathroom allegedly similar to that of King Minos, a figure in Greek legend, did not make him a king. The company of famous and beautiful women like Maria Callas did not make him famous or more attractive. With all his wealth, he was truly a driven unhappy man.

THE MODERN BUSINESSMAN: MEMBER OF THE CORPORATION

Ever since the publication of the book by William Whyte, *The Organization Man* in 1956, the fact became increasingly clear that the modern businessman has to adjust himself to an entirely different set of economic, legal and social standards. Taxes, antitrust actions, prosecutions for industrial bribery, public disclosure of all important business activities (such as an attempt by insiders to "corner the market") have created an entirely different way of life.

In their study of AT&T managers, Bray, Campbell and Grant (1974) described two major lifestyles among the businessmen: enlargers and enfolders. The enlarging lifestyle is oriented toward the goals of innovation, change and growth. The man moves away from tradition and places his emphasis on adaptation, self-development and the extension of influence outward, into the work and community spheres. The enlarger looks for responsibility on the job and is likely also to seek and achieve a position of influence in service organizations. Self-development activities are stressed; thus enlargers are likely not only to read, attend the theatre and keep up with current events, but take night courses and respond to the promptings of physical fitness and health food buffs. The enlarger finds his values have changed so dramatically that he no longer enjoys the company of old friends in the neighborhoods of his childhood.

By contrast, the enfolding life style is oriented to the goals of tradition, stability and inward strength. Rather than pitching his influence outward, the enfolder seeks to cultivate and solidify that which invites attention within his more familiar sphere. He is not a joiner of social or community organizations and when he does enter into such activities rarely seeks an active role. On the other hand, he may be quite active in his church, or in Boy Scout troops, or Little League teams that have their origins in the community. His good works are usually tied to his church affiliation. He values parental ties and seeks to keep a close active relationship with boyhood chums, if possible.

The authors give case histories illustrating the life styles of enlargers and enfolders. Ralph, the enlarger, was twenty-seven when he began with the Bell system, after earning a degree in engineering. Steady promotions occurred. By the seventh year of his employment he was promoted to fourth division level, as an Area Plant Supervisor. This is a staff position where he has charge of statewide budgets and policies.

Ralph was one of three children. He always felt closer to mother than to father. She was ready with moral support, took him into her confidence as though he were her equal on many points. Only in recent years has he felt relaxed with his father.

He was always career-oriented. The degree in engineering was a planned effort to get into management; he felt engineering was the best preparation. He constantly presses himself to exceed the routine activities of daily life. For years he would not purchase a television set "on principle." Instead he bought a set of the Great Books.

Although he had planned to extend his education through night school, job demands have kept him from completing the MBA. Still, he has twelve credits toward the degree and has kept up a steady reading schedule, including both management and current fiction offerings. His wife, whom he met at college, was an English major and since she loves to read he is well-informed on the latest developments in literature.

His marital adjustment has not always been perfect. One factor was the unhappiness of the wife's parents with the many and distant moves the couple had to make. At one time the wife found his time commitments too demanding. She became depressed and stayed with her parents for a few months after their first child was born. Long hours of discussion straightened things out about the fifth year. There was never any question of his devotion to her, or of her devotion to him.

He has gradually drifted away from contacts with his parents. He attends church less often. The couple likes to socialize, they have many friends in the telephone company and they make an effort to cultivate friends who have other professional and occupational identities.

Some people saw in Ralph a future company president or vice-president. He admits to periods of depression when he felt guilty for not having performed as well as he thought he could have.

An example of the second type is Lou, who was twenty-six when he joined the telephone company. Lou is the third son in a family of five; his oldest brother is a hero to him and he was the one who induced Lou to join the telephone company. His most pleasant memories of childhood are of the hunting and fishing trips he took with his father and brothers.

After three years in the Air Force, Lou decided to go to college, thinking that without a degree there was little chance of advancement. He completed college as a business administration major. In his sophomore year he married his high school sweetheart and their first child was born in his senior year. They now have four children.

His work career has not been impressive. After eight years he is still a first level manager. Several times he refused advancement when it meant leaving his home environment.

He hates to read, preferring to learn by doing and nothing

gives him more satisfaction than seeing a job through to a successful conclusion. Lou's life style has always stressed security—the steady accumulation of desirables, such as a car, furniture, then a house. He values a rich family life, loves to play with his children, and seems a perfect husband and father. Most of his socializing centers around his wife's family or his own. He has never taken a night college course and his reading is confined to newspapers, especially the sports pages. He likes to grow things and has a green thumb (the family puts in a full garden each summer). He also has a wood-working shop where he has built some home furnishings from scratch. The wife seems a loving mother. She defers to her husband on most decisions although he lets her manage the family finances. He has been active in church, and related community organizations.

The interviewers did not consider Lou unhappy except for some embarrassment about his lack of advancement. They feel that were he able to reach second level he would feel greatly relieved and would continue at a decent work pace until retirement. They also believe this is the most he hopes for on the work front.

SUMMARY

The businessman's major goal is to make money and to succeed in his business. In former times, great fortunes could be built up by luck, skill and deceit. The Horatio Alger fantasy instilled into American boys was a more likely one a hundred years ago, though even then more failed than succeeded. Yet in the accumulation of large fortunes, of which several examples have been given, the lack of regard for other people and the intense concentration on making money rarely led to much personal happiness. In modern times, the organization man has become the rule; the percentage of those who are self-employed has dropped greatly and is steadily dropping. These organization men have to adjust their life styles to the corporation with which they are associated. The old image of the self-made man who makes millions is still in the back of the minds of many corporation men and can cause a great deal of conflict.

Chapter 15:
The Agony and the Ecstasy
of the Creative Man

One of the most often-disputed questions in regard to the creative man is whether creativity and insanity are closely allied. Certainly so many creative geniuses have either become mad or close to it that it causes little surprise when the facts come out. The British poet Wordsworth once wrote:

> We poets begin in our youth with gladness
> But there comes in the end despondency
> and madness[1]

The French novelist Gustave Flaubert felt the author must be like God, present everywhere and visible nowhere.[2] Yet, as we shall see, while there is madness aplenty among the creative, there is also sanity aplenty. Something is to be said for the ancient Greek idea that the creative genius sees further into reality than the average man and at times this accounts for his personal aberrations.

The title of this chapter is taken from the biography of Michelangelo by Irving Stone. There is indeed as a rule agony and ecstasy in the creative man. It is virtually impossible to do any meaningful creative work without some suffering. But it becomes dangerous to push this observation too far. It is true that if the man wishes to avoid all suffering he will stay away from any kind of creative endeavor. But at the other extreme an excessive amount of pain will inhibit the creative act and lead to suicide and death. The artist (in the broadest sense) has to strike some balance between the two. Many have, many have not.

There is a lot of speculation about where the creative man derives his inspiration. Through the ages the genius has been looked upon as a kind of magician, and his source of inspira-

© 1987 by The Haworth Press, Inc. All rights reserved.

tion as a sort of magic gift. If not taken too literally, this age-old view tends to be confirmed by more scientific psychological research. The creative spark comes early. Men who have done nothing by the time they are thirty are not likely to produce creative work of any great merit. This is why as we shall see over and over in this chapter the creative individual attracts attention when he is still in his teens, sometimes in childhood. In some fields, such as music, almost every musician of note has been a child prodigy, not necessarily as great as Mozart, but often not too far away.

It is not enough just to have a creative spark: it has to be developed. Here comes the other side of creativity, to which usually too little attention is paid: the capacity to work. For the creative individual work may be burdensome, but he goes through with it, in fact cannot live without it. Writers habitually have been writing since they were little boys; painters painting since childhood. They acquire skills in this way which the adult who begins at, say twenty or twenty-five, can never master.

How the creative artist is treated depends a great deal on the times in which he lives. For centuries the artist needed a patron; without one he could not present his work to the world, or be published or even noticed: "Full many a rose is born to blush unseen." No doubt there have been many creative geniuses throughout history who are totally unknown for that reason.

It has happened often enough that a man regarded as great by his contemporaries does not last; likewise many who were disregarded by their contemporaries have been hailed as geniuses after their deaths. Even Shakespeare was not fully appreciated until about a hundred years after his death. The paintings of Van Gogh, who could not make a living during his lifetime, now sell for millions. It is actually rare for a man to be fully appreciated during his lifetime: Picasso is one of the few exceptions. And those who are appreciated may still question the value of their work. Somerset Maugham, whose writings earned him a fortune while alive, always wondered whether posterity would not regard him as a second-class writer. George Bernard Shaw was confident he was greater than Shakespeare but subsequent generations have failed to agree.

Creativity can occur in any walk of life. There are creative physicians, lawyers, scientists, teachers and many others whose efforts are not usually looked upon in that light. Creativity involves the capacity to present something in a novel light and this can occur in any field.

Usually creative men are so involved in their productions that they do not relate well to their children. Many of them do not have children; others find the children get in the way. Except for a field like music, where the child can soak in the atmosphere from his parents, it is rare for the children of creative individuals to shine in the same field.

ELVIS PRESLEY: HERO OF THE BOBBY-SOXERS[3]

Elvis Presley, the King of Rock'n Roll, one of the highest-paid performers in the history of entertainment, was born in Mississippi in 1935, an identical twin; his brother died in child-birth, leaving him an only child. His father was sentenced to jail in 1938 for forgery,[4] leaving Elvis alone with his mother from the time he was thirty months until he was eleven. Without any formal training, Elvis learned whatever music he knew from the radio. At eleven he put on a prize-winning performance, singing a song he had learned on the radio. Around that time he learned to play the guitar and entertained people by singing and playing the guitar.

When he was sixteen, still living with his mother, he went through a crisis of nightmares.[5] Night after night he imagined he was attacked by a mob of angry men. They would circle him ominously as he hurled defiant challenges. A violent struggle would ensue. Elvis would cry out in his sleep and toss about fiercely. Sometimes he would leap out of bed and whirl the sheets about his head. Or he would be wakened violently by an agonizing jolt of pain as he smashed his fist into a wall or tore off a toenail kicking against the sheet. If he did not wake, he might rise from bed in a cold sweat, with eyes open but glazed, and make for the nearest door or window.

Such adolescent nightmares, in one form or another, are quite common. We would interpret them as a fear of his father's punishment for his incestuous wishes for his mother. It is striking that this man, later to be known as Elvis the

Pelvis, who would excite millions of teenage girls sexually, never managed to have a normal sex life of his own. He was far too attached to his mother.

There was nothing Elvis wanted more than a singing career. But nobody would listen to him. Around this time he had his first romance, with a fifteen-year old girl named Dixie Locke. Later it became noticeable that Elvis was somehow fixated on teenage virgins.[6] At that time though, all that could be seen was an innocent date every week.

In 1954 he had his first chance and made his first professional recording. Shortly thereafter he met a Colonel Parker, who became his business manager and helped create the mystique that swirled around Elvis all his life. As one of the most popular singers of his day, he earned more than $100 million by the time he was forty. He had also spent all of it.[7]

There is some mystery in these fabulous earnings. Elvis had no extraordinary voice, he was not an actor, he had no electric personality. What accounts for his success? Primarily he became a symbol for teenage girls, the age on which he was fixated. Just becoming adolescent, the teenage girls tease the boys and are teased. Neither children nor full-grown women, they could identify with this man, who likewise was not full-grown but half-boy and half-man.

Elvis steadily went downhill, became more and more obviously disturbed—going into spiritualism,[8] taking innumerable drugs[9] (he died of an overdose though the official cause of death was "an erratic heartbeat") and indulging in peculiar sex practices of all kinds. His very craziness must have been the most attractive part of his personality, for he simply gave in to every whim of the moment, a way of life many fourteen-year olds find infinitely appealing.

For a long time Elvis remained an extremely infantile person, literally fixated on fourteen-year old virgins. His early liaisons were with teenage girls with whom he would flirt but avoid sex. Among other things, he was afraid of being prosecuted for raping a teenage girl, though he could easily have avoided that by picking older ones but stuck to the fourteen-year-olds.

Many times Elvis and his crew (he had an army of young men touring with him) would play childhood or adolescent games. One was "War," basically a free-for-all on skates.

Bandaids were provided for anybody who got cut. Or, since he liked the movies, he would rent a movie theater for the night and take all his friends and anybody else who wanted to go. This helped cover up his lifelong insomnia.

Another favorite game was a teenager pajama party. After a dip in the pool, the girls would dry his hair, then lie in bed. Elvis would be in the middle. He would tickle one of the girls, make her giggle. Then he would lie down on the bed with an arm around a girl on each side and a third girl lying across his feet. (This is reminiscent of the child who gets into bed on Sunday mornings with his parents.)[12]

In 1958 his mother died and he was heart–broken. Then he was accepted into the army, where his manager decided he should spend the full two years. He was stationed in Germany, which brought about another change in his psyche.

In 1959 he met Priscilla Beaulieu in Germany. She had just turned fourteen. He began to spend evenings in bed alone with her. Eventually she became his wife and the mother of his child.[13]

Still, Priscilla did not alter his fixation on voyeurism and fourteen-year-olds. For quite a while he held big parties where he was supplied young girls. He liked to see pretty girls dressed all in white, when they undressed he wanted them to have white panties. Sometimes his rage at the girls would get the better of him; once he dragged a girl by the hair to the door and kicked her out because she got into an argument with him.[14]

He particularly liked a group of girls who would strip to their panties and wrestle with each other while he, with an erection, stared his eyes out. He accounted for this obsession by recalling an incident from childhood: a moment he had seen two little girls tumbling together on the ground with their dresses rising to show their crotches. He had other voyeuristic fantasies and practices.[15]

Soon the orgies and senseless living led him to drugs to soothe his nerves. He was always an insomniac, sleeping pills were the beginning but he went on to everything, including heroin. In his last years the only book he carried around was the *Physicians' Desk Reference* which he consulted constantly.[16]

Next he turned to spiritualism, especially the theosophists and Madame Blavatsky. This was a revival of the weird and superstitious beliefs of his dead mother. Many spiritualists are quite consciously trying to make contact with the dead; Elvis may have been doing the same, since he was so attached to his mother.[17]

In one dream toward the end of his life, he was on trial for his life. The prosecuting attorney was Colonel Parker. The chief witnesses for the prosecution were Priscilla (his wife) and Red (his friend). All the guys had rejected him. When asked what the dream meant, Elvis replied: "The end is near."[18]

Eventually his wife left him; he was obviously too crazy.[19] One girl followed another. He hired a doctor who plied him with injections (the doctor was later tried for over-prescribing, but cleared). In time an overdose killed Elvis. An autopsy showed eleven different drugs in his body.[20]

Presley was obviously disturbed from the time he was a little boy; in all likelihood as an adult he was a psychotic personality who hid his psychosis behind spiritualism, drugs and stage antics. But the real question is: Why did he achieve such extraordinary popularity in his lifetime? (That popularity has since dwindled considerably, so that for the next genera-tion he will probably be almost unknown.) It was somehow the contact between the immature, overstuffed, voyeuristic hillbilly and the love-starved, sex-crazed-and-denied teen-age girls that catapulted him into the ranks of the highest-paid entertainers.

In Elvis we see one aspect of creativity, especially in the arts, that is rarely considered: the communication between the artist and his audience. Elvis the Pelvis with his wild gyrations on stage, his infantile antics at home, was saying to the girls: don't be fully sexual yet, but try to be sexual. He was teasing the girls with his body, as in his habit of sleeping with three fourteen-year old virgins at the same time; they in turn were teasing him by their pajama parties in which they appeared half-dressed. That such shenanigans led to drug addiction and death was a tragic end to his acting out of sexual immaturity.

WILL ROGERS: "I NEVER MET A MAN I DIDN'T LIKE"[21]

No greater contrast to Presley can be imagined than Will Rogers, the universally beloved comedian who died in an air

crash in 1935. Rogers was born in 1879 in Oklahoma, when it
was still Indian territory. He had Indian blood in his veins on
both sides and was proud of it. In the Civil War his family
fought for the Confederacy; Stand Waite, a Cherokee general, was the last Southern general to surrender, on June 23,
1865.

Will's father was a prosperous rancher and farmer. He was
of such importance to the area that a county was named in his
honor.

The family had eight children, of whom Will was the
youngest. Will's mother died when he was nine, a loss that
saddened him considerably. But his family was very close.
Among the Cherokee families there was more the feeling of
kinship than of just being neighbors. Everybody was "aunt"
or "uncle." Homes were hospitable, warm and friendly.
Often a whole family would drive for miles over the dim
wagon trails to spend a few days with Aunt Mary and Uncle
Clem. It was no doubt this early childhood environment that
Will referred to in one of his most famous remarks: "I never
met a man I didn't like."

Will did not take well to school. He was a poor student
and dropped out at an early age.[22] But he loved horses,
spent a great deal of time perfecting his skills with them, in
particular building up a repertoire of rope tricks which were
later to become the initial base of his entry into the arena of
entertainment.

Eager to try his way in the world, Will and a friend set out
for the Argentine in 1902, with $3,000 his father had given
him.[23] He planned to be away two years, sowing oats in distant and inhospitable places. While abroad he found his niche
in circus life, showing off his rope tricks and wrote home to
his father he was a "contented man." By 1904 he was performing rope-catching acts in vaudeville. In 1908 he married
Betty Blake. They had four children and an extremely happy
marriage through the years. His wife, who wrote his biography, held only adoration for him as a husband, father and
human being.

One day he discovered that in addition to the rope tricks, he
could also keep up a patter of conversation. This soon became
more popular than the tricks. His wit was typically devoid of
arrogance or malice and full of humorous self-deprecation. At

one point he said: "I've only got jokes enough for one miss. I've either got to practice roping or learn more jokes."[24] Or when he failed to get both feet through a loop of rope he would say: "Well, got all my feet through but one."[25]

Soon his wit became legendary and he acquired the sobriquet of "the columnist of the theater." What was most striking about his performance and his life was his absence of guile. When Ziegfield offered him a highly desirable two-year contract, Will declined, saying: "I don't like contracts. You can trust me and I know I can trust you."[26] For years he was one of the outstanding stars in the Follies on Broadway.

Will's forte was to spoof the stuffy and deflate the egotistical. One time he was invited to speak to a group of society ladies; they did not respond to his jokes. He commented on this: "Then two nights later after that fiasco, I went to Sing Sing and did a show for them and I never had as well read an audience in my life. They didn't miss a thing. Ever since I have always felt we had the wrong bunch in there."[27]

His pungent comments aroused so much interest he soon put them into weekly articles, then daily. He compiled the best for a volume issued in 1924, called *The Illiterate Digest* (*The Literary Digest,* since deceased, was then one of the leading magazines). He continued to lampoon those who put on too many airs. When the Prince of Wales kept falling from his horse time after time in the 1920's, Will said: "In my falls I am not fortunate enough to spill any royal blood, but it's my blood and it's all I got."[28] Once, when asked whether his ancestors had come over on the *Mayflower,* he said: "No, they were here before and met the boat." At another time, when asked to make a political speech, he said: "I don't want to go over and then have to go into politics, because up to now I've always tried to live honest."[29] Modest as always, he signed hotel registers, "Will Rogers, Claremore, Oklahoma." When his sister Maude died and was mourned as the sister of Will Rogers, he said: "It's the other way around, I am the brother of Mrs. C.L. Lane, the friend of humanity."[30] Of G. B. Shaw he said: "We've got a great deal in common. Both of us know the world is wrong, but we don't know what's the matter with it."[31] Once on an airplane flight when his wife was frightened he said: "Woman, don't hold on to me. I couldn't be of any help to you."[32]

Although he was always a hard worker he could take time off to relax completely. If he had a free day, he would drive off without any plans. He liked small country hotels and talking to the people he met in out-of-the-way places. He had a human friendly way with strangers and a warm curiosity about what other people were doing and thinking. Brought up in an area that saw a lot of shooting, both for pleasure and in anger, he could truthfully say: "I never killed anything in my life."[33] He once conducted a mock session of the Senate, and when he wanted to discontinue his weekly radio talk shows the entire Senate almost to a man petitioned him to continue.

When asked by Will Durant to contribute to the book, *Living Philosophies,* he wrote:

> I can't tell this doggone Durant anything. What all of us know together don't mean anything. We are just here for a spell and pass on. Any man that thinks civilization has advanced is an egotist. We have got more tooth paste on the market and more misery in our Courts than at any time in our existence. So get a few laughs and do the best you can. Don't have an ideal to work for. That's like riding towards a mirage of a lake. When you get there it ain't there. . . . Live your life so that whenever you lose, you are ahead.[34]

The uneducated Indian cowboy had acquired more wisdom in his short life than many centuries of philosophers. When he died in 1935 in an airplane accident, he was universally mourned.

Though he made a fortune in the entertainment world, Will Rogers never put on the high airs or the craving for publicity and glory so many entertainers possess and that defeats them in their life's endeavors. Again, we see that for the creative man it is not so much the nature of his creative gift (and Will Rogers certainly ranks with Mark Twain as one of America's greatest humorists) as what he does with it. Rogers joked and entertained, but deep down he was a humble loving man without guile or malice who never made any enemy, and lived his life according to his own philosophy, that whenever you lose you are ahead.

SOMERSET MAUGHAM: OF HUMAN BONDAGE[35]

Toward the end of his life, when he was world famous, Somerset Maugham became alarmed at the idea of having a biography written of him. He directed his literary executor not to authorize any biography nor "to assist any person who wishes or attempts such publication."[36] He repeated this wish in his last will dated July 9, 1964, a year before he died: "I direct that there shall be no biography or publication of my letters . . . I earnestly request anyone who possesses any of my letters to destroy them."[37]

Maugham is after all one of the giants of contemporary literature. His book *Of Human Bondage* is widely and justifiably regarded as a masterpiece. Why then all this secrecy, and wish to have his personal life obliterated, rather than make all his letters available and have his biography written and rewritten a hundred times? Here lies the first clue to what he really meant by *Human Bondage:* shame, indelible, ineradicable shame.

Maugham was born in the British embassy in Paris in 1874. His father was a lawyer who handled the British embassy's legal affairs. His mother was born in India and brought to Paris after the death of her father. Her mother, Maugham's grandmother, wrote children's books, edifying tales about orphans and selfish little rich girls who learn humility.

William (that is what the initial W. in his name stands for) was the fourth of four sons; a fifth had died in infancy. His mother was consumptive and at that time it was believed by doctors that tuberculosis in a woman should be treated by encouraging her to bear children. The three older boys were sent away to boarding school in England, as was the custom in those days, and Somerset had his mother to himself from the time he was three. He also had a nurse who shared his bedroom.[38] Father was distant, preoccupied with his legal business. Such a family situation readily predisposes the boy to homosexuality and Maugham was no exception, though his sexual inclinations remained a source of much conflict all his life.

When he was eight his mother died; when he was ten his father died. He was left a small inheritance, enough to later see him through medical school. He was sent to live with his father's only living brother, a Church of England clergyman in his fifties who was married and childless. Another blow. The uncle was properly described as a "very narrow-minded and far from intelligent cleric."[39]

Soon Maugham found relief from his loneliness in books, and developed the ambition to be a writer. He also began to stutter, which he had not done in France. Stuttering is generally considered a sign of impotent rage, which fits in with what we know of his character. In Victorian times stuttering was so poorly understood that doctors sometimes cut off pieces of the tongue of the stutterer on the theory the tongue was too long; fortunately Maugham escaped such sadism.[40]

Maugham was small, not athletic, a stutterer and shy. In the cruelty of the English school obviously his life was not going to be easy. To cope with this dilemma he developed a singular habit, imagining he was someone else. In his frankly autobiographical novel, *Of Human Bondage,* he has the hero say, describing himself: "He took to a singular habit. He would imagine that he was some boy whom he had a particular fancy for; he would throw his soul, as it were, into the other's body, talk with his voice and laugh with his heart . . . in this way, he enjoyed many intervals of fantastic happiness."[41] Perhaps it is this overidentification with the characters in his novel that Maugham never wanted anybody to discover.

Unhappy, he left the school at sixteen. He took a trip to Germany, where he had his first homosexual experience.[42] England at that time was still under the domination of the anti-homosexual law which later sent Oscar Wilde to jail; Maugham was fearful of suffering such an experience. His affair was hushed up. One of his characters said: "Follow your inclinations with due regard to the policeman around the corner."[43] His homosexual inclinations did not become fixed; that was to come much later.

After drifting a while, Maugham decided to go to medical school, which he entered in 1892. Five years later he graduated but the practice of medicine never attracted him; he always wanted to be a writer. Until the middle of World War I he had a number of casual heterosexual affairs.

Several of his stories were rejected. Then came *Liza of Lambeth* in 1897. It was accepted by Fisher Unwin and Somerset Maugham's writing career was launched. By 1900 he had published two novels and a volume of short stories. He was dapper, nice-looking, and getting on in the world. Although he had a publisher and an agent he was still rowing against the current. Yet as his biographer says: "Behind the mask of the Edwardian gentleman there hid the alienated, mother-deprived outsider who lacked a secure grip on his identity."[44] This was to remain true all his life.

In his writings he devoted a good deal of attention to plays. Not until 1907 did he experience much success. But when he did, he became the talk of the town. At one time, four of his plays were running simultaneously on the West End. At the same time he started a liaison with an attractive woman, which lasted eight years; somehow though he had to keep secret the identity of this woman. As he was later to put it: "To the acute observer no one can produce the most casual work without disclosing the innermost secrets of his soul."[45]

Then came World War I. Maugham wrote his masterpiece, *Of Human Bondage* in 1915 and took an active part in the war. On the Flanders front he met the love of his life, Gerald Haxton, who became his secretary-companion-lover.[46] Maugham was forty; Haxton was twenty-two; a typical homosexual liaison. In the meantime Maugham's mistress Syrie (whom he later married) was pregnant. He felt great conflict, which was never really resolved; he hated Syrie until she died in 1954.

The publication of *Of Human Bondage* eventually made Maugham a figure of world reknown. It was clearly autobiographical; some of the sketches of his teachers are so realistic that even their physical aspects can be recognized. The hero has a clubfoot instead of a stutter. He becomes obsessed with a woman he cannot marry and who exploits him; a dramatization of his own inability to find a woman he could love.

After *Of Human Bondage* Maugham wrote many books and short stories but none ever was the equal of his first great achievement. He kept writing until near the end of his life; his last book dates from 1962, three years before his death.

Maugham's homosexuality has been the subject of much discussion. Yet it is simpler than appears. Up to the time he met Haxton in 1915, he was a carefree bachelor, a man about town who was a writer and bon vivant. Then he met Syrie, whom he finally married in 1917, lived with her for ten years, though he soon came to detest her. She eventually revealed his homosexual life to the public.

While he fell in love with Gerald in 1915, he did not live with him until after the separation from Syrie, twelve years later. By that time he was over fifty. He stayed with Gerald until the younger man's death in 1944; then he took up with another young man, Alan Searle, who stayed with Maugham until the latter died in 1965.[47] Thus Maugham spent the earlier part of his life trying to find love with a woman; when that failed, he took up with a young man; when he died, he took up with another young man. Both these young men were weak, ineffectual characters who were virtually slaves to Maugham. In effect, he bought them with his wealth and glamor.

Early in his relationship with Gerald, Maugham placed under the young man's pillow this poem by Yeats:

I turn round
Like a dumb beast in a show
Neither know what I am
Nor where can I go
My language beaten
Into one name;
I am in love
And that is my shame (Italics added)
What hurts the soul;
My soul adores,
No better than a beast
Upon all fours.[48]

Thus the inability to love a woman is his shame, which he dare not reveal. This inability to turn derives from his image of the woman as a hateful, exploitative prostitute, the girl he cannot rid himself of in *Of Human Bondage*. In that book Maugham writes that Mildred, the heroine, accused Philip, the hero, "of every mean fault . . . stingy, dull . . . vain, selfish. . . . Then she turned round and hurled at him the injury which she knew was the only one that really touched him. . . . She flung it at him as though it were a blow. Cripple!"[49]

ISAAC BASHEVIS SINGER: TELLER OF JEWISH TALES[50]

Though both were tellers of tales (Somerset Maugham edited a book with that title), one could hardly imagine a

more vivid contrast than that between Maugham and Isaac
Bashevis Singer. One great work, *Of Human Bondage,* dominates Maugham's output but Singer's represents a more con-
tinual stream, with no one book outstanding. Singer was
awarded the Nobel Prize in Literature in 1978 for his total
achievement.[51]

Singer was born in 1904 in a small town in Poland, the son
of a rabbi. He had one brother, eleven years older, Israel
Joshua, also a writer of some renown; the rivalry with this
older brother played a great role in his life. The family moved
to Warsaw shortly after Isaac was born and lived there until
he emigrated to America in 1935.

He trained for a while to become a rabbi like his father, but
then his passions soon focussed on literature. Although he
lived through the murder of Jews by Germans, Poles and
Russians, world betterment was not his main goal. Instead he
chose two idols: the idol of literature and the idol of love. No
doubt because he was deeply obsessed with love and sex
(which Maugham was not) there is none of the malice and
bitterness either in his life or writings that one finds in Maugham. And yet, until he reached fame in his fifties, his life was
dominated by a poverty and hardship Maugham never knew.

His older brother got him a job as a proofreader on a
newspaper in Warsaw and he eked out a meager living at that
and giving lessons until he left for America. In the meantime
his younger years were spent in pursuit of love. In a humorous piece in *Harper's* in 1979, Mrs. Tova Reich wrote about
"The Mistresses of Singer." She claimed that all over Israel,
Europe and America women were coming forward to an-
nounce they were once Isaac's mistresses. She said even their
husbands boasted about it.[52]

Isaac neither confirms nor denies these stories; he admits,
however, he has been obsessed by sex all his life. Although he
made an early marriage to Runya, by whom he had a son, he
has always admitted that monogamy has been a problem to
him.[53] Still, in 1937, he married Alma Wasserman, and seems
to have been very happy with her, although they have no
children.

His early stories and novels were about another of his obsessions, the spiritual world, with its imps, devils and dyb-
buks. The public did not take kindly to these creatures, so his

early works did not do well. It was only after he began to write about his experiences as a Jew in Poland, and the life of the Jews there, that he began to become popular.[54]

When he came to America he began as a writer for the *Jewish Forward*. But his first big success occurred with the novel, *The Family Moskat,* in 1950, which told the story of a Jewish family in Warsaw up to the time of World War II. It has been said that when Isaac dies the last link to Jewish life in Poland will have been extinguished.

In 1962 he became a vegetarian, which fits in with his emphasis on love; animals too should not be sacrificed to man's cruelty.[55]

Comparing Singer's works with his life, one is struck by the fact he did not really begin his major writings until he was past forty, shortly after his brother died. Then he began to relate the story of the Jews in Poland. At the Nobel Prize ceremony he summed up his philosophy in these words:

> I am not ashamed to admit that I belong to those who fantasize that literature is capable of bringing new horizons and new perspectives—philosophical, religious, esthetical and even social. In the history of old Jewish literature there was never any basic difference between the poet and the prophet. Our ancient poetry often became law and a way of life.[56]

In all, Singer seems to have reached an inner peace and equilibrium in his life which few others have been able to match. Thus the agony of his earlier years has been overcome by the ecstasy of his later ones.

VINCENT VAN GOGH: GENIUS AND SUICIDE[57]

Although now ranked among the greatest artists of all time, Vincent Van Gogh sold only one painting during his lifetime. His brief and tragic life ended by suicide at thirty-seven.[58]

Van Gogh was born in Zundert, Holland, in 1853, the eldest of six children of a poor minister. Before he was born, another boy named Vincent had died in infancy; thus his life began after a severe blow to his parents, which must have influenced their feelings about him.[59] Four years after he was born came his brother Theo, who was to be his lifelong friend, inspiration, confidant and support.

From an early age he began to draw and water-color, but it was not until much later that he was to try painting as a career. In school he showed little ability, so at sixteen he was apprenticed to the Hague branch of the firm of Goupil and Co., art dealers in which his uncle was a partner. Four years later, when he was twenty, he was transferred to the London branch.

In London he fell in love with Ursula Loyer, the daughter of his landlady; it was to be the first of a number of unhappy loves. She ignored him, which made him severely depressed.[60] It is said that from this time on he was melancholic, and became more and more absorbed in a kind of religious fanaticism. He started to lead a secluded life, living alone, seeing nobody. It was then the correspondence with his brother Theo began. In one of the early letters he included a sketch on the title page of *Poems* by Edmond Roche, one of which reads: "I have climbed, sad and alone, the sad and barren dune where the sea laments incessantly, the dune where the billow with its large folds comes to die, monotonous path with tortuous windings."[61] He was already foreshadowing his own sad fate.

He decided that art dealing was not for him. He became a language teacher and lay preacher, then in 1877 worked for a bookseller. His ceaseless drifting had already begun. Since he was the son and grandson of a minister he started to study theology. "If I may become a clergyman and fill that position so that my work resembles that of our father, then I shall thank God," he wrote Theo.[62] But when he was confronted by the Greek verbs he said to one of his teachers: "Mendes, do you seriously believe that such horrors are indispensable to a man who wants to do what I want to do: give peace to poor creatures and reconcile them to their existence on earth?"[63] Soon he had abandoned his studies. During a short period at home, he became enthusiastic about art, writing: "How rich art is, if one can only remember what one has seen, one is never without food for thought or truly lonely, never alone."[64]

Failing at evangelical work, he tried missionary work among the impoverished population of the Borinage, a coal-mining district in Belgium. There he went through a kind of spiritual crisis, left his missionary work and decided to devote his life to art. From then on (1880) until the end of his life he was supported by his brother Theo.

A second disappointment in love came around 1881 when he wanted to marry his cousin Kee, who had just become a widow. She spurned his advances. Perhaps in reaction to that, and constant battles with his father, he went to live with a prostitute, Cristine, and her children, where he stayed almost two years.[65]

When this came to an end he went to Paris to live with Theo. There he met a number of the modern masters, including Toulouse-Lautrec and Paul Gaugin. Under the influence of the Parisian environment, his painting underwent considerable maturation and change. His father's death in 1885 also contributed to his change of style and the deepening of his depression.

Finally he went to the south of France where he was to do his most brilliant work in the last few years of his life. He invited Gauguin to be his guest in his house at Arles. The two quarreled bitterly. One day he went after Gauguin with a razor, then turned against himself and cut off his ear. He took the ear to a prostitute, Rachel, in a brothel he frequented occasionally; she fainted dead away when she saw it.[66]

He was then hospitalized. The whole incident followed the engagement and marriage of Theo and it is obvious Van Gogh's reactions to the loss of his brother were extreme. On top of that, his sister-in-law gave birth to a little boy she named Vincent. This seemed to complete his displacement.

The last period of his life was spent in and out of hospitals. His final physician, a Dr. Gachet, was also an amateur painter, and though he befriended the artist, could do little for him. By this time Theo was also ill and Vincent became convinced he was a burden to his brother and his brother's family. Overwhelmed with guilt and despair, he committed suicide by shooting himself in 1890. Ironically, not long before he had sold his first painting.

The symbolism of Van Gogh's paintings can easily be correlated with his depressed state of mind. He had a deep empathy for sadness and misery and this breaks through in all his works. But for the incomparable genius which makes all his paintings seem to pulsate with life we can offer no psychological explanation. It is also obvious his extremely disturbed sex life contributed to his despair and inconsolable longings for love. There was an obvious homosexual relationship with Theo, as well as with Gauguin; cutting of his ear was a symbolic self-castration. It was not until well past his death that his genius was recognized. Today there is even a Van Gogh museum in Amsterdam.

SHORT LIVES: POETS AND WRITERS IN TURMOIL[68]

Lives such as Van Gogh's are not at all uncommon. These are men who have considerable talent, or as in the Dutchman's case, genius, but are so incapacitated by their mental conflicts, often actual insanity, that they cannot make full use of their abilities. In this section we shall look at the lives of some writers and poets who fit into this category.

Edgar Allan Poe (1809–1849) is generally regarded as one of the most original and brilliant writers in American literature. He invented the detective story and by the free use of his imagination influenced a wide spectrum of writers from Dostoevsky to Dreiser and Nabokov. But his own life was a nightmare.

Born in 1809, to two actors, he was left orphaned at an early age. He was informally adopted by John Allan, a wealthy merchant of Richmond, Virginia. Poe was a good student but when he attended the University of Virginia he gambled so much he had to leave college. He once described himself:

> I am the descendant of a race whose imaginative and easily excitable temperament has at all times rendered them remarkable; and in my earliest infancy I gave evidence of having fully inherited the family character. As I advanced in years it was more strongly developed; becoming, for many reasons, a cause of serious disquietude to my friends and of positive injury to myself. I grew self-willed, addicted to the wildest caprices and a prey to the most ungovernable passions.[69]

He began to write poetry when he was fourteen. He was growing into a romantic, arrogant, rebellious and ambitious boy who fashioned himself after Byron and felt every inch a Southern aristocrat.

Interestingly, his first infatuation was with the mother of one of his classmates, Jane Stanard. She died at an early age of a brain tumor, and he wrote:

> I could not love except where Death
> Was mingling his with Beauty's breath—
> Or Hymen, Time and Destiny
> Were stalking between her and me.[70]

Although he tried to stick to literature his life followed an erratic course. He went to West Point for a while, from which he was duly expelled. His adoptive father disowned him and he went through life always in debt (a common pattern). Soon he took to drink, then added laudanum (opium). He married his thirteen-year old cousin; then she fell ill of tuberculosis, the disease that had killed his parents. He nursed her until her death, then tried romantic involvements with other women, several at the same time. In the meantime, nervous exhaustion, drink, opium and an irregular life took their toll. He died in 1849 at age forty.

F. Scott Fitzgerald[71] (1896–1940) was the voice of the jazz age, the twenties. At twenty-three, he was already a best-selling author. He entered Princeton in 1913, where he did poorly academically but brilliantly as a writer. He also began to drink heavily. *This Side of Paradise* was published in 1920, praised for its youthful exuberance, and made the author a star. He married Zelda Sayre; at their wedding they snacked on champagne and spinach, cartwheeled down the halls, and dived into the fountain at the Plaza Hotel in New York, after which they were asked to leave the hotel. This was a foretaste of their extravagant life style, one that kept him perpetually in debt.[72]

Writing, drinking and carousing, they sailed through the twenties. Zelda had her first breakdown in 1930: eventually she was to die in a mental hospital. High hospital expenses contributed to Fitzgerald's problems.

His wild life style continued. In 1937 Hollywood gave him a contract as a writer at $1,000 a week. There he met Sheila Graham, a columnist, who remained his companion until his death. He died in 1940 at forty-four.

Psychologically Fitzgerald's most interesting novel is his fourth, *Tender is the Night,* published in 1934. It is the story of a woman hospitalized in a psychiatric sanatorium, whose psychiatrist falls in love with her. She is wealthy enough to take him back to the United States where she sets him up in practice in a small town in the east. He goes steadily downhill, neglects his practice, and she finally leaves him.

Psychiatry and psychoanalysis in the 1920's and 1930's were still in their infancy, but they did exist. Fitzgerald with his wild impetuosity and serious alcoholism, must have considered therapy at some point. The novel is a way of defeating the analyst (psychiatrist) by buying him off and destroying him. It is not an uncommon fantasy among analysands today.

John Berryman[73] (1914–1972) was one of a group of poets considered to have had marked influence on the course of poetry: Delmore Schwartz, Robert Lowell, Randall Jarrell, R. Blackmun are others. There is an interesting study of Berryman by his ex-wife, Eileen Simpson, who later became a therapist.

Berryman was the son of John Allan Smith, a bank examiner. His father began to speculate in Florida real estate. After losing a good deal of money, he killed himself; John was then twelve. The suicide had a deep impact on him. His mother remarried and he took her new husband's name, forever after he reproached himself for not retaining the name Smith (although he could easily have changed back at any time).

To his wife, John seemed desperately in need of love, he felt if she did not declare unconditional love for him, he would lose his mind. He was twenty-six and all he had to his name was a fifth of a book. He was a severe insomniac; he and Delmore Schwartz (later to become a complete paranoiac) called Cambridge "Insomnia Valley." Schwartz once said to Eileen: "Poet's wives have rotten lives."[75]

From the beginning John was driven to seek fame. When he met Eileen he was out of a job, broke and dubious of his prospects. Fearful of rejection, he held back from committing his own work to print. When he did so, it was with a combination of arrogance and terror.

Soon alcoholism set in. Yet even when admitted to the hospital in a state of acute exhaustion or alcoholism, he would soon be sitting up in bed working on poems or notes. He always retained his will-to-fame. Yet he also saw the emptiness in himself:

> He wondered: Do I love? all this applause
> young beauties sitting at my feet and all . . .
> one sole beauty only . . .
> she saw through things, she saw that he was lonely
> and waited while he hid behind the wall
> and all.[76]

Eventually Eileen left Barryman. He went on to two other marriages, acquired fame, security, even some fortune. Then he jumped from a bridge and killed himself.[77]

The three writers mentioned here all show considerable similarities: traumatic childhoods, an over-indulgent mother, angry father, a wish for greatness and fame, deep depressions, suicidal thoughts (or actual suicide), recourse to drink and drugs. Yet through all of this turmoil they manage to achieve a great deal.

BEETHOVEN: DIVINE MUSIC AND MORTAL MISERY[78]

Ludwig van Beethoven (1770–1827) is widely regarded as the greatest composer that ever lived. He is one of the few musicians of that day who achieved recognition and financial support for his work while alive.

Beethoven was born in Bonn, the son and grandson of musicians. Though he showed amazing aptitude as a child, it was not until his adolescence that he achieved widespread acclaim. Once he started writing music, his career exhibits no serious interruptions. One masterpiece after another followed, virtually until he died. This in spite of a handicap that would have driven any other man out of his mind, for beginning around 1800, he became increasingly deaf. By 1802 he knew his illness was incurable; by 1818 he was completely deaf. Yet he went on composing, right up to the extraordinary ninth symphony, the last part of which, *The Ode to Joy,* has become the theme song of a contemporary United Europe.

But while his music is always inspired, his personal life was little more than a series of horrors. When he was seventeen his mother died of tuberculosis. His father drank so heavily that Ludwig applied to the court to have his father's salary turned over to him so he could support the family; there were two younger brothers, Karl and Johann. His request was approved by the court so that by the time he was eighteen he was the support of the family.[79] With such a background, the need to support a younger man became the great obsession of his life. The Sterbas, who have devoted a psychoanalytic monograph to the strange relationship with his nephew, have seen in this an identification with his dead mother.

In 1792, with his place in the world of music already secure, he moved to Vienna, where he remained for the rest of his life.[80] Some time thereafter several patrons appeared who supported him with a liberal stipend. Thus he was one of the first musicians in history to have been told: you have nothing to do but compose.

In the early days his piano playing was also incredible. For the most part he stuck to his own compositions though, as one critic put it, "all music performed by his hands appeared to undergo a new creation."[81] Unfortunately after his deafness had gone too far he could no longer play the piano, though he occasionally tried.

With women his relationships were distant in the extreme. He is not known to have ever had an intimate relationship with a woman, although several letters referring to his "immortal beloved" have been discovered. There is even a rumor he had a child by her. But all this is hearsay; so far as the evidence of his contemporaries goes he was a woman-hater.

Like Van Gogh, in his family there was an earlier child named Ludwig who died in infancy; his mother must have been deeply pained and frightened by the experience. Beethoven was always seen as a peculiar child, different from the others, not participating in their games. Of the various portraits of him that have survived, not a single one shows him laughing or even smiling. He was a solemn bitter man, full of violent rages, long-enduring hatreds and imaginary enemies; at times he would even fear being poisoned by evil women.[82] Constantly dissatisfied with his surroundings he would move incessantly from one place to another. His neglect of his appearance was so marked he was once arrested as a tramp, only to be freed immediately when the magistrate found out who he was. Even though his financial situation was not at all bad, at times he would sell the same work to two different publishers. Those were the days before royalties and a composer had to get what he could at the time of sale. His brother Karl who acted as his business agent for a while, also made the double sales without any serious objections from Ludwig. At times he would turn down handsome commissions in a fit of egomania.

The most important relationship of his life was with his nephew Karl, son of his brother Karl. Ludwig, the eternal misogynist, had already expressed strong objections to the marriages of both his brothers but they did not listen. When his brother Karl died in 1816 he entrusted the care of his nine-year-old son to Ludwig, then already famous. Karl's wife Johanna managed to get herself included in the guardianship of her son, which led to endless lawsuits and arguments. The boy was the object of all Ludwig's affection for the last eleven years of his life, while Johanna was the object of all his hatreds.[83] Most of the time Ludwig was declared guardian because of his powerful contacts at courts; it appears his allegations that Johanna was a whore, or a criminal, were grossly exaggerated. When he had charge of Karl he was in seventh heaven but when the boy ran away to his mother, and when the courts turned him over to her, Ludwig sank to the abyss of despair. The boy naturally suffered in this tug-of-war and at one point even made a serious suicide attempt, shooting himself in the temples, but fortunately he survived. The shock of his nephew's suicide attempt was so great that Beethoven died shortly thereafter.[84]

Beethoven's life is full of such deep sorrow that the persistence with which he maintained his composing arouses the greatest admiration. Already deaf, it was only in his music that he could really come to life and express his indomitable will.

When he was near the end he would still go to the piano, even though he could not hear a sound. One critic described him as follows:

The moment he is seated at the piano he is evidently unconscious that there is anything else in existence. . . . The muscles of his face swell and its veins stand out; the wild eye rolls doubly wild; the mouth quivers; and Beethoven looks like a wizard overpowered by the demons he has called up. . . . And, considering how very deaf he is, it seeems impossible that he should hear all he plays. Accordingly, when playing softly he does not bring out a single note. He hears it himself in his "mind's ear," while his eye, and the almost imperceptible motions of his fingers, shows that he is following out the strain in his own soul through all its dying gradations.[85]

While musicians are notoriously temperamental, it should not be thought that all have been as bitter and unhappy as Beethoven. Among the contemporaries, Artur Rubenstein (born 1886), who was still playing occasionally in his nineties, was a pianist who loved people, loved life and loved to play the piano. When he was young, he says, there were many things more important than playing, although he was a child prodigy who had been a sensation since he was six. Good food, good cigars, great wine, women were his main interests. It was only much later in life that he took the piano seriously enough, so that when he was seventy he gave a marathon of ten Carnegie Hall recitals in one season. Genius is one thing; life style is another.

THE ATHLETE

It may come as a surprise to rank athletes with creative men. But the inner dynamics are the same; the differences lie only in the medium chosen. A further distinction is that in sports there is an objective scoring, while in the arts much more subjectivity enters the picture.

Joe Louis: The Greatest Heavyweight[86]

Joe Louis (1914–1981) had the longest reign in history of any heavyweight champion, from 1937 to 1949. The story of his career is told easily enough. First professional fights in

1934, three years later he knocked out Jim Braddock and became the heavyweight champion of the world. During his reign he successfully defended his title twenty-five times, scoring twenty-one knockouts. His record has not been equalled, even by the "one and only" Muhammed Ali.[87]

Louis was born in Alabama in 1914, the seventh of eight children. His father was a farmer who was hospitalized with epilepsy and then disappeared. His mother remarried a man with eight children, so that the family was quite large as he was growing up. His father was the son of slaves who worked on a plantation owned by a man by the name of Barrow. Though the later champion's full name was Joe Louis Barrow he soon dropped the final name.

There is little to tell about his route to the top. He fought, he won and he went ahead. He had no qualms about winning fights. The only complication was that he was black, and in the 1930's there was still a lot of prejudice about black men in athletics. Louis, like Jackie Robinson in baseball, is given a great deal of credit for breaking through the racial barrier.

Once he was champion, however, the heights made him dizzy. An early marriage did not work out well because he was always on the go, and always unfaithful, as he frankly admits. As champion he had his choice of girls and he picked freely from the crop. When he was recognized everywhere as the champ it was a thrill beyond description.[88]

But he could not take victory lightly. As he puts it in his autobiography: "I danced. I paid the piper and I left him a big fat tip."[84] By the big fat tip he was referring to the myriad personal, emotional and financial problems that beset him after a while.

The most persistent problem was taxes. No matter how much he made, he always seemed in debt. This was due to a combination of poor professional advice and unsound investments. When he died he still owed the government about $1.3 million in back taxes.

The next persistent problem was women. Like any Don Juan he had too many. One introduced him to the drug habit, which took a long time to break.[90] Finally he found a California lawyer, Martha Malone Jefferson, with whom he was happy the last few years of his life.[91] Earlier he could not have tolerated a woman like her, but by that time he was tired of knocking around, being sick, having one woman after another, arranging bouts and refereeships to pay back taxes. He even had one brief period of hospitalization in Colorado for paranoid delusions.[92]

During his lifetime he felt he was an inspiration to the black people, and in some ways he was. But that was not enough to satisfy him. Once champion, he wanted everything, and could not get it. So he felt depressed and to overcome that took to women, drinking, drugs—the usual route. His life lasted longer than that of the artists earlier described under *Short Lives* but in all essential respects it was similar: an early achievement, eminence for a while, then a long slide downhill.

Bobby Fischer: Chess Master Extraordinary[93]

In 1972 America was thrilled by two outstanding champions: Mark Spitz, who won seven gold medals for swimming in the Olympics, and Bobby Fischer, who took the chess championship of the world from the Russian Boris Spassky. But while Spitz went on to earn $10 million from his victories, and established himself in a bourgeois profession, Fischer virtually disappeared. When the time came, in accordance with the rules of the International Chess Federation, for a match against the next challenger, Anatoly Karpov, Fischer set difficult conditions which were refused, so he defaulted even though a purse of $5 million had been offered by the Philippines. Since then he has scarcely been heard from. What happened?

Fischer was always an eccentric young man. Born in Brooklyn in 1943, he was deserted by his father at an early age. When he learned the chess moves at seven, he soon abandoned everything else. His first comment was that he was the greatest chess player alive; everybody dismissed this as childish fantasy.

He could never do well in school. His handwriting was so bad as to be virtually unintelligible, and he took no interest in any of the academic subjects; only chess counted.

Again the story of his career is told easily enough. In 1956, at the age of thirteen he won the United States championship, the youngest in history to do so. At sixteen he left high school and devoted all his time to the game. There were some upsets, many victories, and a lot of temperament. Once he walked out of a match because he did not like what was going on. Another time he accused the Russians of conspiring to cheat him (a familiar charge, which may have some truth to it).

Then in 1967 he hit his stride. For five years he was virtually unbeatable. By the time he had beaten Spassky in 1972, he had rolled up the highest score in chess history, using the standard system for scoring developed by Arpad Elo, a midwest professor of physics.

Unlike Joe Louis, Fischer did not start dating; he never seems to have had any kind of sex life. He was always a loner, staying up all hours of the night listening to music, and sleeping all day. He joined a small church sect in California; next he was accusing the leader of fraud. The only book he read was the Bible. When anyone in the chess world tried to contact him, he would not respond.

His behavior became increasingly bizarre. Like Beethoven, he lived only in his art form; away from it he was a severely disturbed human being. And once he had given up chess, the suspicion grew that he was psychotic, with a kind of religious mania. For more than ten years he has not been heard from and understandably the suspicions grow. There are many instances where a creative man who gives up his special area of expertise goes to pieces—Nijinsky in the dance, Ezra Pound in poetry, Delmore Schwartz in writing, Horowitz in music, Ruskin in art—the list could be continued indefinitely. Once Fischer gave up chess he was just a disturbed (no one knows how disturbed) middle-aged man. Whether he will ever try again is questionable.

SUMMARY

In summing up this chapter, four questions have to be put:

1. Why was this man creative?
2. How is/was he affected by success and/or failure?
3. How is the personal life related to the creative achievement?
4. Is the creative man a genius or madman or neither?

1. *Creativity:* In all these men there is a creative spark in their special field noticeable from early childhood. A few are child prodigies, but this is the exception rather than the rule. For the most part the creative ability becomes noticeable in early adolescence. It is then nursed along all through life.

2. *Success and Failure:* The creative man finds it difficult to tolerate either success or failure. If he is successful, it tends to go to his head, and he becomes grandiose, pushing harder and harder. If he fails, he takes it as a sign he is useless as a human being, and gets very depressed. In either case the escape to women, drugs and liquor is common; the hardest thing is to settle down as an ordinary human being.

3. *Personal Life:* The vicissitudes of the personal life, especially the early family experience, break through and have an enormous bearing on what the man does later in life. Somerset Maugham retained all through his life a sense of shame about himself, perhaps related to his stutter, most likely to his sexual fears. Van Gogh felt doomed at whatever he tried.

In their fields the creative men find an outlet relatively free from conflict which they can pursue with pleasure and abandon. The suicidal-psychotic propensities seen in so many of these creative men could not be inferred from their artistic productions.

4. *Genius or Madman:* Some are geniuses, some are madmen, but no necessary relationship between creativity and insanity can be found. In general the creative achievement can lend itself to an expansion of the personality, as with Isaac Singer, or a contraction, as with Van Gogh. The decisive factor is the childhood background; what happens to the man afterwards depends on the interaction between his creativity and this childhood background.

Chapter 16:
Generals Die in Bed

For most of human history, and in large parts of the world today, the average man had to contend with two horrendous evils: slavery and warfare. If he was a slave he had to do his master's bidding until death, which was bound to come soon, especially since the slave became increasingly useless as he got older.[1] If he was a conscript soldier, that too meant a fairly early death.

It was generally estimated that up to 1800 the life span of the average man was about thirty years. But that fails to take into account the accidents of war and nature that decimated entire populations. In the Black Death of 1347 (the bubonic plague) perhaps one third of Europe perished. In Napoleon's 1812 campaign against Russia, of the 600,000 men who made up the Grande Armee of that day, not more than one hundred thousand got out alive.[3]

The facts concerning human sacrifice are frightful in the extreme. In Assam in northeastern India when Rajah Nara Narayna rebuilt his empire in 1565 A.D., he celebrated the occasion by sacrificing 140 men, whose heads he offered to Kali on copper plates since he did not have enough gold to go around. When willing victims were lacking, any man of sound health and body caught abroad after midnight might be snatched away for the purpose.[4]

As is well known, Cortez conquered millions of Mexicans with 600 men. One reason was that the Aztecs had been slaughtering their subject populations to a degree that can scarcely be apprehended today. Bernal Diaz, who chronicled the conquest, stated that 100,000 heads were displayed on the skull rack of Xocotlan, while Andres de Tapia claimed there were 136,000 heads on the skull racks of Tenochtitlan.[5]

Numerous examples could be quoted to show that these wholesale massacres were by no means confined to the past; we have already seen that Hitler and Stalin between them

© 1987 by The Haworth Press, Inc. All rights reserved.

accounted for possibly 100 million deaths in the twentieth century, mostly men.

The general who comes out of such a background is given absolute right over the lives of millions of men. One Russian general in World War II was contemptuous of the westerners' caution in clearing minefields; his practice, he said, was to send the men through and simply accept a certain number of casualties. The Japanese fought to the last man; on Okinawa, they stationed some 120,000 men in the last holding action of the war, and not a single one survived.

War cannot be fought without the loss of lives. The general must weigh the risk he is taking against the probable or possible casualties. Eisenhower, an extraordinarily modest general, once commented that no man whose reputation rests upon the sacrifice of thousands of men's lives can be too proud of his achievement. But most generals care much less.

On the other hand the general at his best must also have a capacity, often a genius, for leadership. He must have consummate organizing ability and he must have a profound command of the technology at his disposal. He must also be courageous beyond the call of duty and must have a cause for which he is willing to die.

Since generals, like other men, are only human beings, they alternate between these extremes—courage and loyalty, leadership and the willingness to sacrifice other men's lives.

It is a byword that military history, with its share of glorious triumphs and brilliant campaigns, is also full of incomprehensible costly blunders. Dixon, in his book on *The Psychology of Military Incompetence* (1976), has arued, with considerable logic, that armies are constructed in such a way that the very qualities which lead a man to get ahead in peacetime incapacitate him for the rigors of war. In peacetime a man has to be obedient, adhere to a rigid discipline, avoid original thinking and conform to the code; in wartime in most respects he has to be the exact opposite. Hence the disasters which have befallen even the greatest generals, like Napoleon and the German general staff in World War II.

How does a general get his men to obey him, since blind obedience is of the essence of military strategy? There has to be a certain bond between the general and his men, a certain unifying psychology which allows them to think in similar ways. If this does not exist, mutiny or defeat will result; such was the fate of the French army in World War II which could easily have defeated the Germans at various stages, but lacked the will to fight.

In their examination of Civil War strategy, McWhiney and Grady (1982) have reviewed the thinking of the Southern generals; their book is appropriately titled *Attack and Die*. The Southerners, as the master race they felt themselves to be, were quite willing to charge even strongly defended positions, and their generals were quite willing to order them to do so. The result was one disastrous defeat after another, defeats so bloody that the army had to fall back on a more defensive strategy after 1863. Thus one of the major causes of their defeat was that they displayed more courage than intelligence.

Why are men, ordinarily so careful of their lives, so willing to die in battle? Not even the strictest discipline could force the suicidal tactics so often seen in war. The extreme in the twentieth century is the kamikaze planes of the Japanese in which the pilot became a human bomb, intent on crashing into the enemy ship and losing his life. For these suicidal missions the Japanese at the end of the war still had 20,000 men ready to die, more men than planes. There must be some kind of denial of reality or a belief in magical or divine intervention (kamikaze means "divine wind") to spur men on. Then again many men, in almost any army, have drilled into them that their highest achievement is to die for their country. MacArthur, in World War II, repeatedly and unnecessarily exposed himself to enemy fire, convinced that to die in battle is man's greatest glory. Such psychology is a reversion to the primitive belief that life involves kill or be killed.

EISENHOWER: AN AMERICAN HERO[6]

Although they all have certain traits in common, every outstanding military commander also has a unique individuality of his own. Dwight Eisenhower, who finally toppled Hitler's dream of a 1000-year Reich, in an age when brilliant feats were almost an everyday occurrence, was distinguished chiefly for his diplomatic tact and his consummate mastery of the techniques of warfare. He was widely loved because he was not arrogant (like MacArthur) or unapproachable (like Montgomery) or flashy (like Patton) and never risked the lives of his men unnecessarily.

As with so many others, Eisenhower's career reached its peak in later life. Born in 1890, one of seven sons, to poor farmers with a Mennonite background, he went to West Point and followed a military career. Nothing unusual came out in his background, yet when World War II broke out General Marshall passed over 366 senior officers and appointed Eisenhower commander-in-chief of the allied forces.[7]

In this role Eisenhower faced two problems. One was the need to make so many egotistical men, like de Gaulle and Churchill, work smoothly in the grand alliance. The other was to bring the pressure of his enormous superiority in men and material to bear on the Germans, slowly and methodically. He managed both, and with great skill.

First came the invasion of North Africa in 1942. Then came his greatest test, the invasion of Europe. Resisting all pressures, especially the Russian, to attack prematurely, Eisenhower bided his time and finally launched the great invasion on June 6, 1944. In less than a year Germany was defeated and Hitler was dead.

An example of the tact Eisenhower used to handle the allied commanders is seen in his relationship with Montgomery. Flush from his great victory at el Alamein in 1942, when he turned back the German general Rommel, Montgomery wanted to end the war quickly by a quick punch into Germany across the Rhine. He was so egotistical that he never even visited staff headquarters; everybody had to come to him. Eisenhower preferred the slow prodding piecemeal assault of the German forces. Finally, and apparently primarily in order to placate Montgomery, he put aside enough forces for an attack on Arnhem in Holland; the result was a disaster. Montgomery remained an excellent battle commander but his strategic ideas were never again given serious attention.[8]

After the war, Eisenhower was the lion of the hour, particularly beloved by the veterans because he had been the most human of the generals. In 1952 he ran for the presidency and held it for two terms, in spite of a heart attack, ileitis and a minor stroke. As a president he was in no way distinguished but he was always well liked. One biographer says of him:

"Dwight David Eisenhower was not born great, nor did he achieve greatness. But when greatness was thrust upon him he met the challenge."[9]

GEORGE PATTON: THE BRILLIANT NARCISSIST[10]

George Patton was one of the most admired generals in the U.S. Army, and also one of the most controversial. He was born in California in 1885, the grandson of a Confederate officer who had died of battle wounds in the Civil War. With other military men as ancestors, it was only natural for Patton to seek a career as an army officer. In 1909 he graduated from West Point.

But Patton was no ordinary officer. He was determined to become a great man. At one point he wrote his parents:

> I have to, do you understand, got to be great. It is no foolish child dream. It is me as I ever will be . . . I would be willing to live in torture and die tomorrow if for one day I could really be great."

Patton was unusual in that he did try to excel at everything he undertook. In the Olympics in 1912 he performed in the modern Pentathlon, taking part in five gruelling events, and finished fifth place among forty-three competitors.[12] In World War I he performed gallantly in battle and was wounded.

Between the two wars he worked hard to perfect his military skills. He became an expert in amphibious warfare, even predicting the Japanese attack on Pearl Harbor. He designed the sabre used by the cavalry, invented a machine-gun sled to give assaulting riflemen more direct support, devised a new saddle pack, and improved the tank. He had even learned navigation and earned a license as an airplane pilot so he could better direct the armed forces in those spheres.[13]

Patton was a wealthy man; in addition, his wife was wealthy in her own right. They had three children and a seemingly happy marriage; all the children went into the military or work related to the military.

Finally the chance of his lifetime came in World War II. After some brilliant action in North Africa, he was reassigned to the Third Army, the most mobile branch of the American forces that were to attack Europe. Once the second front was opened, he again did spendidly, at one point forcing an unexpected general withdrawal of the Germans from Normandy due to the speed of his armor. As a military man he was a sensation.

Then came the dénouement. Once the war ended he was appointed military governor of Bavaria, an assignment totally foreign to his nature. All kinds of stories began to seep out about him. He had already attained unwanted notoriety in Sicily by slapping two soldiers suffering from combat exhaustion, calling them cowards. For this he was reprimanded by Eisenhower and publicly apologized to the troops.[14]

In his post-war behavior he behaved in a disgraceful manner. First he was reported to have said we fought the wrong enemy, we should have fought the Russians. Then he let fly a number of anti-Semitic remarks, together with a general appreciation of the Nazis, who, he said, were after all like the Republicans and the Democrats back home, just another party. For the Jews in the concentration camps he liberated he seemingly had nothing but contempt, agreeing with the Nazi remark they were lower than animals. And then he disobeyed orders by proceeding very slowly, if at all, with the denazification process.[15] Finally Eisenhower had no choice but to remove him from his command. On his way home he had an automobile accident in December 1945 which broke his neck; three weeks later he died in the army hospital at Heidelberg.

Patton was a soldier in the old confederate tradition of *Attack and Die*. At one point he said he preferred to hit hard, "even if I lose ten thousand men in one day instead of sailing along and lose five hundred a day for twenty days."[16] At another stage in his career, in 1919, he expressed his narcissistic overestimation of the soldier. He said:

> We, as officers . . . are not only members of honorable professions but are also the modern representatives of the demi-gods and heroes of antiquity. Back of us stretches a line of men whose acts of valor, of self-sacrifice and of service have been the theme of song and story since long before recorded history began. . . .

Our calling is most ancient and like all other old things it has amassed through the ages certain customs and traditions which decorate and ennoble it, which render beautiful the *otherwise prosaic occupation of being professional men-at-arms: Killers* (italics added).[17]

Thus Patton reveals the ambivalence which lies at the heart of many generals. He recognized he was a professional killer but glorified this in various ways. When needed in the war he did splendidly, though with little regard for the welfare of his men. But once peace was established he wanted to go on killing. He knew he had strutted his hour and would no longer be heard from, a situation he did not want to tolerate. Of him it could be said, as of many generals: "First in war, but last in peace."

MACARTHUR: AMERICAN CAESAR[18]

Like Patton, MacArthur was also a man of contradictions, one man in war and another in peace, though he pulled surprises both ways. He was born in 1880, to a professional army officer who had performed heroically in the Civl War. In fact, the senior MacArthur's exploits became an integral part of his son's personality. The greatest was a charge up the hill at Chatttanooga, in a battle situation where the Union forces were pinned down by strong Confederate forces on higher ground. Unexpectedly the eighteen-year old Lieutenant MacArthur led 18,000 men up the hill and to everybody's surprise defeated the enemy.[19] The incident is important because all through his military life MacArthur was careless of his personal safety and many have remarked it was a miracle he came out alive.

After the Civil War, Arthur MacArthur was sent to the west to fight the Indians so that his son's entire childhood was spent in a completely military atmosphere. He worshipped his father, never considered any career other than the army. In 1900 his father was named military governor of the Philippines, a post his famous son was to occupy thirty-five years later. Douglas adored his father, never believed he could

outdo him, and was completely happy in the Army, notwith-
standing the ups and downs he experienced there.

In 1903 young Douglas graduated from West Point with the
highest grades ever recorded up to then. He played a significant role in three wars. In the first world war he headed the
Rainbow Division which saw more action in France than any
other American unit, and was decorated for bravery; again
his indifference to his own welfare was conspicuous.

Between wars he distinguished himself as superintendent of
West Point, later as Chief of Staff. In 1937, at the age of
fifty-seven, he resigned from the army's active list only to be
recalled a few years later when the war broke out.[20] He was
commander of the Philippines when the Japanese attacked
Pearl Harbor; here occurred one of his major blunders. Even
though he had been informed of the Japanese attack, he did
nothing about the safety of the three hundred planes parked
on the ground and they were promptly destroyed by the alert
Japanese.[21] MacArthur himself was sent to Australia after a
holding effort at Bataan gained some time.

The evaluation of MacArthur's true role in the Pacific War is
made difficult by his arrogance, egotism and megalomania, all
qualities which no one doubted existed in him. Of the 142
communiqués issued by him during the first three months of the
war, 109 mentioned only one solider—Douglas MacArthur.[22]
Although he claimed full credit for the island-hopping strategy
that defeated the Japanese, the Navy thought differently, maintaining that the strategy was a naval decision. When the Philippines were invaded, the command was still divided between
MacArthur and the Navy, with what might have been potentially disastrous results. With the average GI, MacArthur's
arrogance made him immensely unpopular, although he was
probably more careful of lives than any other American senior
officer. In any case it is known he was opposed to the military
concentration on Europe which the allied high command had
decided.

The Korean war, his third, also had its highs and lows for
him. When the Korean-American effort seemed doomed, he
engineered a landing at Inchon behind the Korean lines,
which changed the course of battle at once. But then, certain
the Chinese would do nothing, he extended his lines to the
Chinese border and when they attacked, the Americans expe-

rienced bloody defeats. By that time he was seventy-one and it was odd that an active field command be given to a man of that age, but his reputation was phenomenal. After the Chinese entered the war though, his reputation slipped. He wanted to bomb the Chinese mainland. He wanted to spread a cobalt barrier between Korea and China, thus introducing tactical nuclear weapons into warfare for the first time without thinking through the consequences. He issued interviews to journalists without consulting Washington. Finally Truman had no choice but to dismiss him.[23]

After Korea there is little to relate. MacArthur hoped for a presidential nomination, but it was never to be. The greatest surprise was his proposal in 1955 to outlaw war. He died in 1964 at eighty-four.

To evaluate the man is difficult. Everyone agreed he was extremely vain and self-righteous; in his memoirs he wrote he had never given a command that he regretted. He was also, unlike other generals, quite concerned about his men, especially after the defeat at Bataan, and he was willing to take any risks they took. In this respect, his identification with his father's phenomenal feat at Chattanooga, and later battle wounds in the Civil War, was obviously very strong. But his grandiosity was unbelievable. At one point he said his major advisers now boiled down to two men: George Washington, who founded the country, and Abraham Lincoln, who saved it.[21] Which one he fantasied he was, he did not say.

In his personal life he was, like so many military men, rather shy of women. His first marraige to the wealthy Louise Brooks broke up after a few years. Then he took a Eurasian mistress he kept hidden. Finally in 1937 he married his second wife, Jean, by whom he had one son; this marriage, made late in life, seems to have brought him considerable happiness.

Yet the greatest paradox of all is that his supreme achievement was the drafting of the new Japanese constitution. He modestly wrote: "It is undoubtedly the most liberal constitution in history, having borrowed the best from the constitutions of many countries."[25] The constitution provided for equal rights for women at a time our country did not, it uprooted militarism, created a democratic society and was in fact exemplary in many different ways. What he did for Japan during his occupation is also remarkable. After two years cholera was wiped out, TB deaths were down by 88 percent, diphtheria by 86 percent, and typhoid fever by 90 percent. It was estimated he had saved 2.1 million Japanese lives through the control of communicable diseases.[26]

At a reunion of the Rainbow Division in 1935 this most paradoxical of men said of the soldiers who had fallen in France:

> They died unquestioningly, uncomplaining, with faith in their hearts and on their lips the hope that we would go on to victory. . . . They have gone beyond the mists that blind us here, and become part of that beautiful thing we call the spirit of the unknown soldier. In chambered temples of silence the dust of their dauntless valor sleeps, waiting, waiting in the Chancery of Heaven the final reckoning of Judgment Day. "Only those are fit to live who are not afraid to die."
> They will tell of the peace eternal
> And we would wish them well,
> They will scorn the path of war's red wrath
> And brand it the road to hell.[27]

His biographer calls him "American Caesar"; perhaps had the social circumstances been different he might have gone on to a career like Julius Caesar's. There was clearly a strong identification with his hero-father, whom he strove all his life to emulate. (His brother also entered the military service but died of appendicitis in 1923.) Yet along with this identification there lurked the brilliant love-shy little boy who also wanted other things in life than could be summed up in the phrase: kill or be killed. Was he in the end a happy man?

ULYSSES S. GRANT: AMBIVALENT SAVIOR OF THE UNION[28]

Ulysses Grant, the commander of the union armies in the Civil War, also presents a paradoxical history. Born in Ohio in 1822, the son of a tanner, he was reared in poverty and uncertainty. His father Jesse was always struggling to establish himself. When his children (there were six in all) were grown, he both expected them to sustain him and doubted they could be relied on to do so. He did not feel secure until his son was in the White House.

Grant's mother has always been an enigma to historians. She was stolid, unemotional and uncommunicative. When a reporter tried to interview her during Grant's presidency, she acted as if she had not heard him. Even stranger, she did not come to her son's inauguration as president.[29] Grant's unemotional exterior seems to have derived from his mother.

Even the name with which he had gone down in history is not his real one. His parents named him Hiram Ulysses Grant. But when he entered West Point someone slipped and wrote Ulysses S. Grant; this was good enough for him. He never bothered to correct it.[30] The story is typical of the man's stolidity and total lack of emotion.

With no clear-cut ambition in life, Grant finally decided to enter West Point when he was seventeen. He was a mediocre student, as well as a rather withdrawn young man. At West Point he made no permanent friendships. Drawing and horses interested him more than anything else. He also fell in love with the sister of his roommate, Julia Dent.

For the future liberator of the slaves, it was an odd match, since the Dents traced their ancestry back to the old South and Julia's father still had slaves. But this meant nothing to Grant at the time. His engagement to Julia lasted several years and they were finally married in 1848.[31]

In the meantime he served in the Army although he said quite candidly: "A military life had no charms for me."[32] The Mexican war of 1848 woke him up as he saw battle, noted men were killed and maimed. In his *Memoirs* he reports the war with startling simplicity: "After the battle the woods was strued with the dead. Waggons have been engaged drawing the bodies to bury. How many waggon loads . . . would be hard to guess. I saw three."[33] No feelings, no reactions, no comments.

After several years of soldiering, he saw no future in it and resigned his commission in 1854.[34] There followed years of struggling to establish himself in business with no real success. His last try before the Civil War was in Galena, Illinois, where he opened a leather goods shop. He did not prosper, at thirty-seven he considered himself a failure.[35]

Finally came the war and with it his great chance. But the road from Galena to the general who cut the Confederacy in two at Vicksburg in 1863 was still a long and hard one. The quiet man, wearing an old jacket, slouching and watching, was thought by fools to be a no-account and was represented by others as a drunk. But Lincoln was glad to finally find a general who would fight.

In February 1862 Grant scored the first Union victory by capturing Fort Donelson. After some vicissitudes he continued by capturing Vicksburg in July 1863; at the same time Meade repulsed Lee at Gettysburg. For all practical purposes the South was defeated but determined to fight on to the end.

Finally, in early 1864, Grant was appointed lieutenant general and placed in charge of all the Union armies. He held Lee at bay, while Sherman went on his famous march through Georgia. Not long after, the was over. Grant was the hero.

He was a curious hero. It was Sherman who had devastated the South, with his laconic comment: "War is hell." It was Meade who had defeated Lee. Yet there was evidently a need in the country to glorify one man as preeminently responsible for victory, and Grant was that man.

Although he later became president for eight years, his mission in life had been accomplished in these few years of war. He was the general who had saved democracy, and in 1865 the United States was almost the only democracy in the world. Since the 19th century was also the century when Europeans by the millions streamed into free America in search of better lives, Grant also became their hero. When he finally did make a world tour after leaving the presidency he was lionized wherever he went.[36]

After some years in the War Office, he ran for the presidency in 1868 and was overwhelmingly victorious. He served for two terms, until 1877. These years are generally regarded by historians as the most corrupt and shameful among presidential administrations.

To begin with, there was the matter of enforcing the victory by freeing the slaves and seeing to it they remained free. At first military governments in the southern states did lead to black legislatures and some black prosperity. But the ruling race in the South would not give up, and it was not long before the new amendments were defied in one way or another, and blacks who became too prominent were systematically murdered. Many times the only solution was to have Grant send in troops though he was always reluctant to do so. By the end of Grant's tenure, in 1877, the attempts at Reconstruction were virtually over, and the blacks entered another long period of agony. Grant did not seem to care.

On top of that there were the scandals. Grant did not benefit from the widespread corruption that followed the war, though some of his friends and relatives did. Again he was not eager to prosecute, even though he said: "Let no guilty man escape." It was an era of robber barons and corruption in legislative halls all over the nation, which did not let up for another twenty-five years. One Cabinet officer after another, as well as Grant's personal friends and associates, was implicated in cheating the government of hundreds of thousands of dollars, in some cases, millions. Grant stuck loyally to his friends, as though dealing with old school chums, not with the national interest. By 1875 the vice-president called Grant "the millstone around the neck of our party that would sink it out of sight."[37]

As we look at the historical record, we gain the impression that Grant, lost in his glorious self-image as the savior of the Union, cared about little else. His marriage was on the whole a happy one; there were four children. The welfare of the country involved social and economic considerations beyond his comprehension, as they would be for a later general, Dwight Eisenhower. The only project that emanated from his imagination was the annexation of Santo Domingo; he saw that as a place where blacks could go if they did not get along here. But the Senate would not allow this.[38]

He did not survive long after he left office. His hopes for a third term were obviously unrealistic. In 1884 he developed a cancer of the throat; the next year he died. Before his death he completed his *Memoirs*. His military exploits are covered in this book; his presidential years are omitted.

Lincoln valued him because he was willing to fight without too much regard for losses. Yet this willingness to fight may have come out of his lack of emotion as much as his military ingenuity. Whatever happened, Grant was always unmoved. Garfield said of him once: "His imperturbability is amazing. I am in doubt whether to call it greatness or stupidity."[39]

His biographer offers this evaluation with which we can well concur:

> Grant did not make war for reasons or in ways that ennoble the civil War. He did not rise above limited talents or inspire others to do so in ways that make his administration a credit to American politics. If Ulysses Grant was, in any measure, the concentration of all that is American—and we still believe in democracy, his story is troubling. In fact, it suggests that we must rethink both the worth of war and the uses we make of politics . . .[40]

THE MEN AND WOMEN WHO FOUGHT IN VIETNAM[41]

It is all very well for a Patton to say generals are the descendants of the demi-gods, or for a MacArthur to urge that to die in battle is the most glorious way to end life; the fact is that they live on to a reasonable age while many thousands of the men they commanded die young. For the average soldier war is a situation in which he is confronted with the most primitive of human predicaments: kill or be killed. How does this average soldier react?

On this score there is very little material. But in the most unpopular war America has ever fought, the war in Vietnam, there has been considerable study of the reactions of the average GI. A recent book edited by Mark Baker, offers a series of interviews with the survivors of Vietnam. We would like to quote some of these interviews.

On Initiation

> I was in Johns Hopkins Medical School at the time. As a prank, somebody cut one of the fingers off the cadaver I was working on and kept it. When I went to run in the cadaver, I couldn't account for the finger.
>
> I knew who'd done it. So the next day, while he was doing a dissection on the leg, I took the arm of his cadaver and snuck it out. I put it in an ice chest and drove out to the Beltway around Baltimore. At a toll booth, I stuck the frozen arm out the window with some money in the hand and left the toll attendant with the arm.

This got back to the president of the school, who was Dwight Eisenhower's brother, Milton, a real fucking hawk. He told me to take a leave of absence to reconsider my commitment to medical school. I thought that was probably a good idea. I said, "Great." A week later I had my draft notice. They turned me right in to the Board.[42]

It's just a little town where I grew up. I played some football and baseball like everybody else. I was kind of a hard-ass in school. I didn't know how good I had it then. I took little odd jobs and saved up enough money to buy an electric guitar and an amplifier. I started playing in a band.

Near the end of high school, everybody's saying, "What are you going to do? What are you going to do?" I didn't know. I said, "I'm going to join the service." After I graduated, I went into the Marine Corps. They were supposed to be the best. To me, they were. They helped me grow up. I grew up in Vietnam.[43]

After we got in boot camp, they ask you to put down on some form why you joined the Marine Corps. I put down, "To Kill." In essence, that's what the fuck I wanted to do. But I didn't want to kill every fucking body. I wanted to kill the bad guy.[44]

Baptism of Fire

I saw where the fire was coming from that first time I got shot at. It was like a barn. I ran in there, knocking over shit, looking for the guy, but I couldn't find him. I seen fresh tracks leading to another hooch which was like a little barber shop—There were four gooks standing there. I throw them all up against the wall. I got my M-16 out.

My sergeant comes up. "What are you doing?" he screams. "You can't do that."

"What do you mean? One of these God damn bastards was shooting at me and I'm going to find out which one did it."

"No, you can't do that."

"What, are we playing games?" He made me leave.

"Get out of here, Sonny, You can't do that shit. You ask them. If they talk to you, they talk to you. You can't push them around."

"But, Sarge, they're shooting at me!"

"I don't care. You just can't do it."

"What a place this is going to be."[45]

Grunts

In the mornings in the Nam, when you wake up, you always see the sun coming up. It's really beautiful, but it's cool then and that's when you really want to sleep.

You come down off the hill and there's big rice paddies all around the bottom of the hill. Maybe 10 percent of the company gets across them to the far tree line and somebody opens up on us.

I'm running and running and running. I'm getting dinged at over and over again. Guys are falling, not from getting hit so much as sliding in the mud. It must last at least five minutes. That's a long time to be running with all that shit strapped to you.

I turn around and say, "Jesus Christ, man, cut it the fuck out."

Crack, crack, crack. And you're helpless. A guy gets wounded and you don't hardly want to pick the poor fucker up, because you can't make it across the field yourself. But you do pick him up.

You got a base fire set on the sniper, artillery goes on the son of a bitch and he's still dinging at you, the cocksucker. You're so tired that you just want to lay down in the rice paddy. The only reason you didn't was because most of the guys got off their fucking ass and kept moving. If they had laid down, I probably would have too.[46]

Martial Arts

There was this prostitute that came in. I don't remember the exact story, but I think she had been with a couple of GI's and was caught robbing them. Anyway, two guys had been killed. She had been shot, but had survived. She was on our ward. She was about the same age as me—early twenties. I said to a friend of mine, "Jesus, she's going to die. I hope to hell she doesn't die on my shift, because I don't want to have responsibility for trying to resuscitate her. I don't give a shit what happens to her.

This guy was really cool. He said, "Why do you feel that way?"

"I hate her guts. Whether somebody uses a hooker or not, you're all in the same game and you got to pay the consequences. Only the guys already paid and she might as well pay too." I just hated her. . . .

She died eventually, but not because I didn't do something. But it's hard.[47]

Victors

I know Marines that made more gooks than they killed, just by treating them bad. It's funny when you don't expect to get mercy from anyone, you're very reluctant to show it. So you really breed hideous people over there, for the cause of National Defense. If you sit down here on the couch, it seems ugly. At the time, they weren't ugly. They were the things to do. Considering what else was going on this was nothing.[48]

Victims

Everybody there smoked marijuana with a few exceptions. There were the big drinkers. If you tended to drink, well, you drank, and if you smoked, you really smoked. Everybody did it to extremes, just to get their act together to face the ward the next day or whatever they had to do. By the time I left, I knew doctors who had done heroin. I knew two nurses who went home hooked on heroin.

I tried it about a dozen times. Although I liked the high, I puked my guts out every time. It was a great high. You know that feeling when you're nodding out and you can't keep your head up.[49]

Homecoming

When I came back about six of us were walking through the airport and a girl—maybe eighteen or nineteen, about the same age as me really—she asked me how many women and children did I kill. I told her, "Nine. Where's your mother at?" I thought it was great fun putting her down like that. But inside I felt, "Gees, why is she treating me like that?"

I though I would come home as a war hero, you know. I didn't really want to be a war hero, but I thought I'd get a lot of respect, because I'd done something for my country. Somewhere deep in my psyche I thought that people would react to what I'd done, and say, "Hey, good job. Good work."

My family did. "Hey, great. How many people did you kill?" That wasn't right either. I didn't tell them when I was getting home, because I didn't want a party. But it happened anyway. I couldn't stay at that. I hung out an hour or two. Then I went out with my friends and got fucked up out of my face.[50]

Nothing could more graphically depict the lot of the average soldier in war than these verbatim quotes. Accidental entrance into the service, fighting without quite knowing how or why, the only women available thieving prostitutes, drugs all over the place, killing and being killed. Nor is this war any different from any other. Such has been the lot of the average man throughout history—forgotten, terrorized and murdered.

SUMMARY

Most of our study of the military mind, as is most of the literature, is confined to the generals. A number have been examined in critical detail. Considerable variability is noted, with regard to their achievements, their personal lives, their attitudes to war and their evaluation of themselves. Some excerpts have been cited from the stories of young men in Vietnam, which illustrate the fact that the lot of the average soldier caught in combat has always been bleak.

Chapter 17:
The Searching Intellectuals

Our world has been transformed by science in the past three hundred years. We have reached the moon, moved toward further stars, probed the inner workings of the mind, lengthened life by overcoming a large number of diseases, created all kinds of artificial new substances never dreamed of before—the list is endless. The men who have done this have been intellectuals—scientists. What have their lives been like and what are they like as human beings? This too has been extensively researched and some tentative conclusions emerge.

Although there is no one "scientific personality," certain features appear again and again. There is, first of all, superior intellectual endowment as a child; no scientist springs full-blown from the blue (although there are on occasion exceptions to anything). Second, there is an intense curiosity about the world, or in certain parts of it. Almost invariably stories are told of the scientist's early musing about the world. Einstein, when he was five years old, received a compass from his father. Noting that the needle always pointed in one direction he immediately reasoned there must be something "out there in space" to keep it in that direction. Later he was to translate this childish curiosity into a world-transforming theory of space.

A third characteristic of the scientist is a passionate devotion to work and discovery. He is ambitious and from an early age out to win the Nobel Prize. Max Weber, one of the great social scientists of our time put it this way:

> . . . whoever lacks the capacity to put on blinders, so to speak, and to come up to the idea that the fate of his soul depends upon whether or not he makes a correct conjecture at this passage of this manuscript, may as well stay away from science. He will never have what one may call the "personal experience" of science. Without this strange intoxication, ridiculed by every outsider;

© 1987 by The Haworth Press, Inc. All rights reserved.

without this passion, this "thousands of years must pass before you enter into life, and thousands more wait in silence"—according to whether or not you succeed in making this conjecture; without this you have *no* calling for science and should do something else.[1]

Because of his superior endowment the scientist is accustomed to high achievement early in life. This produces a feeling of self-confidence on the one hand and a sense of discouragement on the other because he may never again reach the level attained earlier. One patient of mine had an IQ of 198 (the highest I have ever seen recorded) when he was seven. He had memorized the entire subway system of New York and had a reading comprehension of fourteen. Naturally he was always far ahead in school, with averages well in the 90's. When he grew up he became a college professor, as might have been anticipated. But he chose a field where publication was difficult and could not manage more than one paper a year. This would have been enough for any ordinary mortal but for him it meant a sense of failure, since he felt he was no longer living up to the promise of his childhood. In a similar vein many scientists, even those with extraordinary feats, often suffer from depressive episodes, or even long-standing depressions.

This last point is particularly important because most scientists draw their main identity from their affiliation with the great discoverers, the great contributors to scientific knowledge who have given us the world as we know it today. When the goals are set so high, realistic exploits, no matter how significant they may appear to the average man, seem like nothing to the scientist.

Looking at the scientists in terms of the three fundamental dimensions stressed in this book—sex, aggression and social role—conflicts appear in all of them. Because of their devotion to work, there is little time for women. Hans Selye, who deplores his two "messed-up" marriages, writes:[2] "When you are truly in love with your career, a feeling of solitude and emotional isolation often results." At another point he says quite simply: "My life is my work."[3] This is a feeling shared by all true scientists and there are few women who can compete with such a love.

Since his field of excellence is in the intellect, the scientist tends to shy away from physical combat and shifts his aggression toward intellectual arguments. This is no doubt why there is so much acrimonious disputation among scientists, most of which never gets into print. Nowadays politeness rules and disagreement is expressed fairly calmly but in former days the vilest accusations were hurled much of the time. Thus in the bitter argument between Flamsteed, the royal astronomer, and Newton, the latter wrote to Flamsteed: "I want not your calculations but your observations only."[4] Falmsteed wrote back calling Newton "Hasty, artificial, unkind, arrogant." To which Newton replied that Flamsteed should "bind his head strait with a garter till the crown of his head was nummed." No doubt many current scientists feel like this about their colleagues but they restrain themselves.

In this social role the scientist has both advantages and disadvantages. As a rule he becomes an academic, less often a researcher for a large company. As such, he is often looked upon as a necessary nuisance. The popular term "egg-head" is illustrative of how a scientist is usually looked upon as an odd curiosity. The poor relationships which have prevailed between science and government since World War II are one consequence of this misperception.

By and large the scientist is seen as happy in his work but not too happy in his personal relationships. Especially nowadays, when science has become so minutely technical, he may find few persons with whom he can communicate. And his mind is so full of his work he can think of little else.

ALBERT EINSTEIN: THE MAN WHO REPLACED NEWTON[5]

Newton's world system lasted about 250 years; then many of its fundamental postulates were replaced by the theory of relativity, the creation of Albert Einstein's mind.

Einstein was born in Ulm, Germany, in 1879, the older of two children. His father was not very successful at his business and moved a good deal, first in Germany, then in Italy.

Einstein had a hard time in his German school. Before he

could get his diploma at the Gymnasium he was expelled with the remark: "Your presence in the class is disruptive and affects the other students."[6] While the details are not clear, he evidently had a hard time with Germanic discipline. In fact, he became so fanatically anti-German that at the age of sixteen, in 1896, he formally renounced his German citizenship. For five years he was stateless. Then he became Swiss and remained so all his life.[7]

With some difficulty Einstein got through the Swiss Polytechnic Institute where he could major in physics. None of his teachers found him outstanding, and perhaps because of that he spent a great deal on his own reading the latest thoughts in physics, some of which were unknown in his school. Even his doctoral dissertation, in 1905, aroused little interest, though this was the year in which his epoch-making paper, "The Special Theory of Relativity," was published. Einstein was clearly ahead of his time.

Unable to obtain a teaching appointment, he finally got a job at the Swiss Patent Office, where he remained for seven years. This also allowed him to marry and father two sons. One later became a professor of engineering, the other unfortunately became psychotic. In this early period, however, those who knew the latter described Ernst as a rather happy man.

Finally in 1907, Einstein became a *privatdozent,* then a professor. Gradually it was dawning on the physicists of the world what a revolutionary view was contained in his papers. In April 1914 he was appointed to the Prussian Academy of Sciences, a prestigious position. When World War I broke out several months later, his family was vacationing in Switzerland and he had to remain without them for the war years. After the war he and his wife were divorced and he married Elsa, the widowed daughter of his father's cousin.[8]

Once the war broke out, Einstein embarked upon a pacifist course, which was to be his hallmark for the rest of his life. His hatred of German militarism remained unabated. Around this time he wrote:

> The ancient Jehovah is still abroad. Alas, he slays the innocent along with the guilty, whom he strikes so fearsomely blind that they can feel no sense of guilt. . . . We

are dealing with an epidemic delusion which, having caused infinite suffering, will one day vanish and become a monstrous and incomprehensible source of wonderment to future generations.[9]

After the war, international acclaim came when a prediction he had made was confirmed by direct observation, in contradiction to what Newton would have predicted. It became clear his system was valid, and eventually it also became clear that his famous equation $E = mc^2$, showing the connection between energy and mass, pointed the way to the release of enormous amounts of energy from the atom; this in turn led to the atomic bomb and the nuclear age.

Einstein was always a typical absent-minded professor. He once said of himself: "I'm not much with people, and I'm not a family man. I want my peace. I want to know how God created this world. I am not interested in this or that phenomenon, in the spectrum of this or that element. I want to know His thoughts, the rest are details."[10]

After the war, a change of personality occurred. This quiet unassuming absent-minded physicist, who liked nothing better than to sit in peace and meditate on the construction of the world, became the lion of the hour. For several years he travelled all over the world, lecturing on relativity to the lay public. In 1921 he was awarded the Nobel Prize, but in the award relativity was not mentioned. At that time it was still a center of contoversy.

Scientifically, the rest of his life represents a kind of anticlimax. In the search for the mathematical relationship between electromagnetism and gravitation, he sought to relate the universal properties of matter and energy in a single equation, in what came to be called a unified field theory. To this he devoted the remainder of his scientific life. In 1929 he published a preliminary version of his unified field theory; in 1950, when he was at the Advanced Institute at Princeton, he published a second. It was immediately but politely criticized by most physicists as "untenable."

Once the Nazis came to power, it was widely believed they intended to murder him. He sought and found refuge in this country at Princeton. But he was again a changed man. A friend wrote:

It was as if something had deadened in him. He sat in a chair at our place, twisting his white hair in his fingers and talking dreamily about everything under the sun. He was not laughing any more.[12]

Einstein's failure to keep pace with the development of physics after the late 1920's has often been noted. He gave the conscious reason as the fact he could not accept the uncertainties of quantum mechanics. In 1926 he wrote:

> Quantum mechanics is certainly imposing. But an inner voice tells me that it is not yet the real thing. The theory says a lot, but does not really bring us closer to the secret of the Old One. I, at any rate, am convinced that He does not throw dice.[13]

Scientifically, his intense resistance to the uncertainties of quantum mechanics and the indeterminacy principle is odd indeed. He, after all, was the man who had shown that absolute space and absolute time were figments of the imagination; why should absolute measurement be any different? Clearly there must have been more at play than scientific exactitude.

In his later years, after he came to the United States in 1953, Einstein was a depressed and relatively unproductive man. When his second wife died in 1936, he commented briefly that "she was more attached to human beings than I."[14] Thereafter he never again took any interest in a woman. In his work he did little; he told an old friend in 1935, "in Princeton they regard me as an old fool."[15] The only thing people knew was that Einstein doggedly opposed quantum mechanics and was going to come up with his own theory. He died in 1955, his later ambitions unrealized.

If Einstein is compared with Newton, some similarities can be noted. After solving the problem of the structure of the universe in terms of the scientific knowledge of their day, they each discontinued contacts with the further development of their work. Newton immersed himself in a religious controversy; Einstein involved himself in a battle against quantum mechanics and statistical causation. It is not too much to suppose that each, in his own way, identified with God and was seeking to divine His ulterior purposes. Neither, by any stretch of the imagination, could be described as a happy man.

BERTRAND RUSSELL: RENAISSANCE MAN OF THE TWENTIETH CENTURY[16]

Bertrand Russell, one of the towering minds of the century, begins his autobiography in this way:

> Three passions, simple but overwhelmingly strong, have governed my life: the longing for love, the search for knowledge, and unbearable pity for the suffering of mankind. These passions, like great winds, have blown me hither and thither, in a wayward course, over a deep ocean of anguish reaching to the very edge of despair.[17]

In his work he traces quite frankly the three great passions of his life. Intellectually, his influence stems from the fact that at any time he had more than forty books in print, ranging over the fields of philosophy, mathematics, science, ethics, sociology, education, history, religion, politics. He was indeed the searching intellectual par excellence.

Yet his most enduring claim to fame lies in his two mathematical works, *The Principles of Mathematics* (1903) and *Principia Mathematica* (with A.N. Whitehead) (1910–1913). These two books for the first time placed mathematics on a sound logical footing, and established a sound logical base for the foundations of mathematics. Ultimately Russell showed that logic and mathematics are one. In his own pithy way he put it that mathematics is the field in which you never know what you are talking about (variables undefined) nor whether what you are saying is true (abstractions divorced from the real world).

Russell's life was as varied and exciting as his works. Born in 1872 to parents who had advanced views on the bringing up of children, they both died before he was four. Their will provided he should be brought up by friends who were atheists. But since his grandfather, then already over eighty, had been prime minister of England several times, this will was easily overturned and Bertrand was brought up by his grandparents. His grandfather was twenty-three years older than his grandmother and died when the boy was still very young so that in effect he was brought up by his grandmother.[18]

The family lived in a country house, Pembroke Lodge, given to them by Queen Victoria. Russell's was an isolated childhood, with innumerable servants but almost no children as companions. There were many peculiar beliefs going around at the time, for instance, it was held that fruit was bad for children so he had to steal whatever fruit he might be able to get. It is not surprising he speaks of almost intolerable loneliness all his life. He was brought up by tutors for the most part until he went to Cambridge, which explains his wide range of reading.

His first and major interest for many years was mathematics. His brother introduced him to Euclid when he was eleven and it felt like his first great love. From then until he was thirty-eight, when he finished *Principia Mathmatica*, mathematics meant more to him than any other intellectual field. After that he gave it up.[19]

He entered Trinity College, Cambridge, in 1890 and was at once recognized, especially by Whitehead, as an extraordinary student. Even though mathematics was his great love, he read philosophy, economics, history and divers other field. His first book, published in 1896 (when he was twenty-four) was on German social democracy. In his dissertation, however, he indicated the direction in which he was going by writing on the foundation of geometry.

The work involved in writing *Principia Mathematica* was difficult in the extreme. In essence he and Whitehead were reformulating the conceptual bases of mathematics, and any such effort had to be tortuously difficult. Many times, he tells us, he thought of suicide when confrronted by knotty problems to which he could see no solution. Finally, though, it was finished and he became one of the world's leading mathematicians.

But then he began to shift. In the first world war he was defiantly opposed to British participation and willingly spent six months in jail for his beliefs, even though he was the grandson of a British prime minister. It is not clear what he gained by this jail sentence, but defiance was part of his nature.[20]

There followed years of travel and works on an almost infinite variety of subjects. The best known is his *History of Western Philosophy,* one of the bases for awarding him the Nobel Prize in Literature in 1950. He expressed himself freely and with great skill on almost every subject: war, communism, relativity, marriage, free love, happiness, religion, power, morals. It was said he normally wrote at the rate of 3,000 unaltered words a day.

After World War II he seemed to view himself as a world reformer. First he helped to organize a conference on the management of the nuclear danger. Later he headed up an international tribunal to "try" the United States for war crimes in Vietnam. Apparently fearless of death, he wrote his own obituary, to be read on the BBC after he died. He passed away in 1970 at the ripe old age of ninety-seven.

Although he was a complete rationalist and wanted to pursue love rationally, his relations with women were generally poor. In his first marriage, to an American, Alys Smith, when he was only twenty-two, his early love soon subsided. One day he suddenly found himself "out of love" with her and discontinued sexual relations. For nine years they remained together while he was writing the *Principia,* with sex reduced to once or twice a year. There followed affairs and marriages after a divorce from Alys. Finally, in old age, he found Edith, to whom he wrote this beautiful poem:

> Through the long years
>   I sought peace.
> I found ecstasy, I found anguish
>   I found madness,
> I found loneliness.
> I found the solitary pain
>   that gnaws the heart
> But peace I did not find.
>
> Now, old and near my end,
>   I have known you,
> And, knowing you,
> I have found both ecstasy and peace,
>   I know rest.
> After so many lonely years,

I know what life and love may be.
Now, if I sleep,
I shall sleep fulfilled.[21]

It is understandable that with a childhood as fragmented as his, he should have wandered through life finding mostly agony, ectasy and loneliness. His major achievement, from 1900 to 1910, in transforming the foundations of mathematics, was too difficult for him to continue. For it he had a substitute parent-couple (Mr. and Mrs. Whitehead) and a nonsexual relationship with a woman, then his wife. This helped to stabilize him. For the rest, he will live on more because of his superb literary skill than for any serious contribution to science. And, of course, by his own admission, he was anything but a happy man.

JOHN KENNETH GALBRAITH: A LIFE IN OUR TIMES[22]

Economic wisdom is very much in demand these days, and because of the wide disagreements among economists, many have doubted that the traditional economic theories still have any validity. Among the most eloquent of the contemporary critics is John Kenneth Galbraith who, for most of his life, we are surprised to learn, was a professor at Harvard. He is also a man who has written so extensively about economics that he has become a popular spokesman for his point of view, which has had considerable influence on various administrations in Washington. In *A Life In Our Times* (1981), Galbraith has told the story of his life.

Although a professor most of his life, Galbraith has also been a government administrator (he was in charge of price controls during World War II), a writer (besides his works on economics he has written several novels and a book on Indian painting), editor of *Fortune,* a politician (one of the founders of Americans for Democratic Action—ADA), and an ambassador (to India). A full life indeed. And through it all his main endeavor has been to put forth a view of economics as based on theories that are traditional but incorrect, urging his fellow economists, politicians and the public at large to wake up to the radically new facts of economic life.

In his autobiography Galbraith indulges in very little intro-
spection. In the foreword he says:

> I have not turned to look within on family and per-
> sonal life, perhaps partly because there isn't much on
> which to grieve. My life has been without the agony that
> sustains interest in such matters and which encourages
> the associated introspection.[23]

While there is indeed little agony in his life, one episode
must have been acutely painful: the death of a son when the
boy was seven. Galbraith must have been deeply pained but
all he says about it later is: 'His steady decline, accepted with
unfrightened calm, is something on which after thirty years I
do not care to dwell."[24] Clearly he and his wife made up for
the loss by having two more children, both boys, in the next
two years.

If internally, except for the death of his son, his life has
been placid, externally it has been full of manifold excitement. Born in Ontario, Canada, he tells us that his father was
a former teacher who never fully rejected his profession and
became a moderately well-compensated township and county
official. Galbraith's mother, "a beautiful, affectionate and de-
cidely firm woman," died before all her children (he and
three siblings were not yet in their teens. This is all we learn
about his childhood.[25]

We do not learn why he went into economics, other than
his rural background particularly qualified him for agricultural
theory and practice. In 1931 he was graduated from Guelph
College in Ontario with distinction, and immediately received
an appointment to the University of California at Berkeley.
From there he went to Princeton, of which he had a low
opinion: "The economics faculty of the time was firmly committed to teaching what a decade of depression had shown to
be irrelevant," is a typical comment.[26] In 1934 he went to
Harvard as an instructor, and remained there, with much time
off for governmental and political activity, until retirement.
Even after retirement he undertook a three-and-a-half year
series for the BBC, on the history of economics, which he
called "The Age of Uncertainty," later published as a book.

It is rather surprising Galbraith tolerated the tedium of

academic life for so long. For his colleagues he usually has little but sarcastic comments on their obtuseness. Milton Friedman is one of his major targets. When Galbraith was nominated for president of the American Economic Association in 1972 he was opposed by Friedman, who argued that Thorstein Veblen had never been president. Galbraith neglects to add that this remark is wholly irrelevant. All he says is: "I learned after the election that this got me by."[27] What he learned from his youth, he says, was that one must be compulsively against any self-satisfied élite, and he regarded the average economics professor teaching the traditional theory of the "free market" as a hidebound fool.

Somewhat late in life Galbraith developed his own major ideas, somewhat reminiscent of Veblen, to whose celebrated book *The Theory of the Leisure Class* he wrote the foreword when it was reissued; he even led a drive to restore the home in which Veblen was brought up.

Galbraith's position is that the image of the free market which economists have inherited is all wrong in terms of modern conditions. Half the production of the country is in the hands of 1,000 large firms which have immense control in creating desires, in settling prices, and in the economic policies pursued by the government. There is, in his words, "a new industrial state." Economics should serve "the public purpose" (another title of one of his books). He has brought forth his ideas in some twenty-five books and innumerable popular articles, which stamp him one of the most vocal advocates of the salutary effects of a properly planned economy.

His liberal views have naturally embroiled him in considerable controversy throughout his life. Apart from the loss of his son, and the early death of his mother, no personal upheaval is recorded. His marriage seems to have been an early and happy one, though he gives few details.

Galbraith divided his life between academia and politics, yet he had a low opinion of both. Of academia he says typically: "The wisest course for the textbook writer is to say faithfully what has been said before with, as embellishment, some minor notes of novelty which the publisher can emphasize in his advertising. This brings the best chance of acceptance."[28] (It is to be noted he never wrote a textbook.) Of the government, he composed what he calls Galbraith's First

Law of Intelligence: "You cannot know the intentions of a government that doesn't know them itself."[29]

Thus his aggression came out in constant argument, both in politics and in academia. Always critical he discovered that the American strategic bombing in World War II had failed to hamper Germany's war production, but his findings were ignored), always sarcastic, he steered his life through both fields, kept his head above water, and maintained a certain kind of unflappable calm. From his book, except for a few minor incidents, he seems to have enjoyed himself immensely.

HANS SELYE: STRESS WITHOUT DISTRESS

The discoverer and explorer of the concept of stress, which plays such a significant role in modern medicine and psychology, is in many ways a typical scientist. In his autobiography he says of himself:

> "Realistic people" who pursue practical aims are rarely as practical and realistic, in the long run of life, as the dreamers who pursue only their dreams. True scientists—even when they become very old—retain a certain romanticism, a dreamy, imaginative habit of mind; they continue to dwell on the adventurous, the picturesque, the unusual; they never cease to be thrilled by the heroic grandeur and infallible consistency of the laws that govern the harmony of Nature in and around man.[31]

Selye, a Hungarian by birth, had plenty of stress in his own life. Born in Vienna in 1907 when that city was the capital of the Austro-Hungarian Empire, he encountered the war and its hardships at an early age. His father was a surgeon; Selye was actually the fourth generation of physicians in his family. When World War I broke out, his father entered the army and stayed away five years. The came the fall of Hungary, which depressed Selye, followed by the shifting of borders, so that his native city of Korodom became Czech. The world war was followed by civil war so that he lived through a lot of shooting. This made a deep impression on him of life's uncertainty and the insignificance of personal property.

His scientific career followed virtually a straightline course. It was only natural he should take his degree in medicine. Less expected, but in line with his interests, was a research degree in organic chemistry, giving him both an M.D. and a Ph.D. His mind was set on research rather than practice, even though his father on his return from the war had reestablished his flourishing surgical clinic and his son could easily have joined him. But as a child he had performed surgical experiments on frogs and chickens in the family home and perhaps this was one root of his interest in research.[32]

A Rockefeller Fellowship was his first introduction to the United States; he spent it at Johns Hopkins. It only lasted a year, then he returned to Europe. There followed the great opportunity: an invitation in 1934 to go to the University of Montreal. He accepted readily and stayed there the rest of this life. (At seventy-one, as he relates in his autobiography, he was still hard at work.)

While a student, he became intrigued by the nonspecific elements in illness. Later he was to rename this the General Adaptation Syndrome and show it represented a course followed by many illnesses. Soon he had also formulated the concept of stress, defining it as the nonspecific response of the body to any demand. The word "stress" was selected because no other word could exactly describe what he saw happening in his laboratory animals. Once he had hit upon the notion of stress and its allied phenomena, his life work was settled. He investigated stress from every conceivable point of view. As he tells it now, almost his entire reading is devoted to the enormous number of articles on stress, research he originally stimulated. The word "stress" has become so familiar, thanks to his investigations, that is is now almost universally used; exact equivalents for it do not appear to exist in other languages. In all he has written thirty-eight books and 1600 technical articles on the topic. He is highly regarded as one of the leading scientists of our time.

In his personal life he experienced considerable disappointment. As a youth, he fantasized making a marriage in which there would be a "kissing of the minds."[34] He married his first wife after a brief courtship in Austria, then brought her to the States. She was studying music but to please him and join him she took an M.D. degree at Montreal. The sharing of interests did not make them happy, and they were divorced.[35]

He married his second wife on the rebound.[36] In his book he says very little about her. They had four children, and the marriage lasted twenty-eight years, but it was never a very happy one. He stayed in it, he says, for the sake of the children. Eventually they broke up. Throughout his work he refers repeatedly to his "two messed-up marriages," which he finds humiliating. His third marriage, after the break-up of the second, was to his assistant, this he describes as very compatible. Like Bertrand Russell, he found love late in life, although he had been searching for it ever since he was a little boy. With his new love he remains ever boyish and ever optimistic, again like Russell. In a summing-up he says:

> I have managed to be happy, and I hope productive, throughout my life, although there were always many difficulties to overcome. But now, at seventy-one, I do not feel at all that I am approaching the sunset of my life. Now, the sun is rising! I have finally reached the peak of the mountain, and the horizons I see from here are wonderful. After many unsuccessful efforts (largely because I am so difficult to live with), I have found Louise![37]

It seems odd though that Louise insists on living on her own income, which she earns by selling her now well-recognized "neobatik" at arts shows.[38]

Selye's complete involvement with stress has made his work life extraordinarily productive. He says he talks and thinks of little else. For the personal roots of this ambition we would have to go back to his relationship with his father. Though he admired his father, he also wanted to surpass him. A memory from the age of three is typical: his father put him on his shoulders and walked out into the sea. Hans was frightened but exhilarated. This was then transformed into the wish to conquer a scientific field.

His very ambition, however, creates a certain amount of stress. He says he is always on guard lest time slip away, making him lose his chance to do everything he wishes. The only type of dream he remembers is one in which he misses his aim. He is always late for the departure of a plane, a meeting or a public address. Sometimes he loses his way in a foreign city. It is always the same general problem and when he realizes he had no chance left to accomplish what he wants, he suddenly wakes up in a sweat. This inner stress, that he will never conquer the entire field, must be another strong root of his tremendous ambition. It is not surprising he coined the phrase for his philosophy of life as "stress without distress."

ISAAC ASIMOV: "A NATIONAL WONDER AND A NATURAL RESOURCE"[38]

Isaac Asimov, the world's leading science-fiction writer, has enjoyed a fabulous career. *The New York Times* has said that he "has probably done more than anyone else to give scientifically illiterate readers a feeling for the excitement and accomplishment of modern science."[40]

He was born in Russia in 1920, and came to this country three years later. Father bought a candy store in Brooklyn, and from then on the family's lives revolved around the candy store, open seven days a week and eighteen hours a day. Because of the depression the store failed and a new one had to be opened up and when it failed, another, and in this way they got up to their fourth store.

Isaac was always very bright in school. At nine he discovered science-fiction magazines and by eleven he was beginning his first experimental scribblings. His first glory was finished in 1938 but it was rejected. After more tries he finally sold a story to *Amazing Stories*. Then only nineteen, his career was launched.[41]

Surprisingly, he became a real scientist. Majoring in chemistry at Columbia, he eventually got his Ph.D. and an appointment to teach biochemistry at the Boston University School of Medicine; one of the professors there had been a fan of his and facilitated his entrance into the faculty.

By 1950, he had published his first book, *Pebble in the Sky,* and two years later his first professorial book, *Biochemistry and Human Metabolism.*[42] Up to that point his earnings from science-fiction stories were meager in the extreme, and his salary was only $6,000 per year. He felt he had come to a dead end. But this feeling was soon to change.

Asimov continued to write and to teach. By 1954 his earnings from writing had passed the $10,000 per year mark[43] and he was invited to be a guest of honor at the World Science Fiction convention in 1955.[44] It was the highest accolade in science fiction.

Trouble at the medical school developed in reaction to his success at writing.[45] One contract he received from the government for a book on blood was arranged as a grant to be paid through the school. When the dean, a very jealous man, got wind of this he refused to pay out the money, on the grounds that professors could not earn royalties while working full time. Asimov, always ready for a fight, pursued the case doggedly.[46] It was soon obvious the dean was merely jealous. The medical school faculty was proud to have him and eventually, in 1979, twenty-four years after his promotion to associate professor, made him a full professor, even though he had not taught at the school for twenty-one years.[47]

Asimov kept a diary throughout his life and his autobiography details many incidents taken from his diary. On the whole, however, it is written like a record of a series of victories. At the end of each year he notes how many books he had published that year and his income from his writings. By 1979, when the autobiography ends, he had published 215 books (including the two volumes of his autobiography), while his income had long since passed the $100,000 per year mark.

By 1958 his income was sufficient to allow him to leave the medical school to devote full time to writing. Around that time he also switched from science fiction to science. His popular presentations of a wide variety of scientific subjects have gained him universal acclaim. The catalogue of his books includes the following topics: (1) science fiction novels; (2) mystery novels; (3) science fiction short stories; (4) mystery short stories; (5) science fiction anthologies; (6) general science; (7) mathematics; (8) astronomy; (9) earth sciences; (10) chemistry and biochemistry; (11) physics; (12) biology; (13) science essay collections; (14) history; (15) the Bible; (16) literature; (17) humor and satire; (18) autobiography, and (19) miscellaneous. Truly an awesome astounding collection.

If looked at as a human being, his story goes a different way. To turn out such a prodigious volume of work most certainly involves a restriction of the personal life, especially since his books are for the most part digests of scientific knowledge accumulated by others, so that his job has been to distill the information gained from books and present it in his own style. He was married at twenty-two and remained married for 32-1/4 (his figure) years, yet it could scarcely have been a happy marriage. When his second child was due, he said to his wife: "It's got to be a girl; if it isn't a girl don't come home."[48] (The first child was a boy.) It is not surprising that his wife developed arthritis and other physical illnesses or that the marriage eventually broke up. His second marriage was to an analyst, Janet Jeppson, who had been one of his science fiction fans, though Janet too was afflicted with somatic ailments. However, by this time, he was world famous and could be more relaxed with her so the second marriage was a happier one.

As Asimov describes himself, he is an extremely pugnacious individual. Speaking of one of his early critics, Henry Bott, he says: "I do not, at any time, accept criticism of my stories with noticeable grace; but had I been a saint, his snottiness would have broken through the barriers."[49] Frequently he enters into intense controversies, expressing considerable eagerness to take revenge. Obviously he has to win; at the end of many years in his autobiography he lists the number of books published and the amount of money earned. Gifted with a phenomenal memory, he seems to like to demolish people with some rare bit of information. At lunch with the editor Tim Seldes in 1967 Asimov bested him on information about Adb-er-Rahman III, the greatest king of Muslim Spain. He includes this anecdote in a chapter entitled: "Asimovian Immodesties.[11] After a long string of obscure facts had been recited to beat him down, Tim said: "Asimov, to choose a phrase at random—you're a *prick*."[50]

There is no doubt Asimov has a brilliant mind and a virtually photographic memory. He became a member of a medical school faculty at an early age. One wonders then why, instead of pursuing his scientific career, which could easily have gone far, he preferred science fiction and popularization. No doubt the need for a quick victory as well as for wide acclaim played a significant role. Once his brother Stan said to him: "I notice, Isaac, that when the conversation does not concern you directly, your eyes glaze over, but that you snap to attention the moment your name is mentioned."[51] And at another point Asimov himself says: "But for me, the essence of life *is* writing. In fact, if I do manage to publish a hundred books, and if I then die, my last words are likely to be, 'Only a hundred!' "[52] At another point he comments that the most interesting thing about him is the number of books he has written, which is not a fair appreciation either but rather points to the underlying psychological conflicts.

He says almost nothing about his sex life. His least favorite story is one in which sex is introduced.[53] When he was forty-eight a prostitute tried to pick him up outside a hotel in New York and at first he did not realize what was happening.[54] No doubt his sex life with Janet Jeppson, his second wife, has been superior to that of the first marriage, yet no real details are given.

All told, a very driven life, but how much happiness he has found is hard to say.

SUMMARY

It is the searching intellectual who has brought modern civilization to where it is. Usually the scientist is completely absorbed by his work, leaving to one side the pleasures other men seek in life. If he is gifted, as many scientists are, his contributions are notable. If he is not, he tends to become frustrated by his lack of achievement. And yet over and over, no matter how great the achievement, we find that the scientist is not pleased with himself. In many ways he tends to be like Don Quixote, "dreaming the impossible dream."

Such a situation creates considerable tension and conflict in the man's life, which is handled in different ways. Einstein virtually gave up after he was fifty, depressed by his lack of interpersonal contacts and his inability to reproduce his earlier epoch-making contribution. Bertrand Russell, after ten years of sexless soul-searing effort, brought to fruition the reformulation of the foundation of mathematics; after that he skipped from one topic to another, unable to recapture the profundity of his earlier years. Love and sex for these men are always a source of tremendous conflict. In a way, the great scientist is hurt by his achievement as much as he is helped, since he is cast into a social role which makes it difficult for him to relate to other people. As a result, most scientists show a strong tendency to fall into depressions.

Chapter 18:
Men Who Help:
Therapists and Priests

Most men are in trouble of some kind, either physical or psychological or both, and do not know where to turn. Historically, only two classes of men have been interested in their fellow-men's difficulties, the therapist and the priest. In this chapter we shall focus particularly on the psychotherapist rather than the medical.

Traditionally the first person a distressed person has turned to is the priest (in the widest sense of the word, including the medicine man and the minister). Even in the sophisticated modern world this is still true.

Our interest here is on the personality of the priest or minister, not of the patient. Why should a man give up worldly ambition, sex, aggression and everything else connected with it and devote his life to helping his fellow men?

In all religions the priest is regarded as somehow "holier" than the parishioner, even though this is often not the case. He must offer sanctuary, or solace, or escape from the world, or compassion, and to offer any of these he must to some extent be above the temptations which confront the ordinary mortal.

Priests can offer consolation in a variety of ways, which can broadly be grouped into positive and negative. From the positive point of view the priest encourages faith, confession, greater holiness, resisting temptation and the like; there is no doubt that any or all of these offer some relief at times. From the negative point of view the priest threatens punishment, especially in the after-life, to which he claims a unique line of communication. To avoid this punishment, certain penances are set out. In order to avoid even greater suffering in the after-life, the churchgoer submits to a lesser punishment here.

This points up another aspect of the priestly caste. Almost

© 1987 by The Haworth Press, Inc. All rights reserved.

all religions (there are exceptions such as some forms of Buddhism and Confucianism) stress the existence of life after death, offering the believer a surcease from the awful fear of death. The reassurance against this fear, guaranteed by proper conduct on earth, is one of the greatest inducements religion has to offer. Even Voltaire, who fought the church all his life, managed to have a Christian burial, apparently not willing to risk total repudiation by the church after he was gone.[1] Certainly the fear of death is one of man's greatest burdens.

Still, the theory of what religion has to offer is one thing, the practical realities are entirely different. "He does not practice what he preaches" has become a cliché, deriving from religious inconsistency. We cannot even remotely sum up the history of religion here, but it requires no proof to show it is full of dissent, conflict, hypocrisy and even, in many epochs, outright murder (of the "heretics" of course).

It is only in reaction to the failure of religion to deliver what it promises that the development of modern psychotherapy can be understood. We really do not know to what extent the promise of an eternal blissful after-life relieved the fear of death in former times, or relieves it now. In any case the reality has been for centuries that religion has divided as much as it has united. Tied to a preposterous theology, which then becomes the *gospel* truth, it has often created more conflict than it has resolved.

Psychotherapy has beocme in its way a secular religion, free from theology, free from supernatural sanctions and punishments, geared to finding happiness on earth. Almost all psychotherapists have taken a strong stand against religion as a cure for human suffering. Large parts of the world no longer have any religion at all, while others, like Sweden, though they maintain an "official" religion, literally pay no attention to it. What we will try to understand are the motives which lead men to practice such a secular religion.

SIGMUND FREUD: THE FATHER OF MODERN PSYCHOTHERAPY[2]

If psychotherapy exists as an established profession, and it does with some 200,000 practitioners in the United States alone, it owes more to Sigmund Freud (1856–1939) than to any other single individual. He established its theoretical bases, elaborated the psychology connected with it, showed how its practitioners should be trained, and demonstrated beyond all doubt its relevance for the human condition.

Freud came to psychotherapy through medicine, largely because there was at that time no other route to follow. Yet from first to last he never ceased to insist that psychoanalysis had no inerent connection with medicine. It was a field in its own right. In his old age he specifically said to his friend, the Swiss minister-lay analyst Oskar Pfister: "I should like to hand it (psychoanalysis) over to a profession which does not yet exist, a profession of *lay* curers of souls who need not be doctors and should not be priests."[3] Note the qualifications here. Freud was well aware he was creating "curers of souls," that is, displacing the age-old prerogative of religion. Whether they were or were not medical men was a matter of indifference to him; but in no case should they be priests. The reasons for this view will be discussed later.

When Freud set himself up in practice in 1886, as a "specialist in nervous disorders" (a title he helped to destroy), virtually nothing was known about the bizarre manifestations of hysteria, tics, compulsions, phobias and other symptoms he had to treat. The manner in which he established psychoanalysis is of tremendous importance, and must be recounted in detail to understand the personality of the therapist today.

Freud was born into an era when medicine was king. Psychology as a profession did not exist, while as a field of study in the universities its main concrete results were in the area of sensory physiology; everything else connected with the human psyche was lost in philosophical speculation. Psychiatry at that time had made virtually no progress since the time of the Greeks. Its practitioners were largely in mental hospitals, where they served as little more than custodians of the incurably insane. No one had any real clue to the nature of insanity.

While Freud pursued hypnosis, minor electric shocks, suggestion and the other techniques of that day in attempts to help his patients, the real change came in two ways; first, scientifically, because he recognized the importance of psychology, and, second, because he underwent a self-analysis, the first really successful self-analysis in history.

The emphasis on psychology is easier to understand because it has become everyday currency today. In 1894 Freud established that neurotic problems (and psychotic as well) represented a defense against unbearable impulses, or what we would describe today as a method of warding off anxiety.[4] This led to various questions, such as what were the unbearable impulses, why did they become unbearable, how did the person manage to defend against them, how were the conflicts resolved, and the like, to which he devoted the rest of his life. Again, all of this had become so familiar it is included in every elementary textbook of psychology; what has been forgotten is that one hundred years ago it was regarded as a ridiculous new doctrine.

Less easy to grasp, but equally vital to the development of the science is the self-analysis. From 1895 to 1902, Freud went through a kind of searching examination of his psyche, which had never been done before in that way. It has been described in a French book by Didier Anzieu, not yet translated into English, but the outlines have been clear for a long time.

Freud's self-analysis involved an exploration of his inner world, of his dreams, of his family relationships and of other intimate details of his life. The paradox is that this man, who in real life was so self-effacing, has in this way become one of the best-known figures in history. There is hardly any incident or meaningful experience in his life which is still unknown.

What came out of the self-analysis was a new conception of man and of human nature. Briefly, it could be put in this way: Man is brought up in a family structure which leaves a deep imprint on him. What the parents do to him in childhood is then internalized in a structure called the superego, and thereafter his life is regulated by this superego in the same way it was regulated by the parents when he was a child. He is also driven by powerful biological impulses—sexuality and aggression—over which he has limited control. Because his parents (and later his superego) forbid him to express these impulses, he experiences conflicts of varying degrees of severity about life. His reason, instead of acting in a clear and unequivocal way, is forced to gloss over his errors and missteps so he will not be published by the parents. As time goes on, he develops an image of himself, parts of which obtain approval, and parts disapproval, from the surrounding world and from his superego. The proportion of approval to disapproval will determine how well or badly he feels about himself.

Mental illness, or psychopathology, as it is called nowadays, results from a lack of development. The "insane" man is not really irrational, his true intentions appear only when we clarify his unconscious motives. Because of the constant fear of disapproval, what is conscious to the person represents only a small part of what goes on inside—the tip of the iceberg, as it has been called. What is unconscious explains the major part of his activity, although this will vary with the degree of disturbance. The more disturbed the man the more he is acting at an unconscious level; the healthier he is, the closer his true motives are to the unconscious ones.

All of this had to be puzzled out by Freud from scratch. And what he did for himself he trained others to do for the "patients." The word "patient" is put in quotation marks because it then appeared that what Freud had gone through was a universal human experience, not confined to "sickness" as such. To call the analytic patient "sick" shows a lack of understanding of basic psychological truths.

As a human being Freud was a typical intellectual of his times. He took his medical degree, married after a tempestuous love affair lasting four years, had six children (the youngest of whom, Anna, became a world-famous psychoanalyst in her own right), wrote many books (probably the most significant collection of writings on psychology published in this century), developed a cancer of the jaw in 1923, when he was sixty-seven, fought it valiantly, was expelled from his homeplace in Vienna by the Nazis, and died in England in 1939. Although many have tried, there is little to relate about his life because the excitement was almost entirely in his ideas.

The fact is that from the beginning of his practice in 1886, to just before his death in 1939, a period of fifty-six years, Freud spent the bulk of his time listening to other people and trying to help them with their problems. What was there about his psyche that led him into this way of life?

At various points in his writings Freud denies he really ever wanted to be a healer, yet for more than half a century he functioned as a healer. His denial need not be taken much more seriously than Einstein's wish, expressed in his old age, that he wished he had been a plumber. The question we are raising at this moment is: What made Freud become a healer? And what kind of a man is drawn to heal in the way that Freud did?

The answer in a sense ties in the psychoanalytic healer with the religious. For the wish to heal comes out of the experience of having been healed by someone else, just as the religious person has had an experience of conversion or mystic illumination. It is in a sense the same as the parental wish: If a man has had a happy childhood, possesses loving feelings toward his parents, when he grows up there is a natural wish to found a family of his own, pass on to his children what he in turn received from his parents. A healer in short is one who has been healed.

Because of the intense struggle for power among psychotherapists, this simple fact has been ignored. Psychological research reveals that the vast majority of mankind are and have been extremely unhappy. They have covered over their unhappiness in a variety of ways, but once they stop covering up and allow a healing process to take place in themselves, the wish to help others can become the dominant one in their lives.

HARRY STACK SULLIVAN: HEALER OF THE SCHIZOPHRENIC[5]

Once Freud showed the way, others followed. A new profession was born, though the names of the practitioners were the same as before (psychiatrist, psychologist, social worker), but the psychiatrist of 1982 bears about as much resemblance to the psychiatrist of 1882 as the airplane bears to the railroad, or the automobile to the horse.

Of all of Freud's followers, Harry Stack Sullivan can be singled out for two reasons: with his approach to the schizophrenic, he made the most important technical advance since Freud, and with the emphasis on cultural forces in personality, he and others made the most important theoretical advance in psychoanalytic psychology.

The schizophrenic, the "insane" man in popular language, had been the kind of patient most resistant to psychoanalytic treatment. Freud himself tried but gave up, hoping some new technical advances would make such patients more amenable to treatment. Others tried (Jung had treated a case of schizophrenia early in the century) but Sullivan was the first to work out a systematic method with which he was able to help a large percentage of those unfortunates regain some semblance of normal life.

Although both became great healers, the contrasts between Freud and Sullivan are quite sharp. Sullivan, whose biographer rather grandiloquently calls the "psychiatrist of America," was born in Norwich, Chenango County, New York in 1892. Both grandparents had emigrated to America from Ireland in an attempt to escape from the famine and oppression by the British; neither one did well. When he was still a little boy, his family moved to the farm, where he was brought up until he went off to college. There is little in his early life to forecast the brilliance that emerged later. He was an only child, lonely, with little stimulation, either intellectual or emotional. Somehow, though, he grew up.[6]

An obviously gifted student, Sullivan won a scholarship to Cornell and enrolled in 1908. There he was unexpectedly involved in some kind of illegal activity; some say he was the dupe for a gang of boys who were stealing the incoming mail. Whatever the truth, he was expelled from Cornell in 1909 and never returned to college.[7]

For the next two years he simply "disappeared."[8] It is presumed he was hospitalized somewhere with a schizophrenic break but no records have ever been found, though many years later he did mention casually to his secretary that he once had a schizophrenic break. It is from this point his lifelong interest in schizophrenia dates.

Two years after his expulsion from Cornell, in 1911 he enrolled at the Chicago College of Medicine and Surgery. This was in the days before the Flexner report led to the upgrading and standardization of American medical schools so that, in effect, the Chicago College was not much above, if at all, a diploma mill. Although he left in 1915 without a diploma, by 1917 Sullivan had been allowed to graduate. He was a full-fledged doctor and could now make his way in life.[9]

However, he was still very uncertain about what he wanted to do. Part of this uncertainty was clearly sexual. Sullivan never married, never had a close sexual relationship with a woman. He was stuck on the adolescent joke he was "waiting for a rich widow."[10] It was well known during his lifetime that he was an overt homosexual, though how much homosexual activity he engaged in nobody knows. He stumbled around for a few years until he found his niche at Shepard and Enoch Pratt Hospital near Baltimore, where he was in charge of a ward of young male schizophrenics.

At that time a diagnosis of schizophrenia was virtually the kiss of death. Less than five years before, Kraepelin, the grand old master of psychiatry, had stated that more than seventy percent of schizophrenic patients are incurable.[12] The vast majority of psychiatrists, then as now, did not have any idea of how to treat schizophrenics and, accordingly, in self-defense decided there was something wrong with the schizophrenic's brain.

Sullivan, actually in agreement with Freud's theories that there is a continuum in the mental life, so that, as he was to put it, we "are all more simply human than otherwise," took the young patients under his wing. He established what we would call today a therapeutic milieu. He had a small ward of male patients cut off from the rest of the hospital; he had no female staff on the ward; he hand-picked the male attendants; and he wanted adequate recording equipment so he could record and conduct research on schizophrenic thought. And he spoke to the patients, treating them psychotherapeutically.[13]

The result was astounding for that time: A large majority of the patients got better, some made complete recoveries. His colleagues, totally unable to duplicate his results, tended to deride him as schizophrenic, but the derision derived obviously more from envy than from objective evaluation.

Sullivan was well aware, though he never said so, that his own hospital experience must have been the major determinant of his success, just as Freud's self-analysis was the major key to his therapeutic endeavors. Sullivan once wrote:

> The graduate of our medical schools, for somewhat different reasons, is so detached from a "natural" grasp on personality that it usually takes him from 12 to 18 months residence on the staff of an active mental hospital to crack his crust to such effect that he begins to learn what "it is all about." The graduate nurse, however,

harassed as she is by upstart interns, inefficient physicians, utterly unmoral male personnel, etc., etc., seems usually too preoccupied ever to make this beginning.[14]

Similar derogatory comments about medicine and psychiatry, in their relationship to schizophrenia, are found throughout his writings. He was clearly aware he had discovered something, thirty or forty years ahead of the field.

After the experience at Shephard Pratt had established him as one of the world's leading authorities on schizophrenia, the rest of his life was somewhat of an anticlimax because he never tried to resolve his personal problems. There is no clear record of what personal analysis he went through; apparently with Clara Thompson, who was herself a novice at the time, and also a colleague. In 1930, he moved to New York; shortly thereafter he went bankrupt. In private practice in New York he was only moderately successful; evidently the brilliance displayed in the treatment of the schizophrenics did not suffice for the treatment of ordinary mortals. He went back to Washington, founded a school, the Washington branch of which later repudiated his theories in favor of Freud, and threw himself into various other activities. But he remained a homosexual, an alcoholic and a most unhappy man. His great and enduring achievement was the demonstration that the schizophrenic can be treated psychotherapeutically. He died in 1949.[15]

The subsequent near-deification of Sullivan as founder of a new "interpersonal" school in contrast to Freud's "biological" school is due more to the need to create a hero than to any inherent truth in the arguments presented.

But once more Sullivan's capacity to heal the schizophrenic came out of his own self-healing process.

CARL GUSTAV JUNG: PSYCHOTHERAPY AND RELIGION[16]

Jung can best be contrasted with Freud and Sullivan because of his emphasis on religion, an emphasis entirely lacking in virtually all his other contemporaries, as well as in modern times. He regarded religion as one of man's natural functions; for those in the second half of life he felt that the problem was always one of religion. Nevertheless this was tempered with a wide-ranging system of psychology, much of which was a reformulation of Freudian doctrines.

Jung was born in Switzerland in 1875, the son of a small-town pastor, and the grandson of a famous man with the same name, allegedly an illegitimate child of Goethe's.[18] He studied medicine, took a position at the Bürgholzli, the famous Swiss psychiatric hospital, where he worked under Bleuler. He married, had five children, and outwardly led a fairly normal life, although recently a book appeared by Sabina Spielrein, one of his former patients, and later an analyst in her own right, which claims he had sexual relations with her and other patients—the great taboo of both the psychotherapist and the religious leader.[19] Jung worked with Freud from 1907 to 1913 and was promoted by Freud to be the president of the International Psychoanalytical Association against the wishes of many analysts. In 1913 Jung suddenly resigned and left the psychoanalytic movement forever.

From 1913 to 1919 he had a spiritual crisis, which he called his Nekiya[20] (the journey of Ulysses to the Sojourn of the Dead). Through this crisis he worked out what seems on the surface to be an entirely different system, then reformulated into a system of psychotherapy.

For Jung life was seen as a series of psychic metamorphoses. From earliest days he had a rich interior life of which no one was aware; he was interested in visions, mystics and other delvers into the supernatural, in addition to the more usual kinds of religious experiences. In therapy the first step is to bring the patient back to reality, and particularly to the awareness of his present situation. From this there emerge a series of steps which finally lead to what he called the process of individuation. As in Freudian analysis, a great deal of emphasis is placed on the dream, though Jung felt that the unconscious was in every respect deeper and less accessible than it was to Freud.

In later years especially, he became interested in psychic experiences which are dismissed by the ordinary analyst as varieties of wishful thinking. He delved into astrology, graphology, the occult, mysticism, alchemy, gnosticism, eastern wisdom, and the like. In 1948, at the age of seventy-three, he opened a C. G. institute in Zurich, to teach his theories to others; it is still flourishing.[21]

Jung has had his followers but his influence has always been greater among the lay public than among the mainstream therapists in the profession.

What we are intrested in is the elements in his personality that led him to spend his life as a healer? There was the deep split in his own psyche, which he had always keenly felt and to which he referred as his divided self. The function of his voyage of self-discovery from 1913 to 1919 was to integrate this divided self and become an individual in his own right; this was his process of individuation. In his work he actually combined the medicine of his famous grandfather and the religion of his father, together with the deep psychological insights he had learned from Freud. He thus succeeded in uniting in one self-image the various strands from the past which had gone into his image of himself as a man. Since all his heroes had been healers in one form or another, it was virtually inevitable he should become a healer himself.

PART IV:
MAN: VICTIM OR PERSECUTOR?

Chapter 19:
Love Is the Answer

It is time to take stock of the main lessons to be derived from the material presented. Throughout, the thesis has been presented that man and his troubles have been forgotten. Everywhere departments of women's studies have been set up; nowhere is there a department of men's studies.

Man has been approached in terms of three facets of his functioning; sexuality aggression and social role. In all three profound problems arise.

In his sex life the man is repeatedly frustrated by a rejecting woman. His mother pushes him away sooner or later. His first girl friend in childhood makes him the butt of jokes, even though this is an experience of profound importance to the little boy. Shortly after he starts school he is separated from his sister and girls his own age. When finally he hits puberty, the conflicts surrounding intercourse are as tormenting as those of the girl. That socially he is permitted to take somewhat more of the initiative than the woman makes little difference.

Marriage likewise becomes a disappointment to man. To confine their sexual relationships to one woman for the rest of their lives is a deprivation many men find extremely painful, much as women are now discovering it is painful to limit themselves to one man. The result is that sexual conflicts in marriage are virtually universal.

In our society man is driven to fight and to achieve. In

© 1987 by The Haworth Press, Inc. All rights reserved.

many areas his attainments have been prodigious. Yet when we look at the inner man, he is full of despair, unhappiness and quite often serious depression. Henry Ford II and Somerset Maugham were in agreement on one point: They did not want anybody to look at their lives too closely.

The man is trained to fight, even though fighting carries with it many dangers. Not the least is that he can be killed or seriously wounded. Yet he is not supposed to show any fear. While dueling is an aberration of previous centuries, modern man is preoccupied with the "put-down." He has to maintain a certain image in the eyes of the world and if he cannot maintain that image, he feels deeply humiliated and depressed. Not as deeply as the Japanese in World War II who, rather than disgrace themselves by surrendering to the Americans, committed suicide by the thousands. Yet deep enough to hurt, and hurt badly.

At the same time the man is unable to reveal his hurt to anybody. He has to hold on to the stiff upper lip for which the British became most famous. Women go to psychotherapists more often, but that is a reflection of the man's inability to show his pain, not of any reflection on woman.

Finally, the social structure forces a man into certain paths. He does not have an infinite variety of life careers to choose from; he just has a few about which he has to make up his mind. Scarce wonder that many men falter by the wayside, unable to decide what they want to do in life, drift, or become homosexual to justify their indecision, or resort to more serious emotional difficulties, such as neurosis or psychosis. In times of economic distress these problems multiply manyfold.

Man of course does not give up. He chooses one of the various alternatives open to him. The average man marries, finds a career, curbs his aggression to become an obedient member of society. But whenever we examine more closely the inner dynamics of his adjustment, large chinks in the armor appear.

In sex he is faced with too much or too little. Don Juan was not a happy man. To pile up sexual conquests resolves the dilemmas no more than a retreat from sexuality. So wherever we turn we find that in sex there is either stress or deprivation. Few men escape.

In the release of his aggression, again the man's fight does not make him happy. If he is powerful, he becomes ruthless, his view of life becomes one of beat the other fellow out or be beaten out yourself.

If he is successful he keeps under wraps the great suffering that was the price of his success. If he is narcissistic, turning in on himself, he remains desperately lonely. If he resorts to crime, usually he dies young. If he remains just an average man, he is apt to find himself described like Solomon Grundy: born on a Sunday, died on a Tuesday, with little to describe in between.

Several social roles available to the man have been considered in more detail. Politicians may be either leaders or power-seekers. "Political promises" are notoriously unreliable, which always makes politicians suspect. Do they mean what they say, or is this just another ploy to get the votes? Politics is also mixed up with corruption, money and crime. There is an aphorism that the politician is the man who has his eye on the next election, the statesman is the man who has his eye on the next generation. There are few statesmen, lots of politicians.

The business of America, Coolidge once sententiously observed, is business. Various business careers have been examined. The Horatio Alger myth is still pursued by many Americans, and on rare occasions realized. Most of the time though it leads to heartache and sorrow. Many men are shortening their lives by dreaming the impossible dream.

Those who choose to enter the military career find themselves in a well-organized hierarchy where they do not have to do much thinking; obedience and discipline are their major ideals. When war does break out, those at the top feel few qualms about sending men to their death; generals, as has been said, die in bed. Through the ages the fate of the average soldier has been a horror; Sherman described every campaign in history when he said, "War is hell." Even the generals who suffer no pain are often as unhappy as the men who carry out their orders.

Our contemporary society has been built up by large numbers of searching intellectuals. They withdraw from the worlds of business and war to pursue science. For them, all too often, the scientific work becomes so fascinating in its own right that they give up a great deal of everything else that makes life exciting. Particularly difficult for them is the relationship to women.

The creative fields attract a great many men. Yet here the problem is particularly acute because of the conflict between the pursuit of art for art's sake and the compromises needed to make a living. A large number of creative men follow a path of hard work leading to success, then dissolution into women, drugs, depression and early death.

Finally, there is the new profession of psychotherapist. Following Freud, who founded the field, men who enter this profession are, or should be those who have had deeply moving personal experiences in their lives. Yet here too the suffering may last many years before it is finally resolved.

What then is the answer? Love. It is possible, despite all the cynicism displayed about it, to reach a meaningful love relationship with a woman which will be gratifying sexually, intellectually and socially.

Occasionally men are found whose early family lives were so harmonious that they could as adults move on to a happy relationship with a woman; among those discussed in this sense were Will Rogers, John Adams, John Galbraith. But this is unusual.

More common are the men who, after various fruitless attempts to find compatibility, eventually end up with a woman who meets their needs and whose needs they meet. Sometimes this happens only in old age, as with Bertrand Russell, or middle age as with Isaac Bashevis Singer. Sometimes though it never happens, as with Albert Einstein, or many of the artists described in this book.

What is important is that instead of, or in addition to the drive for achievement drilled into the boy, the notion of a happy love-match should also be held up to him as an ideal. There is no implication this is easy; no ideal is easy. But at least it points in a direction which offers a solution that avoids the terrible tragedies of the kind that have been described throughout this book.

To train men for a happy love life requires a thoroughgoing restructuring of the family and educational system. That, however, need not come as a surprise, since nothing is more common on the present scene than proposals for such reorganization, whether in the prescriptions for a return to the traditional, or in the cries for outright rebellion.

The physical sciences have made progress by a variety of astounding technical innovations. The social sciences have tried to imitate them, with no success. What they have come back to is a recognition of the crucial importance of love for human happiness, a recognition that has repeatedly been stressed throughout the ages by religious leaders, philosophers and wise leaders everywhere. Then the man, instead of pushing himself beyond endurance, as he does today, will find himself fulfilled and happy. He will no longer be forgotten.

References

Abbott, J. H., 1981. *In The Belly of The Beast*. New York: Random House.

Adams, J., 1973. *The Founding Fathers*. New York: Newsweek

Andrews, F. M. and Withey, S. B. 1976. *Social Indicators of Well-Being*. New York: Plenum Press.

Anthony, J., Kowpernik, C., Ed., 1970. *The Child In His Family*. New York: Wiley

Anzieu, D. 1975. *L'Auto-Analyse de Freud*. Paris: Presses Universitaires de France.

Asimov, I., 1981. *In Joy Still Felt*. New York: Avon.

Baker, M., 1981. *Nam*. New York: William Morrow.

Bartell, G. D. 1971. *Group Sex*. New York: New American Library.

Beach, F. A., Ed., 1977. *Human Sexuality in Four Perspectives*. Baltimore: Johns Hopkins.

Berryman, J., 1977. *Henry's Fate*. New York: Farrar, Straus and Giroux.

Berryman, J., 1981. *The Dream Songs*. New York: Farrar, Straus and Giroux.

Bleser, C., 1981. *The Hammonds of Redcliffe*. New York: Oxford University Press.

Bradlee, B., Jr., Van Atta, D., 1981. *Prophet of Blood*. New York: G. P. Putnam's Sons.

Brady, F., 1977. *Onassis*. New York: Jove.

Brandon, R., 1977. *A Capitalist Romance*. New York: J. B. Lippincott.

Bray, D. W., et al., 1974. *Formative Years in Business*. New York: Wiley

Brod, M., 1963. *Franz Kafka: A Biography*. New York: Schocken Books.

Brodie, F. M., 1981. *Richard Nixon*. New York: W. W. Norton.

Brown, C., 1965. *Manchild In The Promised Land*. New York: Signet.

Bruce, L., 1972. *An Autobiography—How to Talk Dirty and Influence People*. Chicago: Playboy Press.

Burns, J. Mc., 1956. *Roosevelt—The Lion and The Fox*. New York: Harvest Book.

Campbell, A., 1981. *The Sense of Well-Being in America*. New York: McGraw-Hill.

Caplow, T. et al. 1982. *Middletown Families*. Minneapolis: U. of Minnesota Press.

Carver, M., Ed., 1976. *The War Lords*. Boston: Little, Brown Co.

Clark, A., 1979. *Lewis Carroll—A Biography*. New York: Schocken Books.

Clark, R. W., 1971. *Einstein—The Life and Times*. New York: World Publishing.

Cuber, J. and Harroff, P. 1965. *The Significant Americans*. New York: Appleton.

Davies, N., 1981. *Human Sacrifice In History and Today*. New York: William Morrow.

DeMaris, O. 1981. *The Last Mafioso*. New York: Bantam Books.

DeMause, L., 1974. *The History of Childhood*. New York: Psychohistory Press.

Dixon, N. F., 1976. *On The Psychology of Military Incompetence*. New York: Basic Books.

Dubos, R. J., 1976. *The Professor, The Institute and DNA*. New York: Rockefeller Univ. Press.

Egner, R. E. and Denonn, L. E., Eds., 1961. *The Basic Writings of Bertrand Russell*. New York: Simon and Schuster.

Ehrenreich, B. and English, D., 1978. *For Her Own Good*. New York: Doubleday.

Eiduson, B. T., 1962. *Scientists—Their Psychological World*. New York: Basic Books.

Ellenberger, H. 1970. *The Discovery of the Unconscious*. New York: Basic Books.

Erickson, C., 1980. *Great Harry*. New York: Summit Books.

© 1987 by The Haworth Press, Inc. All rights reserved.

Farago, L., 1982. *The Last Days of Patton.* New York: Berkley Books.

Fest, J. C., 1975. *Hitler.* New York: Random House.

Fine, R., 1979. *A History of Psychoanalysis.* New York: Columbia U. Press.

Fine, R., 1981. *The Psychoanalytic Vision.* New York: Macmillan Free Press.

Fine, R. 1983. *The World's Great Chess Games.* New York: Dover.

Fine, R., 1982. *The Healing of The Mind.* New York: Macmillan Free Press.

Fisher, E., 1981. *Eddie—My Life, My Loves.* New York: Harper and Row.

Fisher, R. B., 1977. *Joseph Lister.* New York: Stein and Day.

Flynn, E., 1981. *Errol Flynn—My Wicked Ways.* New York: Berkley.

Franklin, B., 1962. *The Autobiography of Benjamin Franklin* New York: Macmillan.

Freedman J., 1978. *Happy People.* New York: Harcourt Brace Jovanovich.

Freud, S. 1963. *Psychoanalysis and Faith: Dialogues with Oskar Pfister.* New York: Norton.

Galbraith, J. K., 1981. *A Life In Our Times.* Boston: Houghton Mifflin Co.

Gay, P. and Webb, R.K. 1973. *Modern Europe.* New York: Harper and Row.

Gelles, R. J., 1972. *The Violent Home* Beverly Hills, Cal.: Sage.

Gil, D. G., 1970. *Violence Against Children.* Cambridge, Mass.: Harvard U. Press.

Goldman, A., 1981. *Elvis.* New York: McGraw-Hill.

Gomberg, E. S. and Franks, V., 1979. *Gender and Disordered Behavior.* New York: Brunner/Mazel.

Gottfried, R. S. 1983. *The Black Death.* New York: Free Press.

Grady, M. W. and Perry, J. D., 1982. *Attack and Die.* Alabama: Univ. of Alabama.

Graham, A., Jr., 1971. *Age of Industrial Violence, 1910–1915.* New York: Columbia Univ. Press.

Greenacre. P., 1955. *Swift and Carroll.* New York: International Univ.

Harris, M., 1981. *The Heart of Boswell.* New York: McGraw-Hill.

Hass, A., 1979. *Teenage Sexuality.* New York: Macmillan.

Hawke, D. F., 1980. *John D.* New York: Harper and Row.

Hersh, B., 1972. *The Education of Edward Kennedy.* New York: A Dell Book.

Hill, A., 1976. *Closed World of Love.* New York: Avon.

Hite, S., 1981. *The Hite Report on Male Sexuality.* New York: Knopf.

Hite, S. 1976. *The Hite Report on Female Sexuality.* New York: Dell. 1979.

Hosken, F. P. *The Hosken Report: Genital and Sexual Mutilation of Females.* Lexington, Mass.: Women's International Network News.

Hoyt, E.P., 1983. *The Kamikazes.* New York: Harbor House.

Hunt, M. M., 1959. *The Natural History of Love.* New York: Knopf.

Jaher, F. C., Ed., 1975. *The Rich, The Well Born, and The Powerful.* Secaucus, NJ: The Citadel Press.

Jencks, C. et al. 1972. *Inequality.* New York: Basic Books.

Jencks, C. et al. 1979. *Who Gets Ahead?* New York: Basic Books.

Jones, E. 1953–1957. *The Life and Work of Sigmund Freud.* New York: Basic Books.

Josephson, M., 1962. *The Robber Barons.* New York: Harvest (HBJ) Book.

Jung, C. G. 1975. *Letters 1951–1961.* Princeton, N.J.: Princeton U. Press.

Kearns, D., 1976. *Lyndon Johnson and the American Dream.* New York: Harper & Row.

Khrushchev, N. 1970. *Khrushchev Remembers.* Boston: Little, Brown.

Kiell, N., 1964. *The Universal Experience of Adolescence.* New York: Int. Universities Press.

Kinsey, A., et al., 1948. *Sexual Behavior in the Human Male.* Philadelphia: Saunders.

Kinsey, A., et al., 1953. *Sexual Behavior in the Human Female.* Philadelphia: Saunders.

Komarovsky, M., 1967. *Blue Collar Marriage.* New York: Random House.

Kraepelin, E., 1917. *One Hundred Years of Psychiatry.* New York: Citadel Press, 1962.
Kresh, P., 1979. *Isaac Bashevis Singer—The Magician of West 86th Street.* New York: Dial Press.
Ladurie, E., 1981. *The Mind and Method of the Historian.* Chicago: U. of Chicago Press.
Lamb, M. ed. 1981. *The Role of the Father in Child Development.* New York: Wiley.
Langer, W. C. 1972. *The Mind of Adolf Hitler.* New York: Basic Books.
Lichtenberg, J. 1983. *Psychoanalysis and Infant Research.* Hillsdale, N.J.: Erlbaum.
Levinson, D. J., 1978. *The Seasons of a Man's Life.* New York: Ballantine.
Liddy, G. G., 1980. *Will.* New York: St. Martins Press.
Lewis, A. M., 1981. *The Tycoons.* New York: Simon and Schuster.
Louis, J., 1981. *Joe Louis: My Life.* New York: Berkley.
Mack, J. E., 1976. *A Prince of Our Disorder.* Boston: Little, Brown.
Manuel, F. E., 1979. *A Portrait of Isaac Newton.* Washington, D.C.: New Republic Books.
Martin, J. P., Ed., 1978. *Violence and the Family.* New York: Wiley.
McClelland, D. C., 1961. *The Achieving Society.* New York: Van Nostrand.
McClelland, D., 1975. *Power—The Inner Experience.* New York: Irvington.
McFeely, W. S., 1981. *Grant.* New York: W. W. Norton.
McWhiney, F. and Sameson, P. D., 1982. *Attack and Die.* Alabama: Alabama U. Press.
Maccoby, E. E. and Jacklin, C. N., 1974. *The Psychology of Sex Differences.* Stanford, CA: Stanford Univ. Press.
Maccoby, M., 1981. *The Leader.* New York: Simon and Schuster.
Mailer, N., 1981. *Advertisements For Myself.* New York: Perigee Books.
Manchester, W., 1978. *American Caesar.* Boston: Little, Brown and Co.
Mannix, D. P., 1974. *Those About To Die.* New York: Random House.
Marshall, D. S. and Suggs, R. C., 1971. *Human Sexual Behavior.* Basic Books.
Matson, K., 1980. *Short Lives.* New York: William Morrow.
Mead, M., 1961. *Coming of Age in Samoa.* New York: William Morrow.
Mead, M. 1961. *Cooperation and Competition among Primitive Peoples.* Boston: Beacon Press.
Mitchell, G., 1981. *Human Sex Differences.* New York: Van Nostrand Reinhold.
Montagu, A., 1974. "Aggression and the Evolution of Man." In R. E. Whalen, ed., *The Neuropsychology of Aggression.* New York: Plenum, pp. 1–29.
Morgan, T., 1982. *Churchill—Young Man in a Hurry—1874–1915.* New York: Simon and Schuster.
Morgan, T., 1980. *Maugham, A Biography.* New York: Simon and Schuster.
Nagera, H., 1967. *Vincent Van Gogh, A Psychological Study.* London: G. Allen and Unwin Ltd.
Oakes, J., 1982. *The Ruling Race.* New York: Afred A. Knopf.
O'Neill, G. and O'Neill, N., 1972. *Open Marriage.* New York: Evans.
Ouchi, w. G., 1981. *Theory Z.* New York: Avon.
Oxford Dictionary of Quotations. 1966. New York: Oxford U. Press.
Perry, H. S., 1982. *Psychiatrist of America—The Life of Harry Stack Sullivan.* Cambridge, MA: Harvard Univ. Press.
Persico, J. E., 1981. *The Imperial Rockefeller.* New York: Simon and Schuster.
Pescatello, A. M., 1976. *Power and Pawn.* Westport, CT: Greenwood Press.
Rasputin, M. and Durham, P., 1977. *Rasputin.* New York: Warner.
Reich, T. 1979. *"The Mistresses of Singer."* Harper's Vol. 258, May.
Rennie, T. et al. 1962. *Mental Health in the Metropolis.* New York: McGraw Hill.
Rogers, B., 1979. *Will Rogers.* Oklahoma: Univ. of Oklahoma Press.

Ross, J. M., et al., 1982. *Father And Child*. Boston: Little, Brown.
Russell, B., 1967. *The Autobiography of Bertrand Russell*. Boston: Little, Brown and Co.
Schlesinger, A. M., Jr., 1978. *Robert Kennedy And His Times*. Boston: Houghton Mifflin.
Schonberg, H. C., 1966. *The Great Conductors*. New York: Simon and Schuster.
Schonberg, H. C., 1963. *The Great Pianists*. New York: Simon and Schuster.
Selye, H., 1979. *The Stress of My Life*. New York: Van Nostrand Reinhold.
Shaw, S.J. 1976. *History of the Ottoman Empire and Modern Turkey. Vol. 1* New York: Cambridge U. Press.
Shirer, W. L. 1960. *The Rise and Fall of the Third Reich*. New York: Simon and Schuster.
Sherfey, M., 1972. *The Nature and Evolution of Female Sexuality*. New York: Random House.
Simon, J. F., 1980. *Independent Journey, The Life of William O. Douglas*. New York: Penguin.
Simpson, E., 1982. *Poets In Their Youths*. New York: Random House.
Slovenko, R., 1973. *Psychiatry And The Law*. Boston: Little, Brown.
Sorensen, R. C., 1973. *Adolescent Sexuality*. New York: World Mirror.
Spielrein, S. 1982. *A Secret Symmetry*. New York: Pantheon.
Sterba, E. and Sterba, R., 1971. *Beethoven And His Nephew*. New York: Schocken.
Stierlin, H., 1976. *Adolph Hitler*. New York: The Psychohistory Press.
Stokes, H. C., 1974. *The Life and Death of Yukio Mishima*. New York: Farrar, Straus and Giroux.
Strean, H., 1982. *The Extramarital Affair*. New York: Macmillan Free Press.
Talese, G., 1980. *Thy Neighbor's Wife*. New York: Dell.
Thernstrom, S., 1974. S., 1974. *Poverty And Progress*. Cambridge, MA: Harvard Univ. Press.
Tiger, L. 1969. *Men in Groups*. New York: Vintage Books.
Timerman, J., 1982. *Prisoner Without A Name, Cell Without A Number*. New York: Random House.
Tobias, A., 1976. *Fire And Ice*. New York: William Morrow.
Tolstoy, N., 1978. *The Half-Mad Lord*. New York: Holt, Rinehart and Winston.
Troyat, H., 1982. *Catherine The Great*. New York: Berkley.
Tucker, R. C., 1981. *Politics As Leadership*. Columbia: Univ. of Missouri Press.
Tucker, R. C., 1973. *Stalin As Revolutionary*. New York: W. W. Norton.
Ulam, A. B. 1973. *Stalin: The Man and His Era*. New York: Viking.
Vaillant, G. E., 1974. *Adaptation To Life*. Boston: Little, Brown.
Vanggaard, T., 1972. *Phallos*. New York: International Univ. Press.
Veroff, J., et al., 1981. *The Inner America*. New York: Basic Books.
Volkov, S., Ed., 1980. *Testimony—The Memoirs of Dimitri Shostakovich*. New York: Harper and Row.
Wachhorst, W. 1981. *Thomas Alva Edison: An American Myth*. Cambridge, Mass.: MIT Press.
Wickler, W., 1972. *The Sexual Code*. New York: Doubleday.
Williams, H. T., 1981. *Huey Long*. New York: Random House.
Yankelovich, D., 1981. *New Rules*. New York: Random House.
Yee, M. J. and Layton, T. N., 1981. *In My Father's House*. New York: Berkley Books.

Notes

INTRODUCTION

1. Quoted in J. Ross et al. eds. *Father and Child,* p. 524.
2. Wickler, *The Sexual Code,* p. 23, pp. 28–29.
3. In animal groups there is a dominance-submission pattern which maintains order. "Superior" here refers to the dominant animal.
4. Vanggaard, Phallos.
5. Vanggaard, Phallos, p. 168.
6. W.R. Layland, "In search of a loving father" *Int.* Journal of Psychoanalysis, 1981, 62, pp. 215–223.
7. See particularly M. Lamb, ed. *The Role of the Father in Child Development* (Wiley, 1981) and J. Ross et al., eds. *Father and Child* (Little, Brown, 1982).

CHAPTER 1

1. M. Rutter, "Sex Differences in childrens' responses to family stress." In E.J. Anthony and C. Koupernik, eds. *The Child in His Family,* Vol. 1 (Wiley, 1970).
2. J. Lichtenberg, *Psychoanalysis and Infant Research.* Erlbaum, 1983.
3. Quoted in Maccoby and Jacklin, p. 313.
4. Kinsey, *Sexual Behavior in the Human Male,* p. 513.
5. See Y. Cohen, *The Transition from Childhood to Adolescence* (Aldine, 1984).
6. Yee and Layton, *In My Father's House* (Berkley Books, 1981).

CHAPTER 2

1. Quoted in Kiell, *The Universal Experience of Adolescence.* pp. 164–166.
2. In R. Massie, *Peter the Great,* pp. 534–535.
3. Marshall and Suggs, *Human Sexual Behavior.*
4. L. De Mause, *The History of Childhood.*
5. O'Neill and O'Neill, *Open Marriage.*
6. Flynn, *My Wicked Wicked Ways.*
7. Flynn, *My Wicked Wicked Ways,* p. 301.
8. See also H. Strean, *The Extramarital Affair.*
9. Cf. B. Bettelheim, *The Uses of Enchantment.*
10. Gelles, *The Violent Home.*
11. Hunt, pp. 281–284.

© 1987 by The Haworth Press, Inc. All rights reserved.

CHAPTER 3

1. Kinsey, *Sexual Behavior in the Human Male,* p. 237.
2. Kinsey, p. 580.
3. Kinsey, p. 580.
4. Marshall and Suggs, *Human Sexual Behavior.*
5. G. Vaillant, *Adaptation to Life.*
6. See D. Yankelovich, *New Rules.*
7. Kinsey, p. 550.
8. Sorensen, *Adolescent Sexuality.*
9. St. Augustine, *Confessions,* pp. 43–46.
10. Ladurie, *The Mind and Method of the Historian.*

CHAPTER 4

1. Jencks, *Inequality,* 1972; *Who Gets Ahead,* 1979.
2. Jencks, 1979, p. 81.
3. Manchester, p. 37.
4. Veroff et al., 1981. *The Inner American.*
5. Yankelovich, *New Rules.*
6. Cf., Freedman, *Happy People.*
7. Mirra Komarovsky, *Blue Collar Marriage.*
8. Gomberg and Franks, 1979.
9. McClelland, *The Achieving Society.*

CHAPTER 5

1. See Yankelovich, p. xiv.
2. Middletown, 1981.
3. Dollard, *Caste and Class in a Southern Town,* p. 138.
4. Murdock, *Social Structure.*
5. Hite Report, p. 112.
6. Yankelovich, p. 99.
7. Mary Sherfey, *Female Sexuality.*
8. J. Boswell, *Autobiography.*
9. Manchester, *American Caesar.* See also Ch. 16.
10. M. Rheinstein, *Marriage Stability, Divorce and the Law.*
11. Slovenko, p. 349.
12. Robitscher, The Powers of Psychiatry, p. 177.
13. See also Chapter 4.
14. Hite, p. 827.

CHAPTER 6

1. Claire B. Kopp, ed. *Becoming Female.*
2. Ehrenreich and English, Ch. 4.
3. Ehrenreich and English, p. 94.
4. Ehrenreich and English, p. 100.

5. Ehrenreich and English, p. 111.
6. Ehrenreich and English, p. 92.
7. Hosken Report. Reviewed in *Signs,* Summer, 1980, Vol. 5, No. 4.
8. Pescatello, p. 234.
9. *Harper's* Oct. 1981. Article by Barbara Harrison.
10. Freedman, *Happy People.*
11. Campbell, *The Sense of Well-Being in America.*
12. Andrews and Smythey, *Social Indicators of Well-Being.*
13. *Sisterhood is Powerful,* p. 514.
14. See also E. Benedek and E. Poznanski, "Career choices for the woman psychiatric resident." *Amer. J. Psychiatry,* March 1980, pp. 301–305.
15. A. Montagu, *Aggression and the Evolution of Man.*
16. Erica Jong, *Saturday Review,* Oct. 1981, p. 67.
17. Quoted in ibid.
18. See R. Fine, *The Psychoanalytic Vision.*
19. Ernest Jones, *Freud,* Vol. 3, p. 440.
20. T.S. Rennie et al., *Mental Health in the Metropolis,* 1962.
21. R. Fine, *The Psychoanalytic Vision.*

CHAPTER 7

1. Brodie: Nixon, p. 88.
2. Figures vary here. The ones cited are taken from the *Encyclopedia Britannica,* Vol. I, p. 184.
3. L. De Mause: *The History of Childhood.*
4. Gil: *Violence against Children.*
5. The material here is based on James F. Simon: *Independent Journey* (Harper and Row, 1981).
6. Simon, p. 23.
7. Simon, p. 24.
8. Simon, pp. 41–42.
9. Simon, p. 109.
10. Simon, p. 373.
11. Simon, p. 239.
12. Simon, p. 374.
13. Simon, p. 373.
14. Simon, p. 373.
15. Simon, Ch. 28.
16. The material here is based on Carrolly Erickson: *Great Harry (Summit Books, 1980).*
17. Erickson, p. 15.
18. The material here is based on Rene J. Dubos: *The Professor, the Institute, and DNA* (Rockefeller U. Press, 1976).
19. Lower East Side, at 1 Henry St., Dubos, p. 50.
20. Dubos, pp. 48–49.
21. Dubos, p. 91.
22. The material here is based on K. Matson: *Short Lives* (William Morrow and Co., 1980).
23. Matson, p. 239.
24. Matson, p. 244.
25. Matson, pp. 245–246.
26. Matson, p. 235.
27. The material here is based on K. Matson: *Short Lives.*

28. Matson, p. 30.
29. Matson, p. 38.
30. See R. Gottfried: *The Black Death* (Free Press, 1983).
31. Martin: *Violence and the Family,* p. 345.
32. A. Lewis: *The Tycoons.*

CHAPTER 8

1. The material here is based on B. Bradlee and D. Van Atta, *Prophet of Blood* (Putnam, 1981).
2. Bradlee and Van Atta, p. 19.
3. Bradlee and Van Atta, p. 24.
4. Bradlee and Van Atta, p. 15.
5. Bradlee and Van Atta, p. 14.
6. Bradlee and Van Atta, pp. 45ff.
7. Bradlee and Van Atta, p. 55.
8. Bradlee and Van Atta, p. 58.
9. Bradlee and Van Atta, p. 61.
10. Bradlee and Van Atta, p. 82.
11. Bradlee and Van Atta, p. 141.
12. Bradlee and Van Atta, p. 147.
13. Bradlee and Van Atta, p. 350.
14. *New York Times,* May 29, 1982, p. 23.
15. The material here is of course voluminous. For the facts of Hitler's life I have relied on J.C. Fest, *Hitler* (Vintage Books, 1975). For the facts on Stalin I have relied on R.C. Tucker, *Stalin as Revolutionary, 1879–1929* (Norton, 1973) and A.B. Ulam, *Stalin* (Viking, 1973). W. Langer, *The Mind of Adolt Hitler* (Basic Books, 1972) has also been consulted, although some of his interpretations have been questioned.
16. Langer, p. 165.
17. Langer, p. 92, pp. 133–134.
18. Langer, p. 168.
19. Langer, p. 90.
20. Tucker, p. 107.
21. Tucker, pp. 220–223.
22. Quoted in Tucker, p. 449.
23. Fest, p. 720.
24. Fest, p. 593.
25. Ulam, p. 685.
26. Shirer, p. 719.
27. The material here is based on N. Tolstoy, *The Half-Mad Lord* (Holt, Rinehart and Winston, 1978).
28. Tolstoy, p. 1.
29. Tolstoy, Ch. 1.
30. Tolstoy, pp. 18–25.
31. J.J. Shaw, *History of the Ottoman Empire,* p. 184.
32. *Khruschchev Remembers,* p. 307.
33. Catherine the Great, p. 260.
34. The material here is culled from many sources.

CHAPTER 9

1. Clark: *Einstein,* p. 614.
2. Wachhorst: *Edison,* p. 101.

3. The material here is based on Fisher's autobiography, *My Life, My Loves* (Harper and Row, 1981).

4. Fisher, pp. 28–29.

5. Fisher, p. 319.

6. Fisher, p. 350.

7. Fisher, pp. 98–111, 144–159, 295.

8. The material here is based on Andrew Tobias: *Fire and Ice* (William Morrow, 1976).

9. Tobias, p. 128.

10. Tobias, p. 15.

11. Tobias, p. 182.

12. Tobias, p. 146.

13. Tobias, p. 31.

14. Tobias, p. 96.

15. Tobias, p. 139.

16. Tobias, p. 139.

17. Tobias, p. 173.

18. Tobias, p. 174.

19. Tobias, p. 182.

20. Tobias, p. 89.

21. Tobias, p. 91.

22. Tobias, p. 63.

23. Tobias, p. 146.

24. The material here is based on *Ruth Brandon: A Capitalist Romance* (Lippincott, 1977).

25. Brandon, p. 6.

26. Brandon, p. 17.

27. Brandon, p. 27.

28. Brandon, p. 33.

29. Brandon, p. 34.

30. Brandon, p. 55.

31. Brandon, p. 42.

32. Brandon, p. 128.

33. Brandon, p. 158.

34. Brandon, p. 161.

35. Brandon, p. 162.

36. Brandon, p. 164.

37. Brandon, pp. 171ff.

38. Brandon, Ch. 9.

39. The material here is voluminous. The essential facts are taken from the *Encyclopedia Britannica,* Vol. 12, pp. 600–604 and H. Schonberg, *The Great Pianists* (Simon and Schuster, 1963).

40. The material here is based on J. E. Persico: *The Imperial Rockefeller* (Simon and Schuster, 1982).

41. Persico, p. 28.

CHAPTER 10

1. *Encyclopedia Britannica,* Vol. VII, p. 193.

2. *Oxford Book of Quotations,* 476:6.

3. The main facts have been taken from F.E. Manuel, *A Portrait of Isaac Newton* (New Republic Books, 1979).

4. *Oxford Quotations,* 382:17.

5. Manuel, p. 80. The years are 1664–1666.
6. Manuel, p. 24.
7. Manuel, p. 45.
8. Manuel, p. 151, p. 156.
9. Manuel, p. 230.
10. Manuel, Chs. 8 and 17.
11. Stukely and Conduitt were the worshipful early biographers. See Manuel, p. 8.
12. The material here is based primarily on Max Brod, *Franz Kafka: A Biography* (Schocken Books, 1963).
13. Brod, p. 9.
14. Brod, p. 172.
15. Brod, p. 18.
16. Brod, p. 90.
17. Brod, p. 94.
18. The material here is based on John Mack, *A Prince of our Disorder* (Little, Brown, 1976).
19. Mack, forewood.
20. Mack, p. 4.
21. Mack, p. 332.
22. Mack, p. 241.
23. Mack, Ch. 33, pp. 427ff.
24. See F.P. Hosken, *Genital and Sexual Multilation of Females* (Women's International Network News, 1979).
25. The material here is based on Richard B. Fisher, *Joseph Lister* (Stein and Day, 1977).
26. Fisher, p. 21.
27. The material here is based on Anne Clark, *Lewis Carroll* (Schocken Books, 1979).
28. Greenacre, *Swift and Carroll*, p. 227.

CHAPTER 11

1. The material here is based on Claude Brown's autobiography, *Manchild in the Promised Land* (New American Library, 1965).
2. Brown, p. 9.
3. Brown, p. 43.
4. Brown, p. 426.
5. The material here is based on Jack Henry Abbott's autobiographical work, *In the Belly of the Beast* (Random House, 1981).
6. Abbott, p.xvi.
7. Abbott, pp. 6–7.
8. Abbott, p. 5.
9. Abbott, p. 19.
10. Abbott, p. 45.
11. Abbott, p. 57.
12. Abbott, p. 79.
13. Abbott, p. 111.
14. Abbott, p. 6.
15. Normal Mailer: *Advertisements for Myself,* p. 6.
16. Abbott, p. xvi.

17. The material here is based on the autobiographical account Jacobo Timmerman: *Prisoner without a Name, Cell without a Number* (Vintage Books, 1981).
18. Timmerman, p. vii.
19. Timmerman, p. 33.
20. Timmerman, p. 153.
21. Timmerman, pp. 152–153.
22. The material here is based on the autobiographical Archie Hill: *Closed World of Love* (Avon, 1976).
23. Hill, p. 13.
24. The material here is based on *Will: The Autobiography of G. Gordon Liddy* (St. Martin's Press, 1980).
25. Liddy, pp. 208ff.
26. Liddy, p. 30, p. 313 also passim.
27. Liddy, p. 1.
28. Liddy, p. 2.
29. Liddy, p. 12.
30. Liddy, p. 31.
31. Liddy, p. 163.
32. Liddy, p. 237.
33. Liddy, p. 213.
34. Liddy, p. 210.
35. Liddy, p. 307.
36. Liddy, p. 107.
37. The material here is based on O. Demaris: *The Last Mafioso* (Bantam Books, 1981). Demaris' account is based on conversations with Jimmy Fratianno. I cannot vouch for the authenticity of his report, nor take responsibility for any errors that he may have made.
38. Damaris, p. vii.
39. Demaris, p. 4.
40. Demaris, p. 6.
41. Demaris, p. 7.
42. Demaris, p. 153.
43. Demaris, p. 15.
44. Demaris, pp. 2–3.

CHAPTER 12

1. Cuber and Harroff, *The Significant Americans*, p. 49.

CHAPTER 13

1. *Oxford Quotations*, 14:4.
2. For an excellent discussion of this topic see R. C. Tucker: *Politics as Leadership* (U. of Missouri, 1981).
3. The main source used is Doris Kearns: *Lyndon Johnson and the American Dream* (Harper and Row, 1976).
4. Kearns, Ch. 1.
5. Kearns, p. 32.
6. Kearns, p. 342.
7. Kearns, p. 44.

8. In the Billie Sol Estes case (not mentioned by Kearns) Johnson was not personally involved.

9. Kearns, p. 80.

10. Kearns, p. 353.

11. The main source here is Fawn M. Brodie: *Richard Nixon, The Shaping of His Character* (Norton, 1981).

12. Brodie, p. 23.

13. Brodie, p. 37.

14. Brodie, p. 39.

15. Brodie, p. 88.

16. Brodie, p. 99.

17. Brodie, pp. 121ff.

18. Brodie, p. 138.

19. Brodie, p. 153.

20. Brodie, p. 171.

21. Brodie, Ch. 15.

22. Brodie, Ch. 19 and p. 271.

23. See also Liddy, pp. xx.

24. the main source here is Arthur Schlesinger: *Robert Kennedy and His Times* (Houghton Mifflin, 1978).

25. Schlesinger, p. 3.

26. Schlesinger, pp. 14ff.

27. Schlesinger, p. 15.

28. B. Hersh: *The Education of Edward Kennedy,* pp. 111–117.

29. Schlesinger, p. 7.

30. The main source here is T. Harry Williams: *Huey Long* (Vintage, 1981).

31. Williams, p. 841. Whether the story of the meeting is true or false has never been determined.

32. Williams, p. 313.

33. Williams, Ch. 14.

34. Williams, p. 429.

35. Williams, p. 845.

36. The main source here is J.B. Peabody ed.: *John Adams: A Biography in his Own Words* (Newsweek, 1973).

37. Adams, p. 27.

38. Adams, p. 143.

39. The main source here is Maria Rasputin and Patte Durham: *Rasputin* (Warner Books, 1977).

40. Rasputin and Durham, Ch. 3.

41. Rasputin and Durham, p. 96.

42. Rasputin and Durham, Ch. 6 and passim.

43. Rasputin and Durham, Ch. 15.

44. Rasputin and Durham, p. 309.

45. The main source here is Ted Morgan: *Churchill: Young Man in a Hurry,* 1874–1915 (Simon and Schuster, 1982).

46. Morgan, pp. 23–24.

47. Morgan, pp. 66–67.

48. Morgan, p. 138.

49. Morgan, p. 554.

CHAPTER 14

1. Quoted in M. Josephson: *The Robber Barons,* title page (Harcourt, Brace, Jovanovich, 1964).

2. Maccoby: *The Leader*, p. 34.

3. Whyte: *The Organization Man*, p. 68.

4. The material here is based on David F. Hawke: *John D.* (Harper and Row, 1980). The designation of John D. as "the most hated man in the world" is the title of Ch. 36.

5. Hawke, p. 3.

6. Hawke, p. 13.

7. Hawke, p. 14.

8. Hawke, p. 10.

9. Hawke, p. 18.

10. Hawke, p. 16.

11. Hawke, p. 22.

12. Hawke, p. 24.

13. Hawke, pp. 38–39.

14. Hawke, p. 45.

15. Hawke, p. 135.

16. Hawke, p. 224.

17. The material here is based on Carol Bleser: *The Hammonds of Redcliffe* (Oxford U. Press, 1981).

18. Bleser, p. 7.

19. Bleser, p. 5.

20. Bleser, p. 7.

21. Bleser, p. 9.

22. Bleser, p. 10.

23. Bleser, p. 10.

24. Bleser, p. 12.

25. Bleser, p. 14.

26. Bleser, p. 16.

27. Bleser, p. 17.

28. Bleser, p. 18.

29. The source material here is Victor Lasky: *Never Complain, Never Explain, The Story of Henry Ford II* (Richard Marek, 1981).

30. Lasky, p. 30.

31. Lasky, p. 39.

32. Lasky, p. 41.

33. Lasky, p. 49.

34. Lasky, p. 5.2.

35. Lasky, p. 59.

36. Lasky, p. 98.

37. Lasky, p. 146.

38. Lasky, p. 98.

39. Lasky, p. 108.

40. Lasky, p. 146.

41. Lasky, p. 157.

42. Lasky, pp. 207–208.

43. Lasky, pp. 234–238.

44. Lasky, p. 223.

45. The main source here is Frank Brady: *Onassis: An Extravagant Life* (Jove, 1977).

46. Brady, p. 134.

47. Brady, p. 186.

48. Brady, p. 22.

49. Brady, p. 36.

50. Brady, p. 62.

51. Brady, pp. 77–83.

52. Brady, p. 11.

53. Brady, pp. 48–54.
54. Brady, p. 70.
55. Brady, p. 152.
56. Brady, p. 149.
57. Brady, p. 63.
58. Brady, p. 183.
59. Brady, pp. 195ff.

CHAPTER 15

1. Quoted in Eileen Simpson: *Poets in Their Youth,* front matter.
2. *Encyclopedia Britannica,* Vol. 7, p. 380.
3. The source material here is Albert Goldman: *Elvis* (McGraw-Hill, 1981).
4. Goldman, p. 66.
5. Goldman, p. 69.
6. Goldman, p. 96 and passim.
7. Goldman, p. 527.
8. Goldman, Ch. 25.
9. Goldman, pp. 556–557.
10. Goldman, p. 572.
11. Goldman, p. 252.
12. Goldman, pp. 252–254.
13. Goldman, pp. 306ff.
14. Goldman, p. 337.
15. Goldman, p. 338.
16. Goldman, p. 502.
17. Goldman, Ch. 25.
18. Goldman, p. 505.
19. Goldman, pp. 516–517.
20. Goldman, p. 563.
21. The source material here is Betty Rogers: *Will Rogers* (Rogers Co., 1979).
22. Rogers, p. 53.
23. Rogers, p. 62.
24. Rogers, pp. 110–111.
25. Rogers, p. 111.
26. Rogers, p. 137.
27. Rogers, p. 153.
28. Rogers, p. 161.
29. Rogers, p. 171.
30. Rogers, p. 180.
31. Rogers, p. 198.
32. Rogers, p. 200.
33. Rogers, p. 274.
34. Rogers, p. 300.
35. The source material here is Ted Morgan: *Maugham: A Biography* (Simon and Schuster, 1980).
36. Morgan, p. vii.
37. Morgan, pp. xiii–xiv.
38. Morgan, p. 8.
39. Morgan, p. 13.
40. Morgan, p. 15.
41. Morgan, p. 20.

42. Morgan, p. 24.
43. Morgan, p. 26.
44. Morgan, p. 84.
45. Morgan, p. 183.
46. Morgan, p. 190.
47. Morgan, p. 494.
48. Morgan, p. 488.
49. Morgan, p. 197.
50. The source material here is Paul Kresh: *Isaac Bashevis Singer: The Magician of W. 86th St.* (Dial Press, 1979).
51. Kresh, p. 395.
52. *Harper's,* 1979: Tova Reich: *The Mistresses of Singer.*
53. Kresh, p. 23.
54. Kresh, p. 155.
55. Kresh, p. 152.
56. Kresh, p. 411.
57. The material is voluminous. The main source here is Humbert Nagera: *Vincent Van Gogh: A Psychological Study* (George Allen and Unwin, 1967).
58. Nagera, Ch. 20.
59. Nagera, p. 13.
60. Nagera, p. 25.
61. Nagera, p. 27.
62. Nagera, p. 40.
63. Nagera, p. 47.
64. Nagera, p. 49.
65. Nagera, Ch. 8.
66. Nagera, p. 117.
67. Nagera, Chs. 15–20.
68. The source material for Poe and Fitzgerald is K. Matson: *Short Lives: Portraits in Creativity and Self-Destruction* (Morrow, 1980).
69. Matson, p. 303.
70. Matson, p. 304.
71. See note 68.
72. Matson, p. 130.
73. The main source material here is the book by his ex-wife Eileen Simpson: *Poets in Their Youth* (Random House, 1982).
74. Simpson, p. 61.
75. Simpson, p. 31.
76. John Berryman: *The Dream Songs,* #118.
77. Simpson, p. 252.
78. There is voluminous source material. I have drawn on Edith and Richard Sterba: *Beethoven and His Nephew* (Schocken Books, 1971) and H. Schonberg: *The Great Pianists* (Simon and Schuster, 1963).
79. Sterba and Sterba, p. 18.
80. Sterba and Sterba, p. 19.
81. Schonberg, p. 79.
82. Sterba and Sterba, p. 110; Ch. VII.
83. The Sterbas discuss all the battles in great detail.
84. Sterba and Sterba, p. 277.
85. Schonberg, p. 88.
86. The main source material is his autobiography, *Joe Louis: My Life* (Berkley Books, 1981).
87. Louis, pp. 263–271.
88. Louis, pp. 77ff.

89. Louis, p. 251.
90. Louis, p. 233.
91. Louis, pp. 239ff.
92. Louis, p. 240.
93. The main source material is R. Fine: *The World's Great Chess Games* (Dover, 1983) and personal knowledge.

CHAPTER 16

1. I am aware of the tendency among many modern historians to minimize the awful nature of slavery and warfare, but such efforts miss some of the essential misery in human history. The data in this chapter are taken from Nigel Davies: *Human Sacrifice in History and Today* (Morrow, 1981) and W. H. McNeill: *Plagues and Peoples* (Anchor, Press, 1976).
2. McNeill, p. 168.
3. Gay and Webb, *Modern European History*, pp. 529–530.
4. Davies, p. 76.
5. Davies, p. 218.
6. My major source material here is Field Marshall Sir Michael Carver, ed.: *The War Lords* (Little, Brown and Co., 1976).
7. *Encyclopedia Britannica*, Vol. 6, p. 514.
8. Carver, p. 528.
9. Carver, p. 509.
10. Carver: *The War Lords* and Ladislas Farago: *The Last Days of Patton* (Berkley Books, 1982).
11. Carver, p. 555.
12. Carver, p. 556.
13. Carver, p. 558.
14. Carver, p. 560.
15. Farago, pp. 93–94.
16. Farago, p. 86.
17. Carver, p. 566.
18. The main source is William Manchester: *American Caesar* (Little, Brown, 1978).
19. Manchester, p. 14.
20. Manchester, p. 180.
21. Manchester, p. 212.
22. Manchester, p. 230 and also pp. 284ff.
23. Manchester, p. 643.
24. Manchester, p. 479.
25. Manchester, p. 499.
26. Manchester, p. 509.
27. Manchester, p. 157.
28. The main source material here is William S. McFeely: *Grant, A Biography* (Norton, 1981).
29. McFeely, p. 287.
30. McFeely, p. 14.
31. McFeely, p. 42.
32. McFeely, p. 16.
33. McFeely, p. 32.
34. McFeely, p. 55.
35. McFeely, p. 64.
36. McFeely, p. 101.

37. McFeely, p. 406.
38. McFeely, p. 332.
39. McFeely, p. 434.
40. McFeely, p. 522.
41. The quotes here are from Mark Baker: *The Vietnam War in the Words of the Men and Women who Fought There* (Morrow, 1981).
42. Baker, p. 25.
43. Baker, p. 35.
44. Baker, p. 41.
45. Baker, p. 60.
46. Baker, pp. 106–107.
47. Baker, p. 158.
48. Baker, p. 191.
49. Baker, p. 230.
50. Baker, p. 269.

CHAPTER 17

1. Eiduson, p. 115.
2. Selye, p. 218.
3. Selye, P. 198.
4. Manuel, p. 303.
5. The main source is Ronald W. Clark: *Einstein: The Life and Times* (World Publishing Co., 1971).
6. Clark, p. 20.
7. Clark, p. 42.
8. Clark, p. 194.
9. *Encyclopedia Britannica,* Vol. 6, p. 512.
10. Clark, pp. 18–19.
11. Clark, p. 614.
12. *Encyclopedia Britannica,* Vol. 6, p. 513.
13. Clark, p. 340.
14. Clark, p. 532.
15. Clark, p. 533.
16. The main source is the *Autobiography of Bertrand Russell 1872–1914* (Little, Brown, 1956).
17. Russell, p. 3.
18. Russell, I, *Childhood.*
19. Russell, VI, *Principia Mathematica.*
20. *Encyclopedia Britannica,* Vol. 16, p. 36.
21. Russell, front matter.
22. The main source is his autobiographical work *John K. Galbraith: A Life in Our Times* (Houghton Mifflin, 1981).
23. Galbraith, foreword.
24. Galbraith, p. 278.
25. Galbraith, p. 2.
26. Galbraith, p. 18.
27. Galbraith, p. 31.
28. Galbraith, p. 514.
29. Galbraith, p. 396.
30. The source material here is his autobiography *Hans Selye: The Stress of My Life* (Van Nostrand Reinhold, 1979).
31. Selye, p. 31.
32. Selye, Ch. 2.

33. Selye, p. 47.
34. Selye, p. 220.
35. Selye, pp. 222–223.
36. Selye, p. 221.
37. Selye, p. 266.
38. Selye, pp. 266–267.
29. The main source is his autobiographical *In Joy Still Felt: The Autobiography of Isaac Asimov, 1954–1978* (Avon, 1980).
40. Asimov, back cover.
41. Asimov, p. viii.
42. Asimov, p. x.
43. Asimov, p. 22.
44. Asimov, p. 39.
45. Asimov, Ch. 5.
46. Asimov, Ch. 8.
47. Asimov, p. 798.
48. Asimov, p. 26.
49. Asimov, p. 5.
50. Asimov, p. 434.
51. Asimov, p. 181.
52. Asimov, p. 221.
53. Asimov, p. 19.
54. Asimov, pp. 459–460.

CHAPTER 18

1. *Encyclopedia Britannica,* Vol. 19, p. 515.
2. The material is voluminous. The most reliable source is still Ernest Jones: *The Life and Work of Sigmund Freud* (Basic Books, 1953–1957). For the best reconstruction of his self-analysis see D. Anzieu: *L'Auto—Analyse de Freud* (Presses Universitaires de France, 1975).
3. *Psychoanalysis and Faith,* p. 126.
4. "The Defense Neuro-Psychoses"—Standard Edition, Vol. III, pp. 43—68.
5. The best source is Helen Swick Perry: *Harry Stack Sullivan: Psychiatrist of America* (Harvard U. Press, 1983).
6. Perry, Chs. 1–16.
7. Perry, p. 137.
8. Perry, p. 146.
9. Perry, Ch. 19.
10. Perry, p. 165.
11. Perry, Ch. 23.
12. Kraepelin, *One Hundred Years of Psychiatry,* pp. 148–149.
13. Perry, Ch. 23.
14. Perry, p. 194.
15. Perry, Ch. 33.
16. There are many sources available. The most objective is H. Ellenberger: *The Discovery of the Unconscious* (Basic Books, 1970).
17. Jung, *Letters 1951–1961,* p. 553.
18. Ellenberger, p. 661.
19. S. Spielrein: *A Secret Symmetry* (Pantheon, 1982).
20. Ellenberger, p. 670.
21. Ellenberger, p. 677.

PART V:
TEN DISCUSSION PAPERS

Discussion I

Robert C. Lane

This is a book that has something for everybody. A basic text on men written in simple language, its messages are easily understood by all levels of readers, the unsophisticated as well as the sophisticated. It is a treasure of anecdotes that will be talked about for a long time. Like Dr. Fine's many other books, it is rich in philosophy, scholarly, down-to-earth and contains a wealth of clinical material and information: from the pre-oedipal to the oedipal, from the diad to the triad, from mama's darling to father's rival, from boy to man, from son to father, and from father to grandfather.

The first six chapters on sexuality discuss man's fears (of sexual inadequacy), man's defenses (Don Juanism), man's ideals and hopes (the masculine and analytic ideals), man as husband, father, ex-husband and lover, and man's reaction to women's liberation. The main thesis of the book is stated in the preface: "In the extensive literature on human and sexual liberation, there is a startling omission: the psychology of the man." To Dr. Fine, man is not only powerful and strong, independent and free, dominant and ruthless, but also weak and helpless, passive and dependent, submissive and depressed.

Dr. Fine begins his book by telling us that men have as many problems with sex and aggression and with life in gen-

© 1987 by The Haworth Press, Inc. All rights reserved.

eral as women do. Dr. Fine feels in man's striving to be macho, the he-man and have machismo, he must struggle with fidelity versus infidelity and promiscuity, heterosexuality versus bisexuality and homosexuality, and monogamy versus polygamy. He postulates that men are crushed by a repressive childhood that causes them to become emotional cripples in adult life. They oscillate between a woman they can have and do not want, and a woman they want and cannot have. They long for the mother, a woman who is unavailable to them. Man's emotional health is dependent on the nature of his parenting, his parents' relationship with each other, and of particular importance, the mother-child relationship in early infancy. Dr. Fine tells us, man will feel weak and helpless if the mother is destructive and hateful, and strong and loved if the mother is warm and cuddly. A man who had difficulty in his early mother relationship will fear closeness, intimacy and commitment, may never love a woman, and fall ill at some point in his life.

The author offers an excellent description of the boy's developmental stages. He points out that the emergence of the father as an important object making the mother-child dyad of the pre-oedipal period a triad, brings with it deep conflict. The boy's aggressive potential is greatly exaggerated during this phase of life, and both aggression and sexual frustrations reach a high point in the oedipal period. Repression leads to frustration and frustration in turn to aggression, and a search to find the lost object. The intense frustration caused by the loss of the boy's first love object may lead to a withdrawal of affect or even flight from girls. The boy is warned to stay away from girls. Hopefully, he will have a first love affair at five or six and turn to a girl other than his mother or sister. Although the first love affair is more often than not greatly discouraged. If the boy turns to his sister (the author feels this occurs at around eight), he is warned again to stay away and he may well be sent away, according to Dr. Fine.

In adolescence, the boy struggles to disengage, searches for an identity, is conscious of his greater sexual potency, yearns to become a man, while crucially aware of his competition with and fear of his father. He may turn to cults, alcohol or drugs, act out in one form or another, fight, engage in promiscuous behavior, become a jock or body builder, withdraw or throw himself into a fantasy world, become ascetic, or turn to idealistic causes. The road to manhood and fatherhood is a rocky one, with conflict constantly along the path always threatening to disturb man's inner peace.

The typical pattern described by Dr. Fine is that the boy is spoiled by his mother, toilet-trained too early, forced to give up aggression, made to feel guilty concerning masturbation, separated from girls at an early age, unable to come to grips with his sexual maturity, inadequate as a man and, disappointed in his achievements, falls back on neurotic and psychotic defenses.

Dr. Fine quotes percentages and gives examples of man's inadequacy from Kinsey's book on sexual behavior in the human male, the *Hite Report on Male Sexuality,* Marshall and Suggs book *Human Sexual Behavior* and George Vaillant's study on the best and the brightest, "Adaptation to Life." Dr. Fine points out man's impotence and premature ejaculation, and his turning to homosexuality, group sex and swinging in his search for liberation, excitement and passion, as a new experience, and to be free from a poor relationship or marriage. Dr. Fine feels that the latter may be "passing activity," and that man will eventually move on to a more "lasting" relationship. The type of homosexuality Dr. Fine believes most pathological and difficult to alter is "exclusive homosexuality." Many men have what the author calls the "2 women fantasy" (wife and girlfriend, or performing sex with two women) or the fantasy of multiple women (Casanova Complex). When man is unable to perform, he becomes once again a little boy seeking attention from his mother.

Dr. Fine discusses the "myth" promulgated by the Woman's Liberation Movement that man mistreats and uses women, takes advantage of them, is insensitive to their needs, incapable of understanding them, guilty of cruel and inhuman behavior, and to blame for all women's difficulties. Man is presented as "evil" by the movement, using his power and physical strength to threaten and subjugate women, while women are presented as devoted and loving, and helpless against man's physical threats. The truth is closer to the statement that whereas some men are ruthless, and Dr. Fine gives us many examples, women can be provocative, cold, complaining, rejecting, uncommunicative, unresponsive, turned off from the marital bed, and disinterested in sex in general. Whereas infidelity occurs in men, so does it in women. If women have been enslaved, so have men according to Dr. Fine. Man has reacted to marriage by turning to other women, withdrawing, losing himself in work, turning to drink, illness and homosexuality. Dr. Fine feels that the marriage and divorce laws favor women, and there is actually an advantage to the man who has little material wealth at the time of a divorce settlement. To Dr. Fine, the ideal marriage is often a myth. Marriage, more often than not, is like the sequence, "wife refuses husband, husband loses interest in wife," one or the other is tired or busy, one rebuffs the other, and eventually both go their separate ways.

Dr. Fine points out that the liberation movement has lost much of its meaning at this point in time, and it is no longer clear from whom women want to be liberated. He feels women's attack on psychoanalysis is unjustified and that Freud did much to liberate women from their Victorian shackles. Dr. Fine comments on penis envy, an area of considerable concern to the Women's Liberation Movement. He sees penis envy and castration anxiety occurring in both sexes, and points out both of these afflictions can be reduced to a feeling that one's body is inadequate. To him, inadequacy seems more the rule than the exception, and is found among men just as often as among women.

The author's thesis on love is summarized in some very moving passages. He describes how both sexes reach a stage in which the tender and sexual feelings are united towards a person of the opposite sex. For him, the truly liberated person is not one who can have sex with anyone, but one who can have a gratifying love experience with another human being. This is the analytic ideal. Dr. Fine tells us people look to love as a key to happiness and that marriage and a good family life are seen as perhaps the best way of fulfilling one's need for a relationship and communication. Dr. Fine's goal would be to change our hate culture into a love culture.

The next six chapters deal with "aggression," and include man's training to fight, his need to be strong, successful and powerful and how this power can be used both ruthlessly (Hitler and Stalin) and constructively (Franklin D. Roosevelt). The author describes through a number of examples how the road to success is paved with suffering and hardship (Eddie Fisher, Charles Revson, Isaac Merritt Singer, Mozart and Nelson Rockefeller). Next, Dr. Fine turns to the narcissistic man. He tells us narcissistic men are lonely, remaining tied to their mothers, resentful of their fathers, full of rage toward and jealousy of them, and unable to love or find a satisfactory relationship with a woman. The author has some very interesting things to say about the narcissistic man and his examples (Dudley, Isaac Newton, Franz Kafka, Lawrence of Arabia and Lewis Carroll) are indeed fascinating. Dr. Fine next discusses the criminal personality. He tells us there is no evidence that there is a "criminal personality" or to substantiate a "defective brain" in the criminal. He does point out there is a high crime rate in the lower class and that the criminal dies young. This is explained by the early "object relations" and experiences the criminal is exposed to and how these influence his behavior. Chapter 12 deals with the average man and the author gives many examples from clinical practice.

Fighting and aggressive behavior in general are more characteristic of boys than girls in our hate culture. Aggressive needs, like sexual needs, may be forced into repression at a very early age. When this happens ambition, achievement, competition, the need for success and the drive for power in the male may all be hampered. Aggression is necessary for the performance of sexual activity, and when it is repressed the result may be sexual problems. When the need to discharge normal aggressive feelings is not punished, boys will grow up to become aggressive adolescents and then men. The frustration of the boy's normal oral, anal, urethral and phallic-oedipal aggression can lead to severe repression of these drives and inhibitions in sexuality, aggression, work and creativity in general. The fighter's dilemma concerns man's inability to know what to do with his rage. Although fighting and entering dangerous situations are both normal and inevitable in boys, physical limitations and handicaps can and frequently do occur to inhibit the need to discharge aggressive feelings. Factors such as size, strength, speed, motor ability and coordination, as well as intelligence may seriously hinder the boy's and later the man's capacity to engage in aggressive activity. Girls do not have to prove they can fight or be aggressive to the same extent as boys, and therefore difficulties in this area lead to emotional disturbances more frequently in boys than girls.

Dr. Fine correctly brings social class differences to our attention. He points out that whereas learning to fight is essential to being accepted by one's peers in the lower class, ambition, achievement and competition are more essential weapons in the middle class, while "position," which fighting may interfere with, is more important in the upper class. The need to fight, compete with or aggress can be sublimated into a variety of activities including sports, academia, achievement and creative endeavors. The boy needs a male role model from whom to learn how to fight, and the healthier this person is, the healthier the boy will be. The father-son conflict is often a life struggle, and when the son becomes a father, the struggle is repeated with his son and so it goes on from one generation to another.

In conclusion, modern man lacks a group identity more than women in that there is no male movement equivalent to the Woman's Liberation Movement. The many roles modern man must play are bewildering and often lead to emotional problems. Today's society makes more demands on men than women in terms of changing roles and identities. Perhaps this is why men are more susceptible to life-threatening illnesses, psychosomatic difficulties, and have a higher mortality rate than women. The roles of man are forever changing and strong psychological reactions often accompany the role transition from boy to adolescent, adolescent to young adult, single to married, husband to father, husband to ex-husband, married to single again, and father to grandfather. Dr. Fine feels that psychoanalysts have paid little attention to the psychology of man in general and the father in particular.

Discussion II

Dorothy Lander Rosen

Replete with life histories, Dr. Fine reminds us that men as well as women must travel that precarious developmental path from infancy to adulthood. Under optimal conditions the child reaches adulthood having resolved the Oedipal conflict, achieving the psychosexual level of genital maturity. That is, he is able to love, enjoy sexual gratification, work and possess pride and pleasure in his life.

Unfortunately, most often, children are raised by caretakers who, themselves, have not reached psychological maturity. Envy, aggression, competition, neglect are but some of the emotional hardships suffered by children at the hands of the persons upon whom they are dependent. Disappointed in and dissatisfied with their marital relationship the parents cannot nurture, and instead use and/or abuse the child. Dr. Fine reiterates that children raised in such a climate are themselves unable to grow into happy, loving adults.

In this first installment of his work, Dr. Fine stresses the gulf between the analytic ideal and the societal ideal of machismo which guides the child rearing practices directed towards males. Men in our society incorporate an ego-ideal inconsistent with instinctual gratification and emotional well-being. Tenderness and the sexual drive are incompatible. A man might love his horse, but never the woman with whom he has intercourse.

Don Juan is recreated in different garb for each generation. The movie *The Man Who Loved Women* is a recent restatement of the adventure of such a lifestyle. The main character (played by Burt Reynolds) is the supra-analytic patient, and is able to seduce his analyst into abandoning her professionalism and ethics to his charm. The analyst's skills and person crumble. True, Reynolds compulsively flits from woman to woman, but this need stems from both a childhood seduction *and* a love of women which causes him discomfort and, suffer-

© 1987 by The Haworth Press, Inc. All rights reserved.

ing when, shortly after entering a sexual relationship, he is attracted to and loves another beautiful woman. He feels trapped in his relationship and, indeed, it would seem self-destructive for him to remain with one woman. The rationalizations change, the glamorization of the lifestyle continues and the resistance towards acknowledging one's inner life also continues. Dr. Fine discusses the Don Juan character in depth and demonstrates that such a person is fearful of female rejection, leaving each woman before she can leave him. While such a lifestyle enables the man at least to experience sexual gratification, at bottom he is troubled and unhappy.

John Wayne, as noted in the text, was the epitome of macho man, ruthlessly killing the "bad guys," at times not involved with a woman at all, at other times allowing a woman to love him. He was often seen as a "man's man whom women loved," unafraid, lacking compassion, and not beset by uncertainty. But even as he made his last films, his brand of machismo was eclipsed by that modern hero, James Bond. Cool, detached, urbane, he is ever ready to sexually please each beautiful woman and to efficiently destroy every evil man. Bond is armed with highly sophisticated electronic/atomic weapons, and even as we marvel at these great toys (as they are presented), the reality we witness demands that we recognize that our technology has advanced too far for us to insist that our heroes continue to act out these infantile fantasies of omnipotent sexuality and aggression.

Who idolizes these men? Women who have been raised to admire "strong," aggressive men, and men raised "not to show the yellow feather," states Dr. Fine. Efforts to achieve, or to appear to achieve such unrealistic demands leave most men feeling inadequate and unhappy. Dr. Fine uses material from his clinical practice, research studies and life histories to illustrate his percepts. It is not surprising to find that genius or worldly success are no barriers against despair when individuals are raised in despairing, unhappy homes.

Dr. Fine states that the goals of the women's liberation movement are not inconsistent with a more loving relationship between the sexes. Certainly the freeing of a woman to pursue her needs for mastery within society equally frees her from the need to become a "back seat driver," attempting to control the person upon whom she exclusively depends for her social and economic position. There would be less necessity for her to cling to her children, their dependency a rationale for her self-worth, and the need to use her children as penile projections would similarly become obsolete.

It seems odd that only thirty years ago massive propaganda would have us believe that a woman who chose to work after marriage was a pariah, taking jobs away from men and abandoning her "natural role"; a woman who chose to pursue a career was suspect of being unfeminine with all the disdain that image carried at the time. Men, of course, who chose nurturing occupations were similarly suspect and viewed as emasculated. The possibilities for each sex to lead a richer, independent life opens the possibility for each to bring greater richness and understanding into their relationship.

I cannot agree with Dr. Fine that men should earn higher salaries for equal work because their responsibilities are greater. The first reason is purely economic. Should a widow with two children earn more than a single man? Should a man with three children earn more than a man with one child? Financial need has never been a criteria for salaries in our economy, and it is not likely to become so in the foreseeable future. If the principle of lower salaries for women was freely adopted, we would find women hired as cost efficient measures. Much the same situation would occur as when child labor was practiced: men would, by and large, be unemployed while women worked for lesser salaries.

Of equal importance is the role of the working wife in the family. A woman no longer works for "pin money." The contribution of her salary to the household functioning is directly related to the lessening of the unilateral burden of support upon the male. Freed from this charge, the the man has the possibility of spending more time with his family and/or in pursuits bringing gratifications other than financial reward alone.

Evidence suggests this is occurring among working and lower middle class families. When the man's resistance to having a working wife is resolved, he welcomes the freedom that the economic contribution of his wife brings and feels less a beast of burden and more a valued person. The redistribution of family responsibilities can do much to expedite the arrival of the loving society of which Dr. Fine speaks.

A particular strength of Dr. Fine's work which continues into this volume is his commitment to presenting human beings with human feelings, conflicts and attempts at resolution of those conflicts, and not with categories of personality disorders or psychiatric diagnoses within which individuals may be tabulated. In keeping with this, the book is richly illustrated with clinical material.

In accordance with this humanitarian orientation to the study of psychology, he has searched for those values which, if incorporated as societal mores, could change child rearing practices so they would produce a more loving and cooperative society. He has stated these values as the "analytic ideal" in this and other works and presents his ideas as to how a more loving society based upon this ideal might be generated. Dr. Fine has often expressed his adherence to the principle that "it is better to light one candle than to curse the darkness." This volume is the latest manifestation of this conviction.

Discussion III

Simone Sternberg

Dr. Fine has chosen to present the unfolding of the human being in terms of male development and vicissitudes endemic to the male of the species. This work is in part a rebuttal to the heavy attention devoted to female sexuality and the psychology of women in recent years which was in turn a reaction to Freud's initial exposition from a male point of view and mainly focused on the masculine gender. Like the Hegelian dialectic, one can hope that eventually enough redressing will have been accomplished on both sides so we can get on with it and look at the two genders together and in relation to each other. Common sense as well as research studies tell us that neither can function very effectively without the other.

I am grateful to Dr. Fine for having accomplished masterfully an exposition of growing up and surviving, more or less well, with a male identity (and organ) to contend with the rest of life. As the act of writing helps us to understand things better for ourselves, this work has doubtless helped the author, as well as his male readers, to a greater degree of self-understanding. I, as a female reader, found it very helpful to look at male psychology, development and its vicissitudes through Dr. Fine's eyes. Some of his depictions of women pleased me less, however, and I will address these issues later.

On page 4, Dr. Fine talks of the human cost to the man who has achieved considerable success. We know of the often even greater cost to women of achievement, of the price some pay in terms of not getting married, not having children, or needing others to take care of their children. As the author focuses on psychodynamic aspects of the societal injunction for men to be achievers, I am reminded of the literature on fear of success and masochism. The masochist pays up front to enjoy his success afterward, or sabotages the success after it has been achieved due to unresolved conflicts, be they

© 1987 by The Haworth Press, Inc. All rights reserved.

379

Oedipal or pre-genital. For men, fear of success seems to be more Oedipally determined while pre-Oedipal issues might be more salient for women. Both genders, however, are equally victimized by this syndrome.*

In the Introduction, Fine states that most leaders are men (with a few exceptions) and "it can be assumed that there is some biological basis for this differentiation, though again culture can force various changes in it." I would question the biological basis and lean more to cultural and psychological derivatives for explanations to such a complex issue. That women are still mainly reared to be pleasing, both physically and behaviorwise means that many women are in the habit of pleasing other people (the dutiful daughter, daddy's little girl, etc.) and want desperately to be liked. Women tend to be very concerned with what others think of them. If such conditioning is not placed in its proper perspective women will suffer by comparison when corporate and world leaders are counted by gender.

On page 6, when talking about the three poles of male psychology as sexuality, aggression and success, the author states that the mother tends to loom larger than the father in a hate culture. (Why not in a love culture?) It led me to wonder whether the inventors of the game of Chess (the game in which Dr. Fine is an internationally known Grand Master) were from a hate culture as well. The Queen is the most powerful figure on the board. When my son was turning six and in the throes of learning to play this game, he knew that if his Queen is captured, the game is up, so to speak (though he gamely played on).

On page 13 I was fascinated to learn that the chimpanzee Lucy avoided her "adopted father," the psychologist Temerlin, as a prospective sexual partner, but presented herself to other males, presumably human. That the incest taboo might exist in chimps is food for thought. That its strength is psychological is attested by the fact that it holds with adoptive parents as well.

Further in the book, there are numerous examples of forgotten men, both famous and unknown. The book can be

---

*"Fear of Flying High. Fear of Success as an Expression of Sado-Masochism." Workshop with Carol Schultz, NYCPT Symposium, April, 1979. Paper presented with Carol Schultz, Scientific Meeting.

viewed also as a memorial to these men, which I very much appreciated and was tempted to add some "forgotten men" of my own, gleaned through personal experience and through clinical supervision. My initial annoyance to the focus of the book, because after all there are forgotten women with stories equally poignant, was mitigated by Dr. Fine's sensitive recounting of the stories of these men.

However, some of the annoyance remained, particularly at the occasional depiction of women in stereotypical fashion, such as references to women in divorce proceedings. Certainly there are some women who are grasping and try to seek large alimony, houses and other property in divorce settlements, but this is often a last ditch attempt to salvage a pittance of self-esteem. As we know from our work with children, the stealing of money may be equated with stealing love. Obviously divorce is a declaration of non-love, a ripe battleground for all the unresolved hurts on both sides, often magnified by avaricious divorce lawyers with a vested interest in a large settlement for their client. The depiction of the woman of ice, the frigid, ungiving, unyielding woman, was also diturbing to me. That these women exist is well known. (That men exist who are unemotional and ungiving is also well known.) Nonetheless, ice only remains ice in a cold climate. A freezer is particularly good for this purpose. Under conditions of warmth the ice melts. Also, the author tells us that some women do let themselves go to seed after marriage. How sad for the woman, as well as for her family. Perhaps this can also be seen as a symptom of the paucity of the marriage.

On the other side, however, Dr. Fine, to his credit, depicts the terrible injustices inflicted on women throughout history, including the physically and psychologically horrendous effects of cliterectomy and its even worse variants. The overdrawn portrait of some stereotypical women marred for me the obvious care and intelligence the author bestowed on this otherwise estimable and enjoyable book.

From Dr. Fine's discussion of male development I was tempted to extrapolate from my own experience of my son's early years, trying to ferret out those factors which might apply exclusively, or principally to a male child. Freud has told us that the most perfect relationship was that between a mother and her son. (From his own experience, he meant first-born or only son.) I can only state such a relationship has its ups and downs. Parenthood has its joys and sorrows and parenting a boy has its own set. Some of my son's developmental difficulties and hurdles were rendered more meaningful by Dr. Fine's exposition of them.

At the risk of being overly self revealing I remember coming home when Noah was an infant and smelling the babysitter's (a woman in her sixties) perfume on him and my painful pangs of jealousy. Would I have reacted so strongly with an infant daughter? I certainly would have felt as guilty being at work and leaving my precious baby with a sitter.

I remember the pride of the fearless toddler who would venture off to the next room (with no parent in sight) without a backward glance. I identified with my little voyager, wanderer, climber, doer.

In kindergarten, a vamp named Rebecca cast her eye on my son. Their attraction culminated in two marriages in our living room without benefit of Rabbi or priest, but with M & Ms to celebrate. (More pangs of maternal jealousy.) The memory of the sight of Noah's backpack hanging down his chest with four cabbage patch children peeking out, the combined progeny of the happy marriage, is a sweet one. A year later, while still very close, the early disappointment that they couldn't actually live together and share a bed (as they had planned) took its toll and they were merely close friends.

Dr. Fine's discussion of the Oedipal issues for boys reminded me of a family in my neighborhood. The boy, now a strapping fifteen-year old with a scholarship to a prestigious school, is sometimes seen walking with his mother, who looks about forty years old. His sickly father, who stays at home, recently underwent stomach surgery and appears to be recovering. I thought the father was about sixty-five years old but just learned he is in fact eighty. In this family the son is very young and stalwart, the father very old and sickly. One can wonder how much this son has to rein in his aggression and how responsible he might feel for taking care of his mother (and how little he could afford to see his mother as a sexual woman); how in fact the reality interferes with the fantasy and impedes the adolescent tasks of the second individuation, as delineated by Peter Blos, Erikson and others.

At a recent phsychology conference I attended, a paper was given on female latency and identification issues for girls with their fathers were delineated. There was identification with the "real" father as well as with what the father represents; phallic functions, including the work role, assertiveness and aggressiveness, were also discussed. I brought up the issues of the latency male child, relating to both active and passive mother (the mother who works and has a professional identity as well as a maternal one) and the active and passive father (who among other things, might do a lot of the cooking and child caring, a not unusual configuration in today's urban families). I wondered how these issues could be conceptualized within the framework under discussion. Two responses from the audience were telling (and not without humor). One famous male psychologist answered, "He'll work it out." Another said, "As long as he's happy." Ultimately, most children do work it out, happily.

Recently, much attention has been given to custody issues and fathers' needs and wishes to be involved in the lives of their children. We are also increasingly aware of children's need for their fathers as well as for their mothers, throughout childhood, starting from very early on (perhaps from birth itself).

Some problems of father having sole custody of their children are illustrated by the story of Sean, age fifteen, the oldest of three sons presently being reared by his father. Sean was the only one of the three who first tried to live alone with his mother, who is apparently psychotic, when the parents separated a few years ago. When this became impossible, he joined his brothers at the home of his father. This bright adolescent, who has interested himself in Norse mythology, spiritualism and psychology, is flunking out of school and making life miserable for himself and his father, not to mention his brothers. His father has threatened to send him away to a Jesuit school where they will allegedly make a "man" of him. The fierce struggles of adolescence are exacerbated here by Sean's inability to master the Oedipal triangle in a safe and "normal" environment. The struggle with his father has gone beyond his father's ability to contain it. Parenting under normal circumstances is difficult enough. Parenting an adolescent is particularly difficult, not only because of the turmoil within the adolescent, but for what it reactivates of the parent's own adolescence such as unresolved conflicts and authority conflicts with his father. Single parenting is perhaps the most difficult of all, be it for a mother or for a father.

There are further problems for the male child reared by a single parent, usually the mother, who might have to search long and hard for a male identificatory figure. These sons also work it out, sometimes less happily and less well. Child therapy clinics and child therapists fill their practices with such children. However, a male child growing up with a father as single parent isn't necessarily in a better position. As we know from recent child research, if not from common sense, it is far better to have one of each, both mother and father, when growing up. Fine and others have pointed to the need for the father as a conduit from the closeness with mother to the outside world. Martin Bergmann speaks of the need for the male figure to cool down and diminish the libidinal intensity between mother and child.

I am reminded of the story of a male single parent of a little girl. A thirty-seven-year old, intelligent, resourceful black man, former drug dealer with a concomitant lifestyle, is now "single" parenting a two-year-old daughter, the product of a bi-racial liaison. They are living in a Single Room Occupancy hotel. A proud man, he wants to earn a living to escape the dire poverty in which he now exists. He doesn't want to be on public assistance and tries not to think of the temptations of the easy money of his former lifestyle. This man is trying to provide a home and life for his daughter. He is completely devoted to this little girl, a bright, lively, happy child (seemingly against great odds).

How long will this father be able to provide a "good enough" growth environment for his daughter? At what point might it become too difficult, too overwhelming for him? (Conversely, many single women, both black and white, raise sons alone. One could ask if women are better equipped for single parenthood.) An interesting sidelight is that this little girl called her father "Mommy" in spite of his manifest protestations that he should be called "Daddy." Later, with his therapist, he was able to recognize that unconsciously he wanted to be called "Mommy" (he was in fact fulfilling both the mothering and fathering roles and wanted to be seen by his daughter as her only parent). That this child, though lighter in skin tone and female, looks very much like her father, speaks to the second chance men have through their children of both sexes to work through issues of their own childhood and to redeem their adult selves through the parenting role.

In Dr. Fine's chapter on the average man, I was reminded that men from racial, as well as ethnic minorities, are often among the most forgotten. A therapist I was working with in supervision had as a patient the fifty-year-old son of a black father and white mother; he was a bright, sensitive, gifted man. His parents, ardent members of the Communist party, sent him to be raised by a black woman in another city. He ran away repeatedly and at puberty spent some time with his natural parents before being sent for schooling in Russia. After numerous breakdowns and many "comebacks" he died suddenly of a heart attack, just prior to a feared confrontation in yet another rehabilitation program in which he was placed. A sad and lonely life, not without yearnings and hopes for the future. Was his death a response to an ultimate feeling of despair he might have experienced as the last job training program failed? We are only left with our conjectures and a deep sense of loss.

Dr. Fine in his Preface gives us the example of the therapist who manages to overcome his own suffering and is then able to teach others. Perhaps this is a fitting coda to the book: readers, whether male or female, can participate in a mutual human endeavor to relieve their own suffering to a greater rather than lesser degree and in turn pass this knowledge on to patients, supervisees, mates and children.

In closing my discussion, I would again like to thank Dr. Fine for helping me to think and rethink through issues of male psychology. I reiterate my hope that with a better understanding of the issues and needs of both genders we will have an enriched psychology of both men and women, seen in their relationship to and interdependence with each other.

Discussion IV

Norman Shelly

Reuben Fine's book *The Forgotten Man* is painted on a large canvas and with broad strokes from a multi-colored palette. In looking at some famous men, Fine contrasts their public achievements and their inner dilemmas and reveals they all suffered in their human relationships. He also emphasizes the role of the penis from a biological and symbolic perspective, and points out that this aspect of man's endowment has been mostly ignored in the psychoanalytic literature.

Fine expands Freud's statement that "anatomy is destiny" to include how anatomy plays a major role in the arrangements that society makes for the destiny of each of its members. The penis is, and represents, man's narcissistic pride and also his vulnerability. The penis is, and represents, an instrument of love, aggression and hostility. The penis becomes the symbolic "raison d'être" in Fine's treatise in *The Forgotten Man*.

The internal design is determined not only by the developmental phases (oral, anal and phallic) but also by the move from the mother to the father and to the outside world Fine considers the drives of the child in conjunction with the parental reactions to these drives based on cultural ideals (superego) and the unconscious unresolved conflicts of the parents belonging to the same developmental phase as the basic dilemma. He hazards a guess that it it is not only the Oedipal conflict of the child that is at stake in this interaction but "that the intensity of the Oedipal problem is a reflection of the degree of animosity that exists between mother and father, rather than of the biological strength of the drives." When a mother and father hate one another fiercely, as is unfortunately all too often the case, the child identifies with one or the other and develops fierce hatreds as well. When the mother and father love one another, Fine says, the Oedipal wishes surface, but are rather easily handled. Every human being "can best be understood in the light of his or her

© 1987 by The Haworth Press, Inc. All rights reserved.

family background and in this background the feelings surrounding love/hate relationships of the parents are at the
core." Because of the hatred and destructiveness that is so
obvious in our society, Fine concludes, "in general, it can be
said that ours is a hate culture, in which the predominate
mode of relationship of people is based more on hateful than
on loving feelings."

The many rich and insightful observations made by Reuben
Fine stimulated me to associate in many directions. I thought
of the parental conflicts aroused during the different phases of
development and how that might effect the growth of the
child. I drifted to the concept of introjection and their repre-
sentations as they evolve in the clinical setting through transference and resistance. I thought about the resistance to psychoanalytic concepts as applied to our various institutions and
especially in the realm of education. In the light of Fine's *The
Forgotten Man* I pondered the recent Supreme Court's ruling
on homosexuality and its lack of psychological insight.

Each one of my associations could be fully examined in the
light of parenting and how the conflicts of the parents are
visited upon the child. However, I will confine myself to a few
clinical examples. First, I would like to point out that countertransference issues are similar to identification and empathy
issues of parents during different phases of development.
These unresolved countertransference reactions are defended
against and become counter-resistant in the treatment.

The parent who cannot identify with a particular phase
prevents the child from experiencing the phase and cannot
support the child through the inevitable frustration of entering the next phase. Max, who idealized his father, experienced his silence as a sign of strength and longed to emulate
him. He saw his father as having the capacity to be alone.
Max could not tolerate being alone. His masculine prototype
was John Wayne. Max struggled with his homosexual longings. His mother had been very seductive and overprotective.
Her message was "be a man but don't hurt yourself." Max
was caught between his mother and father. For Max, "macho
man" could be alone and did not need anybody. This represented father and his erect penis. On the other hand, he
wanted to lie down with father and take in his penis, as this
would make him a man.

Years ago there was a cartoon depicting a father viewing his newborn child in the hospital nursery. The father was loaded down with a baseball, bat, football and helmet and a catcher's mitt. The dark side of this cartoon was that the baby was a girl. There are times when each parent has an easier time identifying with the sex of a child. The mother, for example, can respond with joy and pleasure to the suckling but then reacts with irritation and anxiety as the little baby boy becomes more independent. At a later stage when he proudly shows her his erect penis she once again responds with anxiety and may belittle him."

Christine Olden, in her paper, "On Adult Empathy With Children," published in The Psychoanalytic Study of the Child (1953) said, "Good childhood or bad, happy or unhappy, if for some reason the adult can allow himself to live with the sufferings of his childhood and reach a degree of reconciliation with them as part of his development; if he is able to 'reflect' or relive the emotions he had as a small child on this or another occasion; if he has managed to work through his early experience (not necessarily in analysis) and come to find it natural in retrospect and remoteness that he did once have infantile needs; if he considers those needs of the past as much of himself as his history is a part of himself; if in the course of growing up, and perhaps with the aide of his sense of humor he has gained some perspective toward those needs—then he can begin to take for granted the child's primitive behavior. Then he will not feel seduced or endangered by being confronted with the manifestations of the primary process. Then he can permit himself to gradually live in the strange fantasy world of children and, by the way of sublimation, to be their guide and enjoy their growth."

I would take issue with Olden's statement that these very important reliving and reworking through of early wishes and conflicts could take place with a formal analysis, primarily because of the countertransference issues involved. At any rate just a cursory look at our society would indicate the impossibility of such a feat in most instances.

There is one association I had in reading *The Forgotten Man* that will conclude my discussion. In the musical *South Pacific* by Rodgers and Hammerstein a penetrating lyric has remained with me because of its simple insight:

You have to be taught to hate and fear,
You have to be taught from year to year,
It has to be drummed into your dear little ear,
You've got to be carefully taught.

And the final stanza:

You've got to be taught before it's too late,
Before you are six or seven or eight,
To hate all the people your relatives hate
You've got to be carefully,
You've got to be carefully taught.

Discussion V

Donald Whipple

I would like to begin by saying how happy I am to have been asked to make a few comments about Dr. Fine's book, "The Forgotten Man." It is tremendously expansive and inclusive, the amount of research that must have gone into this work is truly noteworthy. There are more than 160 citations in the list of references. My first response after having read parts three and four, which were the parts I was asked to review, was that I would like to take off a year from practice and devote my time to reading biographies. What follows are some random thoughts stimulated by Dr. Fine's book. I hope they are not too random and that they may help stimulate others to think further about their reactions to the book.

I found Chapter 13, "Politicians: Leaders or Power Seekers?" to be of particular interest. I wondered why Dr. Fine chose to write about Nixon, Johnson, and the Kennedys and why he left out Roosevelt, Truman, Reagan and others. I am not saying that what Dr. Fine had to say about Nixon, Johnson and the Kennedys was not instructive. Perhaps it is that I would like to read something about all the presidents, since the use and abuse of power is of particular interest to me. I was surprised to read that there is no evidence that Johnson was corrupt. If I am not mistaken, he is generally thought of as having been a rather corruptible wheeler-dealer from Texas. I wonder why, then, a rather common image of him portrays him as worse than the evidence would indicate. It is often said that the course of history might have been different had John and Robert Kennedy lived. This may be true. However, it is possible that if John had lived, he might have gone down in ignominy as the president who got us into the Vietnam war.

Putting these, and numerous other issues that could be raised aside, there is one psychological dimension that I wish to focus on, which is related to power. This dimension is narcissism and its derivative, grandiosity. Dr. Fine did not

© 1987 by The Haworth Press, Inc. All rights reserved.

overlook this dimension. Indeed, he described a number of his biographical personalities as grandiose. I think the issue of narcissim and grandiosity deserve even more attention.

I wonder if one can be a successful politician without being grandiose and power hungry. I think this may be especially true for the higher offices such as governor and president. As we know from our own observation, and from Freud's paper on group psychology, people, in general, have a great deal of difficulty relinquishing infantile omnipotence. We seek to preserve this feeling of omnipotence by identifying with, or submitting to, an omnipotent other. Belief in God helps us deny our helplessness and death. Politically, we want our politicians, and especially our presidents, to be powerful. The president must convey an aura of power and omnipotence. Candidates who are perceived as weak are not elected. A war hero, Eisenhower, trounced his opponent Stevenson in 1952 and 1956. Stevenson was brilliant and rational. However, he was perceived as weak and indecisive. He lacked charisma. In 1960 Kennedy won over Nixon even though Nixon was well-known and had been vice president for eight years. Kennedy was better on television and had more charisma. In 1980 and 1984, Reagan demonstrated he had tremendous charisma. In general, it is true that men who are somewhat grandiose and who convey an aura of self-confidence are more likely to be regarded as having charisma. Thus the slightly grandiose politician is likely to win—as long as he is not extreme and offensive. I am afraid that with television, politicians in the future will be more and more elected on the basis of charisma and television performance, and less and less on the basis of issues.

Dr. Fine mentioned corruption in relation to the politicians he discussed. In my opinion, our political system is almost designed to encourage corruption. House members are constantly running for office as they face election every two years. The main preoccupation of most representatives is to be re-elected. This is less true for senators who are elected every six years. However, both the house and senate seem to be most sensitive to special interest groups. After all, P.A.C.'s and other interest groups are essential sources of campaign contributions.

As Dr. Fine so cogently pointed out, grandiosity is not limited to politicians. We see it in business, the military and among intellectuals. The age of the robber baron may be in the past, but there still are men who amass power and fortune for its own sake. Some of them wheel-and-deal in billions of dollars, embarking on friendly and unfriendly takeovers of major corporations. As Dr. Fine pointed out, great scientists, after having made a great discovery, often do not keep up with the latest developments in their science. They become wedded to their own ideas and refuse to take in new ones from the outside. This is narcissism.

Dr. Fine also pointed out we see the quest for power and grandiosity in all fields. Although he mentioned these motives in relation to the healing professions, I think he was too kind. I think one finds the quest for power and self-aggrandizement just as much among therapists as in other fields. This can be seen in institute politics, factional disputes in the field and among individuals as individuals. Too often, therapists are concerned about how high their fees are in relation to other therapists. In my many years of committee work for various organizations I have witnessed the most brutal power struggles over meaningless positions—meaningless at least in terms of fame or fortune. Law and business are known as competitive fields. Businessmen and lawyers are supposed to compete. Therapists are supposed to be healers. Therapists, however, often annihilate one another with psychological name-calling.

Perhaps lawyers and businessmen are more honest and less hypocritical than many therapists. Dr. Fine pointed out that priests were always thought to be holier than the common man. Some therapists wish to believe that they are better off or healthier than the common man. Certainly, clients and patients wish this to be true. It is often difficult for the therapist to give up this idealization. I must disagree with Dr. Fine who stated that the healer is one who has been healed. It would be great if this were always the case. Too often, the healer has not been healed. When this happens, the therapist ends up with mountains of countertransference. Some therapists refuse to be healed at all, as they refuse to go into analysis themselves. I hope I do not sound unduly pessimistic. Dr. Fine did not separate therapists from the rest of humanity. I think it is important that we, as therapists, from time to time, remind ourselves that we are mere mortals.

I wish to express again how glad I am to have been asked to respond to this most scholarly work.

Discussion VI

Richard T. Symons

Man has been forgotten: inadequately studied and neglected asserts Dr. Fine. In order to rectify this, he has studied man in terms of three primary facets of his functioning: sexuality, aggression and social role. A major conclusion reached from this examination is a realization of the profound difficulties men experience in their lives.

In presenting the problems men face in making their various career choices, Dr. Fine states: "The social structure forces men into certain paths. He does not have an infinite variety of life careers to choose from; he just has a few, and he has to make up his mind. Scarce wonder that many men falter by the wayside, unable to decide what they want to do in life, drift or become homosexual to justify their indecision, or resort to more serious emotional difficulties such as neurosis or psychosis. In times of economic distress these problems multiply manyfold." I am not sure whether I follow his etiology of homosexuality here.

Dr. Fine clearly depicts the effect of aggression on man's social role as producing grave problems: "In our society man is driven to fight and to achieve. In many areas his attainments have been prodigious. . . . If he is powerful, he becomes ruthless; his view of life becomes one of beat the other fellow out or be beaten out yourself. If he is successful he keeps under wraps the great suffering that was the price of his success. . . . He has to maintain a certain image in the eyes of the world, and if he cannot maintain that image, he feels deeply humiliated and depressed."

Various social roles are considered: the politician, businessman, the creative individual, the military man, intellectuals (scientists) and the psychotherapist. Dr. Fine utilizes the psychoanalytic model whereby these social roles are studied in depth. He accomplishes this by examining the lives of individuals respresentative of these careers, focusing on their

© 1987 by The Haworth Press, Inc. All rights reserved.

childhood and family histories. Two important findings emerge from an examination of this material. For one, the vicissitudes of the personal life, especially the early family experiences, break through and have enormous bearing on the man's functioning later in life. For another, close scrutiny of the inner man, in whatever social role, whether successful or not, reveals that he is often full of despair, unhappiness and even depression.

To give but several examples: Studying the lives of businessmen leads to the observation that in the acquisition of great wealth, "the lack of regard for other people and the intense concentration on making money rarely led to much personal happiness." The dream of the self-made entrepreneur and the accumulation of enormous wealth is a powerful motivation. Because its realization is rare and frought with difficulty, "it can cause heartache and sorrow and even the premature shortening of life."

The creative man is particularly conspicuous for the amount of suffering he displays: "If he is successful, it tends to go to his head, and he becomes grandiose, pushing harder and harder. If he fails, he takes it as a sign that he is useless as a human being, and gets very depressed. In either case the dissolution into women, drugs, depression and early death is hardly uncommon."

The scientist's powerful ambition often leads to feelings of frustration and low self esteem: "And yet over and over no matter how great the achievement, we find that the scientist is not pleased with himself. In a way the great scientist is hurt by his achievement as much as he is helped since he is cast into a social role which makes it difficult for him to relate to other people, particularly women. As a result most scientists show a strong tendency to fall into depressions."

Mankind is extremely unhappy and has traditionally turned for help to the priest and, more recently, the psychotherapist. "Men who enter this profession are or should be those who have had deeply moving personal experiences in their own lives. . . Yet here too the suffering may last many years before it is finally resolved," says Dr. Fine.

He asks: "What then is the answer to man's suffering and unhappiness?" The answer he feels is the recognition of the crucial importance of love for human happiness. Thus he believes that "It is possible to reach a meaningful love relationship with a woman which will be gratifying sexually, intellectually and socially." He admits that, in reality, this is unusual. It is far more usual, after various frustrated attempts to find compatibility, to eventually end up as a couple who just satisfy each other's needs.

The prescription of love for man's suffering and depression stimulates two lines of thought in me. The first has to do with man's search for the restitutive relationship. In childhood, boys, while separating from the mother, at the same time feel rejected and wish to reunite with her. They look for reunion in all those ways in which society permits. That is, they want to be like the mother (through identification) or conquer the mother symbolically. They experience the separation as a rejection, causing the general depressiveness in men.

In adulthood, men try to find a woman to take the mother's place. If a man can find such a woman to love him, he can lose his anger towards his mother and love this woman. He has found salvation through love. Love has cured him.

The second has to do with the curative aspects of the positive transference. Freud likens the positive transference, with its affectionate and erotic elements, to a love relationship. It is the positive transference that empowers the analyst to help the patient face and overcome his resistances: to endure and carry on the psychoanalytic process.

However, it is also true that the positive transference serves as a powerful resistance to the psychoanalytic process. The patient, under its influence, wants to put aside the work of analysis and demands immediate satisfaction of his impulses. It seems a riddle in which the positive transference serves both as a resistance and the means by which the work of psychoanalysis progresses.

In his paper, "The Dynamics of Transference" (1912), Freud solves this riddle in the following way: ". . . transference to the doctor is suitable for resistance to the treatment only in so far as it is a negative transference or a positive transference of repressed erotic impulses. If we 'remove' the transference by making it conscious, we are detaching only these two components of the emotional act from the person of the doctor; the other component (affectionate feelings), which is admissible to consciousness and unobjectionable, persists and is the vehicle of success in psychoanalysis exactly as it is in other methods of treatment. To this extent we readily admit that the results of psychoanalysis rest upon suggestion; by suggestion, however, we must understand . . . the influencing of a person by means of the transference phenomena which are possible in his case. We take care of the patient's final independence by employing suggestion in order to get him to accomplish a piece of psychical work which has as its necessary result a permanent improvement in his psychical situation." Once again it can be said that love has cured him; love is the answer.

Discussion VII

Janet Schumacher Finell

Reuben Fine's sketches of famous men are down to earth and read easily and smoothly. He captivates the essence of the individual in his crisp and cogent accounts. In some cases, one might wish for deeper psychoanalytic insights, particularly if one feels a particularly strong affinity for a man he is discussing. His approach, however, permits him to cover a number of different men from different professions and with widely different interests. In this way, his broad-based approach permits him to give the reader a great deal of information about a large number of men. In addition, the reader without any psychoanalytic training can read the book with no difficulty as it is free of jargon and esoteric terminology.

Fine explores the motives of a number of well-known politicians (Lyndon Johnson, Nixon, the Kennedys, Huey Long, John Adams, Rasputin and Churchill). While some of them were motivated by violence, power and were corrupt, others were honest, sincere leaders, dedicated to the pursuit of their ideals. Fine's account of Nixon's paranoid personality was particularly fascinating to me. Nixon overcame a very unhappy family background and drove himself by sheer will to a position of power. His underlying paranoia, however, destroyed his political career. The Kennedys' wealth made them immune to the need to further accumulate money, and Fine succinctly describes their strong persistence and dedication to politics. While he mentions their personally self-destructive behavior, and the many tragedies the family endured, I would have enjoyed more discussion of this aspect of the family profile.

Of the businessmen (John D. Rockefeller, James Hammond, Henry Ford II, Aristotle Onassis), I found myself most interested in and wishing for more information about Onassis, perhaps because of the notoriety he received in his lifetime. Fine stresses the importance of a steady income in the life of

© 1987 by The Haworth Press, Inc. All rights reserved.

the corporate man, but I would add that the corporation has a protective, motherlike quality which fulfills important emotional security needs as well as monetary ones.

The creative men (Elvis Presley, Will Rogers, Somerset Maugham, Isaac Bashevis Singer, Vincent Van Gogh) and artists who led shorter lives (Edgar Allan Poe, F. Scott Fitzgerald, John Berryman, Beethoven) were presented with rich and relevant material. Van Gogh is an artist I have studied and followed, and Fine did justice to the account of his short, tortured and highly productive life. Beethoven's rages, misogyny, bitterness and sorrow and the tragedy of his deafness even while he was still creating exquisite music, was fascinating. Joe Louis seemed a bit out of place followed by Chessmaster Bobby Fischer, but the contrast was certainly of interest.

The workings of the military mind (Eisenhower, Patton, MacArthur, U.S. Grant and men and women who fought in Vietnam) is followed by descriptions of intellectuals (Einstein, Bertrand Russell, Galbraith, Hans Selye, Asimov). I was particularly interested in Einstein's failure to keep up with "the uncertainties of quantum mechanics." His genius could not adapt itself to a changing field because of personality difficulties. Multi-gifted Asimov feared that if he were to die at the time he was interviewed, he would have written "only a hundred books." His brother noted that his eyes glazed over, but he snapped "to attention the moment your name is mentoned." His intense rivalrous feelings toward his father accounted, in Fine's description for his need to produce a large number of books, thus establishing a sense of phallic adequacy.

Fine's belief that "Men Who Help: Therapists and Priests" are driven by good experiences that "A healer in short is one who has been healed," is not in accordance with my understanding of the healer's motivation. Rather, I believe that the healer is driven by rescue fantasies that originally were directed to a family member or members and which gave him an important source of narcissistic gratification. This later becomes an important source of self-worth to the healer and accounts for his dedication to healing others.

I quite agree with Fine's dislike of the pejorative term "sick" often used to describe patients in treatment. This term creates an artificial dichotomy between patient and analyst.

Fine was able to outline the salient elements of Freud's life and contributions, and this is quite a feat considering the great breadth of Freud's contributions and the changes he underwent in his thinking. Fine does not deal with Freud's attitude toward females and female psychology, and I think it is wise that he avoided this controversial topic. His account of Sullivan's struggles with alcoholism and serious economic problems captivated the essence of the man while Jung's spiritual, mystical, occult learnings reflect his idiosyncratic approach to treatment.

"Love Is The Answer," Fine's concluding chapter, reflects his emphasis on the importance of love as a force for health in man's life. He describes man as more fearful of revealing his vulnerability and neediness than women, a finding with which I agree. Traditionally, far more women seek therapy than men when they feel painful anxiety, depression and other distressing feelings. Man's need to feel in control and dominant, however, are the underlying motives for his difficulty in revealing vulnerabilities and may, at times, interfere with his ability to seek love and make a commitment to a relationship. Here we do not see love as juxtaposed with aggression, an element that one might consider the "sine qua non" of psychoanalysis. My preference is to see love and hate as in conflict and alternately moving man toward and away from intimacy with others. I think that Fine's optimistic attitude about the restorative-saving power of love is refreshing in a field that too often focuses too heavily on aggression.

In summary, I found that the book offered interesting reading, and summarized the lives of a number of very interesting men from different walks of life. The forgotten man can read this book with sustained interest and feel restored in a literary world that focuses heavily on women.

Discussion VIII

Margot Tallmer

Many years ago, in a pre-video era, a popular movie titled "My Man Godfrey" depicted a flaky, blond socialite assigned the task, as part of a scavenger hunt, of tracking down a "forgotten man." She, Carole Lombard, cleverly discovers a person in the ash heaps and demands to know if he is indeed a forgotten man.

He replied affirmatively, explaining that such a man is one who lives from day to day. According to Dr. Fine, this assignment would be no challenge at all today, for forgotten men abound. Despite their large numbers though, they have been overlooked and their all too frequent problems persistently ignored. (As evidence of this pervasive slighting, he cites the absence of men's studies in college curricula. I had actually assumed *all* studies were studies of men, save the specific, and few departments of womens studies.) Sexuality, aggression and social roles for men are all seen as areas of potential difficulties. The author resourcefully illustrates his thesis by broadly-based vignettes of men's lives, including despots, geniuses, criminals, fathers of patients and others.

Many of these vignettes extend only to early adulthood; few address the issues of confronting middle or old age in any detail. In fact, Fine notes that creative, innovative spurts often reach the zenith at a relatively young age, never to be equalled later in the life cycle. For men, that is.

Can we then extend his thinking into midlife and the later years and is maturing different for men and women? Is old age harder for the male?

Oddly enough, the answer is probably in the affirmative. Although mature women are demonstrably poorer than men (women are *not* treated favorably by judges—the judicial system is woefully biased against women), are much more frequently the survivor in the marriage, remarry far less often, suffer to a greater extent from depression, and are dealt with

© 1987 by The Haworth Press, Inc. All rights reserved.

more harshly in old age than their male counterparts (women are enjoined through their lives to maintain a constantly youthful appearance, clearly an impossible feat, and are often regarded as sexless objects after menopause), nevertheless, they seem to experience greater life satisfaction than men. The suicide rate, cited in Fine's book, is only partially correct; actually, the incidence for white men continues to rise proportionate to age.

Major losses occur for both sexes in midlife: these include physical deficits, widowhood, retirement and the empty nest syndrome.

Regarding the first event, that is, physical decrements, there seems to be little controversy regarding the many biological advantages of women. Facts are indisputable; universally, men die at an earlier age than women; infant mortality is greater for males; men are more vulnerable to environmental stress and thus die more frequently in epidemics or bombings. Sexual drive, a main area of consideration in the book, is a far greater problem for men in old age, for any waning of potency (and there are definite changes with age) is regarded as a profound assault. Women, of course, do not have to perform sexually in any observable, measureable way. Fine mentions that many women are relieved not to engage in sexual relationships after a divorce; many women are, also, lamentably, forced out of sexual contacts because of the absence of partners.

The loss of a spouse has a greater impact upon the husband. (By the age of eighty, one-third of the men and two-thirds of the women are widowed.) Both widows and widowers actually have higher death rates and higher psychiatric impairment than married couples. The usual age differential in couples means that the woman can probably anticipate widowhood; that is, she has internalized expectable age norms—those events that then occur out of sync are the most distressing. Women have frequently rehearsed this phenomenon with other women and, in fact, have a supportive peer group of other widows available. As we have mentioned, men remarry much more often but women more frequently live with their children, where they can perform useful services. The grandparent role is also more important for the female and permits a degree of close physical contact usually denied to the male.

Finally, in the periods of middle and old age, the work role loses some or all of its importance, forcing one to develop other means of self differentiation. The years around retirement are often the most difficult and crucial in a man's life; clearly voluntary versus involuntary choice is an important variable, as are socio-economic status, the meaning of work, marital status, health and potential resources. Retirement seems to affect morale in many subtle but powerful ways; there is a strong relationship between the working role and suicide in old age. Fewer working males commit suicide than retired ones.

We are seeing today the varied effects of early retirement (fifty-five years and up) and the anger engendered by being "asked" to retire before sixty-five. One element is, once again, that retirement is an anticipated life event but early retirement may be unexpected and thus very stressful. There may be feelings of failing to achieve one's potential—a feeling more likely to occur when the work role is aborted precipitously, leaving less time to ensure a financial basis for security and developing means for sustaining activity. There are few suitable role models since other retired men often appear inferior. Much of the social life of men is work related; that is, unions and labor clubs, and the absence of a group of working colleagues may be keenly felt. If a man's job has been prestigious enough he may continue to confer status on the family after retirement. If he has contributed to society through his work efforts he may welcome retirement. If he has not, there is no longer time for reparations. One cannot straighten things in the future any longer. Also, retirement often offers solitude, solitude that may eventuate into loneliness and excessive aloneness. Those who prevent the emergence of anxiety through frequent activity and socialization may be unable to use the solitude productively.

Retirement for men (women's retirement has been nearly totally ignored by social scientists, save for their responses to their husbands' stopping work—women's *real* work is her family) has been analogized to the putative empty nest syndrome for women. In comparing these two events, women are in a better chronological place than men, since the last child departs before fifty in the usual family. In midlife, both sexes concentrate on morals, the meaning of live, super-ego concerns—issues that have often been shunted aside because of child caring responsibilities. Women can assess personal belief systems, slough off unwanted obligations and concentrate on future steps to be taken, a future that is more extended than the husbands at age sixty-five.

Many women now permit themselves the expression of long inhibited so-called masculine, aggressive impulses, striving for achievement and dominance. They may become more outward in orientation, retrieving some of the child-invested narcissism for personal use. While the wife is enabled to consider aggressive action, freed from many household routines, and also to express the active part of herself, simultaneously the husband may well examine and assess the intense, prolonged absorption in work activities, an absorption that may have resulted in the neglect of interpersonal relationships and inequitable treatment of women.

Men may decide to concentrate on slighted areas, such as affiliation, aesthetics and contemplation. Their own dependency needs, previously projected onto the wife and children, now have to be owned and dealt with. Empirically, we witness many men who decided upon a divorce following the departure of the children, and then, interestingly enough, remarry and start another family. The man's dependency can, once again be projected onto others and sexuality may be enhanced temporarily by the presence of a younger mate. An illusion.

It is manifest that the issue of death must be confronted in old age. David Gutmann has noted that personal death may be easier for a woman who has mothered a child, for the existence of another person has become more important than one's own life. The death of one's child is acknowledged as the quintessential tragedy. Perhaps women, long accustomed to the responsibility for other people's lives, may be better able to accept the notion of their own demise. Children offer the possibility of continuity and this potential may be more accessible to the mother, as the primary parenting figure.

Fine has addressed people in terms of three areas of functioning: sexuality, aggression and social role. We have attempted to extrapolate, albeit briefly, some of these issues into old age and to consider the fate of these events on the elderly man and woman. We are much more optimistic than he is for somehow persons in late life, according to the Harris poll, express themselves as satisfied—that is, they know that senescence is a difficult time but they themselves are content. It is *other* older people they see as having difficulties. Perhaps this is denial, perhaps resignation or perhaps it is an accurate statement of their feelings.

Or perhaps the "forgotten man" does turn out to be William Powell, a suave, dapper sophisticate, and most of us do live as happily ever after as he and the heroine. In any event, the man does not have to be an object of special concern, for progressing through the life cycle in a productive, growth-enhancing, positive way is a Herculean task for all of us. Carole Lombard was also a star in that particular flick.

Discussion IX

Laura Arens Fuerstein

Psychoanalysis is so often presented and experienced as an entity unto itself. It is frequently separated from real life, viewed as vital only in treatment settings, while preserved for a uniquely pathological segment of the population. In *The Forgotten Man* Dr. Fine demonstrates an extraordinary capacity to integrate this insulated and stilted version of this social science and psychology with the essence of man, his culture, and "humanness." More specifically, within the last two sections of the book, the author employs a psychoanalytic perspective to focus upon man's social role and view of himself within a cultural context. He achieves this through an artful weaving of the first two sections which deal with man's sexuality and aggression, with these two final parts: the connective thread is the culture's imprint upon the "forgotten man's instinctual life" which then is played out graphically within his social role.

The author states implicitly that man feels "forgotten" on both an internal and external level. Internally he feels forgotten because of the primordial rejection he experiences by necessity at the hands of the incestuous object/mother. Externally he feels "forgotten" by the culture for two basic reasons: first, because the woman has taken center stage due to recent socio-political events; second, and more importantly, the monolithic culture "forgets" his needs and his feelings, as they are largely dictated by the social role to which he is assigned and/or chooses.

In order to review the section on the forgotten man's social role, it seems necessary to first place this role within the total psycho-biological and cultural context in which he is placed by the author. Man's role as politician, businessman, creative artist, soldier, searching intellectual or psychotherapist has been subject to scrutiny and society's dictates through the centuries (though the role of psychotherapist is relatively

© 1987 by The Haworth Press, Inc. All rights reserved.

new). Historically, the very same culture that has awarded
man with special privleges, so to speak, for being a man (as
opposed to a woman) exacts an emotional price: if one is
permitted to achieve more, or request more for oneself from
a societal forum, then that same forum can demand that he
meet its requirements.

One result is that the man is forced into certain polarized
positions as he leads its electorate, runs its business, creates
its art work, commands its armies, devises its scientific formulations, or treats its emotionally distressed population. For
example, the politician is entrenched between statesmanship
and demagoguery. The industrialist straddles the line between
the "Protestant Ethic" and the lure of corruption. The artist
must strike a balance between the turbulence and suffering
inherent in the self-expression of the pure creative act and the
personal emptiness often found in the "sell-out" to commer-
cial success. The general is programmed to see the loss of life
in war as secondary to the humiliation or possibility of total
extinction inherent in defeat. The searching intellectual sees
himself as pinioned between the position of total mediocrity
or Nobel Prize superhumanness. The psychoanalyst, due to
his incorporating the role of religious healer of the past must
attain a balance between "medicine man" and proselytizer on
the one hand and scientist/artist on the other. A more detailed view of two social roles discussed by the author might
serve to further illuminate his work.

From Dr. Fine's examination of the politician, it might be
gleaned that the path between Scylla (corruption) and Cha-
rybdis (abuse of power) is quite narrow, since both dangers
are so intricately woven into the role he must play: He must
have power in order to lead well, and in order to lead well he
must maintain the support of a large segment of the electorate; this worth is often measured by his capacity to control
violence and maintain an invincible image. Furthermore, the
author conveys the message that the politician's ability to be a
statesman (as opposed to a demagogue) is largely determined
by the amount of love he can experience in his personal life.
Yet, so much of his inner life is inextricably connected to the
demands of the populace he serves. This link in turn, leads to
a sacrifice of intimacy and individuality for the good of the
State.

Dr. Fine juxtaposes politicians who might be considered leaders of principle with those who come nearer to the category of despot. The theme of the book is reflected here as evidence is brought forth to reveal that those men who experienced more love, who felt less "forgotten," were better equipped to deal with the realities and enticements of their career. In turn, they were often (but certainly not always) rewarded with more positive recognition from an historical perspective. In a sense, each of these leaders had some driving force or childhood passion which they were able to effectively activate to maintain a more steady and productive political course. On the other hand, the less loved or forgotten children came closer to being abusers of power and of their office in adulthood. They allowed their passions or modus vivendi to become unwieldy, destructive tools which at times led to their demise within a governmental structure.

An example of the former type of leader is Lyndon Johnson. The author hypothesizes that Johnson was an idealist and champion of the underdog due to some wish to rescue his mother from an abusive father. His Great Society and national policy reforms were probably an offshoot of this fantasy. The Vietnam War was the overwhelming reality to which he ultimately succumbed. Despite this, he could successfully actualize his childhood wish as a leader by benfiting from the stability of a loving wife and family. While there is a controversial opinion about the quality of the Johnsons' marriage and home life (several biographical sources discuss his abusiveness as a husband, for example), the point is made that a sense of domestic equilibrium provided him with a growth-enhancing experience while he served his presidential term.

One of the politicians who might be viewed in contrast to Johnson is Rasputin, viewed by the author as ". . . obviously a fraud who wanted only power and sex . . ." Rasputin is perhaps a caricature of the corrupt politician who abuses his role, reserves a facade of integrity for a coterie of powerful supporters, and exploits the weaknesses of those who defy him. It may be inferred from Dr. Fine's discussion that Rasputin was a forgotten child and man, victim of instability, rejection, and seduction in his youth. Moreover, his feeling forgotten and unworthy ultimately profoundly influenced the course of Russian history (and the world). This effect came about through his influence upon Czarina Alexandra and through his philosophy of "spiritual awakening through sexual assuagement." Through these two routes he engendered a state of self-enhancement and recognition (albeit destructively) as a backlash to his earlier feeling of unworthiness.

The creative artist is confronted with a polarity which is unique to his social role: At one extreme is his creative process and ability and at the other extreme is the public response to his product. His success is defined by the latter element. Hence, whatever the inner gratification or emptiness he may experience through his work, his sense of identity is constantly being either reinforced or challenged by the cultural label placed upon his creations. While his internal dichotomization is a sharply delineated one (agony or ectasy, turbulence or stability), his route to financial success is intricately related to his *product,* not to *what he is.* The paradox which often confronts him is that he is forced to turn his aggression into healthy assertiveness to "sell" his product in the marketplace; yet, he may very well have chosen this social role because it can allow for a greater repression or denial of aggression than some of the other careers (politics or business). Of further significance is the creative artist's capacity to work and to communicate effectively with his audience. Moreover, the degree to which his home environment can nurture his creativity and capacity to work is correlated with his ability to enjoy his success.

The talented performer can be an Elvis Presley at one extreme and a Will Rogers at the other. Elvis' creativity was ultimately superseded by his need for the approval of the audience. The blend of a fine vocal quality with a novel type of showmanship was his offering to the audience. His creativity lay in his capacity to actualize a performance which may have been designed for him in large measure by his agents. However, with his lack of a sense of self, the seduction of his fans' response was too overpowering and he allowed himself to be devoured by it. His ultimate dissipation was a reflection of the emotional price he paid the culture for making him a success on its terms. Will Rogers, unlike Elvis, allowed his creative acts to be a reflection of his inner sense of self and offered them to the audience as such.

It seems important to reflect on a connective thread which is woven through *The Forgotten Man* between man's sexuality and aggression and his social role. The politician must often fuse seductiveness with aggression for which he is rewarded by the electorate. His superficiality and emotional distance are frequently evident and necessary in order to win the favor of the "need-gratifying object," the populace. The creative artist must sublimate his sexuality and aggression; in fact, he often must disguise its more blatant derivatives through the subtlety of his art, in order to win its universal acceptance. The industrialist's sexuality is often manifested in a manner similar to that of the politician; some seduction of the client is frequently present. Likewise, his aggression is often overtly rewarded through the "hard sell," for example.

Distance, superficiality, and insincerity may often supplant intimacy and truth in this social role. On the battlefield the soldier's reward for aggression speaks for itself; his sexuality is a split-off entity, to be expressed at home, if that is possible. The searching intellectual often sublimates his sexual and aggressive drive through his theorizing; however, like the creative artist, he is often confronted with the paradox of needing to assert himself to sell his theories or gain government funding for research while he unconsciously may employ his professional role as an escape route from overt aggressiveness. Finally, the psychotherapist, like the artist and scientist, is required to greatly sublimate his instinctual impulses.

In his concluding chapter the author further accentuates the leitmotif of the book. The predicament of the forgotten man is his confrontation with a culture which impels him toward extreme choices (of "too much" or "too little") within his social role, and powerfully molds his affective responses: one major effect of this is to shift him away from his "self." As this applies to his sexuality he frequently feels caught between the experience of addictive sex used as an opiate to remove him from the pain of intimacy, and the total withdrawal from sex in order to achieve the same goal. In terms of the role of aggression in attaining career success, the forgotten man once again feels shackled: by a compulsion to be ruthless and/or experience great suffering at one pole, and an isolation foisted upon him by virtue of his total narcissistic withdrawal from an aggressive display in his work at the other pole.

Dr. Fine's prescription for man's achievement of an equilibrium between these excesses is love. He advocates that a "love ideal" must be integrated within man's upbringing to equalize and/or surpass the achievement ideal which exists presently. Through this alteration in the boy's rearing, his identity as a potentially loving husband and father would be nurtured and embellished in a gradually progressive manner through childhood. Hence, in adulthood his social role would become more a direct reflection of a "loved and loving" self than an empty mold, largely formed by the mandates of the Culture-Despot: in this way, the man's sense of inner achievement would supersede his compulsion to mechanically gratify an outward definition of success, void of internal meaning.

In conclusion, this book poignantly conveys the concept that man is not simply "forgotten"; he is, rather, forgotten by the culture for what he cannot concretely produce and exhibit to it and he is "remembered" for what he can even if the outward display is a shallow one, based on weak (or no) principles, or skewed values. Related to this is the evolving role of today's woman. She has the potential to play an integral role in the unfolding of Dr. Fine's concept of a new male ideal in two basic ways. First, as she experiences a greater sense of recognition and self-worth within her social role, as a mother she is then enabled to express her love more generously and effectively to her son, who will in turn be better equipped for the adult love-match defined by the author. Second, the evolving woman has a major part to play within this adult love-partnership. As she develops greater positive channels for her sexuality and aggression and a more creative, diverse life style, she presents a model with which her male son and spouse can identify. Moreover, as her own domesticity becomes an integral autonomous part of herself (rather than a fortress to which she is exiled by the culture), she offers her husband the reward of a gratifying expansion of his domestic and paternal role.

In the final analysis the author should be credited with a vibrant creativity of thought which is conveyed throughout the book. The ideas sparked by if offer psychoanalysis to men and the culture as an effectively dynamic vehicle for change. Its potential application to a reconstruction of man's (and woman's) life style, self-image, and philosophy of living is profound.

This final paper offers a clinical application
of some of the issued raised in
The Forgotten Man.

Discussion X

Sanda Bragman Lewis

The feeling of being forgotten has been a very prevalent theme in virtually every male patient I have seen. It aptly describes an important underlying current in their lives. Men feel forgotten by their wives, their children, their parents, siblings, and friends. Those who are not married feel women will not look at them, or that they cannot reach the woman they want. At work, they feel unappreciated and overlooked by bosses and co-workers. If they are men of accomplishment, their successes never seem to be enough; there is always something else they should be striving for.

Every man I have seen in treatment suffers from depressed feelings of inadequacy and failure. Sometimes this is clear from the beginning of treatment; sometimes it emerges only after the treatment has been under way for a while. Sexually, it has been universal that men feel their penises are too small. They also actually feel that their erections are not hard enough and do not last long enough. There is usually an underlying conviction that they are not good lovers, and will not be able to satisfy a woman. If they cannot have intercourse two or three times a day, *and* last all night, they feel they are not really "men." With patients who are overtly afraid of women and stay away from them, these fears are more apparent. However, it has been striking to observe that these fears and doubts eventually emerge even with men who are apparently successful with women.

For example, Frank, twenty-eight, was an attractive, bright, professional man who had no trouble attracting women. He reported no overt sexual problems—to him this meant potency problems or premature ejaculation. He got involved with one woman after another, and always had the complaint that they were not interested in sex. It was his conviction that women just did not like sex. Only after a series of relationships of this kind and exploration of these

© 1987 by The Haworth Press, Inc. All rights reserved.

feelings in the transference was he able to realize that he was afraid to be involved with a woman who could enjoy sex. Partially this was connected to his difficulty grappling with the painful realization that his mother had been quite promiscuous before and between her two marriages. He had turned her into a saintly, all-good mother who was forced to submit to his father, as a way of handling his intense attachment to her. As these issues became clearer in the treatment, it also became more clear that he had very little pleasure during sex. He was so focused on performing properly that he could not enjoy himself. In fact, it was two or three years into the treatment before he revealed that he often could not ejaculate, a point that Dr. Fine rightfully takes up as a symptom of deeper conflict. Eventually, as the patient worked on his anxieties about sex and loving, he was able to make a happy marriage.

Jack, forty-five, is another example of a man successful with women and who, on the surface, had no apparent sexual problems. He was a talented, charming, up and coming businessman, who started treatment because of problems with depression. He was divorced, went out with many women and felt "sex was no problem, there was no need to talk about it." It took two years into the treatment for it to become clear to him that indeed sex was a problem. First, it emerged that he needed to have more than one woman in his life at the same time. And he had to pretend to each that she was the only one. This turned out to be connected to his father who had a series of extra-marital affairs while Jack was growing up.

As he could work out his anxieties and start to relate to one woman, he then experienced a profound loss of sexual desire. He could go for long periods feeling he did not want to have anything to do with sex. It was only while exploring these feelings which were very puzzling and troubling to him that he brought out that when he did have sex, he usually had to have a few drinks beforehand. Although his anxieties around sex and women's bodies had various sources, one important aspect was his deep fear that if he loved one woman she was bound to leave him. As this was worked out in terms of his sense of loss of his mother's love, he was able to re-marry and eventually enjoy his wife sexually, as well as in many other ways. Both he and Frank, the previous patient, had deep fears of rejection by women that took a long time to uncover. Their charm, easy ways with women, and seeming lack of sexual problems made it difficult to see how much they feared that the woman they loved would leave them. Beneath their handsome, accomplished exteriors, they each felt like little boys who could lose mommy if they were sexual.

As Dr. Fine points out in this book, virtually every man has problems in his work life. The more inhibited man will have trouble pursuing a career, getting jobs, and being appropriately assertive. Other men may be very ambitious and aggressive, to the point that even if successful in their career, they may alienate co-workers, bosses and family in the process. I think that Dr. Fine makes a good point when he says that most successful men, when their lives are examined carefully, feel that they have not done enough. What they have been able to accomplish does not seem to count to them. On an unconscious level, they feel it does not count in terms of their fathers. It was very striking to hear Sir Laurence Olivier, one of the greatest actors of our time, say on a Public Broadcasting Service documentary about his life, that he felt he was a failure, and had not lived up to his own standards. In particular, it was a blow to him when he had to give up being the head of the National Theatre in London.

In my own practice, I see a man, Michael, sixty-three, who had been a professor for twenty-five years. He was so filled with self-hatred that he regarded himself as a complete failure ·in life even though his career had been quite distinguished. He was the youngest of three children. His father was an insurance salesman who was domineering, overbearing, and cruel. The father, feeling ineffectual and frustrated in his own work, was very competitive with his son, and tried in various ways to break Michael's spirit. Michael, because of his superior intellectual abilities, was able to get encouragement from teachers at school, and to finally break away from the family. His successes in high school, college, and graduate school were barely acknowledged by his family.

Unfortunately, Michael, when seeking therapy for his feelings of depression and inadequacy, wound up seeing male therapists who repeated with him the competitive, embattled relationship with his father, rather than working it out analytically. One therapist used him for personal favors and socialized with him. The next therapist would order Michael around, and give him advice. If Michael tried to express any anger, the therapist would become antagonistic and threaten to break off the treatment. Both of these experiences ended when the therapists told Michael he could not be helped. They considered him hopeless. Because of Michael's strong sado-masochistic conflicts, each of these therapeutic experiences lasted several years. By the time he came to see me, he had all but given up hope in his life. The self-hatred he had carried with him because of his father's unrelenting contempt, as well as his own unacknowledged rage at his father, had become much worse after these attempts at treatment failed. It took a lot of work for him to begin to feel that the failures in his previous treatment may have been due to his therapists' inadequate training rather than that he could not be helped.

He was just starting to come out of his profound discouragement about himself when his department was phased out because of lack of funds, and he lost his job. It has been a terrible blow for him. Although he always felt he did not do his job well enough, a great deal of his sense of identity and his self-esteem were tied to having such an important position in his field. Without it, he feels completely lost. Further, our culture does not necessarily value the experience of a man his age. Rather, he is looked at as over the hill. Middle-aged men in their fifties and sixties who are without jobs often have a difficult time finding a place for themselves. In some fields, men in their forties start to feel anxious about their security, as they may be regarded as "too old" for a company to invest in. The realities of the culture for a man Michael's age, added to his disappointing experiences in therapy up until now, are all layered upon feelings of rejection and despair that have plagued him all of his life. However, because he had been able to understand in his current treatment some of these long-standing issues, he has not completely given up hope despite this latest blow. His struggle to gain a sense of manhood is a very poignant one.

Some men, no matter how successful, feel that they have done nothing. If they are not the President, Mickey Mantle, or John Rockefeller they feel that they are nowhere. Other men, however, are raised to accomplish little and actually hold themselves back from success. Such is the case of Peter, thirty-two. He came into treatment because of inhibitions in relating to women and problems finding work that he liked. He is an unusually bright, talented young man who has since treatment become a stockbroker. His father, who was skilled in science, never pursued his abilities. Instead he became a skilled laborer. Even there, the father refused all opportunities to advance himself. The father, who had dreams of becoming a world champion boxer, had been hospitalized for psychiatric reasons when Peter was a child. The father was an embittered, frustrated man, a bully to everyone around him. Peter's mother was very narcissistic, and took no steps to protect Peter, her only child, from his father's rage. She also had affairs throughout the marriage which were known to Peter but were a secret from her husband.

Through working on Peter's feelings of inadequacy as a man, and his inability to pursue more assertively his career, it became clear that Peter was raised to do worse than his father had done in his own life. The father was very competitive with the son and treated him with great contempt. Peter, on his part, has been terrified of experiencing his hatred for his father, as well as his love. His hatred leads to feelings of guilt and castration. His love leads to feelings of disappointment and loss, since the father had been unable to respond to him in any kind of loving way. The father, unhappy in his work yet unable to change it, and demeaned by the mother through her affairs, is experienced by Peter as actually being a failure. As such, Peter has felt unconsciously, that it would destroy his father if he were to succeed in his life. As Peter has been able to get in touch with his dilemma, he has realized that on some level it would please his parents if he were to fail. As he has been able to recognize and work on these issues, he has been able to be much more successful in his life.

Dr. Fine puts forth another hypothesis in his book that is borne out in clinical practice. That is, he feels that the Oedipal strivings are made most difficult by the hatred between the parents rather than the strenth of the drives themselves. When the parental marriage is very poor and embattled, the children feel caught between both parents. Love becomes a dangerous experience in such a situation, since the child feels that he is being disloyal to one parent when loving the other. Often parents actively disparage each other and unconsciously try to make the children take sides in the marital dispute. In such a climate, the child has difficulty making appropriate heterosexual identifications. Love becomes a risky and anxiety-filled experience, while marriage may become something to be avoided at all costs. Peter, mentioned above, lived out this dilemma before beginning treatment. His father constantly complained that the mother was not a good wife to him. The mother, for her part, carried on her affairs practically under her husband's nose. Weekends at home were particularly bad, and the parents would often have violent arguments before they were supposed to go out with each other. The fighting ensured that the parents would have no intimacy, sexual or otherwise, with each other.

In this environment, Peter grew up feeling inadequate and impotent. Women were seen as two-faced and untrustworthy. It is only now, after several years of treatment, that he has given up his conviction that if he loved a woman she would leave him for another man. His attachment to both parents is very intense and highly ambivalent. It has always seemed to me that the resolution of his Oedipal conflicts has been made much more difficult by the respective pathologies of each parent, as well as the profound hatred that exists in their marriage. The fact that he has been able to find a career for himself, develop a loving marriage, and trust me as a therapist, attests to a hope for a better life that he managed to keep alive while growing up in a family filled with misery and fear.

For most male patients, the feelings of being forgotten are very difficult to acknowledge. Feelings of failure, despair, and need of any kind are regarded as weak. Tenderness, love, longing, and loss are also experienced as weakening. There is tremendous pressure on men, both internal and external, to be strong, unfeeling and aggressive. By working on these issues in treatment, men are able to get in touch with feelings and wishes inside themselves that they felt had to be denied. As they can look at their feelings of love, sadness, and wishes to be taken care of, they can recognize that these feelings are not by definition weak. They can reflect upon how these feelings and their denial have shaped their lives and try to work out more appropriate ways of handling them. As a result, the guilt, anxiety, and self-hatred they feel is reduced, and they can move toward a more rounded and human sense of being a man. One patient said when he came to treatment that he felt like a mechanical man. He functioned very well, but he had different parts to his life and they were all disconnected from each other. In our work together, we developed the idea that like the Tin Man, in the Wizard of Oz, he wanted a heart. And that is what he got, while feeling a renewed sense of confidence, mastery and a capacity for tenderness.

One of the most important ways of working out men's feelings of failure and inadequacy is to look carefully at the love experiences in their lives, starting with the family. As they can examine the ways they love, how this shows up in the transference, the kinds of women they choose, their sexual fantasies and sexual practices, and their hopes and disappointments, they are able to understand the inner forces that drive them in directions that lead to conflict and misery, often to a self-destructive level. As they are able to recognize and work out these conflicts, their lives change dramatically. With other men they can work through their homosexual longings and their competitive feelings enough so that they can have meaningful friendships and successful work experiences. As their feelings about men and being a man are resolved, they can work on their fears of women, as well as their contempt for them, so that they can move toward more pleasurable and gratifying heterosexual relationships. As their disowned aspects are reclaimed, they no longer feel either forgotten or forgettable. Like the Tin Man, they too can have a heart.